The Cádiz Experiment in Central America,

1808 to 1826

The Cádiz Experiment in Central America, 1808 to 1826

MARIO RODRIGUEZ

University of California Press / Berkeley / Los Angeles / London

This book was designed by Jim Mennick.
It was set in V.I.P Garamond
with display in Phototypositor Codex
and it was printed and bound by Thomson-Shore, Inc.

University of California Press
Berkeley and Los Angeles, California
University of California Press, Ltd.
London, England

ISBN 0-520-03394-9
Library of Congress Catalog Card Number: 76-50256
Printed in the United States of America

1 2 3 4 5 6 7 8 9

To my wife Mildred Shepherd Rodríguez
who has filled my life with so
many rich memories

Contents

PREFACE / ix

1 The Bourbon Legacy in Central America / 1
2 The Glorious Revolution / 28
3 Central Americans at Cádiz / 53
4 The Cádiz Constitution / 75
5 The Experiment in Central America / 101
6 The Second Trial / 124
7 A Conditional Independence / 147
8 The Mexican Connection / 167
9 The Nation in the Cádiz Tradition / 187
10 Federalism and the Abyss / 212

NOTES / 239
GLOSSARY / 275
BIBLIOGRAPHY / 283
INDEX / 307

MAPS
MAP 1. Spanish America in the Eighteenth Century / 10–11
MAP 2. The Kingdom of Guatemala / 82–83

Preface

CENTRAL American liberalism began to interest me when I was teaching at Tulane University in New Orleans over two decades ago. The career of José Francisco Barrundia, in particular, had a meaningful note, especially since it spanned the first half of the nineteenth century. As I prepared my research schedule, there were inevitable digressions. The major one was the writing of *A Palmerstonian Diplomat in Central America, Frederick Chatfield, Esquire* (Tucson, 1964), a study of Barrundia's fierce opponent. With Don Federico out of the way, I was fortunate to receive a fellowship from the John Simon Guggenheim Foundation in 1964–1965, to build up my knowledge of Barrundia's earlier career. Professor John Tate Lanning's prize-winning volume on the University of San Carlos de Guatemala was helpful, since Barrundia was a graduate of its reform program at the end of the eighteenth century. Professor Louis E. Bumgartner, who studied under Professor Lanning's direction at Duke University, further enlightened me on one of Barrundia's peers, José Cecilio del Valle of Honduras.

I did not, however, share anything like Bumgartner's good fortune with the Valle papers; I was unable to find any substantial holdings of a private nature on José Francisco Barrundia. Before 1808 there were only a few fugitive facts available about him: he graduated at the university and undertook a part-time program in law, which he apparently never finished, he also seems to have helped out in his father's commercial establishment, and so on. Without any substantial biographical materials, I had no alternative but to resort to all the documentation that might help me form a judgment of the years before 1808, when the young man was preparing himself for a political career. The situation brightened after May 2, 1808, as the process of liberalization in the Spanish empire opened up new opportunities. More and more, I came to appreciate the importance of investigating the Cádiz story and the famous charter of 1812—a theme that had intrigued me as a graduate student at Berkeley. So, as I familiarized myself with the Cádiz years and patiently read through the municipal records for Guatemala City and other localities in Central America, I was able to appreciate who constituted the political elite in those years. As a recent arrival from the Basque country, Barrundia's father was indirectly connected with the "family" of the Aycinenas in Guatemala.

A great discovery of those early months of research in Guatemala was to find out that José Francisco Barrundia, at the minimum age of twenty-five, had been elected to the first municipality of Guatemala City under the Constitution of 1812. Wondering why this had not been emphasized, I double-checked the secondary references; they mentioned it only in passing, apparently not recognizing its historical significance. Needless to say, I was not so hesitant; and my main concern was to protect my findings until the final completion of the manuscript.

Fortunately, the Director of the Biblioteca Nacional in Guatemala, María Albertina Gálvez, came to the rescue. A friend of mine since 1953, she kept asking me to deliver a formal paper before her organization. Suspecting that she wanted a digest of my Chatfield book, I demurred on the grounds that I did not want to be distracted from my work. We struck a compromise. I agreed to deliver a paper on my findings on Barrundia, providing that she would publish an enlarged version of it: *La Conspiración de Belén en Nueva Perspectiva* (Guatemala City, 1965). Don Arturo Taracena edited the manuscript for me, weeding out many of the non-Spanish constructions that haunt bilinguals. María Albertina Gálvez and Arturo Taracena Flores—two human beings who have unselfishly helped many of us to advance the historical knowledge of their area—are no longer with us. It has been an honor to have known both of them.

As the research on the first constitutional experiment progressed, I recognized that an exclusive focus on Barrundia was perhaps not justified. Many founding fathers of Central America gained their first experience in government at this time. They, too, were exposed to the process of modernization after 1808, a movement which I have chosen to call the Cádiz Experiment. Its roots, as we shall see in Chapter One, go back to the reign of Charles III, from 1759 to 1788.

There is much that is controversial in this book. The Cádiz Constitution still elicits strong statements pro or con among Spaniards today. Central Americans argue vehemently about the corresponding period from

1823 to 1826, one permeated with the aura of Cádiz. I hope that the documentary base of this study will help to convince some, although I doubt that they will be converted. The fact that the Cádiz Experiment was first implemented overseas permits us to inspect its weaknesses and strengths. Central Americans of all political persuasions welcomed the Cádiz Experiment initially, a convincing testimonial to its blend of traditional and modern elements.

The program of Spanish reforms, however, exposed some glaring deficiencies in the governance of Central America that would haunt the area for decades, forestalling the advent of modernization. A severe economic depression prevented any serious reformation of Central American society. Similarly, the states' rights movement that was encouraged by the Cádiz Experiment eventually splintered the vaunted unity of Central America. Nevertheless, the political experience acquired during the Cádiz Experiment had a profound impact upon the future liberalism of the area.

For variety and effect, I have employed Spanish terms rather freely in the text. Their meanings should be self-evident to scholars, and the Glossary at the end of the book may prove useful to the non-specialist reader.

Many institutions and persons have made this work possible. The Guggenheim Fellowship was basic. Furthermore, I have received lesser grants from the Graduate School of the University of Arizona (1964) and the Graduate School of George Washington University (1970). My present employer, the University of Southern California, has provided valuable financial assistance in the preparation and publication of the manuscript. Mr. Bradley Reynolds, a graduate student of considerable talent, has been a faithful bibliographical scout; my colleagues A. Lloyd Moote and John A. Schutz have read portions of the manuscript; and Sandra Wasserman and Janet Crusius have done most of the typing. The final pages were completed in Madrid, Spain, by Miss Susan Hendry. Professor Carlos Meléndez of the University of Costa Rica served as a convenient sounding board for the earlier phases of the study. Mrs. Georgette Dorn of the Hispanic Foundation has checked certain items for me in the Library of Congress.

Space does not permit me to name all the hard-working and devoted members of archival staffs all over the world that have helped me at certain stages of the research. Their organizations are mentioned in the Bibliography. I wish to thank all of them sincerely.

I have dedicated this book to my wife, Mildred, who has been unusually patient and understanding. The same applies to my two chihuahuas, Torito and M'Hijita, who have spent many hours supervising my work on the typewriter and wondering why their master was so grumpy at times.

Of course, I bear full responsibility for the contents of this volume.

MARIO RODRIGUEZ
Madrid, January 1976

I. The Bourbon Legacy in Central America

Yes, good King, this is the glory that will most distinguish your name to posterity. . . . The science of economics belongs exclusively to you and to those entrusted with your authority.

GASPAR DE JOVELLANOS, *December 8, 1788*[1]

GASPAR MELCHOR DE JOVELLANOS, a prominent lawyer from northern Spain, was in his mid-forties when his favorite monarch died. The epitome of the generation that matured intellectually during the reign of Charles III, from 1759 to 1788, Jovellanos was the logical choice of his colleagues in the Royal Economic Society of Madrid to deliver the eulogy for the king. As a student of the Spanish past, he appreciated the significance of the era that had just ended, a period of modernization unparalleled in the history of Spain. It augured well for Spaniards everywhere. Jovellanos had no way of knowing that in the following year the French Revolution would help to reverse the fortunes of his country, especially with a king of lesser stature at the helm.

The Asturian barrister described with pride the numerous reforms of Charles III's rule. To improve agriculture, the regime had encouraged "the establishment of new agricultural colonies, the division of communal lands, the reduction in privileges of the pastoral interests, the abolition of the assize, and the free circulation of grains." In the industrial sphere, it had supported "the propagation of education in manufacturing, the reform of guild administration, the multiplication of industrial enterprises, and the generous profusion of favors and exemptions to the crafts." To stimulate commerce, the Spanish government had insisted upon "the breaking of ancient chains that hampered national trade, the opening of new markets abroad, peace in the Mediterranean, and the periodic correspondence and free communication with our overseas colonies." It had also welcomed "the revival of the people's representation in the perfection of municipal government"; it had changed the objectives of public charity in order to discourage "voluntary idleness," while at the same time opening up "the sources of beneficence in a thousand places for the indigent"; and it had encouraged the formation of economic societies throughout the Spanish world, organizations "dedicated zealously to all objects of the common welfare." With such a "glorious record," Charles III deserved to be called the "father of his vassals."[2]

Moreover, this remarkable monarch had recognized that to bring about permanent change it was necessary to educate his people in the "useful sciences, economic principles, and the general spirit of the Enlightenment." This, after all, was what Spain owed to Charles III.[3] His Bourbon predecessors had developed the nation's economy by spreading the Enlightenment thought of the eighteenth century and by bringing political unity to Spain. King Charles accelerated the process when he deliberately attacked scholasticism's hold upon the educational system of the nation, thus giving Spaniards the "freedom to philosophize." The country's youth responded enthusiastically to the "rule of reason." Jovellanos recalled that even theology had become a science in Spain by returning to the original sources. In law, future lawyers studied ethics, the law of nature, and international law with great benefit to the nation.[4] At all times, the emphasis was on "useful knowledge" and the discovery of practical "truths" that had an immediate bearing upon Spain's prosperity. Hoping to regenerate his people, Charles III promoted the teaching of the "exact sciences, without which one could advance little or not at all in the investigation of natural truths." Elaborating upon this point, Jovellanos reminded his listeners:

> Madrid, Sevilla, Salamanca, Alcalá witnessed the rebirth of their ancient schools of mathematics. Barcelona, Valencia, Zaragoza, Santiago, and almost all the General Studies [institutions] saw them established for the first time. The relevance of the demonstration replaced the subtlety of the syllogism. The study of physics, supported now by experience and calculation, approached perfection; and from it were derived the remaining sciences of its jurisdiction: chemistry, mineralogy and metallurgy, natural history, botany; and while the naturalist observer investigated the basic elements of bodies, penetrating and analyzing all their properties and

characteristics, the authority on politics studied them from the viewpoint of the wisdom that the Creator had deposited in them so as to assure the multiplication and the happiness of the human species.[5]

Another science was needed, however, one that would apply the knowledge of the exact sciences for the benefit of society.[6] This was the science of "political economy," Jovellanos told his audience. And it was Charles III and his talented ministers who provided this "happy revolution" in Spain.[7] Since 1765, King Charles had constantly promoted the activities of economic societies throughout the Spanish-speaking world:

> These bodies raised general expectations concerning their operations, and everyone hurried to enlist in them. The clergy was attracted by the analogy of the objective to their own charitable and pious ministry; public officials joined, dropping for the moment their authoritative trappings; the nobility did likewise, forgetting its prerogatives; and men of letters, merchants, and artisans, shedding their fondness for personal gain and moved by the desire for the common good, also joined; all got together, they considered themselve citizens, they declared themselves members of a general association rather than of their class, and they prepared to work for the utility of their brethren. Zeal and wisdom joined forces, patriotism boiled [within them], and the nation, astonished, saw the hearts of her children turned toward her for the first time.[8]

Discounting the emotionalism of the occasion, the eulogy of Charles III provides a remarkable synthesis of the Bourbon contribution to the Spanish world. Since the beginning of the eighteenth century, this new dynasty, of French origin, had centralized government in Spain to a point that would have seemed impossible to an observer of the Hapsburg era. Moreover, the Bourbon kings revitalized Spanish institutions and aroused a strong nationalistic feeling among Spanish subjects everywhere. This national consciousness pervaded the Spanish and American scenes in the thirty-five years that followed Charles III's death. In addition, Spanish-speaking people committed themselves unequivocally to economic development, a trait that is not usually associated with their character.

Since Spain and her colonies were producers of raw materials, Bourbon planners concentrated their attention upon agriculture. Jovellanos, for example, had mentioned agricultural reforms first in his eulogy; and this was no coincidence. He strongly believed that agriculture should have priority in the Spanish economy, a conviction that he shared with most members of the Economic Society in Madrid. In 1780, the Royal Council of Castile had asked the Society to evaluate the topic of agriculture in Spain, making whatever suggestions it deemed worthy of the government's attention. Throughout the 1780s, its members debated, researched, and studied every possible aspect of Spain's agricultural condition. In 1787, the Society asked Jovellanos, who had been the most active researcher and contributor, to write up the final report. It was published by the Spanish government in 1795 as the *Informe de Ley Agraria*.[9] Translated into many languages, it brought immediate world recognition to Jovellanos.

The Report on Agrarian Law was indeed the "economic bible" for Spanish liberals of the early nineteenth century, as Professor Herr has noted.[10] Although the treatise dealt exclusively with agricultural conditions in Spain, its conclusions had application in Spanish America as well. Heavily documented from a variety of sources, the thought of the French physiocrats prevailed in the *Informe*. Yet, the approach was eclectic; and the investigators drew their information from a plethora of authorities throughout the world and from the time of the Romans forward. Agrarian experts of Rome were cited frequently. Adam Smith was another source; and even agricultural production figures for the United States appeared in the report. Much, of course, came from direct observations of agricultural practices in Spain.[11]

After reviewing the Peninsula's agricultural history, Jovellanos described the many obstacles that had hampered the natural development of Spain's agriculture. Government intervention had been a particularly serious deterrent. Since agriculture had a "natural tendency toward perfection," laws should only have encouraged this trend "not so much by presenting incentives as by removing the hindrances that retard its progress."[12] At this point, the Economic Society of Madrid severely criticized many projects and laws sponsored by the ministers of Charles III because they did more harm than good. Moreover, Jovellanos and his colleagues unmistakably favored laissez-faire and presented all the standard arguments of that time in behalf of the new economic orientation.[13] They allowed, however, that the government could play a constructive role in the development of the economy's infrastructure.

The 1795 *Report* strongly assailed the government's favoritism toward special interests. As the champion of free competition, the Economic Society of Madrid attacked monopoly in general and focused particular criticism on the ubiquitous Mesta, that centuries-old institution that represented the free-range objectives of sheepherders and cattlemen. An unjust monopoly that had prevented the enclosure of Spanish lands, the Mesta hindered the development of agriculture in Spain. Enclosures, the *Informe* insisted, were indispensable for Spain's future. In addition, it recommended the large-scale transfer of Spain's population from urban to rural areas. Moreover, it condemned the trade barriers between districts and provinces in Spain as monopolistic deterrents. The same applied to the tax structure that favored industrial and commercial elements at the expense of agriculturalists. Above all, free trade should be an established national policy in order to stimulate agricultural development.[14]

The inequities of land tenure were by far the major obstacle to Spain's agricultural development. Here, the Society underscored two points: first, the non-utilization of potential land resources and, second, the alienation (*amortización*) of Spanish land to special interests who ignored economic productivity. In either case, they limited the area needed by private enterprise for the development of agriculture and raised land prices to a "scandalous" level.[15]

After a review of all so-called political deterrents, the *Informe* came up with these suggestions. First, public lands (*baldíos*) should be sold to private entrepreneurs, thus helping to populate these areas, raising the standard of living for individual farmers and contributing to the increase of the nation's population—a key prerequisite for economic development. Next, the Crown should encourage town councils (*ayuntamientos*) to sell their commons, offering "free and absolute" titles, or to rent them without inhibiting the tenants—a conscious effort to improve upon the agrarian experiments of 1768–1770.[16] Finally, the *Informe* recommended no further alienation of lands to civil or religious parties. With regard to entailed estates of the Church, inalienable and therefore removed from circulation, the Society urged religious corporations either to sell their lands or to rent them under commercial conditions. The Society hedged somewhat on civil entails (*mayorazgos*), perhaps because it recognized that the opposition of nobles might defeat the entire program. It hoped that the nobility would follow the Church's lead in making their lands productive.[17] On the controversial issue concerning the relative efficiency of large or small properties, the *Informe* did not take an unqualified stand, although it seemed to prefer smaller holdings.[18]

The following statement reflected the Society's view on moral obstacles to the development of agriculture in Spain, those based upon opinion:

> The agriculture of a nation can be considered under two important aspects: that is, with relation to public prosperity and to individual happiness. In

the first case, it is undeniable that large countries, and specifically those like Spain that enjoy an extensive and fertile territory, should look upon it as the primary source of their prosperity, since population and wealth, the basic supports of national power, depend more immediately upon it than on any other of the remaining lucrative occupations, and even more than all of them together. As for the second, it also cannot be denied that agriculture is the easiest, surest, and most extensive means to increase the number of individuals in the state and the particular happiness of each one, not only because of the immense amount of labor that it can employ in its various phases and activities, but also because of the immense amount of work that it can provide for other occupations, that are engaged in the elaboration of its products.[19]

And yet, Jovellanos lamented, modern states have seemingly lost sight of agriculture's priority. In carrying out policies of national aggrandizement, they have favored the "mercantile arts" (commerce, industry, and navigation) at the expense of agriculture. Wars have been fought because of mercantile objectives, ending in treaties and negotiations that further aggravated the development of agriculture—inexcusable conduct on the part of governments in view of the fact that agriculture was the real source of prosperity.[20] Furthermore, the *Informe* urged the Royal Council of Castile to promote the study of "civil economy" in Spain, a science "that teaches one how to combine the public interest with the individual's interest and how to establish power and strength of nations upon the fortunes of their individuals."[21]

The perennial problem of the farmer's incompetence and ignorance was another key moral obstacle. The *Report* urged a pragmatic solution: to educate agriculturalists in the easiest and least expensive way possible, taking into account that Spain did not need learned doctors but rather "practical and patient" men who could work on farms.[22] Two reforms were vital. First, the government should establish institutes of "useful education" in all major cities and towns; the emphasis, in short, would be on vocational education. Second, all tillers of the soil should learn to read, write, and count in parish schools where priests could serve as teachers.[23]

To communicate the latest technology to the Spanish peasant, the *Report* proposed a series of technical manuals (*cartillas técnicas*) written in simple language. Priests and other knowledgeable persons were to encourage farmers to study these valuable manuals, to be prepared by the nearest economic society. In fact, the Economic Society of Madrid urged the establishment and support of economic societies in every province—a recommendation, by the way, that Spanish liberals adopted in the early nineteenth century.[24]

In discussing the physical obstacles that confronted Spanish agriculture, Jovellanos stressed the positive role of government in providing the needed internal improvements—irrigation facilities, roads, canals, ports, and so forth—which individuals could not supply on their own. In doing so, the government should first take stock of available financial resources before determining priorities. Above all, it should not repeat the mistakes made in 1761, when it started many roads all at the same time, only to have them half completed thirty years later. A given road should be finished before starting another one; and priority should go to provincial roads, for without them the large national roads were useless to most Spanish farmers.[25] Spain also needed more seaports to send out her agricultural products.[26] The government could finance these internal improvements by avoiding unnecessary wars—those that involved no real national interests, but only pride. Moreover, the government could economize by dispensing with "vanity" projects, those huge, ostentatious buildings and monuments at the capital that contrasted immorally with the poverty of Spanish villages. The welfare of Spain's people came first.[27]

At this point, Jovellanos outlined an elaborate national system for funding the infrastructure of the Spanish economy. He proposed an annual appropriation derived in part from the savings suggested above or from a special tax levied according to the ability to pay. These funds would be used exclusively for national projects. At the provincial level, a junta would set priorities, levy special taxes if needed, and control the revenue from the sale of public lands.[28] Town governments likewise might assume financial responsibility for their own projects, allowing them to use revenues from the sale of their commons.[29]

Throughout the *Informe*, the Society did not hesitate to condemn the excesses of centralized government; conversely, it extolled local autonomy and the freedom of the individual—an advocacy that in the future might encourage a spirit of federalism in politics as constrasted to the Bourbon penchant for centralism. Jovellanos chided the government for its excessive paternalism when he asked:

> And how can one possibly expect public zeal when the government cuts off all the relations of affection, of interest, of decorum that reason and civility itself require between the whole and its parts, between the community and its members? Entrust those assignments to individuals from the provinces themselves and if possible to individuals selected by them; trust them with the distribution of the revenues which they themselves contribute and with the administration of the works that they alone are interested in; form provincial juntas composed of proprietors, ecclesiastics, members of the economic societies; and then you will see the rebirth in the provinces of

that zeal which seems to have been exiled from them and which, if it exists, only exists where and up to that point that distrust has not been able to penetrate.[30]

Such were the major conclusions of the *Informe de Ley Agraria*. It is clear that the Royal Economic Society of Madrid had taken the assignment seriously and that it had spared no one in pointing out the deterrents to a prosperous agriculture in Spain. It sought real answers and not just another placebo. Its conclusions, representing a consensus of the best minds in Spain in the late eighteenth century, envisioned a thoroughly modern Spanish nation in Europe and in America.

≈

The New World possessions of Spain were by no means an unmixed blessing. The mother country had paid dearly for her empire overseas. It was common knowledge during the colonial centuries that while Spain paid the expenses of empire, her enemies enjoyed the fruits of her possessions. Unable to supply the manufactures needed for the colonial traffic, Spain depended upon foreign sources; and Spanish merchants were only middlemen in the exchange that took place. The devastating competition of the smuggling trade, also controlled by foreigners, was even more debilitating in the long run, making a mockery of Spain's mercantilist theory. This situation was intolerable to the new Bourbon dynasty, nurtured on the economic theories of Jean Baptiste Colbert, the renowned French minister of the seventeenth century.

The Hapsburg predecessor had recognized the problem of control overseas and had supported royal absolutism with enthusiasm. The political realities in Europe and America, however, had compelled him to dilute the theory in order to survive. The extent of the empire itself, the isolation of many of its parts because of stubborn topography and other factors, and the constant challenge of European rivals all contributed to the relaxation of centralist government overseas. Spain's dependence upon colonial support against challengers led her to make concessions to home rule, to the local oligarchies of Creoles (whites born in America) and Peninsulars who dominated the corporations of the New World—the municipalities, the merchant guilds (*consulados*), miners' organizations (*reales de minas*), associations of sheepherders and cattlemen (the Mesta of New Spain, for example), and others.[31] The Bourbons were far more successful in centralizing control throughout the empire, to be sure; but it is doubtful that they ever succeeded in reversing the strong regionalist tradition or in consummating the Second Conquest of America, as Professor

John Lynch has put it.[32] In Central America, at least, Bourbon reformers faced the reality of a strong regionalist sentiment and decided to encourage it in the hopes of strengthening a more general Spanish nationalism, just as recommended by Jovellanos in the 1795 *Report*.

The Bourbon effort to rationalize government in the Spanish-speaking world met with some initial successes, thanks in part to the opportunities provided by the War of the Spanish Succession (1700–1713). Philip V's ministers, for example, were able to impose centralizing policies upon parts of the Peninsula that had supported the Austrian Pretender. The Church likewise yielded to the "regalist" pretensions of the Crown; and with the expulsion of the Jesuits in 1767, the main "ultramontane" supporters of the papacy in Spain, the Bourbons were able to gain control of the Spanish Church.[33]

The centralizing process in the New World began with the appointment of a Minister of the Indies in 1715, followed by the deemphasis of the Council of the Indies. Government was hereafter more direct and expeditious. In the 1770s, the Bourbons increased the number of viceroyalties in America from two to four, while at the same time giving the captaincies-general more independent authority. The intendancy system (1764-1786) further centralized government and improved the defenses of the New World, in theory at least. The new *intendentes*, bureaucrats trained primarily as lawyers, had a multiple assignment: to stimulate economic development in their assigned region, to collect taxes more efficiently, to bring about a fairer dispensation of justice, and to prepare the defenses of their jurisdiction. The intendentes apparently encouraged an increase in regional productivity, but it is not clear whether this resulted from their own efforts or from the general upswing in international trade during the last half of the eighteenth century.

The economic record of the Bourbons was remarkable in every respect. By the end of Charles III's reign, for example, Spanish manufactures constituted over one half of the goods in the colonial traffic, a three-fold increase over past averages.[34] The Bourbons placed greater emphasis upon individual registered ships and eventually abolished the costly fleet system; mail packets improved communications with the colonies, providing additional and dependable shipping space; the government revised commercial duties, usually downwards, and in some cases fees were eliminated as an incentive for development; new ports, both in Spain and in America, were opened to the legal trade; and by 1778, the Reglamento de Comercio Libre permitted supposedly "free trade" between the colonies and Spanish ports. Colonials, however, still had to send their products to foreign markets via Spanish ports, a condition that

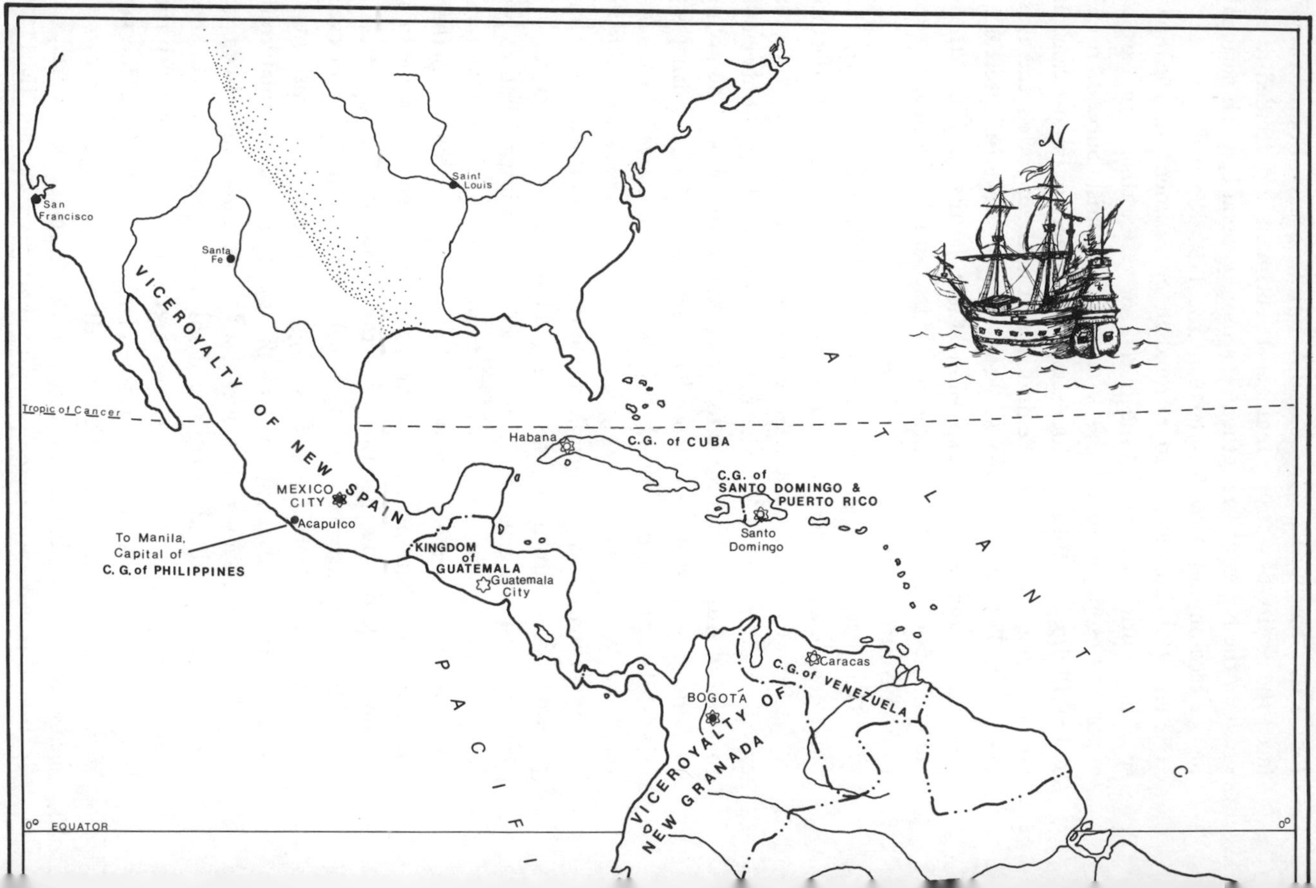
San Francisco
Santa Fe
Saint Louis
VICEROYALTY OF NEW SPAIN
MEXICO CITY
Acapulco
To Manila, Capital of C. G. of PHILIPPINES
Tropic of Cancer
Habana
C.G. of CUBA
C.G. of SANTO DOMINGO & PUERTO RICO
Santo Domingo
KINGDOM of GUATEMALA
Guatemala City
Caracas
C.G. of VENEZUELA
BOGOTÁ
VICEROYALTY OF NEW GRANADA
0° EQUATOR
0°
ATLANTIC
PACIFI

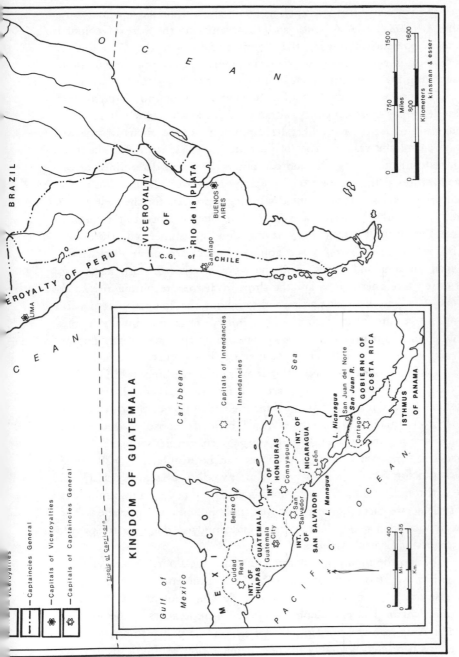

MAP 1. Spanish America in the Eighteenth Century

negated an effective free-trade policy. Spain also authorized new merchant guilds (*consulados*) in America and thus widened the base of colonial traffic. Apparently following the recommendations of the 1795 report, the Spanish government turned more and more to laissez-faire economics, abandoning the Colbertian mercantilism of the early eighteenth century.

The pesky contraband traffic, however, was not molested to any great degree by Bourbon policy, although there was less reason to resort to smuggling under the more liberalized program. It was virtually impossible to patrol the vast stretches of coastline overseas; corruption of royal officials continued as before; and consumers were still determined to get manufactures at the cheapest rates possible. Moreover, the Bourbons, like their predecessors, had to contend with legal pretexts for the contraband traffic, especially the slave trade contract (*asiento*) awarded to the English by the Treaty of Utrecht in 1713. It provided Englishmen with the excuse to frequent Spanish ports, thus enabling them to carry on an illicit traffic in manufactures and slaves. And the right to visit Spanish ports also permitted foreigners to exploit the ships-in-distress technique (*navíos de arribada*), a practice that persisted throughout the colonial period with disastrous results for Spanish economic policy. Legally a ship in distress could enter a port to make repairs, providing no time was wasted and no attempt was made to sell her cargo. If smuggling occurred, officials then could confiscate the cargo and sell it at auction to the highest bidder. The proceeds were divided into three parts: one for the royal officials trying the case, one for the informer, and one for the Crown. The opportunities for abuse were many, especially if royal officials chose to cooperate. Smugglers controlled auction bids; cargoes that were confiscated were small since most of the ship's products had been unloaded on deserted beaches before the arrival in port, thus avoiding taxation entirely. In effect, through *arribadas*, contrabandists ended up paying a minimum tax on their entire cargo, almost as if free trade policies had prevailed. The sale of auctioned goods, not surprisingly, annoyed the regular Spanish merchants of Central America.[35]

To stop the mounting contraband trade, the Bourbons canceled the English slave trade contract in 1750. The problem now was how to increase the labor force for the projected development programs in agriculture. Cuban planters, along with other entrepreneurs in the strategic Middle American area, urged a liberal slave trade policy to help agriculture. Spain reacted favorably to these demands by issuing a royal decree (*cédula*) in 1789 that freed the slave trade in the Caribbean, even to foreigners if they promised not to introduce competitive manufactures—a clearcut example of wishful thinking on the part of the Bourbons.[36] Other cédulas extended the slave-trade concession to Buenos Aires and the Pacific ports. The slave-trade program continued until 1816 for Spanish subjects and until 1810 for foreigners.[37] Thus, Spain had unwittingly supplied outsiders with an excuse to visit her ports in Spanish America; and her colonials developed a taste for legal traffic with foreigners—a factor of no mean importance when the opportunity for independence presented itself. Central America was a case in point.

The leading merchants and landowners in the Kingdom of Guatemala, an area which today includes the five republics of Central America and the Mexican state of Chiapas, viewed their region's potential with optimism: "What a powerful Kingdom it could be! How rich and desirable for the comforts of life and what opportunities it offers to prosper!"[38] And they were right. It was a fertile land, one third larger than all of Spain. Its major problem, however, was underpopulation, one million as compared to almost eleven million people for Spain. Most Central Americans lived on a mountain-plateau complex in the West; another cluster of settlers was found along the Nicaraguan depression that cuts across from the Pacific to the Atlantic via the lakes Managua and Nicaragua to the San Juan River; and the population in the Honduran and Costa Rican highlands was scanty by comparison. Elsewhere the land was virtually empty and the climate hot and humid.

Diversity also characterized the racial makeup of the people in Central America. Two-thirds of them were descendants of the Mayas who did not speak Spanish. The rest were mainly mixed-bloods: Indian and Caucasian (*mestizos*), Indian and Negro (*pardos* or *zambos*), and mulattoes—all of them referred to commonly as *ladinos or castas*. The term "ladino," however, was more cultural than racial, since it also applied to Indians who lived like whites. There were not many pure Negroes, and the whites accounted for some 40,000 families. These Caucasians, however, were the recognized leaders of colonial society and the main proprietors of Central America.[39]

The practical problem in the Kingdom of Guatemala was to redistribute its limited population over an immense area in such a way so that its people could prosper and multiply. Central American planners, moreover, hoped to integrate the Indians by training them to live as members of a modern society.

The Spanish conquistador took over the most important land and resources of Central America and settled down to the peaceful life of the agriculturalist or pastoralist, subjecting the non-whites to his rule. For parts of the sixteenth century, he occupied some portions of eastern Central America, exploiting the placer mines along the Atlantic and in the mineral zone of Honduras. He moved on to the healthier highlands of Honduras and the west when mining declined. The fertility of the Nicaraguan depression attracted many Spaniards. By the end of the sixteenth century, the white elite of Central America looked toward the west for its livelihood.

During the most prosperous times, monoculture characterized the economy of Central America.[40] The large haciendas specialized in the export of cacao for nearly two centuries, a product whose quality was world renowned. It had a market in New Spain (Mexico) and in Peru, but the bulk of the harvest crossed the Isthmus of Panama to European markets. It also got to the Atlantic coast via the San Juan River in Nicaragua. While plantation owners (*hacendados*) stressed the cacao culture, nearby cattlemen fed the labor force, along with other entrepreneurs who supplied the foodstuffs and special needs of the plantation. Thus Central America exchanged its regional products, forming a common market of sorts that was geared to the production of one or two major exports. The Pacific ports also traded to the south in naval stores and other items connected with ship-building. Life was comfortable for white masters (*patrones*) and for many Indians who owned small holdings. In any case, the white patrón was lord of his bailiwick, despite the presence of the royal government's representatives, civil and religious.

The stamp of monoculture had its liabilities, then as today. When world demand slackened or more efficient competitors appeared on the scene, the entire economic structure of Central America felt the pinch. Cacao, for example, could not meet the competition from Venezuela, where transportation costs were less. Thus, Central Americans turned to indigo as their major export; and conditions of the times—the increased demand of European textile industries—encouraged the changeover. Moreover, indigo was a lighter product that could bear the heavier transportation costs to the port of Santo Tomás, on the Atlantic coast, near what is today Puerto Barrios in Guatemala. Another regional common market emerged in which cattlemen and farmers from Honduras and Nicaragua fed the labor force on the indigo plantations in present El Salvador and neighboring areas. Prosperity returned briefly to Central America; but by the end of the eighteenth century, indigo growers faced strong competition from British producers in India, as well as from Cuban planters who had taken advantage of special incentives granted in 1792 by the Bourbon authorities in Madrid. In this case, a Bourbon reform for Cuba had worked against the continued prosperity of indigo in Central America.[41]

Moreover, the indigo industry of the eighteenth century exacerbated a regional rivalry in Central America that had ominous portents for the future—the hostility between Guatemala City interests and the leaders of the outlying provinces, called the *provincianos*. To begin with, indigo was sold at the annual fairs in Guatemala City; the merchants there transhipped the commodity overland to Santo Tomás, where vessels carried it to associates in Cádiz, Spain. The Guatemalan merchants had every advantage.[42] They controlled the best route to the Atlantic port with regards to terrain and market for incoming manufactures; and they were the creditors who financed the indigo harvests. They also manipulated indigo prices and interest rates on loans in their favor. Entrenched in Guatemala City, they exercised a powerful influence upon the Superior Government.

In the 1770s, the provincianos complained of monopolistic practices; and the response of the Bourbon government was immediate and energetic. First, it authorized the indigo growers to form their own corporation so that they could control prices. In 1782, the Crown loaned them 100,000 pesos to start a Montepío, a financial institution similar to a loan association, that could help growers during the critical harvest period. The government also authorized a new location for the annual fairs that was favorable to provincial interests; and, finally, it supported the construction and use of a land route that bypassed Guatemala City to the port of Omoa. This overland route from San Salvador to Zacapa was operational in 1789. The Bourbon authorities, in short, were determined to promote the economic development of Central America's provinces, while at the same time discouraging the monopolistic bent of Guatemala City interests. Moreover, the technique of permitting indigo growers home rule of an economic nature had important implications for Central America's political future.

The merchant bankers in Guatemala City, however, were able to thwart the reforms by gaining the support of leading Spanish officials. Captain General José de Estachería was a case in point. He proceeded to reverse Bourbon intentions in Central America almost singlehandedly from 1783 to 1789. Instead of moving the fairs to Chalchuapa, Estachería ordered them held at a site closer to Guatemala City, where he allowed local interests to set the price of indigo and to monopolize the meat supply at the capital. Provinciano cattlemen and indigo growers protested angrily to the authorities in Madrid. Even tobacco growers complained that the higher cost of meat was hurting their workers. Investigations followed, as might be expected; and Bourbon officials were able to learn how the Captain General of Guatemala had worked at cross purposes with them.[43]

The guilty parties were punished fifteen years later, not a very impressive sign of Bourbon centralized power in the Kingdom of Guatemala. Nevertheless, justice was served. Cattlemen won the right to sell their product in a free market and without restrictions as to locale; and in 1796 Spain authorized the reopening of the trade outlet through Nicaragua via the San Juan River. She also encouraged the traffic through the ports of Omoa and Trujillo in present Honduras.[44] The contraband trade, however, continued to flourish.[45]

Notwithstanding the good intentions of the Bourbon officials in Madrid, the reform program in the area had less than dramatic results. Since 1780 the Spanish government had tried to revitalize the Honduran mining industry with tax incentives and more freedom of action for miners; yet mining failed to prosper, perhaps because of the military distractions that we shall treat below.[46] The colonizing schemes of the eighties and nineties in the vicinity of Trujillo and in northern Guatemala respectively did not succeed in attracting suitable immigrants.[47] The intendancy system, with its laudable objective of fomenting agriculture and economic development in general, was only partially successful, judging from the limited documentation that is extant.[48] The new bureaucrats were apparently conscientious and eager to champion regional interests. It was the Salvadoran intendant, for example, who exposed the unauthorized actions of Captain General Estachería. In Costa Rica, the Cuban-born Tomás de Acosta won over many followers with his enlightened measures to stimulate the local economy.[49] The new intendancies, moreover, set the administrative and political bases of the future states of Central America: León (Nicaragua), San Salvador (most of modern El Salvador), Comayagua (Honduras), and Ciudad Real (Chiapas). The *gobierno* of Cartago (Costa Rica) was treated like an intendancy for all practical purposes because of its outlying location. As the capital of the Kingdom, Guatemala City had a special relationship with its neighboring communities that would determine its future as a political entity.

The Bourbon reforms in Central America did not meet expectations because of external distractions: the perennial rivalry with the British and the disturbed conditions in Europe in the late eighteenth century. A constant, disruptive factor in Central America's history was the English challenge that began in the previous century. Allied with the Indian tribes of the Moskito Shore, Englishmen based in Jamaica nullified Spanish control of the coast while at the same time extracting its valuable wood resources. On occasion, for example, buccaneers made their way down the San Juan River to attack Spaniards who lived in Granada, Nicaragua. The whole effort was profitable; and it became more so in the eighteenth century as Englishmen commenced to settle in the area, exploiting the contraband possibilities with the Spanish colonists in the west.

The English presence in Central America was costly for Spain and diverted government revenues from reform programs to defense measures: the buildup of the naval units, the dispatch of land forces from the west through a no-man's land to the Atlantic, and the attempts to establish a mission system in the barren zone. The expense was prohibitive. The fortifications at Omoa, for example, took twenty-five years to complete at a cost of one and one-half million pesos. In 1782, Spain bolstered her defenses at nearby Trujillo at the sacrifice of much revenue. As a result, Englishmen were ousted from the Moskito Shore; and by the treaties of the 1780s, the British merely held on to a wood-cutting concession at Belize (British Honduras).[50] Yet the military victory was short-lived. By the end of the century, Spain's control of the Atlantic Coast was only nominal. If the defense revenues had been employed in the reform program of Central America, it might have assured the economic recovery of that area. But that was not done.

Mother Nature likewise worked against the reform movement in Central America. In 1773, an earthquake leveled the old capital at Antigua; and in transferring the government to its present site, the Bourbon authorities gave up their revenues for a ten-year period to stimulate the move. The economic situation went from bad to worse with the fall of indigo prices due to outside competition. Moreover, the disruption of the Spanish trade because of the French Revolution and subsequent European disturbances compounded the economic miseries of Central America and held back the reform program.

In a broader sense, the Bourbons were successful in creating a mentality throughout Central America that was receptive to economic progress and the modernization of society. As noted earlier, the Bourbon reformers tried conscientiously to sponsor provincial interests and to deter monopoly. In the process they nurtured a desire for the common good— an incipient nationalism or regionalism. It was their hope that by broadening the economic potential of the area, colonials would prosper and thus reinforce their loyalty to Spain. The mother country, on the other hand, would have received more taxes to meet the expenses of defense and further economic development. The home rule approach, moreover, stimulated a greater sense of local involvement, along the lines recommended by Jovellanos in 1795.

≈≈≈

The ideas of the Enlightenment had a wide appeal to the coterie of intellectuals that lived in Guatemala City in the 1790s. It was indeed a remarkably dynamic and active force of teachers, writers, thinkers, and government officials. Since many of them were *provincianos*, educated at the University of San Carlos in Guatemala City, their intellectual activities influenced the entire Kingdom of Guatemala, not just the capital. Many institutions encouraged the reformers. In addition to the university, the Royal Economic Society, established in 1794, gave them a sounding board. The Royal Consulado (Merchant Guild) of Guatemala, founded a year earlier, listened to their counsels; and the Bourbon officials in Madrid and Guatemala City openly supported their attempts to modernize society in Central America. The major catalyst of the new ideas was the *Gazeta de Guatemala*, a weekly that first appeared on February 13, 1797, and that educated at least two hundred subscribers throughout Central America and Mexico.

In his prize-winning volume, *The Eighteenth-Century Enlightenment in the University of San Carlos de Guatemala*, Professor John Tate Lanning has noted that Guatemalan students enjoyed a modern education that compared favorably with that of contemporaries elsewhere in the world.[51] In medicine, for example, teachers like Drs. José Flores and Narciso Esparragosa were innovators with world reputations.[52] If the Guatemalan university suffered any disadvantage, it was the perennial lack of funds that limited course offerings; and it was a tribute to many professors of the period that they often gave their courses without pay.

A key figure in the curriculum reforms of the 1790s was Father José Antonio Liendo de Goicoechea, a Costa Rican who was a Franciscan. The learned doctor, in 1782, described his teaching methods and evaluated his reading lists for courses that he offered in science and philosophy. It was a report that he sent to the university rector.[53] In keeping with the orientation of the Franciscan Order at that time, the document revealed a thoroughly modern approach to education by a dedicated and popular professor. As editor of the *Gazeta*, moreover, Father Goicoechea reached a wider audience throughout Central America and Mexico, helping to form a social conscience with his many publications. He retired in 1803, at which time his Chair in Philosophy was taken over by Dr. Mariano José López Rayón, a favorite of Father Goicoechea. A Mercedarian friar, Father López was a well-known orator who implanted the eclectic approach to philosophy among his students.[54] There were many other scholars and teachers of distinction at the University of San Carlos. Suffice it to say that the founding fathers of Central America learned about the Enlightenment from first-rate teachers. The *Gazeta* took pride in extolling the qualifications and capabilities of the faculty.[55]

Both Spanish and American-born officials participated in the active intellectual life of the 1790s. Recognizing the university's financial plight, various Captain Generals encouraged the wealthy families to endow chairs or help the institution in every way possible.[56] The Royal Audiencia of the Kingdom of Guatemala, its highest judicial body, provided unqualified support of the Royal Economic Society. In fact, the initial planning sessions were held in the home of Judge Jacobo de Villa Urrutia, a native of Santo Domingo. Educated in Spain and in Mexico, Villa Urrutia was another product of the reform atmosphere of Charles III's reign. He was as sanguine about the role of economic societies as his contemporary Gaspar de Jovellanos. His appointment in 1793 to the post in Guatemala City, moreover, gave him the opportunity to help start the new society there.

Like its prototypes elsewhere, the Guatemalan Society offered a host of prizes to foster the skills of artisans and mechanics and to encourage Indians to learn the latest technology in agriculture. For example, it established a School of Design with a grant from the government. Working closely with the *Gazeta*, on one occasion it sponsored an essay contest on whether or not Indians should wear Spanish clothing. It also commissioned studies on mendicancy and the revival of the cacao industry in Central America; and it collaborated with the Royal Consulado in promoting the diversification of the economy and the development of an adequate infrastructure. Considering the lack of funds, its accomplishments were commendable before 1801. An arbitrary order from Madrid closed its doors, and it did not resume its constructive work until 1811.[57] It should be noted that Creoles and Spaniards worked harmoniously in this organization.

Alejandro Ramírez was another key official who helped spread the Enlightenment throughout the Kingdom of Guatemala and in other parts of the Spanish-speaking world. A Spaniard of humble origins, thoroughly committed to the cause of modernization, Ramírez served in Guatemala from 1795 to 1813, later in Puerto Rico from 1813 to 1816, and then in Cuba from 1816 to 1821. He was an active member of the Guatemalan Economic Society, along with his friend Villa Urrutia; and he went on several missions outside of Central America in behalf of the Society. The American Philosophical Society included Ramírez in its membership. As a contributor to the *Gazeta*, he was a tireless advocate of economic development. He also wrote a treatise on the navigation of the River Motagua. His influence was powerful because he was the secretary to the Captain General in Guatemala City. The residents of the capital held him in high esteem. Later, while he was serving in Cuba, they requested his appointment to the top executive post in Central America. Unfortunately, his premature death voided the recommendation.[58]

It would appear that the Royal Consulado de Guatemala was an anomaly in view of the Bourbons' opposition to monopoly and the support of free competition. Yet, contemporaries regarded the Consulado as a vehicle for reform.[59] Its function was to stimulate the area's economy, promote trade, develop the infrastructure, and handle commercial justice. To be sure, it was an instrument of an affluent white elite, men with fortunes over 20,000 pesos; but it included Spaniards, Creoles, merchants, landowners, retailers, and royal officials from fifteen different deputations throughout Central America. Although the main junta was in Guatemala City, it was not exclusively the tool of Guatemala City interests, although the latter had a powerful voice in policy.[60] The Consulado shared the Economic Society's concern for economic development and enlightened ideas; in fact, some men held positions in both corporations. Be that as it may, in the pre-Independence years, monopoly was not a primary objective of the Consulado membership. If it had been, men like Antonio Juarros and José de Aycinena, whose careers we shall study in subsequent chapters, would not have been members. In resurrecting this medieval institution and modernizing its guidelines and membership, the Bourbons sought to give regional interests a substantial voice in the process of economic development, just as they had done earlier with the indigo growers' association. And once again, it appears that the Bourbon government had heeded the advice of Jovellanos in the *Informe de Ley Agraria* by adopting home rule, or regionalism, as an instrument of reform.

Another example of the regionalist or federal approach was evident in the famous maritime expedition that left Spain in 1803 with instructions to introduce the vaccine for smallpox throughout the Empire. Alejandro Ramírez had been an articulate champion of vaccinations to curb the periodic ravages of smallpox in the New World; and he, of course, welcomed the vaccine to Central America. Since it was planned as a continuous project, the authorities in Madrid outlined a special code.[61] It called for the establishment of provincial juntas for the entire Kingdom, encharged with the responsibility of averting the dreaded epidemics of the past. In every respect, this particular code reflected a progressive stand on public health. Indeed, the Bourbon record in support of modern medical practices was commendable in every respect and deserves much more attention than it has received here.

Published weekly from 1797 to 1816, the *Gazeta de Guatemala* was a powerful instrument of reform in Central America. In the prospectus, the editor wrote that he planned to goad "inactive spirits" into "thinking, discussing, and inventing useful things."[62] Certainly the columns of this spirited periodical confirm the impression that Central Americans were in the mainstream of the Enlightenment. Thoroughly modern and imaginative in its presentation, the *Gazeta* reported and analyzed the latest advances in all fields of knowledge throughout the world. Writers questioned their sources of information critically, and there was no blind imitation or indigestion of facts or points of view. They knew that in 1800 a certain Dr. Benjamin Smith had published a key work on tropical disease in Philadelphia; there were frequent allusions to the works of Descartes, Locke, Condillac, Buffon, Montesquieu, and Rousseau. The *Gazeta* also published histories and descriptions of geographical regions in Central America so as to familiarize readers with their resources. With such stimulating fare, we can appreciate how well the founding fathers of Central America came to know the ideas of the Enlightenment, thanks to the Bourbons' promotion of intellectual ferment overseas.

Political economy was the overriding concern of the Guatemalan *Gazeta*. It favored economic progress throughout Central America at all costs, which meant a continual propagation of modern ideas and a corresponding attack upon all that was retrograde. Freedom of trade was an editorial obsession, and the authorities cited were worldwide. The French physiocrats, because of their concern for the freedom of agricultural interests, received much attention; so did Bernardo Ward, an Irishman who wrote the *Proyecto Económico* while in the service of Spain. In one issue, the editor referred to Adam Smith in the most flattering terms, as "a man with hair on his chest."[63] Throughout the issues of the *Gazeta* its writers kept repeating the phrase, "freedom is the soul of trade."[64]

Forever extolling the unlimited potential of Central America, a veritable paradise astride the two oceans, the *Gazeta*, as well as other publications of that day, fomented patriotism and love for the area. Goicoechea was almost poetic in this regard. He was visibly moved when a periodical in Madrid complimented the Guatemalan journal.[65] On another occasion, he observed that North American artists had been received favorably in England; and he yearned for the day when Central American talents would receive similar recognition in Europe.[66] Moreover, the term "American" was commonplace in the literature of the period, furthering the Creoles' identification with the New World.

Like Americans everywhere, Guatemalans resented the slurs made on their cultural ability or racial makeup. Judge Villa Urrutia—a Dominican, it will be recalled—defended the Americans' ability in science, especially in political economy, "humanity's most glorious struggle" to advance the cause "of the Nation."[67] On that occasion, he was honoring Friar Matías de Córdoba, a Dominican born in Chiapas who had just won an essay contest on how Indians should dress. Father Goicoechea took sharp exception to the statement by the German Cornelius de Pauw that humans, animals, and vegetables degenerated in the New World. This was "insane arrogance" on the part of a European, who had no direct knowledge of the Americas. And there were many examples of this nonsense: the Frenchman Masson de Morvilliers' insulting remarks about the Indians of the New World; and the English historian William Robertson's ridiculous claim that Indians had a limited mentality because they could not think in abstract terms.[68] All of which led Father Goicoechea to observe in his own inimitable and pragmatic fashion:

> It is easy to say: all Americans are indolent; thus the climate makes them that way; the Indians are the most slothful of men in this world; thus, that is how they have always been and it is impossible to make them more alert; the ladinos are neglectful and given to drunkedness; thus, there is a force in the climate they live under that inclines them toward laziness and drink, etc. That is the way of thinking of certain pseudo-authorities, more interested in finding general causes to which attribute defects rather than examining the obvious, simple, and natural means of destroying or reforming them. But a good observer does not form these general rules, nor deduces from them such false results. He says, rather: men are indolent; thus there is a moral defect that keeps [them] from going to work. . . . And so on down the line.[69]

Many writings of that period exposed the weaknesses in Central American society. While exploring the causes of mendicancy, Father Goicoechea noted that monoculture was the root cause since a one-crop economy led to overspecialization and a labor surplus. It also discouraged the diversification of the economy, so essential for increased employment. Since hacendados felt no responsibility for the plight of workers—on the contrary, they preferred to have a surplus of labor at hand—vagrancy and begging were the logical consequences. He urged both the Economic Society and the Consulado to work toward an increased production of indigo while at the same time diversifying agricultural exports for the world market and developing the industrial potential of Central America. In the long term, this approach would relieve unemployment as well as the social and moral breakdown that accompanied it.[70]

Villa Urrutia and Ramírez were sharp critics of underpopulation and the poor distribution of Central America's people, creating the anomaly of poverty in an area of fantastic fertility. They underscored the isolation of Central America's regions from one another because of inadequate communications, insufficient ports, and what have you. To a lesser degree than Goicoechea, they likewise blamed the depression upon overspecialization in indigo; and they suggested the export of at least forty potential commodities, including coffee.[71] As royal officials, they understandably reflected the developmental concerns of the Bourbon government.

In the discussion of Central America's economic development, the Indian received much attention, hardly a surprise in view of his overwhelming presence in the Guatemalan area. A book published in 1789 was frequently cited in defense of the Indians. It was the famous manuscript of José Campillo y Cosío entitled *New System of Economic Government for America*, completed in 1743. According to Campillo, Indians were unable to develop their lands properly because of insecure title; and he defended the Indian against charges that he was lazy and inferior—a stereotype that was patently absurd to any honest observer. To integrate the Indian, he urged the use of Spanish-style clothing and the teaching of Castilian.[72] Father Goicoechea and his colleagues on the *Gazeta* staff repeated these recommendations, and they took pride in those Indians that had demonstrated their ability at the University.[73]

Father Antonio García Redondo, the Dean of the Cathedral Chapter in Guatemala City, prepared an articulate and influential treatise in behalf of the Indian in Central America. Born in Nueva Granada (Colombia) and educated at the University of San Carlos, Father Antonio began his defense by reminding the reader that since the mid-sixteenth century the Indian had been forced to work for the white man in such levies as the *repartimiento*, *mandamiento*, and *mita*. The rationale was that otherwise the Indian would do nothing. Thus, Indian work forces built many roads and public buildings and harvested most of the crops in the New World. In fact, they were the only ones who actually worked. It was therefore specious to call them lazy. All the hacendado ever did was to give them seeds, point out what land they might use, and then collect his share of the harvest. In fact, the Indians were the "least idle people that our republic supports," emphasized the father. At times, to be sure, Indians got carried away at their festivities and drank too much, something that they should be discouraged from doing for their own good. But others should not overlook the reality that "while we eat, sleep, and get fat in *dolce farniente*, these wretched humans of ours are out working hard, perhaps to assure us the fuel for our gluttony." If the Indians "were to awaken one day in a calculating mood, by nightfall they would be rich," prophesied the Colombian priest. Following the criteria of Adam Smith, "our Indians should be rich." But selfish interests were against this. With tongue in cheek, Father Antonio noted: "When the question is asked why it is that these trees do not produce, the farmer does not reply that the tree is slothful and lazy; rather, [the answer is] that the suckers and parasitic plants take away the sap and sterilize it."[74]

Throughout the paper the Dean insisted that the Indian performed a major role in Central America's life. He contributed regularly to his community funds (*cajas de communidad*) in order to protect himself in an emergency; and he supplied over 300,000 pesos annually to the Church, an indispensable subsidy. "Everyone eats and drinks at the expense of the Indians," he concluded. Throughout his defense, Father Antonio García Redondo attacked the wastefulness of the colonial system and its unfairness to the Indian. The emancipation of the natives and the economic development of Central America, in his view, were concomitants. Indian lands had to have value, so that the Indians could reap the profits of their labor. Otherwise, economic progress was a chimera.[75] These were remarkably modern notions, but they were held by many reformers in the Spanish-speaking world.

What motivated this concern for the Indians? It would appear that there was a convenient blend of humanitarian, religious, and economic considerations, and not necessarily in that order. At any rate, these various motives tended to reinforce each other, as we have seen in Dean García Redondo's case. Bourbon planners issued many cédulas in hopes of correcting the abuse of the Indian, with little success.[76] In theory, the intendancy system prescribed a basic education for the natives; yet in Central America at least, very little implementation followed. The Spanish government restored the Chair of Cakchiquel at the University of San Carlos to aid priests in communicating with highland Indians, a futile gesture considering the early history of that course.[77] In the 1780s,

Bourbon leaders ordered the teaching of Castilian to the Indians; but, apparently, there was no follow-through. In 1815 the government repeated the order.[78] Although the Indian program of the Bourbons failed in practice, it nevertheless demonstrated good intentions and set a pattern for future reforms.

The Royal Consulado of Guatemala issued a remarkably progressive document in 1811, which in addition to Indian reforms advocated a wide-scale program of economic development for Central America.[79] The economic picture was bleak, one of stagnancy and depression. Only Indians were working; and the mixed bloods, not very dependable as a rule, were apathetic. The white hacienda owners, moreover, were not efficient in the development of their vast holdings. Most trade was local and characterized by barter. Thirty to thirty-five houses handled the legal traffic with Cádiz via the port of Santo Tomás, totaling about one million pesos. The war in Europe had caused serious interruptions in trade; and an onslaught of locusts had damaged the indigo crops. Contraband trade, as usual, was undermining the legal traffic.

Change was long overdue, reasoned the leaders of the Royal Consulado. To further the development of agriculture, land should be placed in the hands of the Indians. Land ownership and patriotism went together. Without land, no one could feel a love of *patria*; and the consensus of the Consulado was that small properties, worked by their owners, were far more profitable and valuable than large haciendas. The Consulado cited figures for 1808 to buttress this point. Moreover, Indians should have secure titles to their lands if they were to become "useful farmers." And to guarantee this result, the Consulado proposed another home rule device: the establishment of *juntas protectoras* in Guatemala City and in all provincial capitals that would meet once a week, consisting of representatives from royal, civil, religious, and commercial bodies. All provincial units would collaborate in assuring "the improvement of customs, agriculture, and the happiness of the Indians." Since the Indian was an equal, he should be paid fair wages in order to raise him from poverty levels. Moreover, and this reflected the dominant voice of merchants in the Consulado of Guatemala, the Indian consumer should be able to buy from all merchants, not just those who in the past had garnered exclusive franchises from the government.[80] The reference here was to the longstanding practice of allowing *corregidores* (royal supervisors) to abuse their authority in Indian communities by monopolizing the sale of manufactures, working closely with some merchant ally who might even be a smuggler in some cases.

The Consulado's demand for agrarian reform in Central America was indeed aggressive for the times, exposing a deep interest in real economic development. Again, it reflects the point of view of newly arrived Spanish merchants and their Creole offspring, since they put the blame for the depression upon the land tenure system in the Kingdom. A few individuals owned immense possessions "with enormous prejudice to the many who form the mass of the State, and who do not have a palm of land where they can plant some corn."[81] To correct this situation, the Consulado urged the return of lands taken away from the Indians by Spaniards. Furthermore, all hacienda territory that intruded upon Indian or ladino villages should be sold to the residents or to other private parties at a fair price.[82] If hacendados did not cultivate their lands, they should be compelled to sell them at an equitable price.[83] Private parties, moreover, should be allowed to buy communal lands (*ejidos*) as well as the public domain (*tierras baldías*) according to need—a reference to Indian owners. Provincial authorities, moreover, should encourge the planting and harvesting of suitable crops. Again referring to the Indian, the Consulado insisted that new owners of land should not be allowed to alienate their property. Poorer settlers might receive initial subsidies from village endowments and revenues, as well as community funds.[84]

The 1811 document reveals the predominant voice of Guatemala City merchants. It proposed, for example, the abolition of the Montepío of the indigo growers—a request that was rejected by the Spanish government. Merchants also wanted to fix prices at the indigo fairs, again to the prejudice of provinciano interests; and we have already alluded to the proposal of free trade with the Indian villages, as opposed to the compulsory sales (*repartimientos*) by the corregidores and their colleagues.

Reflecting a strong physiocratic influence, the 1811 report asked for detailed surveys of all regions in the Kingdom of Guatemala in anticipation of developmental projects. The Consulado, for example, urged the encouragement of the tobacco industry in Central America, an export that could be sold in New Spain and Peru.[85] It also felt that colonization projects should have priority, despite the failures of the late eighteenth century. With the right type of immigrant from Cuba or from the Canary Islands, the colonization of the empty lands might succeed now, thus making it possible to develop the port of Isabal on the Golfo Dulce, backed by an extensive settlement in the interior. Honduras and Costa Rica, especially Costa Rica's Atlantic Coast, likewise had great potential for settlement and agricultural development. The report went into detail on how this might be implemented. The Consulado also urged the government to encourage cotton production and the development of a modern textile industry in Central America.[86] These were the major recommendations that the Guatemalan Consulado made to their representative in Spain. It reflected the program of an aggressive capitalistic element in Guatemala City that aspired to develop and perhaps to control the regional economy of Central America.

≈≈≈

The economic aspects of the eighteenth-century Enlightenment had a powerful impact upon the Spanish-speaking world, perhaps because agriculture was a prime concern of the reformers. The onset of depression in Central America by the late eighteenth century further encouraged the hopes for economic development. The Royal Consulado went beyond the recommendations of the *Informe de Ley Agraria* on the subject of land reform, anticipating many twentieth-century points. The Economic Society of Guatemala likewise supported the propagation of "useful knowledge," living up to the sanguine expectations of Gaspar de Jovellanos. In the field of social reforms, the program to integrate the Indian was a harbinger of today's *indigenismo*, whatever the motivation may have been. There is little doubt that the Consulado spokesmen favored the Indian because of his potential as a producer and consumer; but other reformers, especially the religious spokesmen, had humanitarian and religious objectives as well. The support of the Bourbon government, moreover, was vital. Royal officials were consciously popularizing "political economy" throughout Central America, encouraging a modern viewpoint and a love, or patriotism, for their various regions. Although many Bourbon reforms fell short of their mark, there were external circumstances that contributed to this failure. On balance, the Bourbon legacy was a valuable one for Spain and the Spanish Empire as the dramatic events of 1808 unfolded.

2. The Glorious Revolution

From this point on, American Spaniards, you shall see yourselves raised to the dignity of free men. You are no longer the same men as before, weighed down by a yoke that was heavier the farther you lived from the center of power, regarded with indifference, harassed by greediness, and destroyed by ignorance. . . . Your destinies are no longer dependent upon Ministers, Viceroys, or Governors; they are in your hands.

REGENCY, *February 14, 1810*[1]

IT WAS nine o'clock on Monday morning, September 24, 1810, and over a hundred deputies had gathered on the Island of León, near the walled city of Cádiz. There was a general excitement in the air that not even the presence of hostile French troops in the vicinity could abate. Spaniards in the port area were about to witness the opening session of their first modern parliament, called The General and Extraordinary Cortes of Spain. It drew up the famous Constitution of Cádiz in 1812 and also coined the political term "liberal" for the world.[2]

The largest group of founding fathers were men of the cloth, thus explaining the strong religious orientation and humanitarian fervor in the halls of parliament. Some deputies were aristocrats; others, members of the armed forces, ex-government officials, judges, lawyers, merchants, and farmers. They were generally men of substance who had been appointed by authorized corporations or had been the victors in recent indirect elections.[3] With the exception of Ramón Power from Puerto Rico, the American representatives on that memorable day were *suplentes*, or substitutes, authorized to represent their home areas until the arrival of the proprietary deputies (*proprietarios*). There were also suplentes for the occupied provinces of Spain. Overwhelmingly moderate and yet progressive in outlook, this distinguished assembly was especially determined to oust the French invaders from Spain, while at the same time establishing the foundation for a modern European nation.

As the crowds shouted enthusiastically "Long live Spain, Long live the nation," the proud deputies filed into the Church where they heard the Mass of the Holy Ghost delivered by the Archbishop Luis de Borbón. As uncle of the missing Ferdinand VII, he added a regal note to the ceremony. He was also the highest prelate of Spain in his capacity as the Archbishop of Toledo and the Cardinal di Scala. His close identification with the Cádiz Experiment gave it much prestige and respectability. After the Mass, the Bishop of Orense, as President of the Regency, offered a brief prayer of exhortation to the assembled deputies. His secretary then asked them to take the following oath:

> Do you swear to uphold the Holy Apostolic Roman Catholic Religion, without admitting any other in these kingdoms? Do you swear to conserve the integrity of the Spanish nation, and not to withhold any means to free her from her unjust oppressors? Do you swear to maintain the [nation's] dominions for our beloved Sovereign Ferdinand VII or in his default for his legitimate successors, and to make as many efforts as possible to free him from captivity, and place him on the throne? Do you swear to carry out legally and faithfully the charge that the nation has placed in your care, guarding the laws of Spain without prejudice to the changes, adjustments, and variations that might be required for the good of the nation?

After answering in the affirmative, the deputies approached in pairs to touch the Holy Bible. The Bishop of Orense then solemnly pronounced these words: "If you do as you have sworn, may God reward you; and if not, may He hold you accountable." The ceremony ended with the hymn *Veni Sancte Spiritus* and the *Te Deum*.[4]

Still in double file, the founding fathers marched to the House of Parliament, overwhelmed by the shouts and praises of the crowd. Their seats were located on the main floor; and some sections on the same level were reserved for members of the diplomatic corps, the nobility of Spain, Army staff officers, government officials, and the wives of the delegates. The general public hastened to the benches on the second and third floors, excited at the prospects of viewing such a historic event. Public sessions had been the rule at the Spanish Cortes from the beginning. Thus, "the people" could add their approval or disapproval to the acts of their representatives; and, for better or for worse, this public influence weighed heavily upon the conduct of Parliament. The picture of the seventh Ferdinand of Spain overlooked the proceedings of September 24; and on the dais below it sat the five Regents. The Bishop of Orense reviewed for the assembly the accomplishments of the Regency since January 31, 1810, when it had taken over the government from the Junta Central. He reminded the deputies of the critical problems that they would have to confront, wishing them well in doing so. At this point, the Regents left the hall.

The impressive accomplishments of the first parliamentary session augured well for Spanish constitutionalism. No less than eleven important decrees had passed by shortly after midnight. The editor of *El Conciso,* perhaps with some exaggeration, noted proudly that the deputies had worked fifteen hours straight without food or rest on that first day. And they finished in one day what ordinarily would have taken months, all within sight of the envious and confused French troops. Bursting with emotion, he told his readers: "Privileged beings of the earth who have witnessed the tender and majestic spectacle that has unfolded on the royal Island of León on September 24, 1810, tell the world if there are words to paint what you saw there, what you heard there, and what you felt there."[5]

A well-organized minority capitalized on the general euphoria of the moment to advance revolutionary proposals. The two delegates from Extremadura, Diego Muñoz Torrero and Manuel Luján, were especially effective. In the first decree, Muñoz Torrero, the former Rector of the University of Salamanca, proposed that sovereignty rested in the people of the Spanish nation, a dramatic repudiation of the position taken by the Junta Central on January 29, 1810.[6] The future Liberals of the Cortes thus seized the initiative. War conditions had played into their hands; the sovereignty of the people, a veritable dogma for the liberal leadership at Cádiz, had gained acceptance in the excitement and good will of September 24, 1810. Other decrees of that date repeated the nation's allegiance to Ferdinand VII, declared null and void his cession of the throne to Napoleon, called for a three-way division of power in the Spanish government, appointed the old Regency as the provisional executive of the nation, confirmed officials in various branches of the government, and proclaimed the inviolability of the deputies.

On the second day, the overseas delegation made a serious bid to advance its interests. Americans proposed that the decree of installation should not be sent to the New World without a statement of concessions to the Americas. The proposal was sent to a committee of ten Americans, one of whom was a Guatemalan. In the afternoon session, the group presented a list of demands to the Cortes: in essence, they asked for effective and equal representation of the overseas territories with the Peninsula. Moreover, to demonstrate the sincerity of the Cortes in a program of equality, the ten Americans urged the granting of amnesty to the rebels overseas. Somewhat surprised by the aggressive and well-organized thrust of the overseas delegation, the peninsular majority, nevertheless, was able to resist the pressure; and, a few days later, it voted to table the American proposals. It preferred to discuss the "American Question" in secret sessions rather than risk a display of dissension in the early days of the Cortes.[7]

Writing from London, José María Blanco y Crespo (known in England as Blanco-White) often compared the Cádiz experience to the English "Glorious Revolution" of the seventeenth century. Others referred to it as "The Revolution," "Our Revolution," and "The Holy Insurrection." There was an awareness everywhere that the Spanish-speaking world was undergoing a dramatic historical change—a process that gained momentum after May 2, 1808.

≈≈≈

The reign of Charles IV (1788–1808) had not been a happy one for most subjects of Spain. Jovellanos described it as a "scandalous despotism;" others called it the Mal Gobierno (Bad Government).[8] To be sure, the contrast between Charles III and his son was not flattering. The father had worked conscientiously to uplift his nation and had entrusted government to highly competent ministers. Spaniards regarded him as an exemplary monarch: religious, proud, honest, loving, and faithful to the memory of his wife. His son, on the other hand, had entrusted many affairs to a *valido*, Manuel Godoy, a favorite who was self-seeking and corrupt. Moreover, everyone suspected that Godoy had made his master a cuckold, an image that Spaniards found especially offensive.

The French Revolution and the rise of Napoleon Bonaparte were key factors in the rapid decline of Spain during the reign of Charles IV, a period of serious drain on the manpower and financial resources of the nation. The worsening economic plight of Spain, as well as the increased demands for revenues and taxes, contributed to the stereotype of the despotic state. It was also a desperate government that resorted to the old techniques of selling titles or granting exemptions of all sorts for a price, further discrediting the rule of Manuel Godoy. He was without question Spain's most hated leader. One of his doubtful programs was the Caja de

Consolidación (1798) which he extended to America six years later. Godoy considered the measure a reform, a refunding program that might consolidate the national debt. Indeed, there was some merit to the program for Spain herself; but in the New World it had the deleterious effect of draining away capital at a time when it was most needed for the economy. Colonials therefore were resentful of the refunding scheme. Peninsulars also disdained what they called "Godoy's sponge" and the "dark mysteries" of the Consolidación.[9]

Americans accumulated many other grievances during the Godoy years. On November 23, 1799, for example, the government arbitrarily disbanded the Economic Society of Guatemala on the flimsiest of excuses. This action, of course, contradicted the Bourbon program of furthering the spread of the Enlightenment. The interruption of trade because of war in Europe was also an expensive annoyance; and the weakening of Spain's naval power at Trafalgar in 1805 added to the isolation of the Spanish colonies. During those years of isolation, moreover, many Spanish officials acted rather arbitrarily toward the subjects under their command, further alienating them.[10]

Against this backdrop of discontent, the historical events of 1808 become more meaningful. On March 18, a Spanish mob attacked the hated Godoy's home in Aranjuez and forced his ouster from the government. Charles IV abdicated on the following day, and Ferdinand VII— "The Desired One," as Spaniards were wont to call him in those days— replaced his father on the throne. Lured into southern France along with his parents, Ferdinand VII became a hostage of Napoleon, who demanded his abdication of the throne in order to give it to his brother Joseph. When the French tried to remove from Spain any prince that might have rallied the Spaniards against them, the bloody events of May 2, 1808, took place in Madrid.

The Second of May marked the beginning of Spain's War of Independence against the French. But it was not just independence from France that concerned Spaniards; they were determined, as well, to prevent ever again the despotism of the previous two decades. Constitutionalism was in the air as writers competed with each other in presenting before the public the type of government that should guide a modern Spanish nation. Spain's subjects overseas were likewise caught in the contagion that would eventually lead to their own war of independence from the mother country. And the developments in Spain after May 2 encouraged the trend.

Accustomed to the continual victories of Napoleon's armies, the military action on the Peninsula surprised and elated Europeans everywhere. It seemed incredible that Spaniards without sufficient arms and munitions could resist the well-trained invaders. Although initially the various *juntas de defensa* suffered reverses, on July 21, 1808, at Bailén, the Spaniards destroyed the myth of French invincibility, inspiring themselves and Europeans in general to continue to fight against French domination. By August 1, 1808, the French had abandoned Madrid and were in full retreat to the Ebro River line. After regrouping their forces, Napoleon's troops went on the offensive. By early December 1808, they were back in Madrid and had recaptured much of Spain. Peninsulars retreated southward into Andalucía hoping to control the enemy by bottling up the passes through the Sierra Morena. On November 19, 1809, however, the French broke the defense line at Ocaña and poured into the south, entering Sevilla in late January, 1810. Before long, they were outside Cádiz, laying a siege that was maintained until August 1812. There was, of course, much more to the so-called Peninsular War—the key role played by English armies, the daring guerrilla raids, and the obstructionism of brave Spaniards behind the French lines.[11]

Regional juntas sprang up throughout the peninsula to fill the political vacuum created by the king's absence. These juntas refused to obey the royal councils of Spain because of a suspicion that those bodies were about to betray the nation to the French. Through rump elections, the elites in each province gained control of their respective juntas. They argued that in the absence of the monarch, sovereignty reverted to "the people." The juntas, of course, did represent the people. However shaky their legal reasoning might have been, there is no doubt that the juntas subscribed to it; and they were not disposed to relinquish even the smallest part of their effective power. In short, federalism had become a fact of life in Spain after May 2, 1808; and it mattered little that the disgruntled Consejo de Castilla and other major councils of Spain regarded the provincial juntas as usurpers of power.[12] The example set by the peninsular juntas, moreover, was not lost on overseas subjects. Charging that the Spanish hierarchy in their midst might capitulate to the French, Creoles easily rationalized their seizure of power in behalf of the absent and beloved Ferdinand VII.

The provincial juntas of Spain soon recognized that some type of general government was necessary. They agreed, therefore, to send two deputies to a Junta Central Suprema y Gubernativa de España. This body met at Aranjuez, just south of Madrid, on September 25, 1808, under the capable leadership of the Count of Floridablanca, one of Charles III's great ministers. The Junta Central proceeded to organize the government and the war effort with dispatch, establishing relations with other foreign powers and seeking the financial cooperation of the colonies. It was highly popular while there were military victories.

This popularity was short-lived, however. As the French marched on Madrid in late November 1808, the Junta Central moved its headquarters to Sevilla. Thereafter it was forever in trouble, as dissident elements blamed it for the military disasters. Although the Junta Central had tried to accommodate the old royal councils by placing them under its jurisdiction, the councillors in question were not particularly grateful, especially since they felt that their jurisdictions were circumscribed in this new arrangement but also because the juntas provinciales defied them with impunity. When the Junta Central moved to consolidate the royal councils in late 1809, the furious councillors retaliated by advocating the establishment of a regency. Moreover, they declared the unconstitutionality of Spain's provisional government. A demoralized military also blamed government meddling for the battlefield reverses.

The major enemies of the Junta Central, as it turned out, were the provincial bodies that had created it. The instructions to their delegates reveal that they had intended nothing more than a confederation government; and, in practice, their dealings with the Junta Central stemmed from the same assumption. With a few exceptions, as Jovellanos tells us, the provincial juntas contributed very little to the maintenance of the general government. Their financial support was limited to military expenses in their own areas, not outside of them. When the Junta Central issued the ordinance of January 1, 1809, that would have made the regional juntas merely defense units, the provincial juntas openly resisted the centralizing move. After the defeat at Ocaña, they were even more defiant, the Junta de Valencia in particular.[13] By late January 1810, the Junta Central was thoroughly discredited in Sevilla and was forced to leave for Cádiz. Along the route to the port, the Centrales suffered humiliation and abuse from the mob. They were made the scapegoats of the military defeats to the French; and they were accused, unfairly it would seem, of corruption and power-seeking.[14]

With so much emphasis upon the negative aspects of the Junta Central's tenure, it is easy to lose track of the constructive measures that it initiated in behalf of Spanish constitutionalism. Beginning in 1809, for example, there was a fantastic intellectual effort in Sevilla on the part of the Centrales and their co-workers, many of whom later served in the

Cortes of Cádiz. They researched every conceivable topic that might come up in parliament: education, religious issues, economic problems and projects, medieval parliaments and precedents, and more. Jovellanos, for example, headed the education committee, and his tireless research and public positions gained wide publicity.[15] Many of the files were taken to Cádiz; unfortunately, others were lost to posterity.

The Junta Central, moreover, was quick to recognize that the colonial relationship had changed since May 2, 1808. Overseas subjects were contributing substantial funds (*donativos*) for the war effort and therefore were in a position to demand concessions from the grateful mother country in the future. Moreover, the Napoleonic government of Joseph I had offered the Americans some representation in the Constitution of Bayonne (July 7, 1808), and in every way was trying to attract the Americas to its banners. To meet the competition, the Junta Central declared on January 22, 1809, that the overseas areas were integral parts of the Spanish nation; in short, colonialism no longer existed in the Spanish-speaking world. In terms of representation, this meant that each viceroyalty (Río de la Plata, New Granada, New Spain, and Peru) and captaincy general (Chile, Cuba, Puerto Rico, Guatemala, Venezuela, and the Philippines) was entitled to one representative on the Junta Central.[16] The provisional government was likewise favorably disposed toward freeing trade relations with the Americas and was investigating that possibility when it fell from power.

The encouragement of constitutional monarchy in Spain, however, was perhaps the most constructive feature of the Junta Central's tenure, thanks in great part to the efforts of Gaspar de Jovellanos. On the constitutional issue, Jovellanos represented the middle-of-the-road position. To his right were the conservatives who lost their leadership when Floridablanca died; they opposed the convocation of a Cortes, arguing that the Junta Central should restrict itself to the defense of the nation and the enforcement of the laws. On the left, the advocates of the sovereignty-in-the-people thesis wanted to create a thoroughly modern Spain at a constitutional convention. Jovellanos and the moderates, who dominated the Junta Central, favored the calling of a convention in order to establish a progressive, yet traditional, regime in Spain. Jovellanos believed that sovereignty resided only in the monarch and that no part of it could be exercised by any other person or body. It was "political heresy," he claimed, to argue that a nation "whose constitution is completely monarchical is sovereign, or to attribute to it functions of sovereignty." The monarch's sovereignty, however, was not absolute; it was limited by the "rights of the Nation." What Jovellanos had in mind was an enlightened monarch like Charles III. Above all, he wanted to prevent the abuse of power in all branches of government.[17]

Strongly influenced by the examples of England and the United States, Jovellanos convinced his colleagues that a bicameral system of government was best suited for Spain. As a buffer between the Executive and Legislature, he favored a "moral power," a Senate comprised of clergymen and nobles. It is important to realize, however, that Jovellanos proposed to include the intellectual elite of the nation among the ranks of the nobles.[18] His recommendations along these lines, as we shall see, influenced the institution of the Consejo de Estado in the Constitution of 1812.

The Junta Central's advocacy of a constitutional convention brought upon it the wrath of the conservatives, adding to the dissident elements that favored the ouster of that government. On two occasions, the Junta Central had declared publicly a date for the meeting of the constituent assembly; moreover, it prepared and circulated the electoral procedures for that convention. It was also responsible for the suplentes system that provided representation for occupied or distant provinces.[19]

Completely discredited by so many enemies and hoping to avert further anarchy, the Centrales resigned their trust. In their last decree of January 29, 1810, they explained in detail what arrangements had been made to convene the Cortes by March 1 if the military situation permitted. It also urged the Regency to send out special invitations to all archbishops, bishops, and grandees to participate in the convention. The Junta repeated the various recommendations of the Constitutional Committee for a three-way division of power, a Senate, and so forth. The Junta's final decree, however, was never printed by the Regency, perhaps to satisfy the various dissident elements that had clamored for the Junta's ouster. Noting the fact of non-publication, Blanco-White reproduced the document in the London paper *El Español*. He hoped that the deputies at Cádiz would take into account its many useful suggestions.[20]

Frequently described as a conservative body, the Regency that took over on January 31, 1810, consisted of five men, all of them Spaniards initially. At the last moment, however, and recognizing that Americans might feel slighted, one Spaniard stepped aside for the Mexican Miguel de Lardizábal y Uribe, who had been sent to represent New Spain on the Junta Central.[21]

In view of the deteriorating military situation, the Regency did a fair job of rallying the Spanish forces against the French and of reestablishing confidence in the provisional government of Spain. As the epigraph to this chapter indicates, the Regency fully intended to follow a generous policy toward the Americas, just as the Junta Central had done. It raised the number of suplentes for the overseas areas to twenty-nine, and it expressed a determination to remove the tribute payments of the Indians. On May 17, 1810, moreover, a royal order circulated in Cádiz that allowed American Spaniards to trade with the English and Portuguese allies of Spain, a concession that had been made earlier to Havana, Cuba. It was now generalized to all the Americas, as the Regency granted the request that Americans at Cádiz had made to the Junta Central.[22] These measures seemed to indicate that the Regency fully expected to bring about a new day of freedom for subjects overseas—a generosity which, of course, would make the Regency more palatable to Americans and Filipinos overseas.

Unfortunately, the Regency soon changed its constructive orientation toward the ex-colonies, thus accounting for its unfavorable image among Americans. Its inability to deliver on the promises made to Americans was the result of an unhealthy dependence upon the moneyed interests of Cádiz, the members of the Consulado de Cádiz. Moreover, these merchants had formed a political arm, the Junta de Cádiz, just at the time that the Regency took over the government. Aware of its importance in the military and financial picture, this new Junta of Cádiz exploited its bargaining power. The Regency had made this possible on March 31, 1810, when it turned over its financial affairs to the Junta, a contract which did not expire until after the Cortes had convened.[23]

As a captive of the Cádiz merchants, the Regency was forced into an anti-American policy. When the Junta of Cádiz learned, for example, of the "free trade" concession of May 17, 1810, its members were apoplectic with rage and demanded an immediate retraction of the grant, insisting upon the punishment of the officials who had permitted it. Much to the chagrin of Americans at Cádiz, the Regency complied with the demands of the Junta of Cádiz.[24] Before long, it also bowed to the Cádiz merchants on the Caracas question. When the rambunctious Junta received news that the city of Caracas had set up its own junta and had refused to recognize the Regency in Spain, it urged immediate action against the Venezuelan rebels, ingrates of the first order. The Regency, of course, danced to the fiddler's tune. On August 30, 1810, it established a blockade of the rebel province and ordered a naval force to implement it.[25] In early September 1810, the Regency instructed the Captain General of Puerto Rico—and presumably other high officials overseas received similar orders—to use extraordinary powers in quashing any demonstration of sympathy for the Caracas movement.[26]

It is not surprising, therefore, that the American delegation was in a combative mood as the Cortes began its sessions. The overseas delegates had come to realize by this time that peninsular promises and declarations of equality for the Americas were so much rhetoric. The assignment of ten representatives on the Junta Central, for example, compared dismally with the thirty-six votes alloted to the eighteen juntas of the Peninsula. And one out of five regents made even less sense to the Americans' concept of equality. The Spanish government, moreover, had determined that there would be fifty-eight overseas deputies in the forthcoming Cortes; yet it only authorized half of that number to serve as suplentes until the arrival of the proprietors. Furthermore, the overseas delegates resented the initial quota of fifty-eight, one deputy for every overseas province, whereas Peninsulars were authorized to elect one deputy per 50,000 inhabitants. This was the major political grievance of the Americans at Cádiz.

The ubiquitous Junta of Cádiz also influenced the decision to convoke the Cortes, an objective that it shared with other provincial juntas of Spain in order to legitimize the provisional government as well as their own authority. In early June 1810, the Junta of Cádiz viewed with alarm the latest intelligence that Ferdinand VII might be compelled to marry Joseph I's daughter, Napoleon's niece. It was urgent, therefore, to convoke the Cortes immediately in order to defeat the French strategy. The jittery merchants agreed to interrupt all sailings to the New World in order to prevent any reaction to the wedding rumors. On June 18, 1810, the Regency announced the convocation of the Spanish Parliament.[27]

Central America's response to the European events described above followed the general pattern for the New World, although in some respects it was more moderate. Perhaps the nature of Captain General Antonio González Sarabia may have had something to do with this. An energetic leader and a sincere patriot, González was determined to root out any evidence of French influence in Central America. For this purpose, he established a special Tribunal de Vigilancia to check cases of subversion. Through forceful defense measures, Captain General González brought security to his jurisdiction—an absolute necessity in the light of propects that Mexican authorities might move toward independence.

General González went out of his way, moreover, to inform Central Americans of the events in Spain and worked closely with local militias and troops. He was an efficient administrator, and Central Americans responded generously to the call for funds. Even the Indians, perhaps without their knowledge, contributed from their community sources to the cause against the French.[28]

Despite the cooperation of Spaniards and Creoles in the defense effort, there was nonetheless a strong undercurrent of rivalry between the Spanish hierarchy and area interests. The Ayuntamiento of Guatemala City soon gave evidence that it wanted to play a free hand. It insisted, for example, upon its constitutional right to take the oath to Ferdinand VII within its own building, much to the annoyance of González and other Spaniards.[29] A key factor that stimulated the competition was the propaganda generated by the Second of May in the Spanish world. The Secretary of the Junta Central, Pedro de Ceballos, had emotionally attacked the "despotism" of the previous twenty years in Spanish history in his description of the May events.[30] Americans, in turn, seized upon this characterization with alacrity in depicting the rule of Spanish officials overseas. In short, it became standard procedure after May 2, 1808, to invoke the Black Legend of Spain's tyranny in the Americas. Sensitive to this stereotype, peninsular officials in the New World responded in kind by attributing disloyal views to their American opponents. It was not just a question of Spaniards versus Americans, because many of the Spaniards identified themselves with local interests.

There was great potential for mischief in this competition between the Spanish hierarchy and area interests. The Ceballos document, for example, had urged González and Central Americans in general to contribute whatever enlightened ideas they felt appropriate to improve the economy and government of the area. In response to this request, the Ayuntamiento of Guatemala City volunteered to assume responsibility for the publication and circulation of documents from Spain. It wanted to impress all of Central America with its initiative and preeminence. Captain General González, however, had different ideas. He printed the documents himself and had them sent off to all jurisdictions with instructions that suggestions should be sent directly to his office. By securing the assistance of the official censor, a Judge of the Audiencia, he thwarted the projected publications of the Ayuntamiento. To be sure, the government in Spain subsequently upheld the rights of the city officials in this particular incident. The fact remains, however, that Captain General González had succeeded at the time in upsetting his rivals' plans, arousing in them a keen desire for relief from this type of arbitrary censorship in the future.[31] Like other Americans, they understandably welcomed freedom of the press at Cádiz.

Given the freer context of the post-May Second period, Guatemalans energetically asserted their rights to the governmental authorities in Spain. In a letter of January 24, 1809, for example, they first proclaimed their loyalty to the Junta Central, while at the same time informing the Centrales that Spanish officials in Central America had never been very imaginative in the past. As a result, the Kingdom had been inadequately developed. This "lamentable system," the municipality insisted, had led the mother country to assume that "American Spain" could be kept down by force and by ignorance, a very fallacious assumption. Such despotism could no longer be tolerated. The Ayuntamiento had no doubt that in future the Spanish government would favor the American view that "virtue and merit" were essential qualifications for all officials serving in Central America.[32]

Sanguine in their expectations of a more active political role, the Guatemalan city fathers, as early as November 15, 1808, had demanded representation in any general government that might be organized in Spain; they were alluding to rumors that a Junta Central might be established soon. When the rumor became reality, they insisted that they should have one deputy on that body. They, of course, were speaking for the Kingdom because they immediately notified all jurisdictions in Central America to contribute revenues for the support of their delegate in Spain—an aggressive stance that annoyed Captain General González. He tried to delay the vote for a Central American delegate, but desisted when he learned that the Junta Central had indeed authorized positions for the New World in the provisional government of Spain. González therefore ordered the ayuntamientos under his command to hold elections. The procedure was traditional: each ayuntamiento supplied three names; then a boy, blindfolded, selected the winning candidate's name. At the capital, they did the same with the three names that had received the greatest number of votes.[33]

Thanks to the events after May Second, municipal reforms became a reality in Central America. Although the Bourbons had supported a more representative municipal order, it was not until the early nineteenth century that the program was widely accepted. After sixty years of inactivity, for example, Comayagua reestablished its ayuntamiento in March 1806. Tegucigalpa's records increase in number from 1804 forward, and it is notable that they already reflected an obsession to separate Tegucigalpa from the control of Comayagua's intendancy. It was during this period that the ayuntamientos of Santa Ana (now in El Salvador) and Quezaltenango (the highlands of Guatemala) commenced operations. On May 5, 1809, when General González announced the elections for a deputy to the Junta Central, the municipal governments of León (Nicaragua) and Cartago (Costa Rica) were incomplete. The impact of the announcement, however, was to stimulate the ayuntamientos of Central America to complete their memberships. The Quezaltenango and Cartago experiences illustrate the revitalization of municipal life in Central America after May 2, 1808.[34]

Because of its talented membership, the Ayuntamiento of Guatemala City established the pace for reform in Central America. The Creole Antonio Juarros, a dynamic and progressive leader who set many precedents for the founding fathers of Central America, was the mayor in 1808. Near the end of his administration, he requested the biennial election of *regidores* (aldermen) and the prohibition against the purchase of municipal offices in the future. At the time, there were four gentlemen who were trying to buy openings in the municipal corporation. Since only twenty-five pesos were involved in the projected sales, the incident that resulted loomed as a battle over principle.

In January 1809, a Spaniard, Gregorio Urruela, replaced Juarros as mayor. He, too, insisted passionately upon municipal reforms. Citing the best authorities against the sale of offices, especially the famous Count of Campomanes of Charles III's reign, Urruela argued that elections produced the best men in the community, those who wanted to advance the interests of the commonwealth. Elective offices, moreover, made it possible to take advantage of everyone's best talents. To settle the matter, Urruela proposed to pay for the four vacancies out of his own pocket, so that henceforth biennial aldermen could be elected—a concession that he was making for the "benefit of the nation." The Ayuntamiento of Guatemala, representing both the Spanish and Creole communities, applauded his generosity and patriotism.[35]

Although General González seemed to be receptive to the move at first, he changed his mind when he was assured by members of the Royal Audiencia and the Royal Treasury that municipal reforms were not needed. The Spanish hierarchy in Guatemala City thus provoked another needless confrontation with a local corporation. The details are not necessary. Suffice it to say that the incident underscored the pettiness and obstructionism of Spanish officials overseas—a persistent criticism of Americans at Cádiz and elsewhere. It also demonstrated the strength and determination of an American corporation to persist against such tactics, especially in the new context after May 2, 1808, all of which prepared the way for eventual independence. After a series of resignations and electoral moves and countermoves, the Ayuntamiento finally established the precedent of biennial elections. It simply would not seat the men who had paid for their positions recently. Despite his anger, and recognizing that the home government would not support his stand, González decided to give in to his opponents. Thus, the aldermen elected in the 1809 elections managed to survive in office for the required two years. In subsequent voting, the elective system for aldermen again prevailed; and elected candidates took their seats alongside the few lifetime aldermen (*regidores perpétuos*) of the former system, working harmoniously with them.[36] Municipal reform, therefore, came to Guatemala City well before it was ordered by the Cádiz government. Other Central American municipalities followed the example set in their capital.

The municipalities throughout Central America voted for a delegate to the Junta Central, a rewarding electoral experience. They chose a Guatemalan merchant, Manuel José Pavón, to represent them in Spain. In fact, the favorites of the election were mostly men who resided in Guatemala City, perhaps because it would expedite matters and save on expenses. In addition to Pavón, the most popular names were those of Vicente and José Aycinena from Guatemala, the Honduran José del Valle, the Nicaraguan Joaquín Arechavala, and the Spaniard Alejandro Ramírez. There were some delays in the elections because of resignations and recounts. In Guatemala City, the feud between the Ayuntamiento and the Spanish hierarchy was responsible for holding up matters; but local interests finally got their way.[37] Although the delegate from Central America never got to serve on the Junta Central, his constituents at least had undergone a valuable learning experience.

The post-May Second period in Central America encouraged a spirit of reform throughout Central America, continuing the trend we have noted in Chapter One. Reestablished in December 1810, the Economic Society of Guatemala became more of a regional instrument in its second period. Under the inspired leadership of two Creoles, José de Aycinena and Antonio Juarros, the Society urged all major ayuntamientos of the Kingdom to send a correspondent to Guatemala City, thus strengthening "the bonds that unite the capital with her provinces" and permitting "us to take advantage of the enlightenment and knowledge of its individuals."[38] The main objective at all times was the propagation of useful knowledge. Father Mariano López Rayón exemplified the reforming spirit of these years. The erstwhile professor of philosophy at the University of San Carlos was working with his Indians in the highlands (Los Altos) of Guatemala, diligently teaching them how to improve their crops. He was remarkably successful, and the Ayuntamiento of Quezaltenango asked him to share his experiments with it. He agreed to do so, and also wrote up Quezaltenango's instructions to Manuel José Pavón, stressing heavily the need for economic development.[39]

The Marquis de Aycinena (Vicente) revived plans in November 1810 to reform the seventeen artisan guilds of Guatemala City, a project conceived four years earlier. The indefatigable Antonio Juarros completed the assignment almost a year later. In addition, Juarros recommended the establishment of a school of painting in Guatemala City, sponsored by guild members. If he had been given his way, the Guatemalan reformer would not have waited until the Cádiz period to eliminate the *estanquillos de aguardiente*, the monopoly franchises for hard liquor, so harmful to workers.[40] In fact, the anti-monopoly feeling was a strong regional sentiment during those years. Central Americans especially resented the onerous tobacco monopoly. Just before leaving office on April 19, 1810, Governor Tomás de Acosta exposed the harmful effects of the tobacco monopoly upon Costa Rica's economy.[41] It is not surprising, therefore, that Central American representatives at Cádiz should labor tirelessly against monopolies of all types.

There were other manifestations of the reform spirit in Central America. A case in point was the establishment of the College of Lawyers on June 29, 1810, whose membership included many of the area's founding fathers.[42] Also, Guatemalans wasted no time in dropping the hated Caja de Consolidación, Godoy's funding scheme.[43] Captain General González encouraged an improvement in the mail service to Costa Rica and from there to Panama City and Lima, Peru.[44] The Marquis de Aycinena cooperated closely with General González in the formation of militias and in counting all able-bodied men from 15 to 45.[45] On the question of subversion, however, there was another aggravating incident between the Spanish hierarchy and local interests. When González formed the Tribunal de Vigilancia, he appointed three Spaniards and neglected to include any American. The implication was not flattering to Central Americans, and the city attorney protested this discrimination. General

González gruffly and arrogantly dismissed the claim, forcing the Ayuntamiento of Guatemala City to register a formal complaint with the Spanish government. Spain disbanded the Tribunal on February 20, 1811.[46]

$$\approx$$

The aldermen of Guatemala City were masters of the medieval "natural rights" doctrine that they had been taught at the University of San Carlos. It was implicit in their demands for representation on the Junta Central, even before that body was formed. It is stated clearly in their letter of January 30, 1810: "Man is free by nature and accordingly all men are equal. Thus all should enjoy a perfect equality of rights in agreement with the first law of nature promulgated by God to all creatures 'That no one dare to interfere with the use of another's primitive rights and that whosoever does the contrary shall be considered a criminal to be punished by the sentence of retaliation.' "[47]

This belief in the divine natural rights of man was fundamental for many Catholic thinkers from the thirteenth century forward. Spanish writers like Francisco de Vitoria, Francisco Suárez, and Juan de Mariana, to name only a few, articulated this sentiment well during the sixteenth and early seventeenth centuries. Revived in the eighteenth century with vigor, the trend was reinforced by the secular "natural rights" doctrine of John Locke and others. At Cádiz, however, it was the Catholic medieval tradition of natural rights and contractual law that predominated, thus making reform and religion compatible in the minds of devout Catholics in Spain and in the Americas.

The letter of January 30 provides a convenient analysis of political and constitutional developments in Europe as seen by an American corporation. Since Ferdinand VII had been captured by the French, the administrator and depository of the nation's sovereignty was absent. The administration of that sovereignty, therefore, reverted to the original constituents—the people, as was the case with the provincial juntas of Spain. In turn, these juntas had decided to make the Junta Central the administrator and depository of the nation's sovereignty until the sovereign returned to occupy the throne of Spain. The Ayuntamiento, moreover, went on to explain the "compact theory" of government: free men gave up part of their liberty to form a government that would provide security; and the administrator of those bits of liberty (sovereignty) was the sovereign, the custodian of the sovereignty. Since the Kingdom of Guatemala had also contributed its bits of liberty to the national pact, it followed that it deserved a just representation on the Junta Central. Two deputies, not one, was the correct representation. At this point, Guatemalans were no longer satisfied with the quota assigned by the Junta Central—a general feeling throughout Spanish America.[48]

The context for the discourse above on the "compact theory" was the Ayuntamiento's receipt of a manifesto, dated October 28, 1809, in which the Junta Central announced the convocation of a Cortes for January 1, 1810, and the beginning of sessions by March 1. Since Guatemala's delegates could not get to Spain by that deadline, the Ayuntamiento was afraid that a new constitution might be enacted without the concurrence of the Central American delegation. There were also rumors that a Regency might take over the government. Citing Condillac among other authorities, the city fathers argued that the smaller the governmental body the greater the possibility for tyranny. Accordingly, they could not approve of a Regency taking over the government. In the event that Parliament convened without Americans present, they continued, this would give one-third of the nation (the Peninsula and adjacent islands) the right to dictate the law to the other two-thirds (Americas)—a violation of the original pact. Moreover, the Guatemalans insisted that only persons familiar with a region should make laws for that area—a point that had been made back in the thirteenth century by Alfonso the Wise of Castile.[49] In short, Guatemalans wanted no tampering with the provisional government of Spain until the arrival of their representatives.

It distressed them, therefore, to learn that a Regency had actually taken over the government of Spain. The deliberations in the city council were extended and heated, but it was finally agreed to recognize the Regency, for expediency's sake.[50] There was, however, a vigorous opposition by a distinguished minority that included the Marquis de Aycinena, Antonio de Juarros, José María Peinado, Luis Barrutia, and Cayetano Pavón, all of them Creoles. This minority believed unequivocally that the transfer of power from the Junta Central to the Regency was unconstitutional, violating Guatemala's sovereign rights. Quoting the Jesuit Mariana on the compact theory, the dissenters hinted that Guatemalans were not obliged to obey a pact in which they had not taken part. As for the alleged justification for the transfer—the pressure of the mob of Spaniards on the route from Sevilla to Cádiz—the minority angrily pointed out that the Spanish nation was not to be confused with the voices and desecrations of a mob. In that emergency, the Junta Central should have given up its authority only on a conditional basis—that is, until the people of the nation could approve the transfer. Instead, Americans were faced with an accomplished fact and "imperative words" that they should recognize the Regency.[51] These were strong statements by responsible men. They provide a valuable insight into the refusal of some South American councils (*cabildos*) to recognize the Regency, thus initiating the Wars for Independence.

Although Guatemalans had some doubts about the Regency government, they were hopeful that the Kingdom's six deputies would be able to represent them effectively at Cádiz. The elections in the ayuntamientos proceeded as before—three nominees and the choice of one by Providence in the form of a boy who drew the lucky name from a container. The results were commendable in that the six deputies chosen were distinguished and well-educated men. Lawyers and men of the cloth predominated. Guatemala elected the priest Antonio Larrazábal; the Costa Ricans settled on the priest Florencio Castillo, an enlightened man who had taught at the seminary in León, Nicaragua. Chiapas finally selected the young clergyman Mariano Robles after the death of the lawyer Sebastián Esponda, the first choice. Nicaragua chose a lawyer, José Antonio López de la Plata, and San Salvador did likewise in the person of José Ignacio Avila. Comayagua elected José Francisco Morejón to represent that province in Spain. All the deputies were articulate and effective spokesmen for provincial interests.[52]

Now, the problem was to get Central America's six deputies to Cádiz as expeditiously as possible. The question of cost—their per diems and trip expenses—was settled temporarily by the allocation of regular tax revenues for that purpose. The understanding was that the provinces would reimburse the royal treasury—a serious problem for the future, given the depressed state of the Central American economy. Captain General González decided that Father Larrazábal should receive 5,000 pesos for the trip; others were assigned lesser amounts, much to the annoyance of the Nicaraguan and Costa Rican delegates. Father Castillo found his protest undermined by the authorities in Cartago, who cut him down to 2,000 pesos as an economy move.[53] The poor Costa Rican delegate had just begun to experience his financial problems, for Cádiz was indeed an expensive place to live.

The distance from Central America and the deficient transportation facilities delayed the arrival of the deputies in Spain. The Chiapas deputy did not reach Cádiz until late 1812, well after the promulgation of the Constitution, although Manuel Llano signed the document as the substitute for the province of Chiapas. Larrazábal left Guatemala City on October 24, 1810. He arrived in August 1811, after a circuitous trip via

Mexico, Honduras, and England. The other four Central Americans were far more fortunate. It remained to be seen what these proprietary deputies could accomplish in the Spanish Parliament.

There is no lack of documentation concerning the aspirations and objectives of Central Americans during the Cádiz era. Take, for example, the instructions given to Antonio de Larrazábal by the Ayuntamiento of Guatemala City.[54] Many ayuntamientos accepted or copied its major provisions, and they were published and widely circulated in Cádiz. There also exists a minority report of aldermen who disagreed with certain statements in the instructions,[55] and there was in addition the Consulado report of 1811, discussed in Chapter One. Special letters from the Ayuntamiento of Guatemala City complement the literature, which provides us with an exhaustive view of colonial sentiments on the eve of the Cortes of Cádiz.

Usually attributed to the regidor perpetuo José María Peinado, the Larrazábal instructions represent the thinking of an articulate group of men who resided in Guatemala City, all graduates of the University of San Carlos. Antonio Juarros and Vicente de Aycinena served on the committee with Peinado; Miguel Larreinaga, a distinguished Nicaraguan jurist, helped to revise the document; and Father Antonio García Redondo, the Defender of the Indians, seems to have cooperated in writing those sections of the instructions concerning Indians. Moreover, many writings of the previous decades had helped form the philosophical orientation of the men who were responsible for the instructions. All members of the Ayuntamiento signed the first part—the political section—on October 16, 1810. Later, four Spaniards, perhaps sensitive to the Black Legend characterization of tyranny in the document's "Introduction," decided to write up a minority report.

Considering the oppressive past of Central America, it followed that the new order would emphasize "philosophy" and "enlightenment" in order to promote "the general welfare."[56] In the "Declaration of the Rights of the Citizen," the Ayuntamiento listed thirty items, some of which resembled points made in its French counterpart of 1789. "Natural law" and the concept of "perfect equality of natural rights" permeate the declaration. The statement also emphasized the security of an individual's property, the hatred of monopolies, the individual's right of mobility, and the need to encourage the immigration of skilled foreigners with capital. All the city fathers agreed with Article 29: "The Americas should not receive from other kingdoms those products that Spain can supply from her soil, nor Spain [receive] from other countries the natural productions which the Spanish Americas supply." The minority of four Spaniards, however, rejected Article 25, calling for "free trade" which the majority in the Ayuntamiento had passed as a "natural right."[57]

The main body of Larrazábal's instructions consisted of 112 articles, which comprised the Constitution desired by Guatemalans. It was much more traditional than the Cádiz version, but it was still modern and progressive in outlook. The main objective was to concentrate political power in the hands of the American elite.

On religious matters, the city fathers were unreservedly defenders of the Holy Roman Catholic Church, even to the point of wanting to write into their instructions the dogma of the Immaculate Conception. They also hoped that the Cortes of Spain would make Santa Teresa de la Cruz, whose life was spent on reform, the co-patron of Spain, along with Santiago. To bring better discipline to the Church, the instructions recommended the convocation of provincial councils for North and South America as called for by the councils of Toledo and Trent. Furthermore, Guatemalans favored the return of the Jesuit Order to Spanish America for educational reasons. They also urged the canonization of Pedro de Betancourt, the founder of the Bethlemite Order in Guatemala. On the relationship between the Spanish Church and the Papacy, however, the Guatemalans took a regalist, or nationalist, position.[58]

The instructions dealt at length with the succession to the throne. On the issue of real power for the monarch, the majority voted in favor of protecting the nation against possible abuses. The minority view supported the divine rights of the monarch; yet, on the possible violation of property rights, it too advocated the restriction of executive power.

The Ayuntamiento disagreed on the type of legislature for the new government of Spain. The minority favored the basic positions that the Junta Central had announced—a bicameral legislature, one popular and the other of clergymen and nobles. The majority, however, voted for a legislature that resembled the Junta Central, that is, a National Supreme Council elected by all the ayuntamientos in the Spanish world. There would be one deputy from each kingdom on the National Supreme Council, serving a term of ten years. All executive appointments would be made in consultation with that body; merit and aptitude would be prime requisites for officeholders. Whenever a noble was qualified, however, he would have preference. A three-quarters vote was necessary to pass laws, and the King might veto a law three times; on the fourth occasion, if approved, the law would go into effect. The National Supreme Council could divide itself into sections, as did the Junta Central, to study and frame laws on sundry topics. Taxes would in no way interfere with the freedom of economic life.

The Guatemalan instructions also recommended a special commission, consisting of two "censors," appointed for life, that would supervise, promote, and write up laws ensuring the nation's prosperity and general welfare. This commission would draw up a *catecismo* describing the social virtues, the obligations of the citizen to the King, to his country, to his countrymen, and to himself. The two censors, moreover, would review the basic principles of the Constitution and the criminal code.[59]

The instructions proposed an experiment in federalism by calling for Juntas Superiores in each of the kingdoms overseas. Every ayuntamiento would send two delegates to the capital city for a five-year term, and the Juntas Superiores would function more or less as their national counterpart, even to the point of having censors to review their legislation. One of the principal concerns of the American Juntas was the "education and promotion" of the Indians.[60] Regional juntas, whose main function was economic, could appoint their interim executives. At the municipal level, two-thirds of the positions would be up for sale, and one-third would be filled by election for a period of two years. Apparently, Peinado, as a regidor perpetuo, had changed some minds on this issue. The minority of Spaniards, on the other hand, voted against the sale of offices.[61]

Except for the "free trade" article, the Ayuntamiento was in general agreement on economic development. Whereas the minority argued for the development of a national market and the promotion of local industry in the belief that nations at different stages of industrialization could not compete equitably, Peinado voiced the American position against the protectionism of the Frenchmen Sully and Colbert. Both sides agreed on the constructive role of government in developing the infrastructure, in the introduction of machinery, and in providing adequate educational facilities. They supported the thesis that agriculture should have priority and that the state should encourage capital investment in agriculture as part of the "social pact between individuals of a nation obligated to help each other."[62] Moreover, the capital of a nation or a province consisted of its money, land, products, animals, and all of its agricultural equipment and know-how. Following the precepts of the *Ley Agraria*, the instructions relegated industry and commerce to a secondary position behind agriculture. They advocated a positive role for government. It should try to diversify the economy, since overspecialization involved risks that might impoverish the citizenry. Government, moreover, should observe the precept that "the interest of the nation is that all her citizens should have useful occupations."[63] In this regard, women should be taught useful skills in occupations that required less strength.[64]

The Ayuntamiento, moreover, advocated a pacifist and non-imperialist policy. Wars were reprehensible, and nations should fight only in self-defense. Military men were unproductive, and too large a military force merely sapped the wealth of a nation. Apparently, the writings of anticolonialists like Adam Smith had impressed Guatamalan readers. Local militias, in which all able-bodied men served, would be a more reasonable and less expensive alternative. The possession of empire, the instructions averred, was of no utility to a nation; on the contrary, it weakened and destroyed a country. It was far better to abandon a territory if it was necessary to fortify it or use "restrictive laws to maintain it as a dependency." Furthermore, the assignment of coast guards to prevent American trade with foreigners was useless and "contrary to natural law."[65]

The Larrazábal instructions encouraged Spain to develop her maritime power by capitalizing upon her topography. She should encourage fishing and related industries, especially ship construction. The Guatemalan municipality recalled with pride the ships that were constructed in Campeche, Mexico, in 1702—they were seaworthy thirty years later, twice the life of ships constructed in Europe. Guatemala had a similar potential.

In the competition with other world powers, Spaniards should practice economies of all types. They should cut down on the number of holidays, for example. Apprenticeships should be reduced to increase a man's overall productivity. Religious men could increase "their utility" by assuming responsibility for educating the nation's youth. Schools should be both vocational and classical in orientation; in either case, "education is the basis for public happiness." Every country should recognize its own genius and potential; and surveys of a region's resources were indispensable.[66]

Part Three of the instructions dealt with the vital problem of taxation. At all times, the Ayuntamiento strongly recommended the streamlining of the financial structure, voting against the expensive and cumbersome treasury system of the colonial past.[67] Estimating the population of the Spanish nation at 28.5 million (18 million in America and the Philippines and the remainder in Spain and nearby islands), Peinado subtracted one-third, those who could not pay taxes, and concluded that 19 million were eligible. The Spanish nation, he predicted, could balance the budget by imposing a tax of 1½ escudos yearly. Practicing some economies, the single tax might even go lower. Local administrative units should be encouraged to apply the ability-to-pay principle. Moreover, by disbanding the costly Treasury Department, leaving its function to ayuntamientos and provincial juntas, the savings would be significant: the buildings could be sold to the highest bidder and many salaries could be eliminated or pared down. With the abolition of the tithe (*diezmo*), parishioners would assume responsibility for their own church expenses. There also could be a reduction in the number of clergymen in Cathedral chapters, while at the same time increasing the number of bishoprics to serve the faithful better.[68]

The fourth and final part of Larrazábal's instructions begins with a quotation from Montesquieu's *Spirit of the Laws*: "All human institutions have the stamp of the century in which they were made." Over the centuries, wrote Peinado, man had been subjected to all kinds of evil, but none worse than the arbitrary nature of social laws that had lost their original content because of ambition, ignorance, and all manner of abuse. Kingships had ended by enslaving the people. There were, of course, many enlightened kings; but, by and large, evil seems to have guided humanity, thus accounting for many barbarous and despotic laws like the use of torture, the confiscation of property, and the favor shown to monopolies and customhouses. Thanks to the enlightened ideas of the century, change was in the wind, and it was to be hoped that the fathers of the nation would "restore man to his original dignity."[69]

The minority report also reflected the strong influence of the Enlightenment. Although the four Spaniards who signed it believed in property requirements for the suffrage, they stood fast against the sale of public office. They favored the King's right to dissolve the Cortes, while at the same time advocating "natural law" and the elimination of arbitrary rule at all levels. Except in religious matters, the minority approved of freedom of the press; and they emphasized the power of the purse as a corrective for executive abuse. The aldermen in question shared the physiocratic desire to conduct surveys, censuses of natural resources, and the assignment of a reasonable single tax. They detested monopolies and favoritism to special corporations since they were alien to "natural law" and the "social pact."[70] They had confidence in provincial juntas and ayuntamientos. They believed, along with Jovellanos, in opening up the nobility to people of merit, and they affirmed, insofar as criminal reforms were concerned, that man was basically good. They even countenanced a jury system of sorts at the local level.[71] They were advocates of freeing interior trade and the stimulation of industries. Tough-minded realists, they felt that their American colleagues were too theoretical in their ideas about free trade with outsiders. The four aldermen believed in the preeminence of agriculture, the need for agrarian reform, and the protection and regeneration of the Indian. They were against the accumulation of large estates at the expense of the small farmer; and they applauded the Greek model of a citizen.[72]

There is no question that Central Americans of the Cádiz era had progressive notions in economic, social, and political matters. As in the *Ley Agraria* of 1795, which apparently influenced much of their thinking, Central Americans were fierce advocates of local autonomy and laissez-faire practices. Although many of their suggestions were traditional and some oligarchical, progressivism was the dominant note. Central Americans, in short, were in step with the ideology and spirit that prevailed at the Cortes of Cádiz.

3. Central Americans at Cádiz

The Spaniards' hurt pride has finally brought about this lamentable consequence. A government with experience in politics would have known how to disguise its resentment and perhaps later it would have avenged itself.

JOSÉ MARÍA BLANCO-WHITE, *August 30, 1811*[1]

The overseas deputies are just seeking the enjoyment of our rights, and in no way [are we trying] to hurt or exterminate the peninsula's national trade, as someone has insinuated without reason: harsh and unjust statements, apparently intended to offend the human heart, and not to enlighten our understanding or make known to us our true interests.

ANTONIO LARRAZÁBAL, *March 29, 1813*[2]

WHETHER treated in secret or in public, the "American Question" had a frustrating impact upon everyone concerned. On September 29, 1810, the Cortes held the first of seventeen closed meetings in which the overseas delegation tried to negotiate a meaningful program of equality. Although the documentation is fragmentary, the major bones of contention are clear enough since they were brought out in the open during the debates of early 1811. One American delegate complained that at the secret sessions Peninsulars had used racist slurs about the people overseas, which confirms other evidence to the effect that the issue of race underlay the controversy over political representation.[3]

The fundamental struggle was one of political control over the new Spanish government. Overwhelmed by Peninsulars, who constituted two-thirds of the Cortes, the overseas delegation had no alternative but to challenge the electoral process that had made it possible. Otherwise, it meant that 10 to 11 million people living on the Peninsula and adjacent islands would dominate the nation at the expense of 16 million inhabitants overseas. This was not proportional representation. By the same token, Spaniards adamantly resisted any attempt to give two and a half to three million whites overseas the opportunity to control Spain's parliamentary system because of their dominant position in the societies of America and the Philippines. This would mean that an overseas white would have three times the political power of a Peninsular.[4]

Thus the issue of race was highly important, for the inclusion of non-whites would always favor the overseas elites. A vague compromise was the result, the decree of October 15, 1810. It reiterated the promise of equality for America and Asia without specifying when that relationship would begin. It also seemed to suggest that Indians and mestizos would be included in the political count. In rough figures, this would mean that the addition of about eight million voters to the white total of two and a half to three million would bring an approximate equilibrium with the Peninsula. That was the compromise of October 15 that haunted the debates of early 1811; and it seems to have been made at the expense of five million Castas in America. In the Cádiz context, a Casta was anyone with an African trace in his background.[5]

Except for one deputy, the Americans and Filipinos that voted for the compromise were suplentes, who because of their residency in Spain might be expected to be more understanding of the European's viewpoint on the political question. Yet they were somewhat uneasy about the compromise they had made, knowing that it could be construed as an unnecessary capitulation to the Peninsulars. When they noticed, therefore, that Spaniards were in no hurry to meet other American grievances in the weeks following the compromise, they began to feel that perhaps they had been duped by their European colleagues. And so they hastened to present eleven propositions to the Cortes on December 16, 1810, in hopes of diverting attention from the sensitive compromise of October 15.[6]

The eleven propositions of December 16 constituted the American Question at Cádiz for the next two years. The first item repeated the substance of the October 15 decree with a significant difference: Americans now demanded *immediate* equality, insisting upon new elections overseas on the basis of one deputy for every 50,000 inhabitants. In short, American suplentes rejected outright the earlier provincial-capital formula. Spaniards argued, on the other hand, that America's equality was prospective: it would go into effect at the first regular Parliament elected under the Constitution. To delay the extraordinary assembly's work until the arrival of the overseas deputies, as proposed by the first American demand, would postpone the freedom of the Spanish citizen. Unimpressed with this argument, Americans suspected that in the meantime Spaniards would pass a constitution to their liking and that issues vital to America and the Philippines would not receive adequate attention.[7]

Propositions 8 through 10 were likewise political in nature. The eighth proposed equality for all governmental jobs, ecclesiastical, military, and political. Number 9 recommended that one-half of all available positions should go to natives of a given region. And the tenth proposal called for the establishment of a consultative junta in each provincial jurisdiction to recommend candidates for all openings. Overseas interests, in short, wanted more say in their government. They did not appreciate the large number of Spanish-born officials in their midst.

On economic matters, Americans were avid adherents of laissez-faire. Proposition 2 advocated the freedom of the entrepreneur in agriculture and industry; number 3 championed the right to export products abroad to Spain, to allied nations, and to neutrals, as well as the freedom to import products on national or foreign vessels. Propositions 4 and 5 repeated these same liberties for the traffic with Philippine and Asian ports. And numbers 6 and 7 demanded the end of monopolies overseas, alluding mainly to those of quicksilver and tobacco.

Proposition 11 had a social objective: Americans asked for the return of the Jesuit Order to the New World so that it could continue its missionary and educational work. This proposition got nowhere among Spaniards. But its mere inclusion in the eleven demands showed that the overseas delegation did not share the Europeans' prejudice vis-à-vis the Jesuits. It will be recalled that Guatemalans had asked Father Larrazábal to do the best he could to restore the Society of Jesus—apparently it was a widespread sentiment in the New World.[8]

By December 31, 1810, the Mexican proprietary deputies, who had arrived recently in Cádiz, agreed to support actively the eleven propositions on the agenda of the Cortes. In the first week of the new year, Parliament voted affirmatively to consider the American demands in public sessions every Wednesday and Friday until finished.[9]

The public debates of January and February 1811 on the American-Asian propositions had a significant impact upon attitudes everywhere, especially considering the wide circulation of the published minutes. Despite careful editing of the speeches, the documentation permitted the reader to catch the innuendoes and points of emphasis. Liberal and conservative Peninsulars were especially sensitive to the Black Legend characterization of Spain's rule in the Americas, one of despotism and tyranny. At first the more enlightened Spaniards claimed ignorance of conditions overseas and pleaded with their American colleagues for more information. But when Americans persisted with the negative stereotype, it noticeably upset such Spanish liberals as Agustín Argüelles, Conde de Toreno, and Alvaro Flórez Estrada. It put them on the defensive. In their replies—and the same rationale appears in their writings later—they argued that it was unfair to blame them for the mistakes of previous generations. Besides, Spaniards on the Peninsula had also suffered bad government and tyranny. The defensive posture of Spain's leading liberals eventually compelled them to elaborate a White Legend paper on the history of the Spanish Empire—a stereotype which the more conservative Peninsulars had supplied in the debates.[10] Such polarization of opinion did not augur well for the American Question.

In the context of Spain's national crisis, Peninsulars tended to regard the American demands as blackmail and treason. Even the moderate newspaper *Semanario Patriótico* of Cádiz hinted in its editorials that Americans were being opportunistic in presenting their eleven propositions to the Cortes.[11] Americans replied that it was unfair to impugn their loyalty to Spain after all the contributions that they had made to the effort against the French. Besides, if the Cortes were to meet these demands, it would help to undermine the insurrection overseas and to guarantee the government further financial support.[12]

Americans were especially sensitive to the barbs of Juan López Cancelada, the editor of *El Telégrafo Americano*. Having spent many years in Mexico, this spokesman for Cádiz and Mexico City merchants was particularly effective in arousing doubts concerning American motives. The fact that there was much truth in what he had to say is what made his editorials so effective. For example, he attacked and ridiculed the alleged sympathy of the Americans at Cádiz for the Indians, mestizos, and Castas, reminding his readers that American whites were all members of that elite who for centuries had victimized the non-whites on their large haciendas. It was thus sheer hypocrisy, for these hacendados to champion the cause of the non-whites in the halls of Parliament.[13] Americans chafed at this characterization, while the editorialist's words swayed many minds in the heated atmosphere of the Cortes.

On January 18, 1811, Parliament was ready to vote on Proposition 1. In response to the Miguel Hidalgo revolt in Mexico, the Cortes agreed to allow the franchise for both Indians and mestizos—a confirmation of what was generally intended in the compromise of October 15, 1810. But on the major issue of Proposition 1—the *immediate* equality of the Americas—the vote was 64 against and 56 in favor. At least 21 Spaniards had voted with the overseas bloc. Although their first reaction was to stalk out of the hall in protest, Americans reconsidered when a Spaniard offered an acceptable compromise: to permit elections overseas according to the desired formula but without postponing the deliberations of congress until the arrival of the new deputies. Another spirited debate followed but the outcome was identical—a margin of 8 votes.[14] In effect, Americans could not enjoy their vaunted equality with the Peninsulars until the first regular Cortes convened. Until then, they would be outnumbered by a ratio of 3 to 1. Considering the Peninsulars' concern for the power question, it was perhaps no coincidence that 3 to 1 was exactly the ratio of American to European whites.

The results of other American propositions were mixed. Proposition 8, giving all citizens a right to seek governmental jobs on a basis of equality, passed by an overwhelming vote. The majority bloc, however, turned down the demand for an equal division of posts for natives and Peninsulars, feeling that merit should be the deciding factor. Furthermore, the majority of Spaniards did not accept the notion of regional juntas to nominate candidates for governmental positions.

On economic propositions, the Cortes granted some concessions. It established the precedent of generosity on specific area demands, especially those of a promotional nature. In order to stimulate the mining industry in Mexico, for example, the Cortes abolished the quicksilver monopoly—a concession that subsequently was generalized to all the Americas. The same occurred with the fishing industry in Mexico and elsewhere. Congress likewise supported the freedom of all agricultural and industrial entrepreneurs, as requested by the Americans. But this turned out to be a hollow victory without the free trade called for in Propositions 3 to 5.[15] Cádiz merchants were again the nemesis of American interests. Considering the nation's financial straits, moreover, there was no action on the tobacco monopoly until mid-1813, by which time it was too late to implement it.

The January-February debates did not solve the American Question, as some authorities have assumed.[16] On the contrary, it lingered on for years. The free trade issue, for example, reappeared on the agenda in April 1811, after only a month's respite. This time the British minister to Spain asked for it as an ally. In the secret sessions that followed, Americans consistently rallied to the cause of free trade; and some minor concessions in that direction raised hopes among the American delegates. The Cádiz merchants, however, quashed the move. Always articulate, López Cancelada published a pamphlet that almost single-handedly defeated the British trade measure. It was entitled *The Ruin of New Spain if Free Trade with Foreigners is Declared.* Armed with an impressive array of statistics, the writer argued convincingly that even Americans did not want free trade since it would inevitably harm local crafts and industry.[17] When the measure came up for a vote on August 13, 1811, no less than 87 Spaniards voted against it. Americans were understandably bitter at these results.[18]

The American delegates at Cádiz presented a key memorial to the Cortes on August 1, 1811, almost two weeks before the unfavorable action on British trade.[19] It is likely that what they had to say in that memorial contributed to the defeat on free trade. The memorial repeated a common stand: the Americans overseas were not rebels; they had acted in self-defense, just as the peninsular juntas had done earlier. Spanish governments, nevertheless, had resorted to a policy of force and of inequality, refusing to permit Americans the same rights as Spaniards. Under these conditions, they had no alternative but to seek independence. Furthermore, to rationalize their mistaken policies, Peninsulars preferred to listen to conspiratorial interpretations about what was happening overseas—that Americans, for example, were mere dupes in the intrigues of Frenchmen, Englishmen, and North Americans. Yet, the real cause of independence, as everyone knew, was "bad government"—a truth that the Cortes should accept and try to correct.[20] Americans would no longer tolerate any governmental acts based upon degrading inequality. To be sure, the Cortes had granted the Americas many useful concessions, but more had to be done along the lines of free trade, the abolition of monopolies, and the permission to establish Juntas Provinciales in the New World. Americans reminded their peninsular colleagues that local interests overseas were able to govern themselves; and Parliament would do well to trust the provinces with their own regional government.[21]

Spaniards chose not to heed this reasoned appeal of August 1, 1811, almost as if they were determined to follow a line of self-destruction for the Spanish nation. They rejected the British trade proposal several days later by an overwhelming margin. Spaniards appeared determined to punish their overseas brethren for their frankness in the August 1 memorial. There was despair in the overseas delegation, and Central Americans shared this disillusionment. The two suplentes, Manuel and Andrés Llano from Guatemala, had signed the August 1 memorial; so had the four deputies from Costa Rica, Nicaragua, Honduras, and El Salvador, who had taken the oath of office on July 11, 1811. The full complement for Central America—six votes—was squarely in the American camp. By that time, moreover, Antonio de Larrazábal's instructions had reached Cádiz; and the overseas contingent knew that it could count on the Guatemalan capital for its full support.[22] Larrazábal arrived in Cádiz on August 12 and by August 24 had taken his seat in Parliament.

The Constitutional Committee had been working on their project for months; and by August 25, 1811, it was willing to discuss its various parts with the Cortes. The Constitution that resulted was a remarkable document when we take into account the adverse conditions under which it was enacted—the French siege of Cádiz, the cramped quarters of the city, the shouting of the crowds at the public sessions, the histrionics of the participants, the frayed nerves of the deputies, and the government's financial troubles. American representatives, moreover, figured prominently in the elaboration of its many liberal reforms. Agustín Argüelles and the Conde de Toreno both emphasized that Americans had sided with them, the Liberales, against the Serviles (Conservatives) in matters of reform. It was only on issues involving the American Question that the overseas deputies had formed a third party in the Cortes.[23]

During the first constitutional period at Cádiz, there were at least five Americans who can be classified as outstanding leaders on the power question and on liberal reforms: one was Ecuadorean, José María Mejía Lequerica, the suplente for the Viceroyalty of New Granada; two were Mexican priests, José Miguel Guridi y Alcocer from Tlaxcala and José Miguel Ramos Arizpe from Coahuila; and two were Central Americans, also priests, Antonio Larrazábal from Guatemala and Florencio Castillo from Costa Rica. Except for Mejía, who unfortunately lost his life in the epidemic of 1813, all of these men lived to play important political roles in their respective countries. Cádiz had been their training ground, and they learned their lessons well.

As deliberations opened on the Constitution, Americans recognized the difficulties they would encounter in furthering overseas interests, especially with no more than about thirty-five votes at any given time. Spaniards had refused to go along with any resolutions that might have kept suplentes on the rolls after the arrival of the proprietary deputies until the maximum of fifty-eight overseas representatives had been reached.

Some Americans were optimistic when Article 6 passed referring to the Castas as Españoles, but it soon became apparent that Spaniards had only intended to give the Castas civil rights and not political rights. In Article 18, citizens were defined as all persons "who on both sides could trace their origin to the Spanish dominions of both hemispheres"—that is to say, the Americas or Europe. Father Castillo noted that since the term "origin" meant birth, it followed that the prohibition could not apply to sons of Africans, born in America—an interpretation which Spaniards rejected outright. At this point, the Costa Rican observed that Negroes, according to the latest scientific findings, could not be denied equality because of their color; the same applied to their "alleged immorality." He hinted, not too subtly, that perhaps Spaniards were just trying to limit America's representation in the Cortes. Despite the innuendo, the article passed by an overwhelming vote.[24] The same happened to Article 22, which stipulated that in special cases of meritorious service an individual Casta might petition the Cortes for citizenship. Americans argued that such an indirect approach was too costly and time-consuming to be effective.[25]

The compromise of October 15, 1810, weakened the American hand in the acrimonious debate over Article 22. The general inclination of American proprietors, moreover, was not to embarrass the suplentes, who otherwise had defended the overseas cause with brilliance. Early in 1811, the Mexican deputy Guridi had hinted politely at the ineligibility of the suplentes to negotiate the October 15 compromise which excluded the Castas from the political franchise. The outspoken Guatemalan priest Larrazábal, however, felt no such inhibition during the debate on the constitution. He flatly denied that the suplentes had any authorization to exclude the Castas. Furthermore, he reminded the Cortes that he had specific instructions from Guatemala City to the effect that no fundamental laws could be enacted by Parliament without the concurrence of Guatemala's proprietary deputy.[26]

The fact that four Americans had voted against the franchise for the Castas did not help matters. Other Americans, including Father Larrazábal, further undermined the overseas position by reflecting the elitist views of their constituencies. The Guatemalan deputy recommended second-class political rights for the Castas: they could elect candidates to office (*voz activa*), he explained, but they could not run for national posts (*voz pasiva*). "Do not therefore deny these helpless people," he pleaded, "the right to name a father who will expose and seek a remedy for their misery." Throughout the speech, he sprinkled many threats, including the reminder of the mistakes that England had made with her colonies.[27] The weakness of the overseas position was obvious, and it is doubtful that even complete unity among American delegates could have changed the vote very much.

Spaniards stubbornly held the line on the Castas issue, convinced that Americans were merely trying to increase their representation in Parliament. Some even charged the Americans of hypocrisy on the race issue.[28] Sensitive to the allegations of illiberality, the great Argüelles admitted that Article 22 did violence to his principles; but, he added weakly, it was better than no article at all.[29] At least Article 22 opened the door to "virtue," by permitting a deserving Casta to petition for his citizenship. This was the official rationale of the Constitutional Committee, and it was enough to satisfy most Spaniards. Diego Muñoz Torrero reminded Americans that they were confusing civil with political rights—a confusion that might even lead to giving women the vote.[30] Weary of the argument, Spaniards closed the discussion peremptorily and called for the vote on September 10, 1811, despite the strenuous objections of three American deputies. The article passed by a vote of 108 to 36. It was a decisive defeat, and all efforts to amend Article 22 came to naught.[31]

To soften the blow or perhaps to salve their own consciences, two Spaniards offered propositions that automatically would have made citizens of all Castas in religious or military corporations. They were sent to the Constitutional Committee for further consideration. Hoping to secure civil rights for the Castas, now that political rights had been denied them, Father Castillo introduced a bill that he hoped might help "to dry the tears" of those "unhappy beings." It proposed that Castas be admitted to universities, seminaries, and religious communities of both sexes, as well as any "other corporations, professions, or jobs . . . in which the quality of Spaniard is required."[32] These bills received favorable action, thus making it easier for Castas to take advantage of Article 22.[33]

The power question still remained, however. It came up again in Articles 28 and 29. The first stated that the basis for political representation was the same for both hemispheres of the Spanish World, and the second limited the population count to families with the political franchise. Father Castillo once again mirrored the American position. Less polite than he had been earlier, he insisted that Castas were Spaniards who lived and were born on Spanish soil. It was not fair, therefore, to treat them as foreigners in their own land; and to refuse to count them politically would in effect make them slaves. It was one thing to deny them citizenship, but it was another to withhold political representation from the Castas. Castillo reminded the Cortes that women, men under 25, and criminals as well were counted even though they were not citizens. Some Americans had voted against citizenship for the Castas, but not a single American opposed the inclusion of the Castas in the political count. To do otherwise would be a gross injustice. It would mean that while a peninsular deputy represented 50,000 people his American counterpart might be the spokesman for double that number or more. Needling his opponents, the Costa Rican cleric wondered aloud if Spaniards were deliberately trying to limit America's representation in the Cortes.[34]

Castillo's colleague from Guatemala City was even more blunt, almost as threatening as the delegate from Buenos Aires who had preceded him. Repeating many of Castillo's points, Father Larrazábal protested the inequality that the articles in question would foist upon America. Sovereignty-in-the-people would be meaningless to Guatemalans if the Cortes did not reflect the numbers of people that resided in the Americas. Under those conditions, Americans would always be outnumbered threefold. The overseas residents did not want superiority over the Spaniards, as alleged by some; on the contrary, Americans had always recognized Spain's greatness and had aided her with money on many occasions. Even our Negro slaves, Larrazábal reminded his colleagues, had contributed to the war effort. "Moribund Spain," the Guatemalan predicted, could not recover without America's help. His speech contained the hint that perhaps the American-Asian bloc might settle for equal votes for the overseas territories and Europe, rather than straight proportional representation.[35]

Annoyed by the heated oratory of their American colleagues, Spaniards proceeded to pass the two articles in question by wide margins. It should be noted that Peninsulars were now admitting openly that they feared American domination of the national government if they relented on the Casta issue.[36]

During the recent debate, an incident occurred that further infuriated Americans. The Mexican Consulado, controlled by natives of Spain, had sent a document to the Cortes containing some uncomplimentary statements about Americans, their racial mix and lack of character. Americans reacted violently and wanted Parliament to take action against the libelous tract. Spaniards demurred and recommended a milder censure statement which thoroughly aroused the overseas delegation. The majority again had its way, while 37 Americans and Asians registered their dissent. All Central Americans voted with their bloc.[37] What made the incident so irritating to Americans was that on other occasions, involving an insult to the Cortes, Spaniards had voted overwhelmingly to censure publications within Parliament, thus ignoring the special courts stipulated in the freedom-of-the-press law. Apparently the Cortes had a double standard, thanks to the majority bloc of Peninsulars.

Article 91 added insult to injury. The majority voted that any Spaniard, living in a given area for at least seven years, could represent that province in the Cortes if elected. To sensitive Americans, aware of the realities in their home provinces, this meant that Spaniards might even infiltrate the overseas delegation. Again, 37 votes were recorded against the measure, and all Central Americans were included.[38]

In Article 222, the Spanish majority also determined that there would be an administrative system for the nation consisting of seven secretariats: one for the Peninsula and adjacent islands; another for the overseas kingdoms; and five topical units dealing with State, Religion and Justice, Treasury, War, and Navy. Americans were in general agreement that there should be more than one secretariat for overseas, and most of them preferred to have separate topical organizations to provide better government for their areas. But the Peninsulars insisted upon national topical units, despite the objections of the overseas contingent. Argüelles' final argument was that a liberal constitution would be a safeguard against abuses; besides, future Cortes, it was agreed, could vary the number of secretariats depending upon experience and conditions.[39]

The Castas issue came up again in Articles 313 and 317, excluding them from local town governments. Again, Central Americans were active in the debate. Father Larrazábal complained that it was a travesty to deny the Castas a function which they had exercised under the old regime. Article 22 pretended to open the door to virtue, yet the two articles in question deprived the Castas of the opportunity to uplift themselves so that they might apply for citizenship. His Costa Rican colleague declared that it was a disgrace for the Cortes of Cádiz, renowned for its liberal reforms, to be less progressive than the old order—a charge that visibly annoyed peninsular liberals. The Nicaraguan deputy, López Plata, proposed some ten amendments to the bill on municipalities, but all were rejected, as the majority of Peninsulars passed the articles restricting the Castas.[40]

Thoroughly frustrated as article by article met the approval of the majority bloc, making a sham of the American Question, the overseas delegation was at its wit's end when Article 375 came up for discussion. It stated that no amendment to the Constitution could be considered for a period of eight years. In theory, this was a commendable article, for it allowed the constitutional experiment a fair trial. But Americans regarded it differently since the article would have the effect of freezing the Castas issue until 1820, thus further delaying America's effective equality in the Spanish Cortes. In a move of desperation, Americans insisted upon delaying the promulgation of the Constitution until the first regular Parliament convened. The new deputies, just elected by the people, would then vote in favor or against the national charter. If the vote were favorable, the eight-year prohibition on amendments would go into effect at that time.[41] The American strategy was too obvious to the majority bloc, who proceeded to quash the move in the customary manner—a display of political force that unnerved Americans. Father Larrazábal was especially distraught as he charged that the article was unconstitutional. It violated, he said, the nation's "exclusive right to make fundamental laws."[42] The Cortes's decision, however, was final.

Many American deputies were quick to recognize that control of the national government was an illusory objective—a realization that heightened their desire for home rule. In the August 1 memorial, it will be recalled, they had asked specifically for the establishment of provincial juntas overseas, urging the Cortes to have faith in the ability of Americans to govern themselves. It remained to be seen, however, whether the Spanish majority bloc would go along with this federalist tendency.

Home rule and federalist sentiments were a fact of life in the Spanish world after May 2, 1808, whether the central governments of Spain liked it or not. The Cádiz regime, therefore, had to proceed cautiously in the presence of the peninsular juntas. After all, they had contributed to the demise of the Junta Central; and it was common knowledge that the Regency had convened the Cortes in September 1810 partly because of pressure from the regional juntas of Spain.[43] To this we should add that some Cádiz deputies were selected by the juntas themselves. Home rule, therefore, was not just an American phenomenom and desire; the overseas delegation could reasonably expect some support from the Peninsulars themselves.

Since Argüelles and Toreno were the recognized leaders of the Cortes, their conception of government had an important bearing on home rule. Both men spoke of *federalismo* with undisguised contempt. As dedicated Spanish nationalists, they wanted to create a strong national state of the entire Spanish-speaking world, based on cherished liberal principles. Theirs was a centralist vision of government as contrasted to the federal concept.[44] Yet, as pragmatists, they understood the need to reconcile the home-rule sentiments of the Spanish citizenry with the nationalist objectives of the nation.

The compromise institution was the Diputación Provincial, perhaps the most important reform in the 1812 charter. According to Argüelles and other architects of the Constitution, these regional units had a function that was basically economic and administrative, serving much as development corporations do today in Latin America. In addition to conducting surveys and recommending economic projects for the region, these provincial deputations kept a close supervision over the fiscal procedures of the municipalities, their educational programs and so on. In theory, the deputations were merely consultative bodies which advised the *jefe político* (political chief) and the *intendente* (royal treasurer), the two appointees of the central government. The other seven members of the provincial body were elected by voters of their respective districts (*partidos*) in a given province. Thus, by blending centralism (the two royal appointees) with federalism (the seven district representatives), the Constitution hoped to balance regional and national interests.

As consistent advocates of economic progress, Americans welcomed the provincial deputation. This reform, in effect, amounted to the institutionalization of the Economic Societies that had flourished under Charles III. In view of their political aspirations, however, Americans desired more than advisory councils. They wanted deputations with an effective political voice as well. Suspicious of centralized power, especially one controlled by Peninsulars, Americans demanded the restriction of the jefe político's authority in local and provincial government. Royal officials on the Diputación Provincial should have only two votes; and they should have to abide by, and execute, the decisions of the majority. Other amendments by the American delegation underscored a fierce determination to be masters in their own houses without dictation from peninsular authorities.[45]

Reacting to the emotionalism of the American deputies and swayed by the nationalistic appeals of Argüelles and his partisans, the majority bloc accepted the centralist argument that provincial deputations, as well as municipalities, were just administrative bodies whose function was to advise the political executive. This version went into the Constitution. All amendments failed by a wide margin, further magnifying the frustrations of the overseas delegation. The implementing ordinance of June 23, 1813, added to the alienation of Americans by further strengthening the authority of the jefe político in the Cádiz system of government.[46]

Refusing to accept the Cortes' decision on diputaciones provinciales, Father Larrazábal reopened the debate on February 7, 1812. The excuse was a letter that he had just received from the Ayuntamiento of Guatemala City, dated July 18, 1811. Conditions were still bad in the Kingdom of Guatemala, the letter informed, despite the enlightened efforts of the new Captain General, José de Bustamante. Guatemalans complained that the real weakness derived from a deficient system of laws that had been drawn up by persons who were not familiar with the Central American area. Americans, they reasoned, were the only ones who could legislate for their regions, so different from Europe. They reminded the Cortes of the recommendation that had been made by John Locke to the effect that all laws should be examined and reformed every century because of natural variations between areas. They contended that the Englishman's statement was indeed applicable to the relationship between Europe and America because of the great changes that had occurred over the years. "We repeat," the Ayuntamiento insisted, "it is not possible to frame suitable laws for the Americas and for the entire body of the monarchy without their help." Furthermore, the city fathers of Guatemala City observed that the social turmoil and moral letdown in Guatemala resembled conditions that had prevailed in France before the onset of anarchy. To prevent chaos, therefore, it was urgent to form regional governments that would correct the situation.[47]

With this sobering document before the Cortes, Father Larrazábal proposed seven amendments to Article 335 on the attributes of provincial deputations that would have changed their nature entirely. His amendments clearly favored federalism. Members of a deputation would have the right to name an interim jefe político upon the death of an incumbent, to appoint officials at certain levels, to make recommendations to the Consejo de Estado in certain cases; and to advise the Cortes on legislation that was needed for their province. The deputation would also have had the right to ask the Cortes to suspend the execution of harmful laws. Finally, Larrazábal's institution would have emphasized the promotion and education of Indians by every means possible. Not impressed by the argument, the Spanish majority rejected Larrazábal's amendments on the grounds that Article 335 had already passed.[48]

The next confrontation between Spaniards and Americans took place when the Constitutional Committee recommended that every administrative unit mentioned in Article 10 should have a provincial deputation. This meant only one unit for the entire Kingdom of Guatemala. Father Castillo argued that such an eventuality would seriously inconvenience Costa Rica in view of the extent of the Kingdom. He urged that another deputation be added that included Nicaragua, Honduras, and Costa Rica, furnishing the Cortes with convincing information in behalf of the proposal.[49] Other Americans complained about the distribution of provincial bodies. In fact, some peninsular juntas likewise objected to their demise; and they argued that it was unfair to erase historical realities. When the Committee reconsidered, it yielded to the peninsular complaints but totally ignored overseas demands for additional deputations.

Americans were shocked at this new display of indifference and discrimination. Father Castillo repeated his request for a second Central American deputation and noted that the Kingdom of Guatemala certainly deserved two units if Spain were authorized to have thirty. The Cuban deputy registered a similar complaint.[50] In no mood to be polite, Father Larrazábal shouted that it was a *monstruosa desigualdad* (monstrous inequality) to give the overseas territories one-third of the deputations (30 peninsular and 15 overseas). He noted sarcastically that the Committee had placated European dissidents but had refused American demands.[51] This observation, plus the requests of other Americans, led the Count of Toreno to recommend an investigation of how many new units were needed overseas. It was decided to add six more provincial bodies, three for South America and three in North America, including one for Nicaragua and Costa Rica with its capital in León.[52] Despite Castillo's recommendation, Honduras remained under the jurisdiction of Guatemala City.

The famous Constitution of Cádiz became the law of the land on March 18, 1812. The overseas delegates signed the document for their respective provinces, despite a keen disappointment over the power question. They simply lacked the numbers to persuade their Spanish colleagues; and the latter, emotional and distraught by the crisis of the moment, were determined to minimize the power of the overseas elites in the Spanish nation. They might concede a few more provincial deputations, but they refused to yield on the Castas issue. Instead, Spaniards succeeded in postponing that thorny question for at least eight years and prevented the inclusion of the Castas in the figures for representation. Argüelles and his supporters, moreover, won the day for their interpretation of diputaciones provinciales as consultative bodies only, a serious blow to the aspirations for autonomy overseas. Indeed, it is remarkable that the Americans affixed their signatures to the final product.

~~~~

Overseas delegates signed the Constitution of 1812 because they were sincere adherents of its major reforms and principles. José María Mejía, for example, took great pride in his contribution to the modernization of the Spanish nation. Along with his American colleagues, he had supported unstintingly the freedom-of-the-press law.[53] It was during the debates on that law, according to the Count of Toreno, that Spaniards for the first time used the term "liberal" in its modern political sense. Americans were constantly identified with the liberal faction at Cádiz. Moreover, they gained many tangible benefits for their respective provinces in the Cortes of Cádiz, so that all did not seem hopeless to them. To be sure, many of these gains were never implemented for one reason or another; but they were nonetheless important as indicators of regional aspirations that would reappear in the future. A review of Central American accomplishments at Cádiz illustrates the type of benefits gained in Spain by American deputies.

Central America's representation in Cádiz was as effective as conditions warranted. The two suplentes, Manuel and Andrés Llano, were well-liked and respected by American and Spanish colleagues. Born in Guatemala, the Llano brothers worked closely together. Andrés, the merchant, often missed sessions because of his business; yet, his popularity was evident in certain elections that were held in Parliament.[54] As a captain of artillery, Manuel had more time to attend the parliamentary discussions. He fervently supported the freedom-of-the-press reform; and he was the deputy who proposed the study of habeas corpus so that this English institution might be adopted in Spain. He also served on the five-man committee that recommended that particular reform to the Cortes. It passed.[55] His most important contribution to the Cádiz Experiment, surprisingly, was in the field of military reforms. Keenly interested in modernizing the Spanish army, he proposed on April 3, 1811, the establishment of a Junta Suprema de Guerra. A few months later, Manuel offered seven bills on military reforms that revealed his expertise on the subject. Throughout his parliamentary career, this Guatemalan officer worked assiduously for military reform—a somewhat unexpected contribution that Central America made to the Cádiz Experiment.[56]

Americans played a more important role in the day-to-day operations of the Cortes than might be assumed from their small numbers. It almost seemed that the Spanish majority hoped to compensate for the overseas defeats on the power question by electing Americans regularly to the monthly posts. Because of their numbers as well as their talent, Mexican deputies were especially prominent in this regard.[57] Three of the Central Americans that served in the first constitutional period received this recognition from their colleagues at Cádiz. Father Larrazábal, for example, was elected to the Presidency of the Cortes for the month beginning October 24, 1811, only two months after he had taken the oath of office. Father Castillo's record was even more impressive. He was recognized no less than three times: first, as Vice-President in the elections of July 24, 1812; then as Secretary of the Cortes on October 24, 1812; and finally as President on May 24, 1813. Manuel Llano served as Secretary for the month beginning on April 24, 1812.[58] This was indeed a respectable showing for Central America: three of the eight men who served in the first constitutional period.

Central Americans at Cádiz took advantage of every opportunity to publicize their loyalty to the Spanish cause in Europe, creating a favorable image of their provinces. Whenever special celebrations were held in Guatemala City, attended by speeches and the striking of gold medals to commemorate the event, these mementoes were given wide circulation in Spain by Father Larrazábal and his Central American colleagues. The new Captain General of Guatemala, José de Bustamante, took over the government on March 14, 1811, and from the beginning, he convinced Central Americans and the Spanish Cortes that he was a loyal supporter of the Cádiz Experiment. Indeed, this favorable first impression of Bustamante and of Archbishop Ramón de Casaus, who also sent medals to Cádiz and who urged the continuation of Indian confraternities, produced some unexpected consequences in a later period. In close cooperation with the Carmelite Order, moreover, Central Americans achieved the objective of honoring Santa Teresa as co-patron of Spain.[59]

Delegates from Central America capitalized on the arrival of ships from the New World to impress Spaniards with their loyalty. Father Larrazábal, in one of his first acts as President of the Cortes, announced the arrival of a ship with substantial amounts of indigo and cacao, as well as 30,000 *pesos fuertes*, to help finance the best guerrilla unit in Castile. Add to this contribution the indigo and the 103,663 pesos that had reached Cádiz four months earlier, as well as other donativos from Central

America, and the conclusion was obvious: not all Americans were rebels who were taking advantage of Spain's distress. Larrazábal went out of his way to point out that these contributions from Central America were being made in a time of economic depression. Even the Negro slaves at Omoa, the most "miserable of all the inhabitants in the Kingdom of Guatemala," had contributed 1,280 pesos to the Spanish cause. Captain General Bustamante had thus emancipated them, and Father Larrazábal urged the Cortes to confirm his actions. It agreed. On February 16, 1813, all six Central American delegates at Cádiz proudly reported the arrival of another aid ship with well over 100,000 pesos.[60]

Spaniards were also impressed with Central America's resistance to the spread of the Hidalgo revolt from Mexico, thanks to the energetic measures of the authorities in Guatemala City. Leading Creoles like José de Aycinena and José María Peinado had cooperated with Bustamante in suppressing the insurrections in San Salvador and Nicaragua. On Bustamante's recommendation, the faithful Salvadoran towns of San Miguel, Santa Ana, and San Vicente were rewarded by the Cortes with new titles and ranks; leading clerics of the area received honors. Nueva Segovia in Nicaragua and the Bishop of León also gained recognition and awards from the legislature in Cádiz.[61] And Guatemala City's Ayuntamiento acquired the title of "Excellency."[62] Because of his expertise in law, as well as his role in the recent pacification of San Salvador, Dr. José de Aycinena was selected by the Spanish Cortes to serve on the prestigious Consejo de Estado. The presence of a Guatemalan on that body, moreover, made it possible for Central Americans to obtain coveted posts in government. The Nicaraguan Miguel de Larreinaga, for example, received an appointment to the Audiencia of Guatemala during the first constitutional period.[63] All of these marks of recognition—and the same was true for other loyal regions of the New World—helped somewhat to offset the disappointments encountered in the American Question.

The individual Central American deputies conscientiously advanced the cause of their own provinces. Florencio Castillo was particularly successful as a lobbyist. He obtained the rank of city for the town of San José, the title of "villa" for Heredia, Alajuela, and Ujarrás, and "Muy Noble y Muy Leal" for the capital city of Cartago. Upon Castillo's recommendation, moreover, the ports of Matina (Moins) on the Atlantic and Punta Arenas on the Pacific were recognized as entrepots for trade. Moreover, Father Castillo established important precedents for the future when he lobbied for the creation of a bishopric at Cartago, a conciliar seminary that eventually developed into a university at the capital of Costa Rica, and the appointment of an intendant to supervise Costa Rica's economy and administration. For this post, he recommended the popular ex-governor Tomás Acosta. Although he did not ask for the establishment of a diputación provincial for Costa Rica, it is clear, nonetheless, that Father Castillo had a vision of considerable autonomy for the area of Costa Rica. Only the bishopric was granted, although it did not go into effect for years.[64] Nevertheless, and this is important for the future history of Central America, the aspirations and the objectives of the various provinces were on record. And natives of those provinces would not rest until they had been implemented.

The Salvadoran José Ignacio Avila strove to advance the interests of his region at the proper opportunity. He proposed the establishment of a bishopric on March 21, 1812, and reminded Parliament that this was not a new idea. It had been recommended to Charles III in 1778 by Archbishop Pedro Cortés y Larraz. His province had a population of 180,000 persons, living in 126 villages and yielding about 40,000 pesos annually in tithes. Since San Salvador was at least sixty leagues distant from Guatemala City, a closer religious supervision was of utmost importance. Moreover, Avila urged the Cortes to condone the establishment of a conciliar seminary in San Salvador, so vital for the area's youth and clergy.[65] We note again the marked sense of autonomy in the future states of Central America: the economic administration of an intendancy which all of them had except Costa Rica; the religious unit of a bishopric that corresponded to a province; and a conciliar seminary for the education of provincial youths. All that remained for full autonomy was the establishment of a diputación provincial.

Mariano Robles from Chiapas replaced Manuel Llano on October 22, 1812, and this enterprising clergyman wasted no time in proposing developmental measures for his province.[66] The abuse of the tobacco monopoly among the Indians concerned him vitally, and he reminded the Cortes that it had gone on record in favor of the natives. In May of 1813, while Father Castillo was President, Robles introduced a slate of eight propositions outlining home rule for his province. He urged the establishment of a conciliar seminary at Ciudad Real de Chiapas, which was already the seat of a bishopric as well as an intendancy. Robles felt that it was now time to establish a provincial deputation in Chiapas. Among the more specific demands, Father Robles requested twelve annual scholarships to help educate gifted Indian youths. He wanted permission for trade through the ports of Tonalá and Tapachula in the district of Soconusco with an exemption of taxes for ten years in order to stimulate economic activity. Moreover, he urged the same incentives for entrepreneurs who improved the navigational facilities of the province. He also recommended the construction of a canal through the Isthmus of Tehuantepec—a project that might attract financial support from the Consulado of Guadalajara. The young clergyman recommended a higher rank for the city of Comitán and for other settlements in Chiapas. Most of these requests were granted during the second constitutional period, thus encouraging the home-rule proclivities of that region. It helps to explain why Chiapas would be the first to break with Guatemala City at the time of Independence.[67]

León, Nicaragua, was likewise disposed to an independent course, especially as the capital of the second provincial deputation in Central America. With the support of Father Castillo, Antonio López de la Plata asked that the Nicaraguan bishopric be allowed to dispose of its tithes without supervision from Guatemala City. The proposal passed.[68] He likewise requested a separate Audiencia for his province.[69] Next, he wanted the conciliar seminary in León raised to the status of university, a demand that was granted but not implemented until 1816.[70] Finally, López de la Plata proposed the construction of a canal through the Nicaraguan area—a request that did not arouse much interest in Cádiz at the time. In fact, it seems that the Chiapas canal project had priority.[71]

The Honduran José Francisco Morejón pushed the objectives of his native Comayagua consistently, and on occasion he worked independently of his colleagues from Central America. He did not join with them, for example, in supporting resolutions to establish special units in cathedral chapters for the education of clergymen in Central America, funded with money that had belonged to the Inquisition. He preferred instead to use these revenues for a special chair of philosophy and canon and civil law in the Cathedral Chapter of Comayagua.[72]

Morejón had to contend with a divided province back home, for there was hostility between Tegucigalpa and Comayagua. Tegucigalpa wanted no part of governmental control from Comayagua and had sent Larrazábal a power of attorney to represent it at Cádiz. Moreover, the actual jurisdiction of the intendant at Comayagua had been cut down in 1782 in the conflict with England, and the key ports of Omoa and Trujillo were placed directly under the Captain General in Guatemala City. The Comayaguan intendant questioned this outdated military decision in 1803, but the Crown did not support him. Hoping to correct the situation, Morejón submitted eleven propositions to the Cortes on

November 22, 1811. First, he insisted that Omoa and Trujillo should respect the authority of the intendant at Comayagua. Morejón's case was convincing if we consider that the ports were only fifty leagues distant from Comayagua, and that the new constitutional order gave priority to local units in controlling their economic development. Besides, Guatemala City was three or four times more distant than Comayagua.[73] The Overseas Committee, however, felt that Morejón had not provided sufficient evidence to prove his case. It therefore suggested that the final decision should await the investigation of the matter by the Captain General of Guatemala in consultation with his provincial deputation.

Angrily rejecting a recommendation that he felt reflected the partisan views of Guatemala City, the Honduran delegate noted sarcastically that he knew what to expect from a decision arrived at in that city. "The interests of the capital," Morejón asserted, "are in continual opposition to those of adjacent districts; the propensity to defraud and oppress these and those is reciprocal." And the capital always has the advantage because "the arm of the government supports it." The Spanish Cortes, however, should defend the weak and prevent the "tyranny of the interior: a lamentable evil, that requires more than an equilibrium of forces; it is necessary to have a movement in favor of the people that until now have been oppressed." The main issue, he concluded, was "to take away from Guatemala those ports that were usurped from the legitimate owner, Comayagua."[74] It would seem that the provinciano's hostility toward Guatemala City was very much alive at Cádiz.

Morejón's displeasure with the Committee's recommendations did not stop there. He had proposed the establishment of a Mining Tribunal that would be under the control of Comayagua's Ayuntamiento. In addition, he had requested a Bank of Savings and Loans with a financial base of 200,000 pesos fuertes to assist the mining community. With regard to the mining corporation, the Overseas Committee suggested that it follow the Mexican model. As for its location, it might well be established in Comayagua if the miners and the provincial deputation of Guatemala decided in its favor. The Committee, however, rejected Comayagua's request for monopoly control of the mining unit and exclusive privileges as inconsistent with the new constitutional order. It seriously doubted that there were resources for the Bank of Savings and Loans in Spain, or, for that matter, in the Kingdom of Guatemala—decisions that did not bring joy to the Honduran representative at Cádiz.[75] In the meantime, the municipality of Comayagua had officially asked for the reincorporation of Omoa and Trujillo. Moreover, it followed Chiapas' lead in requesting a diputación provincial.[76] This request was honored during the second constitutional period, much to the annoyance of Tegucigalpa.

America's role in the Cortes of Cádiz had been aggressive and spirited. Her representatives demanded rights for their newly integrated provinces, the administrative units that were formed by the Bourbons in the late eighteenth century. At this point in their political development Americans were adamant exponents of federalism, who resisted the centralist proclivities of Agustín Argüelles and his supporters. They hoped that the provincial deputation would make home rule possible for them. Yet, their overzealousness and their resort to the Black Legend stereotype proved to be counterproductive, polarizing the two sides on the Castas question. That was a war that the Americans lost irretrievably.

Their sincere commitment to reform and the tangible benefits that Americans received at Cádiz offset somewhat their disappointment over the power question. The Central American record at Cádiz illustrates what concessions were available to the Americas. Moreover, Central Americans also exposed to the world their regional aspirations and their determination to improve their lot. There is no question that the Cádiz Experiment encouraged the spirit of federalism in Central America. In retrospect, it also seems that Bourbon imperial reforms of the late eighteenth century had nurtured the optimism and expectations of the overseas provinces, unwittingly preparing them for the break with the mother country. America's desire for freedom and a more progressive existence, as well as confidence in shaping her own destiny, was abundantly evident in the halls of Parliament. The difficult problem at Cádiz was to satisfy the Americans' dreams while keeping them loyal to the Spanish nation. The Spaniards were not very successful in this regard. The political issue was a serious deterrent that alienated many Americans, but in truth, neither side had displayed a compromising mood at Cádiz. The failure of the free-trade movement and the delays in eliminating the tobacco monopoly further convinced American delegates at Cádiz that their options were being closed off.

4. The Cádiz Constitution

It has horrified me more that it even occurs to anyone to compare the Spanish revolution with the French revolution; this is like comparing the sun to darkness.

ANTONIO OLIVEROS, *June 10, 1811*[1]

There is no Spanish nation without a Constitution. We have taken an oath to the Constitution and cannot interpret it now without infringing upon one article, and consequently without being perjurers.

ANTONIO LARRAZÁBAL, *January 29, 1814*[2]

IN ADDITION to the polarization of opinion on the American Question, so vital to the development of a psychology for independence, the Cádiz Experiment set many precedents for the future nations of Latin America. Judging from the Central American example, the Spanish liberalism that was forged at Cádiz provided key ideological guidelines for a program of modernization and independent existence. There is value, therefore, in analyzing the nature of the Cádiz Experiment to ascertain what attractions it held for Americans. It is interesting to note, moreover, that the failure of liberal leadership at Cádiz already anticipated the trends that plagued the Americans in the establishment of their governments.

Spanish liberalism is a topic that is highly charged with emotion and controversy. This is understandable since it involved an ideological confrontation between the "two Spains," one liberal and progressive and the other traditional and conservative. Thus, much that has been written about the Cádiz Experiment and the Constitution of 1812 has little to do with the realities of that day.[3] If we take the time to read the famous charter carefully and to appreciate the milieu from which it emerged, it will help to dispel, or at least qualify, some of the distortions that have survived to the present.

≈≈≈

There is little substance to the charge that the Constitution of 1812 was an ultrademocratic and Frenchified document that had virtually no relevance to the Spanish experience. On the contrary, the deputies at Cádiz worked conscientiously to blend modern and traditional elements in a meaningful fashion, and their approach was essentially moderate. By twentieth-century standards, it might be argued that the orientation at Cádiz was somewhat conservative, a fact that helps to explain why future politicians of Latin America, of both persuasions, found the Cádiz program mutually acceptable at certain periods in their political life.[4] On religious matters, the Cádiz program was certainly traditional. And this should not be surprising if we recall that the largest group of deputies at Cádiz consisted of clergymen. Thus, the Holy Roman Catholic Church was given a monopoly of religion in the Spanish-speaking world, and no one seriously talked of religious toleration at that time. Some deputies wanted to write into the national charter certain dogmas—the Central Americans, for example, had instructions to this effect. The majority at Cádiz, however, recognized that the Constitution was not the proper place for such items. The Spanish Cortes specifically allowed the ecclesiastical *fuero* in some judicial cases.[5] The *desafuero*, or removal of that privileged condition, was not an issue in Spanish liberalism until the *second* constitutional period in Madrid (1820-1823). Traditionalism characterized the electoral procedures under the Cádiz Constitution: elections were held on church property; masses followed certain acts in the electoral process; and a clergyman was required to serve on the local registration committee. Familiar with the people in his parish, he was best able to judge if the potential citizen was "moral" and "virtuous," as required by the national charter. In a discussion with Agustín Argüelles, Father Larrazábal averred that such a practice was indispensable overseas.[6] Father Castillo underscored the traditionalism at Cádiz when he asked his colleagues for assurance that all foreigners who became Spanish citizens had to be Catholics.[7]

On the representation of estates, however, the Cádiz Experiment veered from the traditional path. The Constitutional Committee explained that there were so many different precedents of estates in the peninsular experience that it would not have been fair to impose one type on all of Spain. Nor did the English system of lords seem appropriate to the Spanish milieu, since it might cause disunion. Instead, the Committee members recommended a representation "without distinction of classes or estates." Besides, they reasoned, clergymen and nobles would be the logical preferences of the voters anyway—a contention that was borne out by the electoral results under the Cádiz system.[8] There was, however, a vestige of the estates' tradition in the Consejo de Estado, where four members of the Church and four of the nobility always had seats. In other matters, the nobility lost its former preeminence. It no longer furnished the only participants in Spanish military schools—a nationalistic reform, by the way, that evoked an impassioned favorable plea from Father Castillo in his first speech to the Cortes.[9]

Some members of the nobility and the clergy resented the abolition of entailed estates (*señoríos*) in Spain, and the debates in Parliament indicated that this was indeed a weak spot in the national fabric. When some grandees threatened that they would not tolerate such a violation of their property rights, the reformers countered with the argument that the nation's agricultural future was at stake.[10] Besides, the confiscation of land was not an issue; it merely involved the elimination of seignorial levies and obligations that would free the Spanish economy, making it possible for private enterprise to flourish.[11] The Cortes preserved the honorary attributes of the former system in order to satisfy the nobility's desire for prestige—a point insisted upon by the American delegation.[12]

It has been commonly but erroneously believed that the 1812 charter left the monarch virtually powerless, a mere puppet. The error results from confusing what happened at Cádiz from 1810 to 1814, when the Cortes was dominant during the absence of Ferdinand VII, with the constitution itself which was not fully operational until the second constitutional period a decade later. Under Spain's "Moderate constitutional monarchy," the monarch was "sacred," "inviolable," and not responsible. His ministers, on the other hand, were responsible to Parliament if they gave the monarch bad advice. As the executive power, the King had full authority to administer the laws and carry out his customary functions. Article 172 placed certain restrictions upon his authority: he could not suspend or dissolve Parliament; he needed legislative consent for certain diplomatic acts; he could not grant exclusive privileges to any person or corporation; and he was not to interfere with private property and rights except in very limited security cases. There were certain personal restrictions as well—he could not marry freely, for example. These were all safeguards that were intended to prevent the abuses of the past.

Under the Constitution of 1812, the King shared in the legislative process by his right to sanction or disapprove of Parliament's laws. This was not an absolute veto, to be sure; but it could have been, for all practical purposes, in the hands of a politically conscious monarch. If he disapproved of a bill, it could not be reintroduced until the following year. The same applied for the second year. If the Cortes persisted for a third year, it then could override his veto by a majority vote. Considering the fact that Parliament changed every two years, however, it is doubtful that legislators would challenge the executive's decision in the third year. The right to sanction, therefore, was no empty gesture; it gave the King effective power.[13]

The Council of State, moreover, recommended what action the executive power should take on laws passed by Parliament. And the forty men who served in that corporation were the most highly regarded personages in the nation, specialists in such fields as economics, law, diplomacy, and public affairs. Since the Church and the nobility always had representation on the Consejo, for reasons noted above, ecclesiastical and military expertise was also present on that body. Twelve of the forty had to be overseas residents, leaving twenty that might come from any place in the Spanish nation. The Cortes initiated the appointment of the councillors by proposing a three-man slate to the King, and the latter chose one of the three candidates to serve on the Council of State for life. Because of the calibre of men in question, the Consejo de Estado constituted a veritable moral force in the nation—very similar to what Jovellanos had had in mind—whose advice could not be flagrantly ignored either by the King or by the opposition in the Cortes. Public opinion would support a monarch's decision to sanction or disapprove of a law if the Consejo de Estado had suggested the action. The creation of this advisory corporation, almost as a buffer between the King and Parliament, revealed the practicality of the men who drew up the Constitution of 1812; they were determined to offset any demogogic tendency that might arise from a unicameral system. And there was much in the institution that was traditional, dating back to the reign of Charles III.[14]

The practical question at Cádiz was whether or not the Consejo de Estado should be fully formed in the absence of the King. After much discussion, Parliament agreed to select only one-half of the corporation, leaving the other half for the monarch's decision in the future. In February 1812, the Consejo de Estado began its operations; it consisted of two grandees, two ecclesiastics, six Americans, and ten others. The men selected were exemplary: twenty of the most talented men in the Spanish-speaking world. They included Ferdinand VII's uncle, the Archbishop; Joaquín Blake and Pedro Agar, who had served with Luis de Borbón in the second Regency; Esteban Varea, the Spanish economist who befriended Americans on the free trade issue; and many other distinguished judges, lawyers, and members of leading corporations in Spain and overseas. Among them was Dr. José de Aycinena of Guatemala City, who had helped to draw up Larrazábal's instructions. The appointment of six Americans to the prestigious council was a significant achievement for the New World. Moreover, two of the five men in the new Regency of 1812 were Americans. Their collective voice determined many key appointments to overseas posts.[15]

The stereotype of the all-powerful Cortes had a basis in fact during the first constitutional period. The Regency, after all, consisted of Parliament's appointees; and the legislators on occasion changed the Regency to assure conformity with their wishes.[16] It is pointless, therefore, to judge executive power under the Cádiz Constitution on the basis of what happened from 1810 to 1814, during the absence of Ferdinand VII. Of course, the Regency was virtually powerless; and the Council of State lacked the effectiveness that it might have had under normal circumstances. The Consejo, nevertheless, did the best it could. It recommended appointments to ecclesiastical and political posts, and its research function in diplomatic matters was commendable. The "usurpation" of Spanish territory by the young United States took much of the Consejo's time. The councillors drafted a policy paper on the Belize issue in Central America. On another occasion, they drew up a highly competent report on the tobacco monopoly. As appointees of the Cortes, the report reflected a captive position—that of the Spanish majority bloc. Yet the Consejo acknowledged the merits of the opposition's arguments, voiced by Father Larrazábal of Guatemala.[17] The tone of the lengthy document reflects that even in this case, the councillors were desperately trying to maintain their independence and prestige under the overweening power of the Cortes.

Elections under the Constitution of 1812 support the contention that traditionalism prevailed at Cádiz. At first glance, the notion of universal suffrage for all males with no property and literacy requirements would suggest a predominantly democratic experiment. Yet Cádiz deputies envisioned a representative system, one that followed the Greek model of "moral" and "virtuous" citizens. All men over twenty-five who possessed those characteristics could vote under the Cádiz system. The listing of those denied the vote, however, was revealing: criminals, men with moral or physical handicaps, bankrupts or persons who owed money to the public treasuries, domestics, the unemployed and those men without any known means of livelihood. Foreigners were eligible for citizenship, but they could not occupy high positions in government. The literacy requirement was scheduled to go into effect in 1830, by which time it was hoped that all citizens would know how to read and write. It will be recalled that clergymen, under the Cádiz system, were instrumental in determining who might vote.[18] In short, mob rule was not the objective of the Cádiz legislators.

Moreover, the electoral system was deliberately indirect. After registration, a voter was eligible to participate in municipal elections. He voted, however, for electors; and these gentlemen, in a second election, were the ones who chose municipal officials. A similar procedure was followed for the provincial and national elections, where citizens voted for electors called *compromisarios*, who then proceeded to choose the parish representatives for the district meeting. At the district meeting, electors were chosen for the provincial meeting; and at the capital of the province, the representatives voted for provincial and national posts. It was a complicated and involved electoral procedure, but it left no room for the demogogue. It was clearly a representative system, and the men chosen for high office were usually distinguished and well-educated. The voters in Spain and Central America, moreover, seemed to prefer clergymen for the political arena.

According to the Constitution of 1812, the Cortes met twice during its tenure for three-month periods. Deputies were not eligible for reelection, and they were immune from prosecution for views expressed in Parliament. Sessions were public except on topics that required "reserve." Deputies could not accept or solicit royal appointments while in office; and they could not assume a governmental post for at least a year after their term was over. The overseas delegation complained that this last regulation discriminated against Americans, forcing them to wait around a full year at their own expense before accepting an appointment. The majority bloc refused to yield on the point.

The Spanish Parliament had extensive powers to pass laws for the nation's welfare. It ratified treaties of alliance and other diplomatic instruments, drew up ordinances for the armed services, promoted all kinds of industry, and removed all obstacles to economic prosperity. The Cortes was authorized to draw up an educational plan for the nation, and it was also responsible for the education of the Prince of Asturias, the heir to the throne. A *diputación permanente* represented Parliament when it was not in session. It consisted of seven deputies—three from the peninsula and three from overseas. Providence selected the seventh member.[19]

In judicial matters, the founding fathers of the Spanish nation strove to protect every citizen from any conceivable abuse. In fact, they were obsessed with this objective, and the Americans were no exception. The legislature and executive were enjoined not to interfere with the exercise of the judicial function. Except for special issues involving the vaunted fuero of the Church and the military, the principle of unified law (a common civil, criminal, and commercial code) prevailed in the Spanish nation. Title V outlined a judicial system with a Supreme Court at the capital and regional *audiencias* throughout the Spanish world. As a concession to the Americas, all civil and criminal cases were allowed to terminate in the local audiencia; overseas bodies had authorization to deal with special appeal cases, thus extending their former authority. New audiencias would be formed in a future territorial division of the Spanish world; each district would be about the same size; and a special district lawyer (*juez de letras*) would be assigned to each unit. The Constitution of 1812 contained many enlightened features hailed by liberals all over the world—including habeas corpus, periodic inspections of jails and more humane treatment for prisoners, and the abolition of torture and other barbaric practices of the past.

Public education was a foremost concern at Cádiz, and here Jovellanos exerted a strong influence upon the legislators. All towns were to have elementary schools where children would learn how to "read, write, and count." They were also to study "the catechism of the Catholic religion, which will include a brief exposition of civil obligations."[20] Catechisms had a wide circulation in the Spanish world. One appeared in late 1810 that subsequently was reproduced in Guatemala City.[21] In many respects, the booklet already anticipated the major reforms of the Cádiz system. It was a popular and effective way of educating the public on their constitutional responsibilities. Newspapers took their educational mission seriously, for they realized that without an enlightened public opinion a modern society was not possible. Spaniards were sanguine about education and what it might do for the Spanish nation. They were forever talking about what an enlightened view might do for their communities.[22]

The Cádiz parliament never finished its educational project. During the second constitutional period, however, the legislators in Madrid completed the educational plan. It was one that received much attention

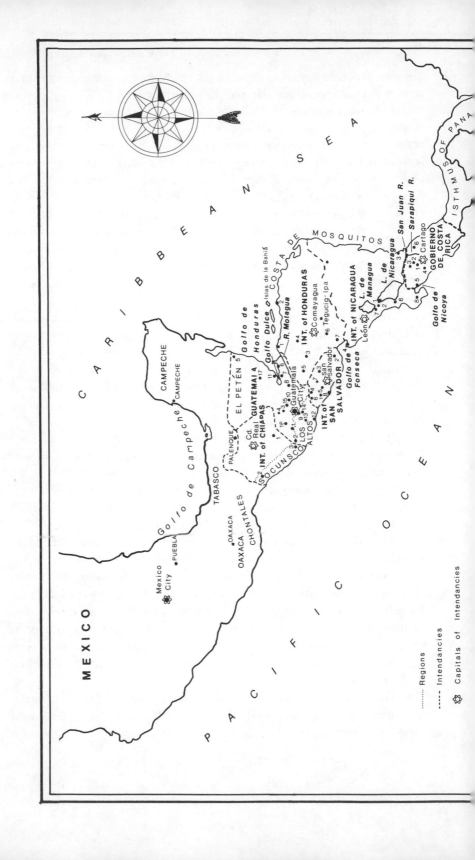

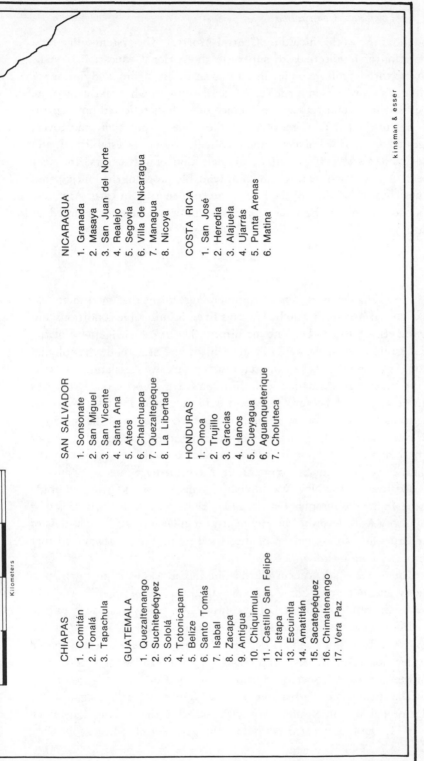

CHIAPAS

1. Comitán
2. Tonalá
3. Tapachula

GUATEMALA

1. Quezaltenango
2. Suchitepéqyez
3. Sololá
4. Totonicapam
5. Belize
6. Santo Tomás
7. Isabal
8. Zacapa
9. Antigua
10. Chiquimula
11. Castillo San Felipe
12. Istapa
13. Escuintla
14. Amatitlán
15. Sacatepéquez
16. Chimaltenango
17. Vera Paz

SAN SALVADOR

1. Sonsonate
2. San Miguel
3. San Vicente
4. Santa Ana
5. Ateos
6. Chalchuapa
7. Quezaltepeque
8. La Libertad

HONDURAS

1. Omoa
2. Trujillo
3. Gracias
4. Llanos
5. Cueyagua
6. Aguanqueterique
7. Choluteca

NICARAGUA

1. Granada
2. Masaya
3. San Juan del Norte
4. Realejo
5. Segovia
6. Villa de Nicaragua
7. Managua
8. Nicoya

COSTA RICA

1. San José
2. Heredia
3. Alajuela
4. Ujarrás
5. Punta Arenas
6. Matina

kinsman & esser

1000

500

Kilometers

0

Map 2. The Kingdom of Guatemala

throughout the world, including Central America. The system called for a corporation of intellectuals to supervise the national educational establishment with a uniform policy in "the sciences, literature, and fine arts." In time, the corporation made recommendations on what textbooks were to be used in certain courses; the choice of authors reflected how up-to-date Spanish scholars were at the time. The corporation, moreover, suggested where new universities and colleges were to be established, and what standards should prevail in the selection of instructors. In every respect, it was a far-reaching and commendable program that anticipated the positivistic curricula of the late nineteenth century in Latin America. National control of the educational system was taken for granted at Cádiz.[23]

≈≈≈

The Cádiz deputies were in complete agreement that the Indian was the forgotten American who had always lived in miserable conditions and that something had to be done for him.[24] The acknowledgement of the Indian's plight was not new in Spanish history. Throughout the colonial period, Spanish officials had written much protective legislation concerning the Indian. It was undoubtedly implemented on occasion; but it was frequently ignored because of pressure from vested interests overseas. Americans at Cádiz chose to emphasize the victimization of the Indian in their controversy with Spaniards over the American Question. The abuses of the *corregidores* and the *repartimiento* sales of worthless goods to the Indians came in for much comment. In the heated arguments, Spaniards who had lived in the New World charged the American Creoles of abusing the Indians wantonly. On occasion, these local elites had preferred compulsory work levies to the payment of regular wages.[25] Regardless of the charges and accusations of blame, speakers on both sides agreed that reform was long overdue.

The men at Cádiz concurred that the Indian was equal to any man in capacity and potential. Some acknowledged that in his present stage of *rusticity*, the result of long-standing conditions overseas that had kept him ignorant and backward, he was at a distinct disadvantage. Father Castillo from Costa Rica argued, therefore, that the Indian should be given special consideration or privileges, even though such a term was not consonant with the new type of society envisioned by the Cortes.[26]

The members of Parliament likewise agreed to legislate against any badge or assumption of inferiority with regard to the Indians. On March 13, 1811, the Cortes voted to abolish the payment of tribute, following the example set by the Viceroy of Mexico a year earlier in order to discourage an insurgency in New Spain.[27] It was a commendable action, to be sure; but it immediately raised the issue of a substitute source of revenue for a nation that was in desperate financial straits. Without some kind of a replacement, the Spanish government stood to lose money, and clergymen would find it impossible to survive in their Indian parishes. The legislators at Cádiz consistently mixed the tribute issue with the question of clerical subsidies. They finally agreed that the Indian as an equal would pay the same taxes as any other citizen; and in certain areas, depending upon local practices, contributions would be collected for parish priests.[28]

The available evidence indicates that the tribute reform was not very successful in practice, certainly not in Central America. The reasons for this were varied. At first, the Indians understandably rejoiced upon hearing that they would no longer have to pay the tribute. When they learned, however, that henceforth they would pay other taxes, just like the whites, it confused and angered them, especially since the clerical subsidies were not dropped. In Guatemala, for example, some Indian villages urged the imposition of the old tribute since it was a cheaper tax; the notion of inferiority apparently did not bother them. Thus, the tribute reform generated considerable resentment among the Indians and led to much instability in Central America.[29] Royal officials overseas also were able to work against the reform. Parliament had been vague on the question of substitute revenues, and this gave treasury officials in Central America an opportunity to procrastinate in the implementation of the reform, especially in view of the limited sources of revenue available to them. They preferred, in short, to stick with a known tax—the tribute— rather than experiment with an unknown tax that was difficult to collect. The Peruvian viceroy likewise decided against the tax reform in the first constitutional period.[30]

Humanitarian motives with regard to the Indians tended to coincide with and reinforce the general program for economic development in the Spanish-speaking world. We have already noted this tendency in Central America; the same was true at Cádiz. The legislators expressed concern about the exploitation of Indian community lands (*ejidos*) by others, such as royal officials and village leaders.[31] They legislated against such abuse. Members of Parliament discussed at length whether or not ejido lands should be divided among the Indians, giving them separate title for their shares. It was the consensus of opinion that the ejido system was too engrained to change. Following the lead of Father Larrazábal, the Cortes also ordered the distribution of royal lands (*tierras baldías* and *realengas*) into individual plots with corresponding titles. In the Americas, the Indians would be the principal beneficiaries.[32]

Much like agrarian reformers of the twentieth century in Mexico and Central America, the Cádiz deputies debated whether or not Indian land-owners should be permitted to alienate the lands given to them by the government. As an inveterate defender of private enterprise, Agustín Argüelles championed the right of the Indian to sell his land. He recognized, however, that powerful neighbors, the Church or large haciendas, might gain possession of Indian lands once they had increased in value. His solution to this problem was to pass laws preventing the sale of Indian property to large corporations. The Merchant Guild of Guatemala, it will be recalled, voted against the Indians' right to dispose of his land. The great Argüelles, however, agreed with his Guatemalan contemporaries that land given to Indians without capital was next to useless since its owner would always remain at the subsistence level. Some kind of subsidy should accompany the land grants to Indians, making it possible for them to get started right. The Regency followed through on this recommendation and ordered political chiefs to arrange for financing by the ayuntamientos and provincial governments. They were authorized to use community resources (*cajas de communidad*) if they were available; the point was to help the Indians advance.[33]

The men at Cádiz expected the American Indian to be a free participant in Spanish society; and among the Central American delegates, fathers Castillo and Larrazábal spearheaded the reform program for Indians. Larrazábal, for example, urged the enforcement of laws against withdrawing money from Indian community savings funds, except for the benefit of the Indians themselves. He was referring here to the common abuse of colonial officials borrowing money from these funds or assigning specific pensions and awards to be paid by them, oftentimes without any relevance to Indian interests. Father Castillo, on the other hand, recommended the use of these revenues, and others that he mentioned, for the establishment of Indian schools. At Cádiz, moreover, many resolutions favored the granting of special scholarships to young Indians, the future leaders of their people.[34]

Father Castillo led the attack against the infamous work levies of the colonial period. The Overseas Committee welcomed his proposition on this issue, convinced that the forced labor system had been destructive for the Indian and was incompatible with his "civil liberty." In effect, it had made a slave of the Indian. The Committee's pro-Indian stand evoked a brilliant speech from José Joaquín Olmedo, the famous literary figure from Ecuador.[35] In vivid terms he described the historical operation of the compulsory work system in Peru and exposed the greedy hacendados who had forged the stereotype of the slothful, inferior Indian in order to justify his exploitation. The *levies* had inflicted great hardships on the Peruvian Indians, even to the point of breaking their spirit. As for the laws protecting the Indian from any abuse, he vehemently accused Spanish officials of "intolerable inobservance." The work levies, moreover, had contributed to the "fantastic depopulation" of the Americas. Such was the despair of the Indian males that they refused to marry or have children. Work levies, concluded the articulate Ecuadorean, had to be abolished.[36] The Cortes agreed, and Castillo's proposition became law.[37]

The crusade in behalf of the Indian was one of the brightest pages in the Cádiz Experiment. Very few voices spoke out against these reforms. When the Peruvian delegate Blas Ostolaza, a clergyman of conservative tendencies, suggested a modified work levy system, Father Larrazábal shamed him as an American for proposing such an amendment to Castillo's bill. Thus, the vote against the *mita* was unanimous, as were other reforms in behalf of the Indian. Although economic development was an overwhelming concern in the passage of these measures, it was not the sole motive that inspired the passionate speeches of fathers Castillo and Larrazábal and of the Ecuadorean Olmedo in behalf of the "forgotten Americans." The sincerity and fervor of their words had a predominantly humanitarian flavor, well within the tradition of Bartolomé de Las Casas, the great defender of the Indians in the sixteenth century.

In fact, humanitarianism characterized the entire Cádiz program of reform, such was the concern for the economic, social, and political rights of each individual in Spanish society, no matter what his color might be. In the debates over the Castas, the legislators alluded frequently to the "barbaric" institution of slavery. It was unfortunate, however, that the Castas issue got enmeshed in the power struggle between Spaniards and Americans, thus limiting the reform program for people of African descent. Except in the political sphere, however, the Cádiz deputies voted to end many discriminatory practices of the colonial past, which made it easier for the Castas to take advantage of the celebrated Article 22 of the Constitution, granting them the right to petition for citizenship in special cases.

Although slavery was discussed at Cádiz, there was general agreement that obstacles to abolition of the institution were too formidable. The Haitian bloodbath of the 1790s was still fresh in the minds of many deputies; there were inadequate funds to compensate slave owners; and the

Cuban slave interests adamantly opposed any open discussion of slavery, feeling that it threatened their economic future.[38] Moreover, the American Question was a serious deterrent, and Spaniards were not disposed to allow American whites to dominate the national government. The abolition of slavery would have an upsetting effect upon the political structure of the Spanish nation.

Nevertheless, the founding fathers at Cádiz heard resolutions for the gradual emancipation of the slaves and the termination of the slave traffic. On March 26, 1811, Father José Miguel Guridi y Alcocer from Mexico presented a list of eight proposals on the emancipation of slaves—a moderate and practical approach to the subject. The Mexican priest maintained that slavery was against "natural law" and repugnant to all enlightened people. Only a few hacendados could hope to gain from the continuation of the institution. Father Guridi urged, however, a gradual program that would not incite social disturbances. As the first step, he proposed the abolition of the vicious slave trade; next, he recommended the freeing of slave children at birth. Father Guridi also advocated a wage system in which Blacks would receive compensation only slightly lower than other domestic servants; and he urged Negroes to buy their freedom under conditions that would be equitable to both their masters and themselves. Other minor suggestions completed Guridi's proposal, which was sent to committee.[39]

A week later, Argüelles presented a resolution to outlaw the slave trade, presumably in anticipation of a British request to the Spanish government on this issue.[40] After abolishing the slave trade in 1807, England pursued a policy of discouraging the traffic elsewhere. Portugal, for example, had promised to end the trade in the 1810 treaty; perhaps the Spanish ally would also follow suit. Coincidence would have it that the great Argüelles had heard the debates in England years earlier, and he took pride in suggesting the reform for his own nation. His bill also went to committee.[41] Because of Cuban opposition, and perhaps the American Question as well, these two promising trends at the Cortes of Cádiz yielded very little. By 1817, Spain terminated the slave traffic; many ex-slaves won their freedom during the Wars for Independence in the New World, fighting on both sides. The Spanish Cortes had set the precedent for this by liberating five hundred slaves at Omoa, Honduras, who had contributed funds to the effort against the French.

The Cádiz Experiment established important precedents for the New World nations with its humanitarian and social reforms, many of which were never implemented. The Central American experience will reveal some of the practical problems that prevented the implementation of these reforms.

≋

A leading objective of the Cádiz period was to bring about the economic development and progress of the Spanish nation. Determined to eliminate all obstacles to prosperity, the legislators freed Spanish agriculture from entailed estates. They gave life to provincial deputations whose main function was the promotion of economic well-being; and, as enthusiastic supporters of laissez-faire economics, they attacked the problem of monopoly in industry and labor. Jovellanos had documented the Cádiz mentality in the famous *Report on Agrarian Law* of 1795.

There were certain inconsistencies, however, that annoyed the overseas delegation at Cádiz and many Spanish leaders as well. War conditions encouraged the deviations in economic policy. Because of expediency and the lack of a substitute revenue, the tobacco monopoly was continued by the Spanish government, as the only viable and profitable tax resource it had. The Cádiz merchants, for their part, thwarted the desire for free trade by exploiting the government's dependency upon them for ready cash. Throughout the minutes of the Cortes of Cádiz there is an undercurrent of dislike for the greedy city merchants; and many Spaniards shared the Americans' resentment toward a small group of businessmen whose presence accounted for the inconsistencies in economic policy.

As Minister of Hacienda, Esteban Varea consistently spoke out in favor of free trade and even the abolition of customs houses. He railed against the disastrous effects of the tobacco monopoly, insisting that supporters of such a program had no place in a modern Spanish nation.[42] His election to the Consejo de Estado was a source of comfort for all the members of the overseas delegation at Cádiz.

Both Larrazábal and Castillo had specific instructions from their constituencies to oppose the tobacco monopoly at all costs. In fact, Larrazábal was the recognized leader of the opposition to continued government control of tobacco. After listening to the committee's report, Father Larrazábal presented his case to the Cortes, basing himself on facts and figures that had been sent to him by the Ayuntamiento of Guatemala City. According to his documentation, which covered a five-year period, the expenses for maintaining the monopoly in the Kingdom of Guatemala had been 50 percent. Even 10 percent for administrative costs was exorbitant, he reminded his colleagues. Besides, it was against reason to permit the King to be the only "merchant" of that commodity. Before 1767, for example, Guatemala used to send about 300,000 pesos fuertes to Spain annually. Since the establishment of the monopoly, however, deficits were the rule; and Guatemala depended upon Mexico for a subsidy of 100,000 pesos yearly. This subsidy had ceased in 1810; and it was doubtful, Larrazábal continued, that it would be forthcoming in the future. "Freedom is the soul of commerce, and the foundation for the prosperity of the state," the Guatemalan concluded; and monopolies (*estancos*) were the enemies of that freedom.[43] The Guatemalan deputy joined some of his colleagues in publishing a document that demanded the end of the tobacco monopoly. It was authored by José Canga-Argüelles, another Spaniard whose economic views pleased Americans.[44] The Council of State, however, recommended the continuation of the tobacco monopoly because of the nation's financial straits.[45] In mid-1813, the anti-monopolists finally got their way; but by then it was too late to implement the free tobacco program in the first constitutional period.

It will be recalled that a free trade law did not pass during the debates of January and February 1811. It failed again at mid-year when the British minister asked for it. The British government revived the issue almost immediately when it volunteered to mediate between Spain and the insurgents of Caracas and Buenos Aires in return for permission to trade with all concerned. Under this plan, the insurgent regimes promised to recognize the Cádiz government and to make contributions to the war effort against France. The American delegation at Cádiz, of course, fully supported the British mediation proposal. Since the project had military implications, on this occasion the Cádiz merchants were not able to frustrate the move. Blanco-White was not entirely pleased with the proposal since it seemed to emphasize the English commitment to use force against the Venezuelans and Argentines in the event that they did not comply with the terms of the convention.[46] There the matter rested until mid-1812, when the English minister proposed the addition of the Mexican insurgents—an unfortunate request that had the effect of undermining the earlier agreement. Spaniards refused to accept the Mexican insurgency under any conditions, especially since there was a legitimate Spanish government in Mexico.[47] Thus British mediation failed, and Americans again were reminded of their differences with the mother country.

The free trade issue came up again in late March of 1813, when a Philippine deputy proposed the revival of the Manila-Acapulco trade. Fathers Castillo and Larrazábal mounted the attack against the expected monopoly traffic between "four merchants in Manila and an equivalent number in New Spain." Father Castillo remarked how ludicrous it was to deny such traffic to the ports of Central America. The real issue, he said, was free trade. He asked rhetorically, Why shouldn't America trade with Asia? The answer: because it harmed national factories and encouraged the extraction of specie. In his rebuttal, Father Castillo maintained that he could not comprehend why Chinese goods coming into Acapulco were any more ruinous to America than the same goods coming to Veracruz on the Atlantic via Cádiz. As for the extraction of specie, the Costa Rican delegate insisted that the argument represented outmoded economic thinking. He lectured that economists of note had discovered that "specie is a commercial product like the rest," and the price of money depended upon the supply and the demand. Furthermore, money should not be given any more importance than it deserved in order to avoid difficulties. Since no one could predict accurately what would result from the exchange of goods from Asia to America, he maintained that the trade should be open to all ports.[48]

Father Larrazábal followed with a trenchant defense of America's right to free trade. His argument reflected the common desire of Americans to free themselves from unreasonable restraints. "Natural rights," he began, "are inherent to man, and their possession is not left to the discretion of laws." Through many pretexts, despotism had changed the laws and thus deprived man of his rights. Selfish interests, for example, had prevented the trade of the overseas territories of Spain with the rest of the world, a traffic which Americans hoped to gain now that their land was an integral part of the Spanish nation. Spain should no longer regard the overseas area as colonial possessions. Instead, it should follow the policy of Alfonso the Wise in opening up the national commerce to the universe. Parliament should also remember the words of José Campillo y Cosío to the effect that Spain should not follow the selfish interests of merchants but should heed the views of statesmen who would take into account everyone's interests. At this point in his presentation, the Guatemalan cleric excoriated the unproductive middlemen at Cádiz for enriching themselves "by increasing the value of goods needed by Spaniards overseas, and decreasing the value of their exports." This was unfair; the Spanish government should promote an advantageous traffic between Americans and foreigners if for no other reason than "the right of every living being to supply his needs with the least amount of work possible."

Father Larrazábal bristled at the thought that the Cádiz merchants represented the "national trade"—a system by which all foreign goods were routed through Cádiz to the overseas markets; yet all ports in

Spain traded directly with foreigners. This discrimination was unconscionable. If peninsular ports were required to trade through the port of Cádiz, Larrazábal noted, "they would shout to the skies complaining of injustice." Yet, "this system is the tyrant overseas," and Americans deserved better. They should be allowed to trade with Europe and Asia like their peninsular counterparts—in an equality that would put an end to monopoly and contraband.[49]

The majority bloc felt the sting of these candid remarks by Central American representatives, but it did not change its mind, despite the Regency's recommendation for "free trade." Two of the five regents were Americans.[50] By the spring of 1813, the rebellion in Venezuela had been quashed, and French pressure on the peninsula was under control. There was less reason to listen to American complaints, as Spaniards chose to believe that Americans merely wanted to take advantage of the mother country. There were also innuendoes that Americans had been unpatriotic in carrying on trade with foreigners—charges and allegations that upset the Guatemalan representative at Cádiz.[51]

Americans despaired of the Spanish connection as their major economic plank failed—a despair exacerbated by the appearance of the Instructions for the Politico-Economic Government of the Provinces, on June 23, 1813. It is ironic that Father Castillo was President of the Cortes when this ordinance became law. As the war came to an end on the peninsula, the Spanish nation was on the verge of anarchy; there was considerable disobedience of the law and many governmental decrees were not implemented. It was desirable, therefore, to have a unified and efficient government—the intent of the above-mentioned ordinances.[52]

In the context of the American Question, however, the June instructions pared away whatever hopes the overseas provinces might have entertained for regional autonomy. Although ayuntamientos still maintained their constitutional prerogatives, the new ordinances placed them more directly under the jefe político. Even in situations involving the diputación provincial, town governments reported to that provincial unit via the political chief. The provincial assemblies likewise came under stricter control; if they had a complaint to make to the Spanish government, it would have to go through "the conduct" of the jefe político. The only concession made to provincial interests was the promise that when the situation returned to normal there would be a separation of military and political authority.

Since political chiefs, in the past at least, had always been Peninsulars, American delegates understandably resented this new encroachment on two institutions that they had hoped to control. Father Larrazábal promptly questioned the Constitutional Committee on its decision to route complaints of the diputación provincial through the presiding officer of that corporation, opening up the possibility for all manner of abuse. The chief, for example, might distort the deputation's letter if it were a transgression in tax collection, one in which he might have a vested interest. The Cortes had labored consistently to eliminate "the despotism and arbitrariness" of the old regime; now the Constitutional Committee proposed to open the door in a "scandalous manner" to the same crimes. All citizens could petition the government under the Constitution of 1812; and yet, the new instructions of June 1813 took this right away from a provincial assembly. If jefes políticos within sight of Cádiz prevented "the circulation and implementation of the Cortes' decrees," Larrazábal noted with emphasis, "you can imagine what will happen in the faraway overseas provinces." It had already happened in his own Guatemala, the cleric added.[53]

Agustín Argüelles arose to answer Larrazábal's objections. Although he recognized the Guatemalan's experience in these matters, he still believed that the new constitutional system would deter any open defiance of the laws by a political chief. If a diputación provincial could challenge a political chief's every move, government would come to a standstill. The new instructions might be abused, to be sure; but at least they would bring more "vigor and energy" to government. Public opinion would provide the corrective to any abuse; and government thus would be united and efficient. Otherwise, Argüelles concluded, government would consist of "federations" and there would be constant squabbles between deputations and political chiefs.[54]

Astounded at the unconstitutional basis for the Argüelles' position, Father José Miguel Ramos Arizpe from Mexico decided to challenge the Spanish liberal leader. He asked tellingly: If the Constitution could impose restraints upon the King of Spain, including the moderating effect of the Consejo de Estado, why should not the same hold true at the local level with jefes políticos? To permit otherwise would mean the introduction of "military tyranny into the political sphere"—the blind obedience of the soldier who follows orders without question. The meeting ended on that note. A few days later, Ramos Arizpe again complained of the unconstitutionality of a certain article in the instructions. At the same time, he sharply rebuffed Argüelles for his ignorance of American history. Argüelles, however, did not relent when the Mexican cleric presented new examples. Spaniards pushed the article through in the usual manner.[55]

Furious at this new display of arrogance toward American interests, Ramos Arizpe could not resist shaming Agustín Argüelles, supposedly such a great liberal. The Mexican minced no words in totally condemning the ordinance of June 1813. Father Larrazábal shared his colleague's frustration and anger. Nevertheless, on June 16, 1813, he introduced a few propositions that might salvage something for the Americas. One proposition passed a few days later; it insisted upon high qualifications for the position of political chief—a statesman in every sense and a native of the province. This was a key concession that made the entire ordinance somewhat palatable.[56] Father Castillo added two other propositions that gained approval; all decrees from Spain had to be delivered to both the jefe político and the provincial deputation, thus guaranteeing the publication of orders from the Spanish capital. A second resolution stipulated that in the absence of the diputación provincial, the ayuntamiento at the capital should be authorized to receive governmental orders with the understanding that it acknowledge them immediately.[57] These were significant measures that assured the implementation of the government's will and protected the governed as well.

The Constitution of 1812 was hardly the work of fuzzy-minded doctrinaires, Frenchified or otherwise. On the contrary, it was the effort of pragmatists who were determined to create a modern Spanish nation while taking into account its traditions and experiences. The role of the Church as described in the Cádiz charter was clearly traditional, and the preservation of the ecclesiastical fuero was realistic given the circumstances of the times; even the blend of centralism and federalism within the institution of the provincial units might have been a commendable arrangement in a less polarized context. The protection of individual rights, an efficient administration of justice, and a progressive orientation in education—to mention only the highlights of the reforms contained in that constitution—reveal the indebtedness of the Cádiz legislature to the Bourbon reforms of the late eighteenth century. The adaptation of the Council of State to the Cádiz milieu demonstrates this point graphically.

As the Cortes settled down to its regular business, it concerned itself with framing the specific ordinances that would put the objectives of the government into effect. In the social field, the legislators, both Spaniard and American, were agreed that something had to be done for the Indian. They were, in effect, precursors of the Indianist movement of the twentieth century. Facing the problem of the Indian realistically, for example, they discussed alternatives on agrarian reform and whether land titles could be alienated. Vested interests, as well as Indian opposition, however, defeated the enlightened objectives of the legislators. Very little was done for the Blacks because of the threat to the political power structure of the Spanish nation. The unwillingness of Spaniards to meet American demands for equal free-trade conditions, as well as the delay on the tobacco monopoly, further alienated the overseas contingent at Cádiz. The Instructions of June 23, 1813, brought the American Question to a dangerous threshold; and, however necessary they may have been in Europe, the fact is that the Instructions convinced many Americans that there was no future in continuing to maintain bonds with the mother country. There was still the possibility, however, that if the political chiefs of the future were natives of their provinces, regional autonomy might come closer to reality.

≈≈≈

If the Cádiz Constitution was such a well-conceived blueprint for a modern Hispanic society, why then was it destined for failure at this time? José María Blanco y Crespo (Blanco-White) suggested an interpretation which can be documented. From the perspective of London, this native of Sevilla, who knew most of the Cádiz leaders, suggested that liberal leaders themselves undermined their own experiment. Needless to say, this interpretation does not appear in the often-quoted works of Argüelles and Toreno.

The tragedy of Cádiz—and we shall see it repeated in Central America—was that the leaders of reform were too sensitive for their own good, a characteristic sharpened by the conditions of the day. The harassment of the French siege, the unruly shouting of the spirited galleries of youthful leaders, the cramped quarters of the port city, the inflation and the financial straits of the government, the rebellion overseas, and the frayed nerves in the Cortes provided an explosive context for the Cádiz Experiment. These circumstances fed the ambition, the pride, and paranoia of the liberal leaders who ended up destroying their own creation. Blanco-White called them the "oracles" of the Congress, whose self-esteem was continually being hurt or needed to be fed.[58] The debates on the American Question reflected this conclusion dramatically, as Spanish liberals reacted emotionally to the Black Legend stereotype. Liberal leaders likewise alienated Peninsulars, especially among the moderates who voted consistently with them. These "oracles," or perhaps it would be more appropriate to call them the "brain trust," were so brilliant and so superior to everyone else that they gave their colleagues in the

Cortes an inferiority complex. Obsessed with their own righteousness and exactitude—and they were right most of the time—the "brain trust" literally pulverized any deputy who dared to question it in Parliament. As time passed, a certain "arrogance of power" prevailed at Cádiz which polarized not only the overseas delegation on the American Question, but also Spanish deputies of moderate and conservative persuasion. Since the same pattern emerged in the Central American scene years later, there is value in considering what incidents evoked the ideological confrontation, which contributed to the defeat of the Cádiz Experiment in Spain as well as in America.

From the first days of the Cortes, the liberal leadership was on the defensive about the sovereignty-of-the-people doctrine—an understandable reaction since it ran contrary to the thinking of the former Junta Central and such popular statesmen as Gaspar de Jovellanos. When someone challenged the dogma, the "brain trust" struck back with fanaticism at (conservative) *serviles*, those vile and servile creatures who preferred to live under tyranny. Their rivals eventually retreated to an equally emotional stance, as the war against the French came to an end. And this polarization did not help the Cádiz Experiment. The liberal leadership bears a large responsibility for the situation.

On that memorable night of September 24, 1810, the old Regency marched back into the halls of parliament to take an oath to the new government. There was one notable absence, however; the Bishop of Orense had not returned, allegedly because of illness and the late hour. This venerable cleric from Galicia, Pedro Quevedo y Quintano, was a patriot with impeccable credentials. Spaniards everywhere admired his tenacious stand against the French. As a man of principle, the Bishop of Orense firmly believed that sovereignty lay in the monarch as much as in the people. He could not in conscience take an oath that might violate previous commitments to his monarch—a position that won him the undying hatred of the liberal leaders. Because of the Bishop's popularity, they dared not arrest him in the early days of the Cortes; the tension subsided on February 3, 1811, when the Bishop swore allegiance to the new government. Later he signed the oath to the Constitution of 1812. In the process, however, he appended an *Exposición* which, in effect, stated that he did so under protest, especially since his bishopric had lost its entailed estates. Blind with anger, Argüelles and his faction had the good bishop exiled and his benefices taken away from him. Even the most tyrannical government in the world could not have acted so outrageously, scolded Blanco-White from London; one might just as well be living in

Constantinople, without any constitution.[59] He was correct, of course. The faithful bishop had been forced into exile; from Portugal he had no alternative but to defy the government openly in the final months of 1813. The impetuous action of the "brain trust," moreover, alienated many devout Catholics who otherwise would have continued to support the Cádiz Experiment.

Another member of the old Regency, the Mexican Miguel Lardizábal y Uribe, also generated a cause célèbre in the early months of the Cortes. Although he took his oath to the government on September 24, 1810, Lardizábal subsequently published a "Manifiesto" that criticized the liberal leaders of the Cortes. In hard-hitting language, the Mexican regent questioned the sovereignty-in-the-people doctrine. Like the Bishop of Orense before him, Lardizábal emphasized that sovereignty originated in both the monarch and the people, not just in the people at the expense of the monarch. To think otherwise, the Mexican insisted, might lead to a turbulent, democratic government.[60] This prospect, by the way, had prompted some deputies at Cádiz to question Article 3 of the Constitution, and to force a guarantee from the liberal leaders that no democratic experiment was intended.[61] Oversensitive egos in Congress, however, were not disposed to forgive a Mexican who was making this point at a time when the American Question was heating up the atmosphere in Cádiz. It should be noted, moreover, that Lardizábal had specific instructions from Quezaltenango and Guatemala City to protest any drastic changes in the government during the absence of their deputies—a point which Father Larrazábal had raised in connection with the October 15, 1810, compromise on the Castas.[62]

To punish the American upstart, the exalted leaders of Spanish liberalism proceeded to ignore the freedom-of-the-press law, one of their great reforms. According to that law, seditious and libelous statements would be studied first in a provincial censorship board (*junta de censura*), and later a national junta would review its decision. In Lardizábal's case, the provincial unit chose to condemn his publication; but the national junta reversed the decision on the grounds that there was nothing seditious in the writing, although the author had been impolitic in raising certain issues. To the "oracles" in the Cortes, this verdict was unsatisfactory. They chose, therefore, to bypass their creation by appointing a five-man tribunal to pass final judgment on the case. As expected, the Cortes' tribunal voted to condemn and burn the offensive document, forcing the ex-Regent Lardizábal to go into exile. Scandalized at the entire operation, Blanco-White reproduced all the pertinent documentation in

El Español in order to expose the unconstitutionality of the decision. He noted that two of the judges, at least, had had the intestinal fortitude to question the majority decision.[63] The sensitive liberal egos responded in similar fashion to other publications that challenged their wisdom.[64] All these incidents documented the same arrogance of power among the liberal leaders at Cádiz—a touchy "brain trust" indeed.

The persecution of the Bishop of Orense raised the religious question at Cádiz, one that should never have intruded itself because of the makeup of the Cortes. In this emotional context, the reform of the religious orders and the abolition of the Inquisition took on a different coloring, and anticlericalism was the unfortunate result. Most religious men at Cádiz agreed that these reforms were long overdue and that the procedures of the Inquisition had to conform to the new constitutional system. For this purpose, Cádiz legislators chose to return to the practice that prevailed before 1478, that is, when the bishops performed the inquisitorial function. Special attention was placed upon the liquidation of the Inquisition's assets and positions with a minimum of upset and with utmost fairness. Central Americans joined with other delegates to convert former positions of the Inquisition to more constructive educational purposes.[65] Only a zealot could have complained of the final arrangement.

Extremists, however, had the final say. To inform the public of the reforms passed, the Cortes ordered the decree on the Inquisition to be read in the churches of the land for three consecutive Sundays, along with a *Manifiesto* explaining the reasons for the reform. It was an adequate explanation which was signed by the Secretary of the Cortes, Father Castillo from Costa Rica. Some religious leaders, however, infuriated by the treatment of the Bishop of Orense, refused to read the documents to the public. The first incident of defiance occurred in Cádiz. The "oracles" again were bloated with power. Noting that the Regency elected to temporize, because it recognized that matters were getting out of hand, the leaders of the Cortes chose to appoint a new executive body. It included such distinguished men as Luis de Borbón, Pedro Agar, and Gabriel Ciscar, who had been serving in the Consejo de Estado. The presence of Ferdinand's uncle, the leading prelate of Spain, on the new Regency, softened the blow somewhat. The real point, however, was the arbitrary dismissal of the former Regency.

The crisis came to a head on March 8, 1813, when the Papal Nuncio publicly encouraged the bishops of Spain to disobey the government on the Inquisition decree. There was no alternative but to dismiss the Pope's envoy; and Cardinal de Borbón, as President of the Regency, expelled him from Spain for meddling in governmental affairs.[66] There was no question about it now; anticlericalism had become a fact of life in Spain—the results of a confrontation that the liberal leadership had incited.

The Cortes also made the mistake of adopting a vindictive policy toward the collaborators with Napoleonic government (*afrancesados*) as the war came to an end in 1813. For one reason or another, most Spaniards had decided to remain in French-occupied territory, not because they liked the French but because it was home to them. Collaborationism, therefore, was a matter of degree, and only the worst collaborationists should have been punished. The xenophobia at Cádiz, however, put all afrancesados under the same cover—a serious mistake that in time would work against the success of the Cádiz Experiment. Many afrancesados were the real leaders in their respective provinces; a vindictive policy toward them gave them no alternative but to fight the liberal cause with a vengeance.[67]

By mid-1813, Spain was on the verge of anarchy. There was alienation throughout the land, and it was obvious to Blanco-White that the "oracles" had undercut their power base with irresponsible actions. With uncanny accuracy, he predicted that the liberals would lose the fall elections for the first regular Parliament of Spain.[68]

≈≈≈≈

After a brief session in Cádiz, the regular Cortes moved to Madrid in January 1814. It was unable to accomplish much during its short tenure; after all, its predecessor had done so much in three years. The regular Parliament elaborated on such legislation as the separation of military and civilian authority at the provincial level—a reform that was anxiously awaited overseas.[69] The deputies in Madrid spent much time in seating their colleagues and in checking the validity of election results, given the widespread disturbances of the previous fall when elections took place. Moderates were still numerous in the Cortes; but it soon became evident that conservatives had a working majority in Spain's regular Parliament. The galleries, however, were still overwhelmingly liberal; and Madrid's young men soon singled out their favorites and enemies. Among the favorites were such Spaniards as José Canga-Argüelles, the economist; Francisco Martínez de la Rosa, one of Spain's great literary figures; and Isidro Antillón, a distinguished geographer. Most Americans in the regular Cortes were suplentes, who could serve until the arrival of the proprietors. Two of them captured the imagination of the galleries: fathers Antonio Larrazábal of Guatemala and José Miguel Ramos Arizpe from Mexico. The great Mejía had died in the previous year during an epidemic at Cádiz.

Father Larrazábal was a strict constructionist in the regular Cortes at Madrid, reminding his colleagues frequently that a certain action violated such and such article of the Constitution. On January 20, 1814, he joined Canga-Argüelles in challenging the Bishop of Pamplona's election to the Cortes on the grounds that the national charter forbade the reelection of former deputies. The galleries cheered the liberal leadership, but the vote went against the supporters of the Constitution by 74 to 66. That night a large band of Madrid's young men serenaded the homes of Father Larrazábal and his partners "to thank them for their efforts in defense of the letter of the Constitution." The crowd's cheers pierced the night air of Madrid in favor of the Constitution, Ferdinand VII, "His adorable Uncle, the Regent Cardinal Borbón," and "National Independence."[70]

The tide, however, was turning against the liberals. More and more deputies chose to interpret the Constitution of 1812 loosely, provoking the desperation of Larrazábal's quotation that introduces this chapter. The liberals recognized that they were fighting a delaying battle. Frustrated at this turn of events, Father Ramos Arizpe shouted at his colleagues that Americans loved the Constitution of 1812; and he warned them that if anything happened to that charter, "the American deputation would leave this beautiful soil forever."[71] An ungrateful Ferdinand VII subsequently imprisoned the liberal leadership, including fathers Larrazábal and Ramos Arizpe.

Ferdinand VII returned to Spanish soil on March 25, 1814. He lingered on in Valencia rather than marching into Madrid. In Valencia, he received a petition signed by sixty-nine deputies of the regular Cortes, pleading with him to throw out the hated Cádiz Constitution. Because of opportunism or perhaps the clerical issue, ten Americans signed that document. No Central Americans, however, betrayed the constitutional order of Spain.[72]

5. The Experiment in Central America

The invitation is no one else's business but my own.

JOSÉ DE BUSTAMANTE, *September 18, 1812*[1]

The sudden flash of light dazzles them, upsets them, throws them into a dangerous state of anxiety . . . inflaming and irritating the sentiment for independence.

JOSÉ DE BUSTAMANTE, *May 18, 1814*[2]

EVERY ten minutes a cannon shot reverberated throughout the city reminding Guatemalans that at eight o'clock that morning Captain General José Bustamante y Guerra would present his copy of the Constitution to the crowd assembled in the Plaza Mayor. The day was Thursday, September 24, 1812, exactly two years since the Spanish Cortes had begun its memorable task. When Bustamante raised the charter in a gesture of presentation, the troops fired into the air. From the Plaza Vieja a detachment of artillery replied with a cannonade of its own—the signal to launch the parade along a select route through Guatemala City. It was a remarkable sight: "The presence of such a brilliant entourage, the stately air of the marchers, the happiness that beamed in their faces, the gaiety of the large crowd, the adornments on the houses, the general pealing of bells, the din of the artillery, and the pleasant harmony of the military bands, produced a grandiose effect, a sublime picture, that charmed spirits and brought tender tears to all eyes."[3]

Representatives from all the leading corporations and military bodies of the capital and its environs participated in the procession: the colors of the Muy Noble y Leal Ayuntamiento de Guatemala led the parade; the Royal Audiencia of Guatemala surrounded José Bustamante, its President; the religious and military units passed solemnly in review; and a group of Indian justices, bearing the insignias of their respective villages, played simple tunes in honor of the Constitution. Reminders of the absent King were everywhere, especially in the Plaza Mayor, where his picture dominated the large ceremonial platform. When the marchers returned to the main square, they took their assigned positions. At this point, three secretaries alternated in reading the Constitution of Cádiz to the people of Guatemala City. Everyone was quiet, listening attentively to the articles of the long-awaited charter. One reporter observed: "It seemed more like a religious act than a civil ceremony."[4]

When the reading was over, the members of the Ayuntamiento got up from their chairs and threw out some 500 pesos worth of coins that had been struck for the occasion, electrifying the spectators. Six of the coins, however, were set aside for later delivery: one for the Spanish Parliament, another for the Regency, and one each for Antonio Larrazábal, José Bustamante, Ramón Casaus, and José Aycinena. Engraved on one side was an open book surrounded by bursts of light and highlighted by the words "Justice" and "Equity." On the edge the inscription read, "for the political constitution of the Spains." The back side of the coin had the Ayuntamiento's coat of arms with the words "City of Guatemala, 24 September."[5] San Salvador likewise celebrated the occasion with dignity and pageantry, evoking the acknowledgment of a grateful Spanish Cortes.[6]

A Vice-Admiral in the Navy whose exploits around Montevideo had won him recognition for leadership, José Bustamante y Guerra took over the top executive post in Central America on March 24, 1811.[7] The first impression that he made upon Guatemalans was highly favorable. Professing admiration for the constitutional experiment in Spain, this native of Asturias assured his constituents throughout Central America that he was in complete sympathy with regional aspirations under the new system of government. In a letter which the Ayuntamiento of Guatemala City passed on for him to the other municipalities of the kingdom, Bustamante urged them to write any suggestions that would help the area to prosper. These words and this gesture of cooperation were a welcome sign to the leaders of Central America. At last it seemed that they had a conscientious administrator in Guatemala City, one who understood the serious economic and social problems besetting the region.[8]

A man of action, Bustamante wasted no time in trying to match his words with deeds. Recognizing that the depressed condition of the lower classes in the city posed a threat to law and order, he advanced measures that might help to preserve the peace. He recommended, for example, a system of street lighting, and that reform in Guatemala City dates from his administration. He urged the appointment of more magistrates to handle the increased court loads in the wards of the city and asked for more nightwatchmen, as well as larger facilities for prisoners. Reviving a reform of 1803, he ordered the establishment of a College of Surgery to train young doctors for their home communities under a system of special scholarships that were granted by the white municipalities. The city fathers of Guatemala City and Quezaltenango acknowledged the value of this latter reform. The problem, as usual, was the lack of financial resources to implement the recommendation.[9] To curb public drunkenness, Bustamante advocated the abolition of *aguardiente* (brandy) stalls. He also recommended setting aside special pastures in order to assure an adequate meat supply for the city—a suggestion that was acted upon immediately.

The city fathers tried to implement these varied suggestions as finances permitted. Because of the opposition of liquor franchise owners, most of them Spaniards, only a compromise was possible on the brandy measure. It was agreed that twelve stands, centrally located for control purposes, would supply the city's demand for liquor.[10] In another compromise, the municipality voted to cut expenses by assigning aldermen to nightly patrols in each of the city's twelve wards.[11]

Much of Bustamante's time was spent on defense, preparing Central America against the possible spread of Mexico's insurrection. By mid-1811, only Lima and Guatemala City on the mainland of Spanish America had escaped the fact of insurrection. The threat of José Morelos's forces in southern Mexico, moreover, required a strong defense in the highland provinces of Chiapas and Quezaltenango. Ayuntamientos everywhere cooperated fully, organizing local militias and trying to curb rumors that might alarm the citizenry. In Guatemala City, young men enlisted in companies called Volunteers for Ferdinand VII. Captain General Bustamante on many occasions commended the loyalty of these regional units.[12]

Despite the harmony of Spaniards and Creoles in the defense effort, the contagion of revolution possessed San Salvador in early November of 1811. The uprisings spread to León and Granada, Nicaragua, in the following month. According to the official explanation, Napoleon's spies incited these insurrections, operating from the United States as a base. Their objective was to provoke hostility between Europeans and Americans. The Guatemalan city council circulated this interpretation throughout the kingdom, urging Spaniards and Creoles to work together against the French strategy. It was a convincing story, at least to Costa Ricans. Usually close with their money, they offered two thousand pesos to find the French agent who had stirred up matters.[13]

Throughout these disturbances, Bustamante heeded the advice of the Ayuntamiento of Guatemala City. It urged a moderate policy toward the insurgents in order to win back their allegiance—a tactic that José María Peinado, for example, had recommended in early 1811 to contain the Mexican movement of fathers Miguel Hidalgo and José Morelos. The underlying assumption, or fear, was that an Indian uprising might stir up the Castas and thus upset a society dominated by a white elite. Bustamante could understand this point, and he especially heeded the advice of Peinado and Dr. José Aycinena. These gentlemen, in turn, went to San Salvador to serve as government leaders—Aycinena as the new intendente and Peinado in a lesser capacity. When the former left for service in Spain, Peinado assumed direction of the intendancy. By rewarding the faithful elements in the Salvadoran area, normalcy was restored; and the Spanish Cortes, it will be recalled, confirmed these rewards. New disturbances, however, broke out in León and Granada, Nicaragua, on December 13 and 22, respectively. The reluctance of the Granadians to accept amnesty from the Spanish authorities in Guatemala City infuriated Bustamante, leading him to reconsider his policy toward insurrection in Central America.[14]

During his first year in office, Captain General Bustamante had been a constructive element in Guatemala, working closely with his American colleagues. But a metamorphosis took place in late May of 1812, giving rise to a new Bustamante, that ogre known by all school children in Central America as the author of the Terror Bustamantino in the pre-Independence days.

As early as October 1, 1811, there was a harbinger of the future breakdown in relations between Bustamante and his Guatemalan colleagues. It involved the touchy issue of censorship. At the time, the Ayuntamiento was preparing to send out publications to other municipalities in Central America that included letters from the Llano brothers in Cádiz and Bustamante's statements favorable to constitutionalism. When Bustamante asked to review the manuscripts in question, he let the printer know that in the future he wanted to see all materials before they were published. Fearing that censorship was back on its doorsteps again, the Ayuntamiento sent a committee to discuss the matter with the Admiral. Dr. José Aycinena was in that group. Courteous and apologetic, Bustamante assured the committee that he had not intended to suppress any publication; he was just curious about what was being published. To reassure his Creole friends that he was a sincere constitutionalist, he announced to the committee that he was about to set up the appropriate tribunals under the freedom-of-the-press law. Believing his apology to be sincere, the Ayuntamiento sent off the publications to their destinations, documents that pictured Bustamante as a champion of the constitutional system.[15] Guatemalans preferred to gloss over the incident. They had gotten a glimpse of the real Bustamante, but they assumed that it was an aberration.

The aberration returned with a vengeance, however, in late May of 1812. The resistance of the Granadians, which lasted until April of that year, convinced Bustamante that Americans were insincere and fundamentally disloyal to Spain. The only way that Spanish rule could be maintained in the New World was by a mailed-fist policy. Perhaps the American Question, which was raging at the time, had contributed to this change of heart. All readers of the *Diario de las Cortes* could not help but take sides in the polarization that was occurring in Cádiz. It does not seem to be a coincidence that other leading Spanish officials of the Church and the Audiencia, those born in Spain, came to share Bustamante's deep distrust of American motives in this period and joined with him in frustrating their aspirations for a free society. Although many of the incidents that contributed to polarization were trivial, they were nonetheless significant in the process of alienation that produced the independence of Central America.

Good news from Spain appeared in the *Gazeta* of May 23, 1812. Father Larrazábal reported on the promulgation of the Cádiz Constitution, a new Regency had taken over the executive branch of the government, the Duke of Wellington and his allies had defeated the French at Ciudad Rodrigo, and José de Aycinena was selected as one of the six Americans to serve on the prestigious Consejo de Estado. A special mass to commemorate the news seemed to be in order, all leaders in Guatemala City agreed. There was disagreement, however, on who should extend the invitation to the religious function. The Ayuntamiento felt that it was its prerogative; but Bustamante thought otherwise and acted unilaterally. What irritated the city fathers was that the article in the *Gazeta* had stated that the mass was agreed to by the "ecclesiastical and secular *cabildos.*" This was not true. Bustamante had not consulted the city council at all; and when reminded of this fact, the testy Asturian refused to retract the statement in the publication. Faced with such stubbornness, the Ayuntamiento decided to let the incident pass.[16]

A more serious incident arose from the celebration in honor of the Constitution of 1812, described at the beginning of this chapter. According to orders from the Cortes, Bustamante should have worked closely with the Ayuntamiento of Guatemala City in preparing for a three-day celebration to take oaths to the Constitution. Again, the Vice Admiral acted unilaterally. The invitations to the ceremonies were exclusively his business. With the directness of a military mind, he ordered two cavalry corporals to post the invitations officially, thus bypassing the American municipality. This was hardly an auspicious beginning for the official Cádiz Experiment in Central America. As the ceremonies for the Cádiz charter came to a close, the Ayuntamiento of Guatemala City sent an official protest to the Spanish government denouncing Bustamante's unconstitutional procedure. All pertinent documentation accompanied the letter.[17] Dr. Aycinena witnessed both affronts to the 1812 city council before leaving for Spain to become a member of the Consejo de Estado.

≈≈≈

Bustamante's feud with the leading Creoles of Guatemala City did not interfere with his determination to implement the Constitution of 1812 as soon as possible. On October 10, 1812, a Junta Preparatoria met to discuss the electoral instructions from Spain and to review the suggestions that had been received from various municipalities in Central America. The Junta included Bustamante, Archbishop Casaus, a few members of the Ayuntamiento, and other distinguished gentlemen, mainly Spaniards. The prime mover of the Junta's report of November 11, 1812, however, was a Creole, José Cecilio del Valle, a graduate of the University of San Carlos and one of Central America's most creative minds.

His presence on the Junta requires an explanation, especially in light of Bustamante's change of heart with regard to the Guatemalan elite. A native of Choluteca in western Honduras, José del Valle was an ambitious and calculating young man who had ingratiated himself with Bustamante's predecessor, Antonio González de Saraiva. Highly recommended and trustworthy, Valle rose steadily in the Spanish bureaucracy; his consuming ambition was to become a judge in the Audiencia. By mid-1812, young Valle was serving as Bustamante's unofficial secretary. This close connection between the Honduran and the Asturian, moreover, helps to explain why the latter restored Tegucigalpa's status as an *alcaldía mayor* in 1812.[18] It is also conceivable that the provinciano, considered an upstart opportunist by the so-called "family" of Guatemala, may have nourished the break between Bustamante and the Creole leaders of Guatemala City. In short, we have here the origin of the two parties that emerged on the eve of Central America's independence. The late Professor Louis E. Bumgartner attributed Valle's cooperation with Bustamante and the "Spanish faction" to personal ambition.[19]

In hopes of expediting the elections that would inaugurate the constitutional order, the Junta Preparatoria made some pragmatic adaptations of the instructions from Cádiz. Thus the first set of elections, those at the parochial level, were completed by the end of 1812. This was not true for the national elections, however, for reasons to be discussed shortly.

The Spanish Cortes had been generous in allocating twelve deputies to Central America, following the formula of one representative for every seventy thousand persons. The assumption was that Central America had a population of 840,000. Yet, the Merchant Guild's estimate in 1811 was 686,666 (Indians and whites), which would have meant only ten deputies for the Kingdom of Guatemala.[20] What accounts for this generosity? It seems that Central American deputies in Spain were persuasive in the absence of accurate census figures. The Junta's willingness to accept the figure of twelve deputies, moreover, reflected its desire to give the Kingdom of Guatemala a maximum representation. Perhaps Valle's personal influence may have accounted for this acquiescence. It is particularly interesting to note that at this point in his Central American career, Bustamante had not yet assumed his totally vindictive pose toward the area.

The smoldering Castas issue, which had preoccupied American delegates at Cádiz, was not important in the Central American elections of late 1812. There were some isolated examples of discrimination in Nicaragua, but elsewhere the Castas were allowed to vote. Recognizing that the qualification of illegitimacy would be the real stumbling block, especially in Guatemala City, the Junta took the position that all registrants would be given the benefit of the doubt in these initial elections. There simply was no time for lengthy investigations and dossiers on each citizen.[21]

Because of the number of deputies authorized by the Cortes, the Junta divided Central America into twelve voting provinces, each with a capital seat where the selection of deputies for the Cortes and the local provincial deputation would take place. Five of these voting provinces were in modern Guatemala: (1) Guatemala City, Amatitlán, and Sacatepéquez; (2) Chiquimula; (3) Chimaltenango; (4) Quezaltenango and Totonicapam; and (5) Vera Paz and El Petén. A sixth province included the Guatemalan area of Escuintla and Suchitepéquez and the modern Salvadoran zone of Sonsonate. There were two more provinces, which are now in El Salvador: (7) San Salvador and Santa Ana, and (8) San Miguel and San Vicente. The four remaining provinces were: (9) Chiapas, with its capital at Ciudad Real; (10) Comayagua and Tegucigalpa, with the former as the head city; (11) Costa Rica and Nicoya, with Cartago as provincial capital; and (12) Nicaragua with its center at León.[22]

As for the two provincial deputations that were authorized for Central America, the Junta made the following assignment of districts that could send representatives. The Guatemalan unit included: Guatemala City, Ciudad Real, Comayagua, San Salvador, Quezaltenango, Sonsonate, and Chimaltenango. The Nicaraguan deputation had district representation from León, Granada, Segovia, Villa de Nicaragua, Nicoya, and from two districts in the highlands of Costa Rica.

The electoral procedures followed the constitutional requirements closely. In setting the date for elections, the Junta announced that the executive officers would consult with their leading religious official: for example, in the capital city area, Bustamante and Archbishop Casaus determined the date of both the parochial and national elections. In the four intendancies, the intendente and the provincial bishop (or highest dignitary) would do so; and in smaller units, the corregidores or alcaldes mayores would work with the highest ranking religious official. Except for the Guatemala City area, the documentary evidence for the first constitutional elections in Central America is scanty. It suggests, however, that the electoral machinery set up by the Junta Preparatoria worked much better than anyone had reason to hope for, considering the limited experience of the constituencies.

The Guatemala City elections were almost flawless. Bustamante announced that on November 22, 1812, there would be voting for a total of twenty-five electors for the entire city, meeting in four parochial juntas. He presided over one of the juntas; and three aldermen, including the Dean of the Ayuntamiento, chaired the other meetings. Then, on November 29, the twenty-five electors gathered to select the two magistrates, twelve aldermen, and two city attorneys (*alcaldes, regidores,* and *síndicos*) for Guatemala City.

The results of these first elections were impressive. The graduates of the University of San Carlos predominated in the municipal corporation, representing the leading Spanish and Creole families of the city. The old elite continued its control of the municipality, although younger men were very much in evidence. Some of them were destined to play key roles in the future history of Central America and Guatemala. For example, José Francisco Barrundia won his first election at the age of twenty-five, which was the minimum under the Constitution of 1812. His colleagues included: Sebastián Melón, a Spaniard, as Mayor; the dynamic Antonio Juarros, as Dean of the aldermen; the lawyers Eusebio Castillo, Manuel Beltranena, and Alejandro Vaca (Nicaraguan); and Francisco Salmón, Lorenzo Moreno, Domingo Pabón, Juan Bautista Asturias, Pedro Batres, José Francisco Valdez, José García Granados, Félix Poggio, Manuel del Castillo, and José Urruela. The corporation chose as its secretary José Francisco Cordoba, a student of law and a future leader in the cause of Central American independence, like many of his colleagues in Guatemala's first constitutional government.[23] The tradition of balancing Creoles and Peninsulars in the city government seems to have been maintained in these elections. The lack of unknown surnames also suggests that the artisan elements in Guatemala City did not bother to participate in these elections to the same extent that they would in future contests.

The constitutional muncipal corporation commenced its sessions in early December of 1812. It compiled an outstanding historical record during the first constitutional period, and it was the major unit that was operational at all times. Because of a concentration of talent in Guatemala City, drawn from all parts of the Kingdom, it followed that its dynamic Ayuntamiento should set precedents for the outlying provinces. For almost a year, before the provincial deputations of Guatemala and Nicaragua began their operations, the Ayuntamiento also functioned as the representative for the entire kingdom. It assumed the responsibilities of the provincial deputations vis-à-vis both the Spanish hierarchy in the area and the authorities at Cádiz.

The first constitutional body of Guatemala City deserves to be called the Juarros Administration, because Antonio Juarros thoroughly dominated that corporation with his leadership, energy, and drive. Historians have forgotten his active role as a precursor of Independence, perhaps because Juarros died a few years before that movement. Contemporaries, however, fully appreciated his talents and leadership qualities. Young Barrundia, for example, learned much from him, serving with him on the

Ayuntamiento and on many committees, as well as in the special militia unit called the Dragones. Not only was Juarros the main instigator of reforms in the Ayuntamiento, he was also the spokesman for Creole interests in the conflicts with the Spanish hierarchy. The Juarros Administration, moreover, set important precedents for subsequent constitutional governments in Guatemala City.

A note of excitement and eagerness characterizes the minutes of Guatemala's constitutional municipality from its first session on December 7, 1812. Its members were anxious to reform their environment and to implement "our wise constitution." Suspecting that they would have a hostile executive, Juarros moved to take an oath of secrecy concerning the deliberations of the municipality. In addition, they agreed to defend *"el misterio de la Concepción Purísima de María Nuestra Señora,"* underscoring the traditionalism of the Cádiz-type of constitutionalism. The assignment of committees followed the requirements of the Constitution, and regidores were placed in charge according to their recognized skills. Young Barrundia, still a law student at the University of San Carlos, was assigned to head the education committee. The pattern was for a regidor to go outside of the corporation to enlist the services of knowledgeable citizens on a given theme. The regidor in charge of the Public Health Committee, for example, would ask the head of the public health service or some other medical doctor to serve on his unit.[24] In this way, larger numbers of people were brought into the experiment in self-government that unfolded around a city's admininistration.

The constitutional city government felt a serious responsibility for educating the public to the advantages of the Cádiz Experiment, a new order whose main objective was to correct the abuses of the past. It was a tireless champion of the freedom of the press, especially against the authoritarian Bustamante. The city fathers complied with the suggestion from Cádiz that their major square be renamed Plaza de la Constitución. Furthermore, at their own expense, they offered to erect a monument in the main square and asked permission from the Spanish Cortes to declare the area in its vicinity an asylum. Juarros, of course, made this motion.[25] Municipal leaders insisted upon the immediate publication and announcement of decrees from Spain in order to keep the public informed of the latest innovations. The publication and circulation of key documents about the Spanish constitutional system was a vital contribution to the area's education. The Ayuntamiento likewise kept the rest of the Kingdom posted on the news from Mexico, constantly pressuring Bustamante for this information.[26] In its various projects for public entertainment, the regidores recognized that the educational objective and the maintenance of law and order worked hand in hand.[27]

Despite a limited financial base, the city fathers experimented with the educational system in the city, using its school San José de Calazans as the model. Barrundia headed this particular experiment and recommended two reforms to his colleagues. First, he felt that mathematics and sciences should be stressed at the primary level; and secondly, he urged an open competition for the teaching posts. Thus, qualified teachers were hired; and in September of 1813 the city fathers proudly witnessed the first public examinations under the new program. So impressive were the results that Juarros proposed that in future examinations students should be examined on their comprehension of the Cádiz Constitution. His colleagues agreed. They also authorized Barrundia to publish one hundred copies of a "political catechism" that had circulated earlier in Spain. Older students were expected to commit this manual to memory—an excellent question-and-answer compendium of the new system and its principles. The Ayuntamiento paid for its publication.[28] A copy of this manual is on public display at the Museum in Antigua, Guatemala.

Hoping to enlighten the community on municipal government, Dean Juarros proposed holding public and open sessions of the city council meetings, following the example of the British and Spanish parliaments. In addition, he argued that the regidores would benefit from the ideas of knowledgeable citizens who might speak to a given topic. Barrundia and others supported the Juarros resolution. It did not pass, however, because of worsening relations with Captain General Bustamante. Nevertheless, the proposal established a precedent that did materialize during the second constitutional period in Guatemala.[29]

Staunch supporters of economic development and an open society, the Guatemalan leaders believed firmly that laissez-faire economics was basic for the return of prosperity to their City and area. The regidores continued the pattern of liberalizing the guilds of the city to meet the demands of the new order. They made it easier for new businesses (bakeries, for example) to be established without complicated licensing. Above all, they strongly upheld the Bourbon policy of a free meat supply for the city, a reform that vested interests had fought with considerable success. They therefore reaffirmed the stand against meat monopoly. There was also much concern in the city council about the development of an adequate infrastructure for the economy in the City and in the area now known as Guatemala. The regidores worked hard on such projects as the maintenance of adequate and sanitary water resources, the provision of public health facilities, the encouragement of agricultural and pastoral activities to provide the city's food supplies, and the promotion of the latest technology by awarding prizes to farmers and craftsmen. In this connection, the city council associated itself with the Economic Society and the Royal Merchants Guild of Guatemala.[30] Juarros and his colleagues, for example, welcomed the Cádiz decree of June 8, 1813, which encouraged the establishment of "Chairs in Civil Economy" to teach the best methodology in the economic field. In 1814, Francisco García Peláez offered a paper in competition for the chair. He defended the economic ideas of none other than Adam Smith.[31]

≈≈≈

Offsetting these positive strides of the new constitutional system in Central America was the stubborn resistance of the Spanish hierarchy. It seemed to envy and resent the Americans' initiative in reform and their devotion to constitutionalism. The old Ayuntamiento of 1812, it will be recalled, had suffered two insults from Bustamante during its final days. The Juarros Administration, of course, was well aware of these encounters.

The clash between Bustamante and the contitutional leaders did not take long to materialize. Anxious to get Central America's deputies to Spain by September 1, 1813, the opening date for the first regular Cortes, the city fathers questioned Bustamante on why he had not issued the call for the national elections. They also wanted to know the latest news from Mexico. Bustamante came to the municipal meeting of December 22, 1812, to answer these points. His affected politeness notwithstanding, the Asturian ended up telling his listeners to mind their own business. He alone was responsible for those issues.[32] Although angered by this graceless outburst, the regidores contained themselves long enough to give Bustamante a second chance. On December 24, they again urged Bustamante to issue the call for elections; and while awaiting the reply, Juarros was authorized to draft a strong statement of grievances to the Spanish Cortes.[33] The corporation was unanimous in its support of this action. Both Spaniards and Creoles felt insulted by the Asturian's arrogance. When Bustamante ignored the second request, the constitutional government convened on January 2, 1813, to review Juarros' draft. Everyone agreed to sign the strong protest on the following day, January 3, 1813. Someone apparently leaked the contents of the Juarros document to Bustamante; and on January 3, he issued the call for the second series of elections, obviously hoping to forestall a serious reprimand from Cádiz. To protect himself, he notified the Ayuntamiento of the convocation on January 5, that is, after the fact.[34] Since the Cádiz instructions stipulated that an executive was required to consult the ayuntamiento at the capital *before* calling elections—as opposed to the Valle regulations for November 1812, which allowed a jefe político to do so in consultation with the highest prelate—the regidores voted in favor of sending the Juarros protest to the Spanish Parliament, just to show that body what a perverse and unconstitutional man headed the government. Father Larrazábal was sent a copy of the protest. Moreover, Dr. José de Aycinena, who left for his post in Cádiz on January 12, 1813, promised his friends on the municipal corporation that he would seek a "remedy for the evils that afflict us."[35] He made this statement at the farewell party they gave for him.

The Juarros document of January 3, 1813, is a damning indictment of arbitrary Spanish officials overseas. It underscores Bustamante's lack of civility in talking to the Municipality in a "language which Spaniards should not have to hear from their governing officials." The delay in calling the national elections was unconscionable in an era when everyone anxiously awaited "the use of his rights . . . interrupted for so many centuries." The following quotation expressed a grievance common to Americans everywhere, not just those in Guatemala:

> Executives in America have been accustomed to treating these vassals as they might be authorized to do with a colony of slaves, because the distance from the throne and the difficulty in seeking recourse, allow their actions to go unpunished. A succession of centuries has engrained in them an absolute and despotic command, and it is not easy for them to reconcile themselves to the new system into which they are compelled to enter and which drastically clips their old authority and practices.
>
> Sir, this is the real cause; the ulterior motive, and the sole origin for obstructing the elections of deputies and the establishment of the [provincial] deputations. Sir, they do not want the people to take their grievances to the throne via the majestic conduit of their representatives, nor do they want to share authority or give up attributes that have been their exclusive preserve.[36]

But Bustamante, the hard-headed naval officer, persisted with the strategy of delaying the national elections during the months that followed. Although the parishes chose their electors (*compromisarios*) by January 10, 1813, these gentlemen were not able to gather for their elections until February 7, delayed by the lack of authorization from Bustamante. The district and provincial meetings were likewise held up by technicalities that an understanding executive might have overcome. When finally elected in March 1813, the deputies to the Spanish Cortes could not proceed to their destination because Bustamante refused to free the revenues they needed for trip expenses and per diems. In an equally exasperating act of obstructionism, he delayed the opening sessions of the Guatemalan provincial deputation until September 2, 1813, and those of its Nicaraguan counterpart until November 21, 1813. Again, a cooperative chief would have allowed the suplentes or a smaller quorum of provincial deputies to carry on business until the arrival of proprietary deputies from the faraway districts.[37] In a technical sense, Bustamante was not entirely responsible for the problems that arose. They merely provided him with a legal pretext to thwart his rivals on the Ayuntamiento, who were constantly prodding him to expedite the elections, convoke the provincial deputations, and advance the elected deputies to the Spanish Cortes. In the national elections of December 1813, by way of contrast, the entire process was completed within a month's time. Conditions had changed by then, and both provincial deputations were actively supervising the operation. The chief could no longer control the process unilaterally, as he had done in the first elections.[38]

Despite the earlier promise to implement the freedom-of-the-press reform, Bustamante resorted to the tactic of delay while at the same time intimidating the two city printers, Ignacio Beteta and Manuel Arévalo. Nothing could be published without the chief's prior scrutiny.[39] Juarros and his companions tried to force the issue, but it was all in vain. Their only recourse was to forward yet another protest to the Spanish government. Suspecting that the authorities at Cádiz would not condone further delay on the cherished reform, Bustamante finally allowed the Nicaraguan Censorship Board to begin its work on November 21, 1813, and the Guatemalan unit, two days later.[40]

Another form of executive obstructionism, which the deputies at Cádiz recognized as a serious problem, was the practice of withholding a decree from the public. The Cortes, therefore, ordered that all decrees had to be made public within three days of receipt (*toma de razón*); otherwise, serious punitive measures would be taken. To assure itself of compliance with the law, the Guatemalan Ayuntamiento proposed to the Cortes that it would willingly receive and record a decree's date of arrival in Guatemala City, turning these books over later to authorities in Spain for their perusal and collation. It will be recalled that Florencio Castillo from Costa Rica had made a similar proposal at Cádiz. In both cases, the goal was to prevent a jefe político like Bustamante from defying the law by concealing it.[41]

Another bone of contention between the Asturian and the Guatemalan aldermen concerned the quarterly visits to the jails in the area—a responsibility that belonged to the provincial deputation and which the city fathers discharged until that body began to function. The intent of the Constitution was clear: to assure a prisoner of his rights by speeding up his trial, by prohibiting any abuses while he was in jail, and by impoving the conditions of his detention. A pair of regidores joined the judges of the Audiencia on these visits. Their investigations were carried out conscientiously; some jailers were fired because of abuses, and others were required to introduce better measures of sanitation. The reform, in short, worked in Guatemala City as it was intended by the legislators at Cádiz.[42] Bustamante resisted these corrections.

A more serious conflict arose over the type of trial that should be given political prisoners. As a naval officer, Bustamante preferred the decree of October 6, 1811, that applied to war conditions in Spain. All cases of subversion (*infidencia*) had to be tried in a military court. The Ayuntamiento's attorneys disagreed, arguing that in non-combat areas like Guatemala the cases should be tried by the Audiencia. The issue became emotionalized due to the presence of Granada's municipal authorities in the city jails. The Guatemalan aldermen felt that the form of encarceration should be more decorous. Bustamante, as might be expected, refused in no uncertain terms to give special treatment to men whom he considered rebels. In the long run, the Ayuntamiento's lawyers turned out to be right on the subversion controversy; even Bustamante suspected that the Spanish legal system under the Constitution of 1812 would never condone his summary treatment of political prisoners. Until the courts corrected the situation, however, many prisoners languished in jails for years; some even died. The insistence upon treating Granadians as common prisoners infuriated many Central Americans against Bustamante and Spanish rule in general. It led to renewed uprisings and plots in Guatemala City in December 1813, and in San Salvador in January 1814. Bustamante would never admit that his policy on subversion was a major factor in causing this ferment and alienation throughout Central America.[43]

Steadfast defenders of the Constitution and their own prerogatives, the aldermen of Guatemala City had disagreeable moments with other leading Spanish officials, including the Archbishop Ramón Casaus. A native of Aragón, Casaus perhaps encouraged Bustamante's suspicions about the loyalty of Creoles because of his earlier experience in Mexico when the Hidalgo rebellion broke out. He was wary of American motives. The issue between the Archbishop and the Municipality concerned the quarterly visits to jails and whether the reform applied to religious prisoners. Casaus simply would not accept the latter point; he insisted that there were no jails in a technical sense on ecclesiastical property. The Ayuntamiento, on the other hand, reminded the Archbishop that the legislators at Cádiz had included the protection of religious prisoners as well. The tireless Juarros defended the Ayuntamiento's position with brilliance. It was outrageous, he argued, to deny clergymen, an exclusive and sacred group in society, the protection of the Constitution when that defense was granted to the scum of the earth. The aldermen, including Barrundia on one occasion, fought their case tenaciously, defending such prisoners as the Indian philosopher Dr. Tomás Ruiz. They even caught Casaus in some patent falsehoods, as when he denied that any prisoners were being held. Moreover, the Archbishop's language with the Creole corporation resembled the caustic tones of his Asturian colleague. It shocked the aldermen, leaving them no other alternative but to register a protest with the Spanish government. Juarros, as usual, drafted the new complaint to the authorities in Spain.[44]

The constant quarreling between Bustamante and the Ayuntamiento of Guatemala City exacerbated the division between Spaniard and Creole. With the pettiness of a sick mind, the Captain General went out of his way to antagonize the aldermen on issues of protocol. For example, he would not recognize the Ayuntamiento's title of "Excellency," which the Cortes of Spain had granted to the City. Moreover, other corporations, dominated by Spaniards, took the same delight in alienating Americans on these small points. Although the Audiencia had the same title, it refused to consider itself an equal to the Ayuntamiento. Members of religious corporations sent lower-ranked clergymen out to greet the Ayuntamiento at religious functions, although its rank required a more important prelate to receive municipal authorities. The Audiencia would not write directly to the Ayuntamiento, only indirectly through a scrivener. There were other slights of this nature, which taken in the broader context, were helping to develop the psychology of independence among Americans. Further complaints made their way to Spain against the Audiencia and the Ecclesiastical Cabildo, providing a damning picture of obstructionism by Peninsulars in the area. In the meantime, the Ayuntamiento conducted itself prudently and constitutionally, refusing to accept letters from the Audiencia that showed disrespect. To correct the defiance of the Ecclesiastical Cabildo, it applied economic pressure of a sort by reducing the number of sponsored functions in local churches, a reform that was long overdue. The reason for implementing it at this time, however, was directly linked to the affront mentioned above; and the Archbishop understood this point.[45] The Ayuntamiento simply refused to participate in functions where the Captain General planned to discriminate against them on seating arrangements.

≈≈≈

Hopeful that the provincial deputations might be functioning by July 1, 1813, as scheduled by the Cortes, the Guatemalan Ayuntamiento sent out a circular to expedite the arrival of district representatives.[46] Four proprietarios and two suplentes had reached Guatemala City by July 20; and if Bustamante had permitted these men to function as a quorum, the Guatemalan provincial deputation (D.P.) would have had a longer active career. He withheld permission, however, until the delegate from Quezaltenango was able to find a replacement for his parish. This was not until September 2, 1813.[47] The Nicaraguan D.P. opened its doors on November 21, 1813. By comparison to subsequent deputations, we have only fragmentary evidence about the functioning of these two corporations. Much of the documentation, especially because of the conflict with Bustamante, was perhaps deliberately destroyed; and the governmental policy of erasing the evidence of the first constitutional period also took its toll.

The Central American deputations, like the Ayuntamiento of Guatemala City, consisted of distinguished representatives from each of the seven districts. The deputation in Guatemala was comprised predominantly of religious men, following the pattern we have already noted for Spain and Central America. Dr. José Matías Delgado of San Salvador and Dr. José Simeón Cañas of Sonsonate, were two leaders of Independence that served on that body; their fellow priests were Mariano García Reyes (Chimaltenango), José María Pérez (Quezaltenango), and Bruno Medina (Comayagua). Eulogio Correa, the delegate from Chiapas, likewise may have been a priest. If so, the only non-priest was the merchant Manuel José Pavón, representing the city and Sacatepéquez. By comparison, the Nicaraguan body consisted mainly of hacendados, two from Costa Rica and five from what is now Nicaragua: Joaquín Arechavala, a leading cattleman since the late eighteenth century, and his colleagues Domingo Galarza, Pedro Chamorro, Vicente Agüero, José Carmen Salazar, Anselmo Jiménez, and Agustín Gutiérrez.[48] A distinct advantage for the Leonese group was a cooperative chief who supported regional aspirations—the intendente Juan Bautista Gual, an infantry colonel with some forty years of service.

The Guatemalan deputation attempted to function normally within the context of alienation between the Ayuntamiento and the Spanish hierarchy. It took over the quarterly jail visits from the regidores, and it worked closely with them on economic and financial matters, reviewing the books of all the ayuntamientos in the province. The Nicaraguan unit did likewise.[49] The support of the Guatemalan D.P. assured the victory of the free-meat advocates in the City, and may have forced Bustamante's hand on the establishment of the juntas for the freedom-of-the-press law.[50] Its commitment to economic development has been documented adequately with regards to Comayagua, Honduras. Father Medina proposed a questionnaire for his district in order to ascertain the potential for the textile industry. The Intendant of Comayagua sent the document to officials under his jurisdiction. The report from the Ayuntamiento of Comayagua was enlightening. The textile industry in that city, it said, might succeed if steps were taken to eliminate the coyote menace in the vicinity. A definite asset was the unemployed female population. Noting that in such countries as Holland, England, and Germany, textile industries required at least four times more women than men, the regidores averred that this requirement could be met easily. There were about five hundred women available for such an industry. This increase in economic activity, moreover, would encourage marriages, increase the population, and improve "the morality of the people."[51] These were dreams that did not materialize, unfortunately.

The Nicaraguan D.P. provided strong support for economic development in its jurisdiction, reviving the Bourbon program of 1796 to open up the Atlantic traffic via the San Juan River to Granada on the Lake of Nicaragua. In addition, Jefe Gual and the Nicaraguan deputation had grandiose ideas of developing the north central highlands in the vicinity of Nueva Segovia, where it was believed that the mining and tobacco industry might thrive. For this purpose, Gual appointed two assistant jefes políticos, one for the northern and another for the southern jurisdiction at Granada, pending the approval of the Spanish government.[52]

The Nicaraguan D.P. was a dedicated advocate of its own autonomy and separation from Guatemala City, in true provinciano style. The distance from Guatemala City to León was more than sufficient reason for establishing an Audiencia in the south, it maintained. Moreover, this would provide better government for the jurisdiction. The D.P.

suggested that if Comayagua wished to join the unit, it would be welcome—a suggestion that Florencio Castillo had once made at Cádiz. The Nicaraguans also raised the standard complaint that the government in Guatemala City listened only to local merchants. That was why the long-standing developmental projects for Nicaragua in the San Juan area and elsewhere had never materialized: the trade monopolists at Guatemala City were against it. In short, Nicaragua's future could never be realized while it was a dependency of the former capital.[53]

The Costa Ricans shared the provinciano attitude toward Guatemala City, while at the same time not feeling too comfortable under the control of León. Although the Nicaraguan D.P. recommended an intendancy for Costa Rica, Gual voted against it on the grounds that a population of 39,000 did not warrant the additional bureaucracy. Nevertheless, he allowed the recommendation to go forward. Although Father Castillo had received many concessions for his constituents in Costa Rica, the implementation of these measures was another matter. Bustamante, for example, was not favorably disposed toward them. He closed the traffic between Panama and Punta Arenas on August 7, 1811, despite the objections of Costa Ricans. When he learned later that Costa Rica had gained permission from the Cortes to open up the port at Punta Arenas, he stubbornly kept it closed. Costa Ricans were angry and bitter. In typical provinciano style, they accused the selfish Guatemalan Consulado of working against the "pious designs of our wise Constitution."[54] Outnumbered two to five, moreover, Costa Ricans were not happy with the Leonese connection. They referred to the Nicaraguans on the D.P. as *"antagonistas, egoístas"* (selfish, egotistical rivals). They felt convinced that Nicaraguans had worked against the establishment of a bishopric at Cartago and had ruined the trade of both Matina and Punta Arenas. Unquestionably biased assertions, they demonstrated nonetheless the exaggerated localism of the colonial period, now venting itself in the Cádiz Experiment.[55]

The program of constitutional reform in Central America was only a limited success, as far as most governmental units were concerned. Because of Bustamante's tactics of delay, many corporations had their tenure shortened so that not many of their ambitious objectives had a chance to materialize. Moreover, if the Spanish hierarchy had been cooperative, such as Jefe Gual was in the Nicaraguan D.P., perhaps the results would have been more impressive for the region as a whole. In reviewing the first constitutional period, the emphasis should be placed upon the record of the Juarros Administration because of its longer tenure and exceptional makeup. Faced with the obstructionism of the Spanish hierarchy, the city fathers intensified their commitment to constitutionalism. In fact, their defense of the new order was perhaps the most notable long-term consequence of the Cádiz Experiment in Central America. Moreover, throughout the acrimonious quarrels with Spanish officials in Guatemala City, they never abandoned hope in their cause. They sincerely believed that the government at Cádiz, the creator of their "wise Constitution," would inevitably correct the situation in their midst. That is how much faith they had in the Cádiz Experiment. Juarros in particular was a veritable Don Quixote in his defense of the Constitution and of the American cause.

Considering the polarization over the American Question, it was perhaps unrealistic for Guatemalans to expect any relief from the Cortes of Cádiz. Yet they had high hopes that Dr. José Aycinena could convince his colleagues in the Consejo de Estado to recommend the dismissal of Bustamante, who was such an obstacle to implementation of the new system; and that Father Larrazábal and his American colleagues would certainly sustain their protests and demand an effective reversal of the situation.

The optimism of the Guatemalan aldermen, however, turned out to be misplaced, for the government at Cádiz chose to temporize. On September 30, 1812, the authorities reviewed the protest made by the pre-constitutional Ayuntamiento concerning Bustamante's unilateral action on the celebration for the Constitution of 1812. The reply of the Cádiz government was that the Ayuntamiento was to be congratulated for maintaining harmony with its chief on that glorious occasion—a pusillanimous statement that enraged the Juarros Administration. The aldermen replied caustically that the government had settled nothing with its letter. They would have to continue to suffer the arrogance of their jefe político superior.[56] From optimism the mood began to reverse itself ever so slightly. There was still hope that the protests of the constitutional municipality would receive a different treatment.

They were mistaken, however. A month later, the Spanish Cortes replied to the Juarros letter of January 3, 1813, the one that accused Bustamante of holding up the national elections. This reply thoroughly disillusioned the city fathers. The Cortes commended Captain General Bustamante and his Junta Preparatoria for its contribution to orderly elections in the Kingdom of Guatemala. For reasons that are not clear, the

Cortes chose to overlook the main point of the grievance: namely, that Bustamante had deliberately delayed the announcement of the second election until the last minute. Apparently, the polarization over the American Question was still having its effect upon the thinking of Peninsulars. The record of the Cortes showed that Bustamante had been a champion of constitutionalism, thanks to the euphoric statements of the 1811 Ayuntamiento; and it was difficult to believe that the Asturian naval officer could have changed so drastically. That at least must have been the reasoning behind such a decision.[57]

The unfavorable replies from Spain reached Guatemala City shortly after the provincial deputation held its first session. It is not difficult to imagine how pleased Bustamante was to learn that he had the full support of the Spanish government. Appreciating the detrimental impact that the Juarros letter might have on his subsequent career, Bustamante had written to the Regency concerning his doubts about the constitutional experiment in Central America. His argument now was that the region could not possibly sustain twelve deputies to the Spanish Cortes, hinting that perhaps the number should be lowered. Bustamante's observation was essentially correct. The depressed economy of Central America could not support such a large delegation. The Asturian's motive in making the statement, however, is suspect; he wanted to justify his policy of withholding funds to advance the elected deputies of Central America to Spain. In short, he was covering up one plank of his obstructionist program. It is also interesting to note that the Ayuntamiento had received word—possibly from Larrazábal—that some of Bustamante's relatives had served on the committee that favored admonishing the Creole-dominated Ayuntamiento of Guatemala City. This sounds farfetched; yet, it is possible that Bustamante's brother, a member of the Consulado de Cádiz, might have exerted some influence in the case.[58]

The Creoles in Guatemala City were overtaken by even greater despair upon receiving a copy of the Instructions of June 23, 1813, which increased the authority of the jefe político at the expense of the provincial deputation and the Ayuntamiento. They erred, however, in believing that the new Regency, headed by Luis de Borbón, had been responsible for these ordinances that violated the spirit of the Cádiz Constitution.[59] This was beside the point, however. As Americans, they viewed the situation as desperate: the two corporations which they expected to dominate, and did in practice, were now mere instruments of executive power, the likes of a Bustamante. It is not surprising, therefore, that in the waning months of 1813, many Guatemalans were starting to think in terms of

Central America's independence. This is the proper perspective for understanding the celebrated Belén Conspiracy of December 1813 in Guatemala City and the renewed outbreaks in San Salvador during January 1814. The leading figures in those plots were key men in their respective ayuntamientos. José Francisco Barrundia, for example, was implicated in the Belén Conspiracy. Fortunately, he managed to escape before Bustamante's men were able to arrest him.[60]

Armed with the Ordinances of June 23, 1813, Bustamante wasted no time in letting the Diputación Provincial know that he intended to dominate the corporation. He rejected outright the suggestion by Dr. Cañas that the D.P. should function as a legislature, permitting only one vote for the jefe político.[61] Acting as dictator of the provincial unit, Bustamante left its members with no other alternative but to register a strong complaint with the Spanish government. Moreover, the D.P.'s strong indictment of Bustamante received considerable publicity because it was published in *El Universal* in Madrid, evoking unfavorable editorial comment about the Asturian. On March 2, 1814, the Cortes had considered the complaint signed by five members of the Guatemalan D.P. They accused Bustamante of delaying the installation of their body for three months, of frustrating the election of deputies in some provinces so that "witnesses of his conduct" would not proceed to Spain, of violating the freedom-of-the-press report, and of failing to permit the singing of the *Te Deum* during the installation of the D.P.[62] Angry at this unfavorable publicity, Bustamante hoped that Archbishop Casaus might investigate the ecclesiastics who had signed the document, so damaging to his honor. He seemed to be especially angry at the charges made against him by fathers Larrazábal and Arizpe in Spain.[63]

The enemies of José Bustamante y Guerra, who were many, finally got a hearing. Soon after arriving in Spain, José de Aycinena exposed the arbitrary conduct of the jefe político superior in Guatemala City to his colleagues in the Consejo de Estado and in the executive. It was thus decided to remove him from office in early 1814. To save face, the proud Admiral let it be known that he was in poor health and had asked to be relieved from duty.[64] The city fathers, however, knew better. They had received a letter from Larrazábal on February 18, 1814, announcing the arrival of a new captain general. He was Fernando Miyares, a field marshal, who had served in Maracaibo, Venezuela.[65] Creoles rejoiced throughout Guatemala.

There was still one more ray of hope emanating from Spain—the announcement that there would be a separation of the military and political functions of the executive power. A captain general would perform military duties, while a jefe político did the rest. The Cortes had indicated on September 12, 1813, that only recognized champions of the new constitutional system could be hired to serve as executives, thus preserving harmony among Spaniards everywhere. José de Aycinena warmly supported this new policy, as did his colleagues on the Consejo de Estado.[66]

Accordingly, a member of the Guatemalan Ayuntamiento suggested the candidacy of Vicente Aycinena, the second Marquis of that name; and his colleagues supported the motion unanimously. An exceptional man, more easy-going but just as enlightened as his brother José, Vicente de Aycinena had always labored conscientiously for his region. He won the appointment on January 25, 1814, and Larrazábal was jubilant in announcing the selection.[67] Everything seemed to have been reversed: the hated Bustamante was leaving office; the Marquis de Aycinena was to serve as jefe político of his own region; and Antonio Juarros had just been elected to serve Guatemala in Spain as one of its deputies. The faith in the Cádiz Experiment had finally borne fruit.

José de Bustamante bemoaned Spanish policy in Central America with a bitterness that defies description. He was convinced that a permissive stance in Central America would merely promote independence. Like many Spaniards who had been polarized on the American Question, he maintained that Spain needed to root out all subversive elements overseas, especially the clerics and lawyers who represented the leading families of America. By sending them back to Spain, the masses overseas would be deprived of leadership, which, in turn, would assure the continuation of Spanish rule. A mailed fist and imperial vigilance were the solutions to the colonial problem.[68]

6. The Second Trial

Americans are called rebels, and some insolent person dared say that our unwillingness to vote was the most damaging and serious proof of it. Let the nation know that we refused to vote, not because we are disobedient or seditious but rather because we do not choose to be perjurers of the Constitution, weaklings in defense of our rights, and traitors to those lands that gave us substance from the moment that we first saw the light.

AMERICAN SUPLENTES, *Madrid, 1820*[1]

IN THE famous royal cédula of May 4, 1814, Ferdinand VII explained to his subjects why he opposed the Constitution of Cádiz, in a beguiling exposition that contains the standard arguments against reform. He was preparing his people for a return to the practices of the past.

Before leaving Spain in 1808, the King recalled, he had ordered the convocation of a Cortes for the sole purpose of raising money to defend the country. The order was ignored, thus making possible the governments of the Junta Central, the Regency, and the General Cortes. By calling for a convention without "Estates," Parliament commenced its existence with the usurpation of the King's sovereignty, pretending all the while to be speaking for the "general will." A handful of seditious persons proceeded to strip the monarch of all of his power, equating the King's rule with despotism. To achieve their objectives, the usurpers capitalized on the violence and shouting of mobs and followed the model of the French Constitution of 1791. They abused the freedom of the press; they intimidated the Bishop of Orense; and they substituted the word *nacionales* for *reales* (royal), just to flatter the people. Fortunately, those evil days were over. Spaniards knew that their old system was good, not despotic. Liberty, individual security, and the royal will would prevail from now on.

The King knew how to take care of his people, and the Cortes would sanction his laws.[2]

═══

It is common to think of Ferdinand VII as a reactionary who turned back the clock on Spain's progress during the interregnum from 1814 to 1820. This is not entirely accurate. When he returned to his country, Ferdinand had to use men who had served at Cádiz and whose political persuasion ranged from moderate to conservative. It was not politic for him to bring into his government the *afrancesados* who had collaborated with Napoleon, the nation's enemy. Moreover, since governments rely heavily upon trained and experienced bureaucrats, it is not surprising that many of the leading administrators at Cádiz continued to serve the country: Martín Garay and Esteban Varea are cases in point. They were both well-liked by the American delegation in the first constitutional period. Furthermore, Ferdinand VII assigned Miguel de Lardizábal Uribe to head up the Ministerio Universal de las Indias, a unit that was revived at this time. Lardizábal was the Mexican Regent that the "oracles" had exiled from Cádiz. The Consejo de Indias likewise reopened its doors; and one of its appointees was the distinguished Guatemalan liberal, José de Aycinena, who won the respect and esteem of his king. Ferdinand VII decorated him with the Cross of Isabel la Católica. A fortunate appointment for Central America, it underscores the fact that there was not a complete break with the Cádiz Experiment during the interregnum, as many believe.[3]

The Spanish government faced some serious problems in the postwar era. The nation was virtually bankrupt and much of the Empire was in rebellion. To bring peace to the Americas, Ferdinand's ministers urged upon him a policy of reform and reconciliation. As Minister of the Indies, Lardizábal recommended the appointment of more Creoles to positions in both America and Spain. The King's Consejo de Estado agreed with this suggestion. Like its Cádiz counterpart, it fully discussed the basic reform of "free trade" in order to win back the allegiance of Americans. This imaginative approach was an alternative course of action until June 1818, when the King voted against the revision of Spain's mercantilistic system. That he later turned to an iron-fisted policy vis-à-vis the Americas should not obscure the earlier, peaceful overtures of his government.[4]

As part of the reconciliation program, Miguel de Lardizábal circulated a "Manifesto" throughout the New World, inviting Americans to present statements of their needs or grievances to the government. In return, he urged them to give up their "destructive war." Independence, he said, was "an impracticable chimera" and could only bring them economic ruin.[5] The King, moreover, was expecting to convoke another Cortes, and Americans should be prepared to send their best men to Spain—an expectation that never materialized during the interregnum.[6] A royal cédula of June 13, 1814, asked American deputies still in Spain to present their instructions and other requests for reforms to Minister Lardizábal. Only two of the former deputies from Central America complied, the Nicaraguan José Antonio López de la Plata and the Costa Rican Florencio Castillo. To assure implementation, they repeated many of their former requests. López's petition for an inter-oceanic waterway through Nicaragua got nowhere, especially since there was a preference at the time for a route through Panama. Castillo's bill on the port of Punta Arenas was put into effect by July, 1815.[7]

Of the Central American deputies elected in late 1813 who went on to Spain, three submitted petitions to the Lardizábal ministry. Fernando Antonio Dávila, for example, asked for support to stimulate the depressed agricultural condition of Chiapas, his province. The Honduran Santiago Milla urged the establishment of a mint in Comayagua, arguing that Guatemala City was too distant from the source of silver. Such a reform, he alleged, would frustrate the sale of contraband silver at Belize and would obviate the need for the annual subsidy of 100,000 pesos from Mexico. The dossier on Milla's request was still circulating as late as November 5, 1817. The most ambitious presentation of demands was made by the deputy from Quezaltenango, Father José Cleto Montiel. He wanted an intendancy, a bishopric, a seminary, and an Audiencia established in Quezaltenango; there was obviously no point in being modest! After Father Montiel's death, the Ayuntamiento of the highland city denied that it had authorized such demands. It seems that the denial was probably to placate the irate authorities in Guatemala City.[8] The highlanders, of course, craved such autonomy, which was expressed in the national period as the State of Los Altos.

Despite the good intentions of Minister Lardizábal, Ferdinand VII's aversion to the Cádiz Experiment was an obstacle. His government revived many of the old institutions that were anathema to liberals, notably the Inquisition, press censorship, and the return of the Jesuit Order. In political terms, the emphasis was put on direct, military government overseas. Ferdinand's Spain did not allow the separation of political and military authority, a reform passed in the final months of the constitutional era. The King also insisted that the municipalities return to the status quo ante 1808. In fact, one royal order demanded the restoration of the pre-1808 bodies with the personnel that was serving at that time. Ferdinand VII's government also made it mandatory to erase all the documentation of the Cádiz years.[9]

Presumably ill and disillusioned, Captain General José de Bustamante recovered hastily from his despondency when he learned of the King's decision to stop the constitutional experiment. Rejuvenated by the news—he no longer mentioned his illness—Bustamante initiated the "Terror" with a savage vengeance. Delay was no longer the strategy of the day. Now it was deliberate speed to reverse the pesky constitutional order that his Creole rivals loved so much.[10] Thoroughly enjoying the assignment, he reminded Ferdinand VII that he had never been an admirer of the former system. He assured his King that Americans were treacherous people who had to be treated forcefully. To prove how disloyal and subversive they were, as well as to punish the outspoken Father Antonio Larrazábal who had maligned him in Spain, Bustamante sent an edited version of the latter's Instructions of 1810. Through the footnotes of that piece, which we have analyzed elsewhere, the Asturian naval officer intentionally cultivated the impression that the Guatemalan Creoles were all devotees of French revolutionary thought. In short, he was capitalizing on Ferdinand's aversion to the French Revolution.[11] Sick with revenge, Bustamante recommended that all the men who had signed the Instructions of 1810 should not be allowed to serve Spain again with the exception of the four Spaniards who later submitted a minority report.[12] Assuming that Bustamante's information was correct, the King issued the cédula of March 31, 1815, that followed the Asturian's recommendations. Thus men like José María Peinado had to give up their posts. Since the Marquis de Aycinena and Antonio Juarros had died by this time, the order merely blackened their memory. Still not satisfied, the spiteful Bustamante called out the people of Guatemala City on December 22, 1815, to witness the public burning of Larrazábal's Instructions by the executioner.[13] Bustamante likewise insisted upon the removal of pictures from the Ayuntamiento's building that honored such champions of constitutionalism as Antonio Larrazábal, Manuel José Pavón, and José de Aycinena. He took pleasure in harassing the leading Creole families of Guatemala, especially the merchant house of the Aycinenas. He saw to it that the Ayuntamiento's title was reduced once again to that of "Señoría"; and in public ceremonies, he discriminated against the aldermen by favoring other units and persons who had the same rank.[14]

According to the investigation (*residencia*) held of the Bustamante years, the Audiencia found the Captain General guilty of contributing to the death of an American by the name of José Mariano Argüelles—a revealing charge, indeed. Bustamante's sick mind imagined that Argüelles, living in Campeche, Yucatán, was actually José Francisco Barrundia, the young regidor who had escaped after the Belén Conspiracy. Urging the Campeche police to arrest Argüelles, he further asked them to bring him overland to Guatemala City. Argüelles died en route to Guatemala at Palenque, a pestilential and "unhealthy site." Bustamante's error consisted of not relaying pertinent information about Barrundia that might have prevented the death of Argüelles. He had forgotten to mention that Barrundia was a redhead. Argüelles, of course, was not.[15]

The more progressive elements of the interregnum finally caught up with Captain General Bustamante, forcing his dismissal from office. From December 1813 until March 28, 1818, however, the "Terror" was in effect. Assuming that they still had rights—and it should be recalled that Minister Lardizábal had supported the interests of the New World in the earlier years—Guatemalans appealed to higher authorities for redress. Composed mainly of Peninsulars, the Audiencia of Guatemala listened to the grievances; and resenting the authoritarianism of Bustamante, it recommended relief for the defendants—a decision that infuriated the Asturian. He turned upon the Audiencia's judges (oidores) on November 18, 1815, urging the Spanish government to punish them for abetting subversion in Central America—a mistake that he would learn to regret. More importantly, Bustamante had an articulate and persuasive enemy in the Council of the Indies who reviewed the literature against him. It was Dr. José de Aycinena who provided his colleagues with first-hand information on Bustamante's personality and capacity for vindictiveness. The Consejo de Indias, as a result, demonstrated concern at the Asturian's "strange conduct" in office and the vicious manner in which he had implemented the cédula of March 31, 1815. Moreover, the councillors learned that Bustamante in the earlier days had been a friend of constitutionalism, contrary to what he had told the King. Aycinena also vouched for the ability and character of José María Peinado, the former Intendant of San Salvador who had lost his post because of the above-mentioned order. The Council of the Indies thus advised the Crown to rescind the 1815 cédula, reversing Bustamante's program of hate in Guatemala. The royal order of June 13, 1817, announced the change in policy, along with the decision to replace Captain General José de Bustamante.[16]

Other aspects of the "Terror" met with the disapproval of Ferdinand VII's government. The decision on the wartime subversion cases in the Spanish courts supported the Guatemalan contention and thus led to the release of political prisoners that Bustamante had persecuted by trying them in military courts. Fugitives like José Francisco Barrundia could come out of hiding once the royal cédula was officially posted. Father Antonio Larrazábal was released from prison in the governmental moves of 1817, thanks in great part to the intervention of his good friend Dr. José Aycinena. Needless to say, Bustamante was horrified at the reversal of policy, which he thought deserted a faithful servant and encouraged the independence of Central America by allowing former subversives to reappear in the area.[17]

Although José de Aycinena's presence on the Council of the Indies led to Bustamante's dismissal, it was also due in part to the alienation of his own countrymen on the Audiencia of Guatemala. In the 1820 residencia, the judges virtually threw the book at him, finding him guilty of practically every charge that was brought up. Bustamante had slighted the Audiencia's rank of "Excellency" on several occasions, he had forced his presidency upon the judges, and had issued orders without consulting them. Whenever he did consult them, it was usually after the fact (charges 22, 26, and 32). There were many more transgressions: mail censorship and the use of evidence acquired in this manner in the courts (charge 30); abuse of prisoners (charge 33); failure to enforce laws favorable to Indians (charge 38); laxity on crime and vagrancy (charges 36 and 40); the publication of articles by sycophants that in most cases were written by him (charge 42), and so on. Bustamante, in others words, had alienated too many people during the Terror, and they turned upon him with a vengeance that was almost poetic justice.[18]

On August 19, 1817, Captain General Bustamante informed the Ayuntamiento of Guatemala City that his successor would be Carlos Urrutia, according to an order from the Secretary of War dated May 18, 1817. He made no mention at all of the uncomplimentary cédula that had reversed his program in Central America, thus refusing stubbornly to implement its pardons. In his correspondence to home authorities, he complained bitterly that the Council of the Indies had conspired against him, "my honor, my character, and my conduct."[19] Even though Guatemalans already knew the contents of the document, Bustamante savagely resisted making public the offensive cédula that announced his disgrace and restored his enemies to public office. He actually used troops to prevent it.[20] Thus, when Captain General Carlos Urrutia took command, the royal will still had not been obeyed, and Bustamante's enemies languished in prison. Attempting to smooth feelings between the Ayuntamiento and his predecessor, Urrutia asked the aldermen to pay the

Asturian a courtesy call before he left the city. The corporation agreed, only to be rudely insulted by the ex-chief. This hostility and rivalry carried over into Spain for the next few years. Once the hardliners in Spanish policy returned to favor with the King, they arranged to promote José de Bustamante to the post of Director General of the Navy. The end of the interregnum, however, thwarted those plans.

There were some constructive features in the interregnum period, despite the vindictiveness and hard feelings we have noted. Bustamante was dismissed from office, and the record of the constitutional patriots was set straight. The Granadian prisoners and many others tried for subversion finally gained their freedom, although some had perished in jail before that. Bustamante's successor Urrutia was a veritable saint by comparison to the Admiral, and he worked harmoniously with the city fathers. Thus, the confidence of the aldermen began to pick up. There was talk of revitalizing the militia forces; José Peinado resumed his post as Intendant of San Salvador; and the annual examinations of students at San José de Calazans were held regularly. At the urging of educators in Spain, plus the active sponsorship of the Nicaraguan jurist Miguel Larreinaga, the Ayuntamiento of Guatemala City encouraged the introduction of the educational program outlined by the Englishmen Andrew Bell and John Lancaster. It was an imaginative and inexpensive educational system that had a widespread appeal in the Spanish-speaking world. Among other things, it permitted students to teach each other. It was another illustration of the Cádiz Experiment's indebtedness to English reforms.[21] The fact that this particular innovation materialized during the interregnum of Ferdinand VIII, moreover, reveals that the impetus for reform had not been extinguished entirely, as we are sometimes led to believe. By 1819, however, the hardliners in Spain had convinced the King that the problem of the Americas could only be settled by force. The Spanish government thus prepared to send a large expedition to the New World to stamp out the rebellion.

Assignment to the American expedition was not popular among military leaders in Spain; and their discontent inspired the famous coup of January 1, 1820, at Cádiz, known as the Riego Revolt. The rebels demanded the restoration of the 1812 charter. The success at Cádiz, moreover, strengthened the hand of Colonel Rafael Riego and General Antonio Quiroga. Unable to counter the increasing pressure of the military, Ferdinand announced to his people on March 7, 1820, that he wanted to rule them as a constitutional monarch. The advocates of constitutional order cheered this turn of events. In the next two weeks, a Junta Provisional issued the necessary instructions for holding elections and set July 9 as the opening session of the Cortes in Madrid. In a manifesto of March 31, Ferdinand VII urged the Americans to join with their European brethren in a spirit of "union and harmony."[22]

The exciting news of the restoration reached Guatemala City via Havana within two weeks, reawakening hopes that constitutionalism would not be thwarted again in Central America.[23] A genuine believer in the Cádiz Experiment, Captain General Urrutia instructed all officials in Central America to take the oath to the Constitution on July 9, the day the Cortes would open its doors. Election instructions followed a few weeks laters. In Guatemala City, the election for a constitutional ayuntamiento was completed by late July. The national series followed in August 1820.[24] Central Americans had not forgotten their earlier constitutional experience.

Once apprised of the events in Spain, the regular Ayuntamiento of Guatemala City demanded the immediate implementation of the Constitution. Its attorney, Mariano Aycinena, was especially aggressive in this regard. The brother of José and Vicente and spokesman for the family's mercantile establishment, Don Mariano proposed that Larrazábal's picture be put back up again in the council room to honor "his heroic firmness" in defending the Constitution of 1812 and "our undeniable rights."[25] Father Larrazábal had returned home by this time. In fact, he served in the Junta Preparatoria for the elections of 1820; and in November of that year he was elected to the rectorship of the University of San Carlos.[26] Guatemalans had a veteran legislator in their midst, whose insights on government proved to be valuable during the second constitutional period.

Until the installation of the Guatemalan Diputación Provincial on September 1, 1820, the Ayuntamiento served as the advisory body for Captain General Urrutia. At the extraordinary session of June 28, 1820, it was agreed, for example, that the Constitution would be read in its entirety on July 9 throughout the Kingdom. In addition to sending out five hundred copies of the proclamation announcing the event, the city fathers advised their executive to speed up the reestablishment of constitutional rule in Central America by such measures as the installation of the Censorship Board (*Junta de Censura*) to put into effect the freedom-of-the-press law; the immediate revival of the 1814 D.P. to serve until the new one was elected; and the holding of elections everywhere in the region of Central America. To remove all vestiges of the old order, the Ayuntamiento recommended the destruction of the whipping post in the main square, replacing it with a monument in honor of the Constitution.[27] As we have noted, there was an instant revival of constitutionalism in Guatemala City, following the precedents of the earlier experiment.

On July 26, 1820, the newly elected Ayuntamiento of Guatemala City assumed command and continued the progressive lead of its predecessor. Just as in 1812, the elections had brought into office the leaders of the Spanish and Creole communities. Mariano Aycinena, for example, returned to his post as syndic or attorney of the corporation. The other syndic was the lawyer José Venancio López, who had been elected regidor in 1814 but was subsequently imprisoned by Bustamante for his alleged implication in the Belén Conspiracy. Both lawyers were aggressive leaders in the Ayuntamiento. They were prime movers in forming a two-party system in the national and municipal elections later in the year. José Antonio Larrave and Manuel Ramírez were also barristers who served as regidores. Ramón Ramírez won the post of Mayor (*Alcalde 1*); Francisco Arrivillaga was the Vice-Mayor; and José Azmitia and Juan Barrundia (the brother of the 1813 regidor) were two more outstanding figures in the constitutional municipality. José Francisco Córdoba regained his post as secretary. By this time, he had finished his law degree at the University of San Carlos.[28] Once again the Cádiz system had produced excellent results in Guatemala City.

Conscious at all times of the precedents set by the Juarros Administration of 1812–1813, the new corporation set out to capture its vitality and imagination. The regidores agreed to form a detailed census of their respective wards, and they immediately established all the committees assigned to ayuntamientos in Article 321 of the Constitution. Juan Barrundia and Juan Antonio Español headed the special committee on Agriculture, Industry, and Commerce, ably assisted by such knowledgeable outsiders as Dr. Juan José Batres, Mariano Herrarte, and José Francisco Barrundia. This same pattern of inviting citizen experts to serve on committees according to one's expertise applied to other units as well: Public Health, Public Works, Hospitals, Municipal Ordinances, Archives, Education, Finances, and so on. Responsible for the general welfare in their jurisdictions and for assisting the magistrates (*alcaldes*) in maintaining order, all the regidores conducted daily patrols in their wards with a sizable body of assistants, usually Indians from the outlying villages.[29] We note again that the experiment in self-government worked satisfactorily in Guatemala City, where there was an adequate number of talented people to cooperate. Although the evidence from other parts of

Central America is fragmentary, it too indicates a satisfactory outcome in places where political leaders cooperated with the local citizenry.

In Guatemala City and its environs the acute economic depression was a threat to political stability. Unemployment was high, and there was a high incidence of vagrancy, homicides, crime, and public drunkenness. Despite Bustamante's innovations of 1811, the situation worsened from 1817 forward. The more advantaged elements in society feared that the lower classes might go on a rampage against them.[30] The elections of late 1820 reflected the economic malaise of the times. By contrast to the earlier constitutional period in which the artisans had been passive, these skilled workers were no longer willing to allow the upper classes to dominate politics. The makers of cotton goods (handicrafts) resented the large-scale introduction of cheap English cottons, either through contraband from Belize or by official permission on occasion. This competition harmed local artisans. Elections thus became more meaningful and spirited; and aspiring politicians now had an issue that might propel them into power at the expense of Guatemala's traditional leaders who favored free trade.

To contain the instability that threatened society in the area, the syndic Aycinena proposed to his colleagues the immediate establishment of the Cádiz judicial order. *Jueces de letras*, men trained in law, were to take charge in each district, thus minimizing the prerogatives of the former magistrates. In the ayuntamiento preceding the restoration of the Cádiz Constitution, Aycinena had gotten nowhere with his suggestions for law and order; but in the constitutional municipality of 1820, he had full support from his companions, including the alcaldes of the City.[31] This unanimous stance in the Ayuntamiento convinced Captain General Urrutia that it was time to implement judicial reforms. The Guatemalan Diputación Provincial strongly concurred with this decision.

The details of the Ayuntamiento's accomplishments in 1820 need not detain us long; it followed the inspiration of the 1812–1813 corporation. The aldermen urged the reestablishment of the Junta de Censura in connection with the freedom-of-the-press reform; a free meat supply was once again assured to the denizens of Guatemala City; and the Public Health Junta was reactivated on October 5, 1820. The aldermen also revived Juarros' 1813 project to build a bridge across the Motagua River; and the educational system in the city continued its progressive orientation.[32]

A key development of 1820 was the beginning of a two-party press in Guatemala City which had a wide circulation throughout Central America: *El Editor Constitucional* and *El Amigo de la Patria*. Like their predecessor, the *Gazeta de Guatemala*, both periodicals were powerful educational instruments that spread the ideas of the Enlightenment and thus conditioned minds toward independence. Dr. Pedro Molina, the Protomédico of the Kingdom, directed *El Editor*, which began to publish on July 28, 1820. He was ably assisted by a coterie of colleagues who gathered together at the home of the Spanish priest José María Castilla, including José Francisco Barrundia, Domingo Diéguez, and Manuel Montúfar—representatives of liberal Spanish and Creole families in Guatemala. Their rivals called them *Cacos* (thieves). The opposition paper, *El Amigo,* was the production of the resourceful José Cecilio del Valle, whose intimate connection with the hated Bustamante made him a natural target for the writers of *El Editor.* They too dubbed Valle and his followers with an uncomplimentary name, the *Bacos* (drunks).

Their rivalry notwithstanding, the two periodicals complemented each other in propagating the Enlightenment throughout Central America. As a medical man, Pedro Molina wrote a column on education that ran for many issues, indoctrinating his readers with the best hygienic and nutritional practices throughout the world. There were other articles that dealt with morality and civic virtue in effective manner. Valle's periodical was similar in character. Both papers frequently reproduced key documents from Spain on constitutional questions or on Central America's economic conditions and potential reforms. Valle's defense of the Indian was exceptional, along with practical suggestions on how to improve his lot. A common theme in both papers was education; and the frequency of articles dealing with economic issues underscores the importance of "political economy" in the fabric of Spanish liberalism.[33] Through these pages the tradition of the old *Gazeta de Guatemala* prevailed. The influence of the University of San Carlos likewise continued. Now it was the students and not the teachers who were educating the public to the process of modernization.

Political power and ambition was the main motive for the rivalry of the two periodicals, hinging on Valle's intimate relationship with the hated Bustamante. Representing the leading Spanish and Creole families of the City, Molina and colleagues could not bring themselves to forgive Valle for his outright sycophancy of the Asturian. They recognized, moreover, that Valle was a dangerous adversary because he was so brilliant; he seemed to be a man who could lull the people into a given position and then betray them. He could not be trusted on the basis of his past record of opportunism. Valle's arrogance, egotism, and eccentricities made it even easier to be his enemy.

A perennial opportunist, however intelligent, Valle prepared for his candidacy in the elections of December 1820. He knew that many people resented the political dominance of the "families," so he attacked them for being selfish with others. In a deliberate bid for the artisan vote, he went out of his way to stress the free-trade proclivities of the local elite. Valle, of course, would support a tariff—an issue that was attractive to artisans and Spanish merchants. In effect, Valle maintained his identification with the "Spanish faction" of merchants, adding now the artisan elements. As an Honduran, Valle had an appeal to citizens of provinciano origins as well.

Although Valle's stand on tariffs was opportunistic and not consistent with his overall economic philosophy, his rivals were guilty of the same tactics. *El Editor Constitucional* took a mixed position on the free-trade issue before the elections, hoping to attract votes for its candidates.[34] Yet after the elections, Molina and company consistently favored free trade, to no one's surprise. Be that as it may, the artisans were not deceived; they voted for Valle, who won the mayoralty race in the Ayuntamiento of Guatemala City.

The Honduran's political victory was a turning point in his career because it committed him irrevocably to constitutionalism and eventually to independence. As a minion of Bustamante, Valle had done exceptional work in drawing up the electoral instructions for the first constitutional elections of 1812. Now, independent of the Asturian, he had an opportunity to convince the doubters that his conversion to constitutionalism was natural and sincere, well in keeping with his personality and philosophy. The Valle municipality of 1821 carried on the tradition of its predecessors with one significant difference. No mayor had previously dominated his corporation as Valle did from January 2 to May 14, 1821. His role paralleled that of Antonio Juarros in the 1813 corporation—a dynamic leader who explored every possible means of improving the lot of his constituents.

To convince the artisans that he meant to keep his promises, one of Valle's first measures was to encourage new industries in order to relieve unemployment. He suggested that the paper and glass industries had a chance to thrive in the community.[35] A few months later, his municipality agreed to send for the skilled personnel and the machinery to begin the new factories, instructing the Guatemalan deputy in Madrid to lobby for these concessions. Although a substantial investment was involved, Valle suggested floating a patriotic loan to obtain funds. Since the Indians were certain to gain from the reform, he thought that perhaps some of the funds might come from their community treasuries.[36] Valle cooperated closely with the Economic Society, a connection that in his particular case dated back to the first constitutional period. An indefatigable worker, Valle revised the Ordinances for the artisan guilds (*gremios*), bringing them up to date, much like Juarros had done earlier. Artisans, of course, felt that the Mayor was their champion.[37]

The Honduran's prolific mind explored every problem and challenge with remarkable insight. He proved to doubters that he was not only a gifted writer and thinker but also a man with unusual executive capacity. Advocating fiscal economy wherever possible, Valle proposed to his colleagues a special project for a municipal tax, based on the ability to pay. It would replace the old system of numerous duties for all types of services, simplifying tax collection without sacrificing revenue.[38] Sanguine in his support of education in all forms, he welcomed qualified persons in the community to write or speak on the subject of educational reform. For its part, the Ayuntamiento agreed to support the publication of a special paper that provided news of the municipality's discussions and projects.[39]

In the field of crime prevention and treatment of prisoners, Valle's record was not entirely impressive. Although he supported the Cádiz program in defense of individual prisoners, he also devised a plan to use informers on crime in their assigned wards. Valle felt that vagrants should be put to work on public projects, thus benefiting society as well as themselves. Some of these ideas were traditional, not progressive. In fact, the Diputación Provincial of Guatemala rejected the use of informers (*zeladores*) on the ground that they were actually spies, infringing upon the liberty of the individual. Although the Ayuntamiento protested the decision, Chief Urrutia supported his D.P.[40]

On May 14, 1821, José del Valle submitted his resignation in order to accept the position of Judge Advocate of the Army in the Kingdom of Guatemala. His old friend Bustamante had made the recommendation; and Valle, still the opportunist, did not hesitate to accept the position.[41] His influence in the Ayuntamiento remained, however. For all practical purposes, he had just taken on another position. He continued to work on various committees, finishing up projects that he had initiated. At all times, he displayed a drive comparable to that of Antonio Juarros in the first constitutional municipality of Guatemala City. He served as one of the forty-eight judges (*jueces de hecho*) in the revised freedom-of-the-press law of October 22, 1820. The new system provided for a Junta Protectora in Mexico City, rather than the old Junta de Censura in Spain. Moreover, the forty-eight judges took turns serving on juries to examine violations of the freedom of the press in their community.[42] All the while, Valle continued to publish *El Amigo de la Patria*, winning for himself a well-deserved reputation as a savant throughout Central America. The constitutional experiment had become a reality in his country, convincing Valle that it could work. Henceforth, he would sponsor the Experiment at every opportunity. Even the doubters changed their minds about him.

≈≈≈

By contrast to its short-lived and inhibited predecessor, the Guatemalan Diputación Provincial flourished during the second constitutional period thanks to cooperative political chiefs: first, the sickly Carlos Urrutia and his replacement Gabino Gaínza, who took over on March 9, 1821. Moreover, the documentation is sufficient for a change to provide us with a meaningful insight into the problems besetting the Cádiz Experiment in Central America in the months preceding Independence.

To begin with, the elections in late 1820 were turbulent by comparison to the ones held at mid-year. More people were interested in voting, and the facilities were not always adequate for the larger numbers. The competition for office led to irregularities in getting out the vote; and it may be that for the first time elections went out into the rural areas. The existence of large numbers of Indian voters, moreover, encouraged fraud on the part of officials who were determined to maintain themselves in office at all costs, even if it meant denying the suffrage to substantial numbers. The alcaldes-mayores and corregidores, many of whom had purchased their positions during the old order, were not anxious to give up profits from supervising their Indian wards. They defied the authorities in Guatemala City with impunity. Charged with reporting all violations of the Constitution, the Diputación Provincial investigated the infractions and advised the jefe político superior on what corrective action to take. It consistently urged the enforcement of the voter's constitutional right at all costs. There were so many irregularities in the elections before Independence that the Guatemalan D.P. had little time for constructive projects in the economic sphere.[43]

Alarmed at the region's instability, the D.P. advocated the prompt implementation of the judicial reforms and the assignment of a juez de letras for all districts of Central America. There was, however, some opposition to the reform. The magistrates of ayuntamientos felt that they were being stripped of much of their authority. The Audiencia claimed that it was unconstitutional for the D.P. and the Jefe Político to name the judges for the districts. And Valle himself, perhaps to ingratiate himself with his political followers, argued that the judicial system was too expensive for Central America at this time.[44] Determined to restore law and order, however, the Deputation urged its Political Chief to stand his ground for a reform that was fundamental to the entire constitutional structure. Moreover, the D.P.'s appeal to the Spanish Cortes was successful; political chiefs overseas were allowed to appoint interim judges. The way was cleared to select thirty men to serve as judges within the D.P.'s jurisdiction. To expedite matters, there was no attempt to draw up new districts; the D.P. simply modified an occasional district here and there in order to get the judicial system functioning.[45]

In addition to the insistence upon the Indian's right to vote, the D.P. discouraged the Valle municipality from tapping the community revenues of the Indians. It insisted that a 5 percent interest had to be paid for such loans instead of the customary 2 or 3 percent, a decision that irritated Valle and his colleagues.[46] On the troublesome issue of the Indian tribute payments, the D.P. favored their elimination. In return, however, Indians were to make some type of contribution to the government, just like any other citizen. Indians protested this decision. Whenever they became unruly, a military detachment moved in to uphold the law. Under no conditions would the Diputacion Provincial sanction a return to the lower tribute contribution, as suggested by some Indian leaders. Since the Nicaraguan D.P. had a similar record, it was obvious that the Indians did not get tax relief under the Cádiz system.[47] In fact, life did not change much at all for the Indians because there were no revenues to implement the ambitious developmental plans of their white leaders in Guatemala City or León.

The relationship between the Guatemalan Deputation and other corporations offers certain insights into the functioning of the Cádiz Experiment. Friendly with the first constitutional municipality of 1820, the D.P. shared its determination to start the new order on a sound footing. Mariano Aycinena and his colleagues, for example, came up with recommendations to avert electoral frauds such as those that occurred in early December, forcing the D.P. to void the elections and to call for a new series a few weeks later—the contests won by Valle and his friends.[48] The Valle administration of 1821, by comparison, was continually at odds with the D.P. mainly because it distrusted the Honduran's motives in opposing the establishment of judicial districts. Moreover, Valle's municipality resented the D.P.'s close financial supervision and restraints.

It will be recalled that members of the Deputation rejected the informers plan on ethical grounds. In general, they too could not forgive the Honduran for his intimate connection with Bustamante, who had humiliated the first Guatemalan D.P. The Secretary of the organization in particular—Domingo Diéguez, who supported Pedro Molina—wasted no love on the controversial Valle.[49] That members of the Guatemalan Deputation worked well with Mariano Aycinena and not with José del Valle indicates how generally the Honduran was hated because of his relationship with the former tyrant. If the provinciano spirit had been consistent, the D.P. should have been pro-Valle and against Aycinena, a recognized leader of the "families."

The tension between Spaniards and Creoles that was so evident in the first constitutional period continued into the second trial, thus paving the way for independence. There were some deviations, however. The hostility between the D.P. and the Royal Audiencia transcended the Peninsular-American syndrome since by this time new appointees were usually Creoles. Rather, the bone of contention derived more from the Audiencia's diminished authority and prestige under the Cádiz system. The judges deeply resented having to share their rank of "Excellency" with the Ayuntamiento of Guatemala City and the Diputación Provincial as well. The protocol issue reflected the deemphasis that annoyed the legal experts. They objected, for example, to the D.P.'s constant requests to certify documents on infractions of the Constitution, as if they were mere law clerks. Another example of their opposition was the delay in presenting *ternas* (three names for each post) for the judicial districts on the grounds that the Political Chief and his advisory corporation had no constitutional authority to make these appointments. The real annoyance was due to the fact that they would have to share duties with the new judges. Furious at this obstructionism, the workings of an "occult hand directed by perhaps sinister motives," the Nicaraguan Cabeza de Vaca vehemently condemned the conservative "serviles" who were resisting the implementation of the Constitution. As in Cádiz, the political use of the term "serviles" became fixed in the vocabulary of Central Americans. The protocol issue surfaced once more in connection with the quarterly visits to prisons. The judges had the temerity to suggest that members of the D.P. refrain from using hats on those visits, which was their sole prerogative. Exploding with anger, the D.P. accused the Audiencia of overlooking many abuses of prisoners that were forbidden by law—the use of the ball and chain, for example. The Deputation reported these infractions to the Spanish government.[50]

The protocol question strained relations with the Ecclesiastical Cabildo for the same reasons that it had in 1813–1814 with the Ayuntamiento of Guatemala City. Peninsulars would not concede the same type of *asistencia*, or greeting, to an American corporation even though it held the same ranking as a corporation dominated by Spaniards. Therefore, the D.P., like its precursor in the first constitutional period, simply refused to attend functions in which there was discrimination against Americans. The Deputation got along very well, on the other hand, with Archbishop Ramón Casaus, who was most cooperative in matters of education for girls in convents.[51]

There was one exception to the persistent squabbling between Spaniards and Guatemalans during the second constitutional period: notably, the splendid cooperation of the political chiefs Urrutia and Gaínza. A sincere constitutionalist, Urrutia worked well with his Deputation and was willing to turn over effective power to it when he was sick, which was most of the time. His replacement also chose to treat his D.P. as a legislative body and not just an advisory corporation as intended by the Cádiz Constitution. Because of these circumstances, the Guatemalan D.P. operated as an effective legislative body whose executives followed through in carrying out the majority's wish. The Audiencia angered the D.P. on one occasion by exposing this unconstitutional behavior. An expert in law, Dr. Cabeza de Vaca admitted the correctness of the accusation; later, however, he defended the D.P. on the grounds that Urrutia had approved of the measures, as was the prerogative of executive power.[52]

Since the pattern described above continued into the national period, it had important implications for the future. It helps to explain, for example, why Central Americans chose their special type of Senate in the national government and the equivalent units in the state governments where the executive and upper legislative body shared executive functions of government.

A crucial break between the D.P. and officials of the Royal Treasury developed over the Tariff Law of October 9, 1820. This tariff (*arancel*) was a cherished liberal reform that at long last freed the internal trade of the nation by dismantling all of the interior customs houses. Officials were to collect duties and sales taxes (*alcabalas*) only at the ports of entry on the coast. There would be checkpoints elsewhere to discourage contraband and to assure the payment of duties by all foreign traders. The Deputation hailed the new tariff system, so necessary to prevent the excessive charges of the past.[53]

The head official of the tax service was uncooperative, however, provoking hostility between Americans and Spaniards only a few weeks before Independence. Arguing that his unit would lose money if it dismantled the interior customs houses, Agustín Yzaguirre further complained that Central America's topography was not suitable for the new tariff law. Moreover, there were no funds to finance the move to the coast. He should have added that his officials, living comfortably with their families in the highlands, were not willing to move to the hot and pestilential ports of Omoa and Trujillo. Furious at this new form of official obstructionism, the Guatemalan D.P. urged its chief to move energetically against the recalcitrant bureaucrats in the treasury department. Gaínza then issued an ultimatum: if treasury officials did not proceed to their new posts, other men would be sent in their place at their expense. He also pointed out that they were vulnerable to prosecution for dereliction of duty.[54] That was the situation on the eve of Independence in Guatemala City—a financial weakness that proved insurmountable for the new government of Central America.

The dramatic assertion of regionalism in the months preceding independence turned out to be a bad omen for both the Guatemalan and Nicaraguan provincial deputations. At Cádiz we noted Comayagua's irritation with the rule of Guatemala City. When José Tinoco received Urrutia's orders to hold elections in August, 1820, the Intendant of Comayagua conferred with the members of the Ayuntamiento and decided against sending a delegate to the Guatemalan D.P. Instead, Tinoco assumed the title of jefe político and ordered the establishment of a diputación provincial for Honduras. The seven-man deputation proceeded to carry out the area's business. In short, there were three D.P.'s in Central America by the end of 1820.[55]

The provincianos on the Guatemalan D.P., interestingly, were hardliners on this display of regionalism by Honduras. They felt that Comayagua's defiance had to be stopped firmly. The lawyer Antonio Rivera feared that Comayagua's example would precipitate a similar move by the people of Quezaltenango. Having lived there for eight years, he knew the highlanders' ideas and attitudes. Dr. Cabeza de Vaca was a veritable militant on the Honduran issue. Bolstered by the strong sentiments of the D.P., both Urrutia and Gaínza let it be known that they would oppose continued disobedience by sending a sizable military expedition to Honduras. In the meantime, letters were written to key people in Comayagua, pleading with them to listen to reason. An effective tactic of the Guatemalan D.P. was to suggest that perhaps the Honduran capital could be moved from Comayagua to Tegucigalpa, since the climate was so bad at the former site! The Comayaguans got the point; they capitulated. After disbanding their D.P., they held elections to send a representative to Guatemala City.[56]

Sentiments for home rule did not die in Comayagua, however. On May 14, 1821, the government in Madrid agreed to permit the establishment of a D.P. in every intendancy, thus reawakening Comayagua's aspirations. Its officials notified the Intendant of Chiapas at Ciudad Real. On August 10, the Ayuntamiento of that capital announced that it would hold elections for a diputación provincial. Although the Intendant of Chiapas notified Gaínza in Guatemala City of these elections, he was clearly presenting him with a fait accompli.[57] Acting upon the same news from Spain, the Salvadorans commenced their preparations in early September 1821, to establish their own provincial deputation. The feeling prevailed throughout Central America that this was the only way open to local citizens if they expected to guide their own program of economic development.[58]

Although the documentation for the Nicaraguan D.P. is fragmentary, it appears that the issue of regionalism prevailed there as well. The Nicaraguan deputy in Madrid continued to advocate a complete break with Guatemala City, as well as other objectives that Nicaraguan deputies had requested earlier, such as the canal project. By the second constitutional period, moreover, Costa Rica openly resented the Leonese connection and blamed Nicaraguans for their economic plight and the failure to establish a bishopric. Costa Ricans were now insisting that they should have their own D.P., given the inability of their two deputies to accomplish much in León.[59]

The process of disintegration was well underway by the time that Independence came to Central America. The Cádiz Experiment was not the cause of the tendency toward fragmentation. It merely gave regionalist proclivities in Central America an opportunity to assert themselves during the second constitutional period.

———

Liberals everywhere, and especially in the Mediterranean area, followed the reform program in Madrid with considerable interest. As was the case at Cádiz, the emphasis was upon modernization. The influence of the Englishman Jeremy Bentham and the Frenchman Benjamin Constant was notable in the second constitutional experiment.[60] Reasserting the importance of foreigners whose capital and "know-how" was necessary in the Spanish-speaking world, liberals in Madrid promised foreigners many exemptions and concessions.[61]

From the viewpoint of Central American independence, it was the negative developments in Madrid that reinforced the strong feelings of alienation. To begin with, the instability of peninsular life—the uprisings and terroristic attacks—made Americans wonder about the desirability of continuing the peninsular contact, especially since there was doubt concerning Ferdinand VII's conversion to constitutionalism.[62] Moreover, anticlericalism in Spain, which Americans had abhorred near the end of the Cádiz period, was now a fact of life as the desafuero denied ecclesiastics any special treatment. The banning of the Jesuit Order from the Spanish-speaking world and the elimination of most monastic orders confirmed the impression that Spanish liberals were punishing the Church.[63] Disturbed by the suppression of those units, Mariano Aycinena proposed to the regidores that the Bethlemite Order, founded in Guatemala, should be made an exception to the law because of its educational and social work.[64] The complete desafuero of the military also passed the Cortes of Madrid. Later when the Consejo de Estado learned of Agustín Iturbide's successful reception in Mexico and Central America, it counseled the King not to apply the desafuero overseas. It thereby showed an appreciation for the significance of that particular measure among Americans, especially those living in Mexico and Central America.[65] Moreover, Spaniards at Madrid were no more disposed to make concessions on free trade, political representation, and the tobacco monopoly than their counterparts at Cádiz. Polarization was in the air again, and Spaniards insulted the overseas delegation by assigning them no more than thirty substitutes. José Sacasa, the suplente for Guatemala, tried to rally the Americans and Filipinos against the alloted figure; but he decided at the last minute not to boycott the Cortes as originally planned. Some representation in Madrid was better than none, he reasoned.[66]

Sacasa's career in Madrid was a source of irritation for his constituents in Central America. Angered by the Parliament's unwillingness to satisfy American demands for more suplentes, he insisted vociferously that the overseas areas be allowed one deputy for every 70,000 people, the same quota allotted to Spaniards. When Peninsulars moved to table the resolution, Sacasa protested and was literally forced back into his chair. At the first opportunity, Sacasa reported this insult to his constituent ayuntamientos in Central America. There were strong reactions to the incident in Guatemala City, Quezaltenango, and Santa Ana.[67]

Despite the progressive record of the Cortes at Madrid, Spaniards failed to meet the demands of the Americans to any appreciable degree. In fact, the Cádiz experience by comparison was much more gratifying to Americans because it avoided anticlericalism until the final months of that period. In either case, the alienation of the Americans was an established fact, which made the break with the mother country only a matter of time. Illustrating this point was the set of instructions drawn up in Guatemala City on December 6, 1820, for Julián de Urruela, the Guatemalan deputy in Madrid. The principal authors of the document were Mariano Aycinena, the Ayuntamiento's syndic, and Domingo Diéguez, a regidor who subsequently served as the Secretary of the D.P. Both men supported *El Editor Constitucional*.[68]

Although a detailed analysis of this document would be rewarding, it would merely repeat what has already been covered in earlier chapters. It brought up all the grievances that were included in the American Question. These were the points that Larrazábal and Castillo, among others, had raised at Cádiz on many occasions. In fact, the hard-hitting style of the prose in Urruela's Instructions bears a striking ressemblance to the language used by Antonio de Larrazábal in the parliamentary debates at Cádiz. It is my contention that Mariano Aycinena and Domingo Diéguez wrote these pages under the supervision of their good friend Padre Larrazábal, who recently had taken over the post of Rector at the University. The instructions insisted that Article 22 on the Castas had to be changed, that twenty Americans should be the quota on the Consejo de Estado (Father Castillo's point), and that Americans should be allowed to fill one-half of the jobs in their regions. Free trade was a natural right; the tobacco monopoly was a travesty; and so on. In effect, Guatemala City's aldermen were sending an ultimatum to the Spanish government: If Spaniards persisted in denying Americans those demands that they had made frequently at Cádiz, the only alternative was independence. The Ayuntamiento of Guatemala City approved these instructions almost nine months before the official declaration of Independence. These demands, however, had been in the air for years; and it was clear that the process of alienation was reaching the point of no return.

El Editor Constitucional and *El Amigo de la Patria* were preparing their readers for the end of the dependency upon Spain. By stressing the need for effective economic development and consistent constitutional government, Valle in his way was contributing to the revolutionary mentality. He took pride in the fact that other European nations were welcoming the liberal experiment in Spain.[69] Molina and company were far more direct, making the point frequently that the distance from Spain was a deterrent to the proper functioning of the constitutional order.[70] No longer writing for voters, *El Editor* consistently favored free trade in the months preceding Independence.[71] In June 1821 Molina reproduced the controversial fable about a trip to the moon which, in effect, labeled Ferdinand VII as a tyrant who deserved to be overthrown.[72] Because of its seditious nature, the Junta de Censura in Guatemala City was asked to scrutinize the publication. The Junta rejected the petitioner's accusation, not a surprising verdict if we consider that Molina and Barrundia were members of the board who reviewed it.[73]

El Editor Constitucional kept its readers informed on constitutional developments and writings. It quoted the Frenchman Abbé de Pradt on the need for mother countries to emancipate their colonies so that they might grow up peacefully. "Oh, if Spain had only adopted those counsels," wrote an editorialist, it would have avoided the useless slaughter of "unfortunate Spaniards and Americans who have perished in war."[74] In another issue, Molina reproduced the first installment of Richard Price's observations on "civil liberty" in his native England and in the former English colonies, discussing the reasons for the American Revolution of 1776.[75] Throughout the pages of *El Editor*, writers took issue with the Spanish government for referring to American insurgents as criminals just because they wanted independence. Why should the Spanish government use such a term when Charles III had aided English colonials who sought the same objective? Although the argument was somewhat contrived, it reflected nonetheless that the fact of independence was not too far away from Central America.[76]

Molina's periodical was not sympathetic to plans of establishing feudal monarchies overseas, headed by Bourbon princes. The Mexican delegation in Madrid proposed such an arrangement, involving three kingdoms overseas: two in South America and one to the north that included Mexico and Central America. Spanish pride apparently vetoed the scheme at the last minute. When Pedro Molina learned of a similar project, he attacked it point by point in *El Editor*. Throughout the discussion, it was clear to the reader that Spain's financial condition was so precarious that she could not be of any further help to her former possessions. By contrast, the image of Mexico was one of affluence. The implication seemed to be that a connection closer to home might offer a solution for Central America's dream of economic development.[77]

The victories of Mexican revolutionaries turned the tide in Central America, and *El Editor* thrilled its readers with reports of battlefield successes at Oaxaca and Puebla. On September 3, 1821, the periodical changed its name to *El Genio de la Libertad*, words that significantly had first appeared in the fable of the trip to the moon. Independence was on everybody's mind. On September 15, 1821, a special issue of *El Genio* announced the victory at Tehuantepec, as well as the news that Ciudad Real in Chiapas had opted for independence, hoping that their colleagues in Guatemala City would do likewise. Then followed these banner lines: *Long Live the Sovereign Guatemalan People! Long Live Their Liberty and Independence*.[78]

That was basically how Independence came to Guatemala City. The Syndic Mariano Aycinena informed the Ayuntamiento of Guatemala City and Chief Gaínza of Mexican developments on September 4, 1821. He assured them that the petition gatherers in the City—Barrundia, Molina, and the rest—wanted to preserve the governmental leadership intact—a statement that has been interpreted as an inducement for Gaínza to accept the fact of independence.[79] Gaínza was receptive, and he yielded to the inevitable by the evening of September 14. He ordered representatives from the government and various corporations to meet on the following day, the fifteenth of September, 1821.[80]

Three months later to the day, the news of Guatemala's independence reached Madrid. Central Americans there were ecstatic. They gathered at a banquet sponsored by Mateo Ybarra, Guatemala City's deputy, to toast "in prose and verse," the independence of Guatemala and of the entire universe. Even Dr. José Flores, the famous surgeon of the 1790s, joined his colleagues in the toast. His advanced age, however, kept him from partaking of the food at the banquet. José Aycinena was present; so were the deputies from Chiapas (Fernando Antonio Dávila), Chiquimula (Luis Hermosilla), Comayagua (Juan Esteban Milla), Nicaragua (Toribio Argüello), and many others, including representatives from Yucatán. José Sacasa, the source of our information, likewise attended. Most of the participants signed a declaration addressed to the "Future National Congress of Guatemala." Sacasa noted with perception the importance of having such intelligent men as Miguel Larreinaga and José Cecilio del Valle in the service of the new government.[81]

7. A Conditional Independence

> Guatemala dreams with a surfeit of ambition, forgetting that she does not have anything to eat or to wear, and that an independent power, or republic, needs many millions to support itself.
>
> JOAQUÍN LINDO, *October 1821*[1]

GUATEMALANS poured into the streets of their capital city on September 15, 1821, anticipating important decisions from the special meeting called by the Jefe Político Superior. The latest reports from Mexico added to their expectations: another victory for Agustín Iturbide and the move by Chiapas to join the revolutionary cause, the first province in the Kingdom of Guatemala to take this step. A small band of enthusiasts generated interest in the activities of the day by assuring Guatemalans that the "people's presence" at the Royal Palace was a guarantee for the glorious cause of Independence. No less than fifty-six notables participated in the discussions on that memorable occasion, representing the major officials in the civil, ecclesiastical, and military administration of the Kingdom. The crowd cheered them on as they filed into the meeting place, while the band played and fireworks added to the hilarity and excitement. The explosions brought even more people to the scene. Everyone was shouting with emotion "Long Live Our Independence."[2]

Popular influence was a key factor in the Declaration of Independence that was signed on September 15, 1821, as attested to by Article I of that document. The "Cacos"—José Francisco Córdoba, José Francisco Barrundia, Pedro Molina, and his wife—helped to attract the crowds. *El Genio de la Libertad* was a key instrument in their campaign. These so-called leaders of the "people" published a *voto particular* in which they suggested what measures the assembly might take on September 15. The fact that most of their recommendations passed indicated the extent to which the agitators had succeeded in manipulating public opinion on Independence Day.[3]

There were many distinguished spokesmen for Independence at the famous hearings. The erstwhile champion of Spanish constitutionalism and representative of the University of San Carlos, Father Antonio Larrazábal, added a note of historical continuity to the occasion. His colleague from the university, Dr. Mariano Gálvez, was another bright star in Guatemala's future. Santiago Milla and José Francisco Córdoba represented the College of Lawyers; and Drs. José Maria Castilla and Antonio García Redondo, men of enlightened views, were there as delegates of the Cabildo Eclesiástico. Fray Juan de San Diego, a leader in education and social welfare, was the spokesman for the highly regarded Bethlemite Order; Miguel Larreinaga added stature to the men who favored Independence as a *Creole* representative of the Audiencia. Mariano Aycinena was the Ayuntamiento's lawyer; and Father José Matías Delgado and Antonio Rivera Cabezas were members of the Diputación Provincial. All of these gentlemen spoke eloquently in their advocacy of Independence, cheered on by the wild enthusiasm of the crowd. Those who equivocated or opposed Independence were jeered menacingly by the "people," which was the fate of Archbishop Ramón Casaus.

Nationalistic predilections have colored the numerous studies on the Declaration of Independence. From the standpoint of a break with Spain, it was a statement of *absolute* independence on the part of the men who signed the document: Gabino Gaínza, the members of the Deputation, two secretaries of the Assembly, authorized representatives of the Ayuntamiento, and José del Valle, the author of the document. On the other hand, the statement of September 15 was *conditional* in the sense that it anticipated the approval of the rest of the Kingdom. Because Chiapas had already joined Mexico, and suspecting that the other units might have different views, Gaínza and company felt that it was incumbent upon them to ascertain the will of the former provinces. Did they favor Independence? If so, what type of government did they want? To answer these questions, Article 2 of the Declaration of September 15, 1821, urged the provinces to hold elections for deputies to represent them at a constituent assembly in Guatemala City on March 1, 1822.

Despite occasional disclaimers of the Spanish past, the Declaration of Independence maintained continuity with the Cádiz Experiment. There were only slight modifications to meet different conditions. The electoral system remained intact, although now each deputy represented 15,000 people in Central America. Article 4 guaranteed the Castas the franchise, a bone of contention with the old regime that was more emotional than real in the Guatemalan experience. Article 3 permitted the use of the electoral juntas that only recently gathered in the provincial voting before Independence. Gabino Gaínza still functioned as Jefe Político Superior. His D.P., however, expanded its membership at least twofold and changed its name to Junta Provisional Consultiva, functioning as it had before. Chiapas was given another deputy, in hopes no doubt of luring her back into the fold. The Marquis de Aycinena, the third to hold the title, was added to the representation for Quezaltenango. Honduras profited from the added presence of the articulate José del Valle; Nicaragua from that of Judge Miguel de Larreinaga; and Sonsonate and Chimaltenango from the votes of Angel María Candina and José Valdés respectively. In due time, Costa Rica likewise had representation on one of the most distinguished bodies that had yet been formed in Central America. Purporting to represent all of Central America, the J.P.C. was theoretically a consultative unit in the Cádiz tradition. Yet it followed the practice of its predecessors and shared executive power with Gabino Gaínza, who made this possible by permitting the Junta to assume the prerogatives of a legislative body.

The Declaration of Independence of September 15, 1821, evinced the same concern for Spanish anticlericalism that was evident in nearby Mexico. Central Americans were unquestionably in favor of the plank of "Religión" in the Plan of Iguala and the protection of ecclesiastical fueros. Article II of the Declaration of Independence specifically mentioned the usefulness of the clergy in maintaining harmony within the nation and in minimizing disruptive factionalisms.[4]

After opening its sessions on September 17, 1821, the Junta Provisional Consultiva completed the assignment of committee chairmen according to expertise and interest. José Cecilio del Valle preferred finances and developmental matters. As a member of the cloth, the Marquis de Aycinena had invaluable connections with Archbishop Casaus in Guatemala City and the ecclesiastical authorities in Nicaragua. A viable electoral law for Guatemala City and its environs exposed another aptitude and interest of his. Miguel de Larreinaga utilized his talents in law and education for the benefit of the nation. He also assumed the delicate task of bringing Nicaragua into a government located in Guatemala City. In other words, Chief Gaínza had a respectable collection of men to advise him on the problems of establishing a new nation.

Following the example of the Spanish Cortes, the J.P.C. opened its sessions to the public and invited outside experts to help man the numerous committees. The public's cooperation was exceptional. As so-called advocates of the people, the "Caco" activists presented various petitions to the Junta—three of them, in fact, by September 27, 1821. One asked for the dismissal of military chiefs, whose hesitancy about Independence made them untrustworthy. Another demanded the prompt exit of these officers from Central America, since they were a threat to the security of the area. Finally, Barrundia urged the reform of Article 3 of the Declaration of Independence. It was against the "rights of the people" because many of the men who had served in the electoral juntas before Independence were not in favor of the new order. It was imperative, therefore, to elect new boards who were sympathetic to Independence.[5] The J.P.C. concurred with the proposals, especially since other governmental units in the area had made similar complaints.[6]

Gabino Gaínza has not been a favorite among Central American historians, leaving us with an unfair image. Contemporaries, however, thought highly of him, at least in the early days after Independence. Barrundia, Molina, and Córdoba in their private vote, for example, had urged the Assembly to promote him to the rank of Lieutenant General of the Independent Guatemalan Army, a suggestion that won the support of the Ayuntamiento of Guatemala City and other bodies. The Junta granted the request, honoring Gaínza's constructive work. Cooperative at all times with his advisory corporation, before and after Independence, Chief Gaínza left a favorable impression of the Cádiz political system and its potential.[7]

A dispute arose between "Cacos" and "Bacos" over the issue of open or closed meetings for the J.P.C. Resenting the ubiquitous writings of Molina and friends, the regidor José Antonio Larrave objected to the constant circulation of their petitions, allegedly in behalf of the "people" but in fact serving their own political objectives. Larrave maintained that petitions should originate with syndics of the city government.[8] The Ayuntamiento of Guatemala City agreed that the J.P.C. should not have any more public sessions than necessary since it had a disturbing effect upon public order. If a citizen chose to present useful proposals to the J.P.C., he should be able to do so without having to accumulate further signatures.[9] Sharing the municipality's concern for disorder, the J.P.C.

voted to close its meetings to the public on the grounds that the shouting and speech-making that accompanied the presence of the "people" was demeaning to its prestige.

El Genio de la Libertad mounted the attack against the retrograde decision. Contrary to what was alleged in some quarters, the public did not hinder the corporation's work; it kept the Junta from making such errors as Article 3 of the Declaration of Independence, rescinded by the Junta's members. Besides, shouting in public served a useful purpose, judging from the parliamentary proceedings in Spain, France, and England. The people wanted to preserve their democratic Junta, remembering their heroic contribution to the events of September 15. The adversaries of an open society were unnecessarily impatient. Opposed to a secretive Junta, the people hoped that it would at least keep its doors open during legislative business.[10] While the controversy was transpiring, a group of artisans demonstrated in favor of closing the meetings to the public—a "Baco"-inspired act. Rising above partisan considerations, however, the J.P.C. changed its mind and accepted a compromise. Whenever business was governmental or executive, the sessions would be closed; if legislative, they would open to the public.[11] That ended the matter, a political skirmish that fortunately was brief.

In keeping with the precedents of the Cádiz Experiment, the Junta welcomed the enlightened opinion of the citizenry in all its deliberations. Valle in particular strove to give the Junta's work the greatest publicity, covering its sessions faithfully in *El Amigo de la Patria*. At his insistence, Gaínza agreed to sponsor a bi-weekly publication of the *Gazeta del Gobierno*.[12] Pedro Molina's periodical likewise focused attention on the Junta's labors.

In a circular dated October 3, 1821, the J.P.C. urged the political deputations of the four intendancies (Chiapas, Comayagua, León, and San Salvador) and the municipalities of the provincial capitals to propose all measures "that they judged useful in consolidating the new government." It instructed the regional corporations to provide monthly accounts of all incidents that ran contrary to "the new system," and further asked them to organize militias in their regions, sending reports every month on the progress of defense efforts. Following the tradition of the Junta Central in Spain, the Guatemalan counterpart requested information from the deputations on how best to protect agriculture, stimulate industry, extend commerce, and perfect the tax system in their localities.[13]

The Junta's faith in the enlightenment of the area's municipalities was more than justified if we consider a perceptive analysis written by the

Ayuntamiento of San Vicente in what is now El Salvador. Furthermore, this document has the merit of outlining the major problems besetting the governmental corporation in Guatemala City during the final months of 1821. It noted that the nation's condition would remain precarious until March 1822, because of the lack of revenues and the troops to defend it. Isolated from world contact and trade, the country needed defensible ports and troops that were loyal to the cause of Independence. The trouble was compounded by the fact that many provinces had not chosen to acknowledge the J.P.C.'s directorship.

These were hard truths, evident to any serious observer. To correct the situation, the city fathers of San Vicente recommended a loan to meet the Junta's expenditures. It might also encourage the Montepío of Indigo Growers to provide some financial contribution, while continuing the collection of the tithes at half rates. For the defense of the area, the government needed an armed force of from five to six thousand men, over and above the support of local militias. The aldermen also urged the continued fortification of Trujillo and Omoa and the appointment of patriotic men to responsible posts. Moreover, the nation had to have a navy to carry the mail and to make contacts with allies in the Americas. An alliance with Agustín Iturbide of Mexico and Simón Bolívar in South America was worthwhile, indeed indispensable. Above all, the nation should commit itself irrevocably to absolute freedom of trade, "destroying the frightful and exorbitant duties demanded by the latest decrees of the Spanish Cortes."[14] The reference was to the Spanish Tariff of 1820.

Central Americans were in general agreement that the break with Spain was necessary, although they might not be of one opinion on future plans. The independence movement in Guatemala City on September 15, 1821, had in mind the reunification of the entire region under the authorities of the old capital, thus explaining the conditional nature of their national charter. Moreover, the terminology and spirit of the Declaration underscored Guatemala's determination to continue with the Cádiz Experiment.

The decrees of the provisional junta for Central America likewise gave this impression to the world. But the problems facing the young nation were formidable; even the city fathers of San Vicente could see that.

━━━━
〰〰〰

Since the end of the eighteenth century, Central America had lacked an adequate financial base for the developmental programs advocated by many of its leading thinkers. In the context of a continuing depression, it was perhaps illusory to establish a new nation. Enlightened leaders could not work a miracle. Economic recovery was an objective that required nurturing for decades under the most optimum conditions. Any extraneous, divisive factors would just postpone the implementation of well-conceived projects.

The Junta Provisional Consultiva worked long hours planning a viable financial structure for Central America, and José del Valle's fertile mind focused on this assignment. The Honduran suggested that perhaps the government might enter the open market to sell commodities for revenue purposes.[15] The harsh reality was that a defiant Spanish bureaucracy had brazenly ignored establishing the Spanish customs and tariff reforms of 1820 and thus created a serious vacuum in the financial base of the Central American government. Moreover, it was next to impossible to collect money. It was not feasible for political reasons to reinstate the alcabala on internal trade without incurring the wrath of the citizenry who had learned to hate the onerous excise tax. We have noted above what the city fathers of San Vicente had to say about the duties imposed by the Spanish tariff system, charges that in fact were not excessive. The truth was that trade in Central America was at a standstill; any charge whatsoever would be considered suffocating in a depressed economy.

What other sources of revenue were left? The restoration of the Indian tribute was hardly worthy of a new, enlightened nation, especially considering the Indians' expectation of relief. Without much choice, the J.P.C. argued that the Indians should pay a *contribución* (in lieu of and equal to the former tribute) until the future congress determined otherwise.[16] The exigencies of the times forced this decision upon the Junta's members. Even Father José Matías Delgado favored imposing momentary sacrifices on the Indians to meet the financial crisis of the government. Over the centuries, the whites had been conditioned to rely upon the Indian for financial help. The Junta agreed, for example, to borrow funds from the Indians' community treasuries—a well-established practice of the colonial period.[17]

What aggravated the financial situation in Central America was the departure of many Spaniards who had accumulated capital over the years of their stay. They were leaving the area as fast as they could arrange their affairs. In addition, Spanish bureaucrats who did not subscribe to Independence received a two-month severance pay—a serious imposition upon the exhausted coffers of the Treasury. In another petition from the "people," José Francisco Barrundia lamented the exodus of specie from

Central America, much of it smuggled in the carts of the departing families. He demanded the payment of an export tax on all wealth taken out of the country—35 percent on gold and silver and 20 percent on pearls and precious stones.[18] Although sympathetic to Barrundia's protest, the Finance Committee imposed a tax of only 10 percent on the first category and 4 percent on the second. José del Valle justified these charges by arguing that since an individual had a right to move—*loco-motivo* as the English called it—a tax on his wealth was in order. "Capital is not solely the product of the man who formed it," Valle explained. "The Society in which he made it also cooperated in its elaboration by protecting its producer, seeing to it that this capital was respected, facilitating the changes that it went through, and encouraging its increase with purchases."[19] Just how much revenue derived from this exit tax is difficult to say in the absence of documentation, but it does not appear to have been much.

As the financial condition of the Gaínza government worsened in the last months of 1821, Valle recommended that it should have priority on the agenda. This was on December 15, 1821, and the J.P.C. agreed.[20] Revenue collections were at a standstill. There was no trained corps of treasury officials; and, more importantly, no money to pay salaries for those positions. Finally, on February 13, 1822, Valle's Finance Committee presented a customs schedule and tariff for Central America. Lower than the Spanish duties of October 1820, the Valle tariff still followed the liberal orientation of its predecessor. The problem was one of implementation, aggravated by the political decision to join Mexico. Until the authorities in Mexico City announced their pleasure, in addition to the deterrents mentioned above, the vacuum in the collection of revenues at the ports of Central America was an embarrassing problem for the officials in Guatemala City. Without revenue, moreover, the J.P.C. had little effective power in its administrative and judicial structures. Although its members conscientiously appointed *jueces de letras* for the districts of Central America, the judges were unable to take over their assignments for want of salary. Even in Guatemala City, there was a constant hassle between the J.P.C. and the Ayuntamiento over the salaries for the judges. The regidores argued that there were no available resources to pay for them.[21]

A final illustration reveals the frustration of the Junta's membership on money matters, bringing forth some strained logic about public drunkenness. Valle and his colleagues on the Finance Committee maintained that drunkenness was on the increase throughout Central America, degrading the present generation. The causes for this condition were as follows: the lack of a liberal education to show the citizen what his true interests were, and the authorities' failure to punish offenders. For humanitarian reasons, therefore, the Committee recommended the establishment of elementary schools with the best curricula available. Secondly, all committees of "Agriculture, Industry, and Commerce" should foment these "three origins of all wealth" in their respective municipalities, thus increasing employment and improving the standard of living. Thirdly, judges should inflict meaningful penalties on alcoholics, keeping statistics on the incidence of drunkenness. Getting to the crux of its proposal, the Committee requested a monthly tax of ten pesos on all licensed *chicherías* that sold the common drink of the lower classes. To make it appear like a reform, the chichería stalls were to be out in the open and not in alleys; they were to close at 6 P.M., effective February 15, 1822. Such a system was bound to produce less drunkards than under the old order of free chicherías, established helter-skelter throughout the City. Since the more expensive aguardiente (brandy) was under the franchise system, the Committee's recommendation had the added merit of bringing uniformity to the liquor business. The estimated revenue for the City alone was set at 24,000 pesos. If extended throughout the region, it would be a boon to the exhausted treasury of Central America, reasoned the committeemen.[22] The J.P.C. passed the tax without trouble. No one seemed to care how the chicha-drinking public might react to the increase in the price of their potent beverage.

By sending out circulars to all the provinces of Central America, the Junta Provisional Consultiva assumed the leadership of the new governmental unit. It recognized that its existence depended upon an imaginative leadership program and the selling of unionism to its component parts, not an easy assignment considering the historical record we have been presenting. To generate interest in the forthcoming congress in Guatemala City, the J.P.C. thought it helpful to circulate the constitutions of other countries whose provisions might be useful to the deputies. Everyone was familiar with constitutional monarchy because of the Cádiz experience. Republicanism, however, was another matter. Santiago Milla, therefore, suggested reprinting the Venezuelan Constitution, and Gabino Gaínza supported the Buenos Aires Charter that had been written by Dean Funes of Córdoba. The chief had witnessed the favorable reception of the Argentine document while in Spain. In either case, both constitutions applied to a republic. By circulating a republican constitution throughout Central America, the Junta gave the impression that it favored this type of government; and this did not set well among supporters of the monarchical alternative.[23]

In early November 1821, José del Valle proposed a special committee to consider the best means of uniting Central America. Although this study group did not last long, it was nonetheless the precursor of the many unionist movements of the national period. Various priests served on the committee, including the articulate José Maria Castilla. In fact, his friends Barrundia and Molina were also members, scheduled to visit Mexico City where they would sound out support for Central American union. Other missions were to proceed to Comayagua, León, and other cities. Considering the assignment of the "Cacos" Barrundia and Molina, men of republican sympathies, it appears that this first unionist effort had in mind the establishment of a federal republic, one that would appeal to home-rule sentiments of the provinces. The J.P.C. also assigned its most influential people to handle the correspondence of a given province. For example, the Marquis de Aycinena, as a leading clergyman, had a persuasive edge in dealing with the activist Bishop Nicolás García of León, Nicaragua. As a Nicaraguan himself, Miguel Larreinaga took over the mail from Granada and Masaya; and so on.[24] The turn of events in late November, however, cancelled the unionist movement for the moment; and the various missions did not go to their destinations as planned.

The Junta Provisional Consultiva never had much control in Central America during its tenure except in areas where republicanism was strong. The Salvadorans, for example, were staunch supporters of Independence and felt grateful to the J.P.C. for encouraging the establishment of their diputación provincial.[25] On the other hand, in Quezaltenango the Junta's efforts were fruitless. Hoping to dissuade the highland city from following the example of Chiapas, it authorized the formation of a Junta Gubernativa Subalterna in Quezaltenango, an offer made on November 17, 1821. It was a day too late; the highlanders had already joined Iturbide's Mexico.[26] As for Chiapas, the break with Guatemala City seemed irrevocable. There was little interest in rejoining the former capital, especially since it could not offer the advantages of the connection with Mexico City.[27]

Elsewhere in Central America, the defiance of the Junta Provisional Consultiva stemmed from the provincianos' historical distrust of the ex-capital, leading to some maneuvers in the balancing of power that were to become endemic in Central America's future.

Comayagua's desire for home rule has already been noted. Her leaders declared their independence on September 28, 1821, from both Spain and Guatemala City, announcing their adherence to the Mexican Plan of Iguala.[28] The former Intendant José Tinoco now sported the title of Jefe Político Superior of the self-styled Captaincy General of Honduras. Not surprisingly, Tegucigalpa refused to follow Tinoco's lead and so notified the authorities of Guatemala City. The ports of Omoa and Trujillo and the towns of Gracias, Llanos, and Cueyagua likewise reaffirmed their loyalty to the J.P.C. They all cooperated with Guatemala's military maneuver to protect Tegucigalpa by ordering the Commandant of Chiquimula to assume command there with a respectable contingent of troops. Another tactic of the J.P.C. was to assign the tobacco revenues to the loyal constituencies, denying their use to Comayagua.[29] There was also serious talk about making Tegucigalpa the new capital of a Honduran D.P.

The climate of opinion was hawkish in Guatemala City, especially in the ranks of the "Cacos." The Hondurans José del Valle and Santiago Milla also favored military intervention. When news reached the City in mid-November of 1821 that Omoa and Trujillo had reversed their allegiance because of a coup, Gabino Gaínza was furious. He angrily denounced this threat to the "commerce and public treasury." Comayagua's "unjust oppression" had to be met by force; and his J.P.C. agreed with him.[30]

The Comayaguan government was no match for the determined Guatemalans, as Colonel Simón Gutiérrez's forces brought Omoa and Trujillo back into the fold. His expeditionary force entered Tegucigalpa triumphantly on December 16, 1821. This brief display of force was enough for the Tinoco government; it recognized that the only chance for survival was to make a personal appeal to Agustín Iturbide in Mexico City. In the meantime, the two governments in Honduras would coexist.[31]

Perhaps Tegucigalpa might have formed her own D.P. if Guatemala City had been able to sustain its independence. It did not, however; but the faithful city of Tegucigalpa was rewarded with the rank of "City" and the title of "Patriotic."[32] Approving the proposal of José del Valle, the J.P.C. further agreed that in the future Tegucigalpa should not be dependent upon Comayagua for anything.[33] As the political currents changed in favor of a connection with Mexico, the authorities in Guatemala City decided to leave the Honduran question for the Mexican government. Thus, coexistence became the rule.[34]

The Nicaraguan pattern was similar to the Honduran. The Leonese authorities resisted the overtures from Guatemala City, the hated ex-capital. The chief, Miguel González Saraiva, with the approval of his D.P. and Bishop García, issued a proclamation on September 28, 1821, announcing León's "absolute and total independence from Guatemala." The statement also proclaimed Nicaragua's independence from Spain "until the clearing of the present clouds."[35] Two weeks later came the announcement of absolute independence from Spain and Nicaragua's adherence to the Plan of Iguala in Mexico.[36]

Despite reassuring letters from Gaínza and others in Guatemala City, the Leonese persisted in their independent course, while at the same time expressing the desire to coexist peacefully with the Guatemalans. Their rationalization for the break with Guatemala City consisted of many arguments, some of them already familiar. First, experience had taught Nicaraguans that governments based in Guatemala City always favored the people there at the expense of the provincianos. The distance from Guatemala City, moreover, caused serious delays in the settlement of judicial and military matters. These hard facts could not be changed, regardless of the type of government chosen. Arguing that Guatemala lacked the resources to form a viable political unit in such an extensive area, the Leonese pointed to its limited and ignorant population, as well as other liabilities. The harsh fact was that Guatemala could not even defend herself from invasion. Mexico, on the other hand, had the requisite resources. Its Viceroyalty had supplied an annual subsidy of 100,000 pesos to meet the deficits in the governmental and defense requirements of the former Kingdom of Guatemala, a compelling reason for the decision to join Iturbide's government.[37] Besides, Nicaraguans wanted no part of a republican form of government which was the J.P.C.'s objective, thanks to the influence of a few "Geniuses." The reference was to the writers of El Genio de la Libertad in Guatemala City—Molina, Barrundia, and others.[38] The opening quotation in this chapter by the Honduran Lindo also questioned Guatemala's capacity to survive as a viable nation.

Despite the urging of the militants in Guatemala City and the irritation of the Leonese rejection, the J.P.C. voted against the use of force in Nicaragua. Barrundia, Molina, and Córdoba attacked the "Spaniards" González Saraiva and Bishop García as the enemies of Central American independence in the pages of their newspaper El Genio. This publication and letters by the "Cacos," including those of the Honduran Santiago Milla and the Costa Rican Pablo Alvarado, created much ill feeling against the Leonese government throughout Central America. Moreover, this propaganda confirmed the suspicion that a republican minority was paving the way for a governmental experiment of its liking. The anticlerical note in reference to Bishop García further offended many devout Catholics in Central America. Moreover, there was no question that the Leonese were annoyed by the propaganda barrage. They formally complained to the J.P.C. about the offensive remarks in *El Genio*, implying that perhaps the Junta de Censura should examine them as a violation of the freedom-of-the-press law. As judges on that body, Barrundia and Molina disqualified themselves; but no one seemed eager to replace them in order to pronounce judgment on the offensive selections.[39] Since the Junta Provisional Consultiva did not discourage the attacks upon the Leonese government, it gave credence to the suspicion that it fully supported the militants.

By capitalizing upon the disobedience within the Leonese jurisdiction, the J.P.C. pursued a divide and conquer tactic in Nicaragua. The City of Granada, and later that of Masaya, refused to go along with the declaration of September 28, the "cloudy" pronouncement. They reaffirmed instead their loyalty to Guatemala City on October 4, 1821. At the request of Granadians living in the City, the J.P.C. authorized the establishment of a Junta Gubernativa Subalterna for Granada. Furthermore, it ordered the transfer of the tobacco factory to the loyal city, the same tactic that had been employed against Comayagua.[40] The lawyer Eusebio Castillo was added to the J.P.C. as the representative for Granada's jurisdiction. The authorities in Guatemala City chose as jefe político in loyal Nicaragua Víctor de la Guardia and gave him instructions to work closely with Crisanto Sacasa, who led the defiance against León. On January 4, 1822, La Guardia took command of his post, despite the threats of Colonel González Saraiva in León.[41] As in Honduras, coexistence was the rule until a decision were forthcoming from Mexico City.

Costa Ricans seized upon the opportunity to assert their own home-rule aspirations. The only uncooperative town was Heredia, which consistently favored the Leonese government. The rest adopted a more or less noncommittal position vis-à-vis the power struggle between León and Guatemala City, seeking their own advantage. Guided by republican tendencies, San José was usually in favor of Guatemala City. Under the Pacto Social, Costa Ricans formed their own Diputación Provincial; and in fact they asserted their own sovereignty until such time that they opted to join another political unit. On December 1, 1821, Costa Ricans ratified the Pacto de Concordia, which established the Junta Superior Gubernativa de Costa Rica. The Junta consisted of seven popularly elected members; its President served a three-month term; and it resided three months of the year in each of the four major population centers of Costa

Rica. The Spanish Constitution of 1812 was the model for the Pacto de Concordia, as scholars of that country have noted. Many of its clauses and references—as on religion and citizenship—appeared first in the Spanish prototype. Moreover, the constitutional experience of the Costa Rican municipalities and provisional governments provides an overwhelming testimonial to the impact of the Cádiz Experiment in this quarter of Central America. The system did work to the satisfaction of most Costa Ricans.[42]

The political panorama as seen from Guatemala City in the final days of 1821 was not at all attractive. Chiapas' defection was definite, and its satellite Quezaltenango seemed to be following the same course. Comayagua's aspirations were quiescent for the time being, contained by Guatemala's military move. It was hoping for a solution from Mexico City, while its neighbor Tegucigalpa had made good its secession from Comayagua. León had sustained its separation and was also waiting for a favorable verdict from Iturbide, unable to stem the secession of Granada and Masaya and the opportunistic neutrality of the Costa Ricans. The Junta Provisional Consultiva, as a matter of fact, had a limited jurisdiction at all times that included future El Salvador, some of what is now Guatemala, and wedges of influence elsewhere in Central America, especially in the centers of republicanism. In view of the dismal financial picture, a change in political strategy was not out of order.

The pressure of Mexican events was a constant factor in the Independence of Central America. At a later date, Gabino Gaínza averred that Guatemala might have remained at peace if it had not been for the military successes of the revolutionaries in Mexico.[43] There was rejoicing throughout Central America at the opportunity that was thus provided to separate from a mother country that was no longer desirable. Moreover, in the provinces, the prospects of relief from control of Guatemala City made the connection with Mexico even more attractive.

As we have seen, in the early months of its existence, the J.P.C. favored the establishment of a unified nation, possibly a republic. The negative reaction from Nicaragua and Honduras, therefore, was a deep annoyance to Gaínza and the men who surrounded him. The emotionalism that had been generated by the "Caco" leaders and their organ *El Genio de la Libertad* fed Gaínza's disappointment with the other provinces of Central America.[44] The militant "Cacos," Barrundia and Molina especially, interpreted the pro-Mexican moves of León, Comayagua, and Chiapas as arbitrary decisions forced upon fellow Central Americans by Peninsulars who opposed the notion of Independence. They viewed the opposition to their political dreams as a conspiracy of Europeans who opposed the cause of the Americas.[45] For this reason, Barrundia and his colleagues had presented their petitions against Spanish officials unfavorable to independence. Determined to secure the area for the new order of things, they asked permission to establish tertulias patrióticas, clubs whose primary objective was to enlighten the public about all measures favorable to the common welfare. For all practical purposes, the tertulias functioned much like the economic societies of the earlier period. In the context we are now discussing, however, they were overwhelmingly political in nature. The first Guatemalan tertulia patriótica commenced its operation in mid-October of 1821. It was strongly unionist and republican in sympathy. The J.P.C. counted heavily upon the tertulia's support for the program against separatism in Central America.[46]

Although *The Genius of Liberty* hailed the exploits of Agustín Iturbide at Independence, it reversed its stand on Mexico when reports from there began to stress the establishment of constitutional monarchy. *El Genio* protested that the Plan of Iguala and the Treaty of Córdoba were not to America's interest. A Bourbon prince would be monarch, and this European would favor his compatriots from the Old World for governmental positions and titles of nobility. While Europeans liked an ostentatious monarchical system of government, the Americans of the New World preferred a spartan republic, such as those that had been set up in the United States, Venezuela, Chile, and Buenos Aires.[47] It will be recalled that in the early days, Gaínza evinced an interest in the establishment of a republic, judging from his favorable comments on the Constitution of the Buenos Aires regime.[48] *El Genio's* emphasis on the dichotomy of European versus American, however, must have given him some cause for thought. After all, he was born in Spain.

The pro-Mexico movement turned out to be irresistible even to the denizens of Guatemala City. A strong Mexican faction developed in the Ayuntamiento that included Mayor Mariano Larrave, a "Baco," and Mariano Aycinena, a former "Caco." The Aycinena connection with Iturbide and other key Mexican officials was a decisive factor in the political events of late 1821. The "families" were beginning to commit themselves to the Mexican cause. As Molina and Barrundia sensed this shift in allegiance, they broke their ties with the Aycinenas. The "families" were now their rivals who preferred constitutional monarchy as opposed to an

American republic; these ingrates were "Nobles" and "Serviles"—synonyms for the conservative opposition in the future political history of Guatemala and Central America.

The tide was against the Republicans, who were hopelessly outnumbered in the waning days of 1821. The realities of the moment dictated their defeat. Most provinces of the old Kingdom had declared themselves for annexation to Mexico. Thanks to the Cádiz Experiment, constitutional monarchy was popular and acceptable to most Central Americans, who saw no reason to experiment with an untried system of republicanism, especially since the monarchical form promised to achieve the same liberal goals. In addition, Mexico's vaunted wealth might be useful in priming the depressed economy of Central America, a sine qua non for a viable nation. These facts of life convinced the heads of families in Guatemala City, for example, to vote overwhelmingly for union with Mexico in a poll taken by the Ayuntamiento in the final weeks of 1821.[49] The miserable state of the J.P.C.'s finances was also a factor of some weight.

A final determinant, if any other were really needed, was the ubiquitous threat of Mexican power. At the time of Independence, officials from Oaxaca, Mexico, reminded Guatemalans that their best interests lay in joining the Plan of Iguala; any other course would just delay the establishment of an effective government in Guatemala City. Besides, an independent country to the south of Mexico might threaten its security and provoke a military retaliation. These insinuations reached Guatemala City in early October of 1821.[50] Iturbide himself wrote a letter on October 19 that for all practical purposes amounted to an ultimatum. Pointing out the weaknessess in the Declaration of Independence of September 15, Iturbide declared his opposition to the "mania of republican innovations" in the Americas. As he saw it, the antidote was constitutional monarchy. That is why he offered the Mexican throne to a European Bourbon. Guatemalans would certainly gain from the connection with the Mexican Cortes. In his letter to Gaínza, Iturbide mentioned that the Mexican delegation in the Cortes of Madrid had proposed the creation of three overseas monarchies, each headed by a Bourbon prince. One kingdom, he noted, was to include Mexico and Central America—an interesting revelation that suggests a connection between the Iturbide movement in Mexico and the proposal to erect feudal monarchies overseas. The Mexican leader reminded Gaínza that a division of his was marching toward Central America to protect the cause of "Religion, Independence, and Union"—the slogan of the Plan of Iguala.[51] Other letters of the period confirmed the impression that Iturbide was planning to frustrate the J.P.C.'s program to reincorporate the former provinces of the Kingdom of Guatemala.[52] These bits of information nurtured the defiance of Guatemala City and hastened the annexation of all Central America to Mexico.

Fully comprehending the insinuations in the Mexican correspondence, the Junta Provisional Consultiva in Guatemala City yielded gracefully to the inevitable, striving to save face in the process. It argued initially that it lacked authority to annex Guatemala to Mexico; therefore, it took action to expedite the reunion of deputies in Guatemala City, where the Constituent Assembly would make the proper decision. With Iturbide's letter of October 19 in hand, Gaínza and his advisors decided to ask all the ayuntamientos in their jurisdiction to hold open meetings in which the assembled citizens could express themselves on the Mexican issue. The replies were to reach Guatemala City by the end of the year at the latest. On January 2, 1822, the J.P.C. met to consider the results, an overwhelming vote in favor of annexation to Mexico. The rhetoric notwithstanding, it was clear that by January 5, 1822, the Guatemalan government had come around to the point of view of the provincianos.[53]

Although the outcome was never in doubt, the Mexican issue posed a serious threat to public order in the capital city during the final days of 1821. The hostility between the "Geniuses" and the pro-Mexican faction was nearing the breaking point on November 27, 1821, when José Oñate arrived in the city, bearing letters from Iturbide.[54] To the sound of music and fireworks, the pro-Mexican elements regaled their visitor on the night of the twenty-ninth, winding their way happily through the streets of the city and shouting in favor of the Plan of Iguala and the impending union with Mexico. The enthusiastic leaders of the parade sought out the homes of Pedro Molina, José Francisco Barrundia, and José Francisco Córdoba where they shouted uncomplimentary epithets and threatened the leaders of the Republican cause. On the following evening, a pro-Guatemala crowd attended the tertulia patriótica at the University. It was a spirited session; afterwards the republican demonstrators took to the streets with enthusiasm and vociferous shouts in behalf of Central America's absolute independence. An unsympathetic patrol headed by Mayor Mariano Larrave clashed with the demonstrators. Although versions of the incident differ, there is no doubt that two patriots lost their lives, one of them Pedro Molina's brother-in-law.[55]

Fearing a complete breakdown of order in the City, Gaínza prohibited any further sizable meetings, especially at night. Thus, the tertulias had to close their doors.[56] Normalcy returned to the capital when the leaders of both factions moved away. By the end of December, the elections were finally held, having been cancelled earlier. No Mexican forces had yet invaded the area, as many believed would happen.

Gaínza's commitment to the Mexican cause was unshakable when the J.P.C. met on January 2, 1822. He was no longer optimistic about Central America's future. On the contrary, he now maintained that it lacked the attributes to form an independent and sovereign nation, repeating the arguments of Nicaraguans and Hondurans that in earlier months had annoyed him. Guatemala was too extensive and too poor. Its depopulation would always be a liability. There were no adequate ports, and the coasts were too distant and unhealthy. There was no navy, no commerce, and no revenues. Guatemala's only salvation was to join Mexico; and now was the time to annex herself to the northern power, while things were still stable.[57] The members of the J.P.C. agreed with their chief; but the deliberations lasted a few days longer on related issues. José del Valle was especially eloquent on the constitutional questions involved. He appeared determined to have the record show him as a defender of Central America's sovereign rights. His words did not alter the final decision to join Mexico, however.

On the matter of representation in the elections for the Mexican Cortes, Gaínza yielded unwillingly to José del Valle. The Mexican authorities had stipulated that every three districts should choose two deputies to Parliament. Valle complained that this was unfair by comparison to the popular representation of the Cádiz Constitution.[58] He argued that until Mexico City acknowledged Guatemala's annexation, the Cádiz system should remain in effect for the impending elections to the Mexican Cortes. The J.P.C. supported Valle's stand; and Gaínza, despite some misgivings, went along with the decision. He hoped that Iturbide's government would accept the deviation on grounds of expediency, which it did, by the way.[59] Valle and colleagues also calculated that Guatemala should have at least one-fourth the number of deputies in the Cortes, following the figures of Alexander von Humboldt (6 million Mexicans and 1.5 million Central Americans). Thus, Guatemalans again marched to the polls to elect deputies to the new Mexican Cortes, using the familiar Cádiz system. They were to elect one deputy for every 27,000 people.[60]

Once the decision was made to join Mexico, Gaínza would brook no opposition. His action appeared to be an admission that the J.P.C. had acted without authority on January 5, 1822, whereas earlier there had been a meticulous concern for the fact that the projected Guatemala City congress was solely responsible for the Mexican decision. An order of January 9, 1822, forbade anyone from questioning the decision in any form. Pedro Molina and José Francisco Barrundia challenged the constitutionality of Gaínza's edict, as members of the Junta de Censura. They argued that Gaínza had only intended to include seditious remarks concerning the annexation decision and not any theoretical discussions about the merits of the governmental system. Refusing to budge on the matter, Gaínza cited precedents from the Cádiz experience to prove his point. Thus, a determined executive held at bay the advocates of republicanism in Guatemala.[61]

If the Junta Provisional Consultiva's expectation was the reversal of the disintegrative process in the former Kingdom of Guatemala, its optimism proved to be unwarranted. Nothing positive in that direction happened in the next few months. On the contrary, the provincianos' spirit of defiance infected even the districts that had been loyal to Guatemala City. Sololá, for example, demonstrated against further control from Guatemala City.[62] The governments of Comayagua and León continued their independent ways, hoping that in time their envoys would influence the authorities in Mexico City to grant them bona fide home rule. The tobacco monopoly was an explosive issue. All governmental units held on to what they had, awaiting orders from Mexico City. What annoyed Comayagua and León, however, was that their Mexican mail passed through Guatemala City. Their complaints prompted Iturbide to assign those two governments temporarily to the Captain General in Puebla, Mexico.[63]

The continued tension with the authorities of Quezaltenango was understandable since the Gaínza government insisted upon its former authority over the highland area. Moreover, since mid-November of 1821 Quezaltecos had been conducting a campaign to influence other towns in the highlands to follow their lead in joining Mexico. Even Antigua, Guatemala, had received such an invitation, much to the annoyance of Gaínza and his colleagues in the nearby capital.[64] The subversion campaign continued into the month of December. Once Guatemala City voted to join Mexico, Gaínza moved to control the tobacco revenues in the highlands, arousing a spirited opposition from Quezaltenango.[65] On February 5, 1822, the regidores of that highland city beseeched General Vicente Filísola to protect them against the Guatemalans by sending Mexican troops there. Filísola refused to step up his advance into the highlands just for that purpose, but he cautioned both parties in the dispute to keep the peace and work in harmony.[66]

Usually faithful to Guatemala City, the Salvadorans immediately challenged the annexation decision. They argued that only the constituent assembly indicated in the Declaration of Independence (September 15, 1821) had authority to do so. Nor were they willing to accept the verdict of the ayuntamientos. In effect, the Salvadoran D.P. was breaking the connection with the former capital.[67] By December 25, 1821, it sent out an invitation to other Central American governments asking them to join in forming an assembly that would resist the Mexicans and erect a republic.[68] The Guatemalan leaders cautioned the districts within their jurisdiction not to pay attention to the blandishments of the Salvadoran government, now headed by Father José Matías Delgado, a former member of the J.P.C.[69]

The Guatemalan Junta reached the nadir of its political life in early February of 1822, as the defiant Salvadorans vied with it in attracting towns and cities within the Salvadoran area. This was especially true in the district of Santa Ana, the subject of a tense correspondence between the two rivals. Then came the news that the towns of Quesaltepeque and Ateos had been attacked by a body of Salvadorans. Gaínza prepared to move instantly, pleading with the J.P.C. to give him approval. Although the members of the Guatemalan Junta cautioned restraint, they yielded to their Chief on February 6, 1822, when he repeated his request for authorization to attack San Salvador in the event of aggression upon loyal towns.[70] Civil war was on the horizon as both governments alerted their military forces. It remained to be seen what effect the Mexican connection would have upon these frightening developments on the Guatemalan-Salvadoran border and throughout Central America among the defiant provincianos.

8.   The Mexican Connection

It is sheer nonsense to attack a free people; the cunningness and brilliant style with which these theories are presented to the public by perturbers of order are already known; we should not deceive ourselves, because the world understands that there is no stable prosperity in a nation without these bases: constitutional monarchy, laws that are analogous, union amongst each other, [and] liberties that are just.

AGUSTÍN ITURBIDE, *January 30, 1822*[1]

ALTHOUGH Iturbide joined the Mexican insurgents in the Plan of Iguala to rid the country of Spanish rule, he was never sanguine about his allies. As a supporter of constitutional monarchy, he distrusted the "Democrats" and their darling ideas about republicanism. When the Spanish government refused to honor the Treaty of Córdoba—that is, no Spanish prince of the Bourbon House would accept the Mexican throne—Iturbide's followers took the initiative. By mid-1822, Mexico's military hero and native son became Agustín I; it remained to be seen, however, whether his commitment to constitutional monarchy was sincere or not.

The operations of republicans in Central America deeply concerned Agustín Iturbide. His principal informant on these matters was Mariano Aycinena, a resourceful lawyer who shared identical misgivings about the republican agitators in Guatemala City and in the feisty province of San Salvador. The cities of San Salvador and San Vicente in particular had to be watched carefully, Don Mariano cautioned, suggesting that a Mexican intendente could be sent to control subversion in that province.[2] When Iturbide learned of the disturbances that wracked Guatemala City in late November and early December of 1821, he hastily blamed the militant republicans for the trouble: "I never imagined that the democratic furor should decide upon such a scandalous break."[3] To protect Chiapas from republicanism, he ordered a Mexican division to proceed there as soon as possible. For various reasons, the military move did not materialize in October 1821. Two months later, however, Iturbide sent Brigadier General Vicente Filísola and his troops to protect all provinces in Central America that had annexed themselves to Mexico. Gaínza also received instructions to withdraw his troops from Honduras in order to assist Filísola's maneuvers against San Salvador.[4]

The freak appearance of a naval force off the Salvadoran coast gave the republican threat in Central America much more attention that it actually deserved. The naval commander in charge was the irascible Lord Thomas Cochrane, later Earl of Dundonald, who announced his preference for "popular federation" rather than constitutional monarchy. As might be expected, the fiery Scotsman's presence excited republican leaders. One of them was Aycinena's old friend José Francisco Córdoba, who hastened to the Salvadoran capital to verify the rumor that circulated in January 1822. Gaínza's censorship moves during that month were perhaps prompted by the disquieting prospect of a republican invasion from the sea.[5]

Perhaps from want of documentation, Lord Cochrane's biographers have not dealt with his appearance in Central America to any extent, a sharp contrast to his career in South America. After quarreling with José de San Martín over money matters, Cochrane deserted the Chilean expedition that had invaded Peru. In Central America, he was offering to sell rifles and cannons to the Salvadoran republicans. The sources conflict on how many weapons were involved. Be that as it may, it was Cochrane's presence off the Salvadoran coast that was the significant factor, since it bolstered the confidence of republicans throughout Central America. At a celebration in San Salvador, a Nicaraguan witness heard the following *vivas*: "Long live the liberals, Long live a free San Salvador, Long live Cokrane, Long live the Republic; Long live Democratic Government."[6]

Although Aycinena doubted that Cochrane's intervention would amount to much, it irked him nonetheless that the incident might embolden the "false patriots" in Guatemala City, an allusion to his former allies Barrundia, Molina, and Córdoba. Aycinena's letter of January 18, 1822, included the name of José Cecilio del Valle among them, perhaps because the long-winded Honduran was stalling the annexation process by quibbling over constitutional details. As a result, he hindered Gaínza's efforts against El Salvador, which led Aycinena to recommend the dissolution of the Junta Provisional Consultiva and the formation of a diputación provincial. Furthermore, Aycinena asked for a money grant of 100,000 pesos annually to cover military expenses in Central America.[7] By implicating Valle as a false patriot and republican, Mariano Aycinena perhaps influenced Iturbide's decision to jail Valle for his alleged participation in Mexico's "Republican Conspiracy" of August 27, 1822. At any rate, Mexican intelligence believed this to be the case, even though the truth may have been otherwise.[8]

Iturbide's reaction to the threat in San Salvador was forceful and imaginative. As indicated earlier, he called for the withdrawal of troops from Honduras in order to assist Filísola, whose mission was to head for San Salvador "in the event that Lord Cochrane tries to embark" or committed some act of "piracy."[9] The imaginative phase of Iturbide's reaction was a public relations program to ascertain opinion in Central America. He wanted to know who the leaders were in each province and what political ideas they had. Furthermore, Filísola had instructions to create a favorable image of Mexico and its key personages. Iturbide urged him to promote union in Central America and to impress its citizens with the importance of sending their best men to serve in the Mexican Cortes. A good tool for enlightening the people in that region, Iturbide noted, was the tertulia patriótica. Filísola and his men should play active roles at the gatherings of these clubs stressing "the progressive acts of the Government, the advantages of union, and the impossibility of Guatemala supporting herself without our help." Through the press and in his correspondence with the area's leaders, Filísola should attempt to produce an enlightened view of Mexico's constitutional experiment. Influenced by Aycinena's evaluation, Iturbide likewise doubted that Cochrane would make the mistake of landing in Central America in behalf of republicanism. Besides, constitutional monarchy, in Iturbide's opinion, was far superior to the republican rival; and he urged Filísola and his agents to stress the point that liberal reforms were attainable in a monarchical system.[10] Central Americans appreciated this point because of their participation in the Cádiz Experiment. Moreover, the secessionists in Nicaragua and Honduras decried the leveling tendencies and the republicanism of a few "geniuses" in Guatemala City. The Mexican annexation, in short, was far more popular throughout Central America than present-day nationalists would like to admit. In those days, moreover, contemporaries regarded Agustín Iturbide as a great hero, the Bolívar of the North.

In form and in spirit the Mexican connection represented a continuation of the original Cádiz Experiment. As issues arose, Mexican and Central American leaders often referred back to the laws and precedents of the first constitutional period. In the tradition of Cádiz, clerics played a prominent role in government and maintained their fuero. It will be recalled that the desafuero in the Cortes of Madrid had alienated both Mexicans and Central Americans, evoking one of the three guarantees of the Plan of Iguala. In addition, there was a concern for religious orthodoxy and the preservation of the dogmas of the Church, as was the case at Cádiz. The strong Catholic stance, however, should not obscure the fact that the major thrust of the Mexican period was progressive, one of reform. Nor should Iturbide's subsequent resort to arbitrary government distort the historical reality of the days that preceded the abandonment of constitutionalism.

Mexican and Central Americans, moreover, followed constitutional developments in Spain and often appropriated the reform measures that were being enacted by the Cortes of Madrid. Independence from Spain was a fact of life, to be sure; but the ideological bond transcended national borders. Freedom of the press continued, and the Mexican Cortes put into effect Madrid's new committee version of correcting abuses, described in the previous chapter. In fact, Gaínza insisted upon the new model in his argument with Barrundia and Molina over the January 9, 1822, edict on censorship.[11]

The dogma of the people's sovereignty permeated constitutional developments in Mexico City, where procedures mirrored the liberal Cádiz tradition. For example, laws had to be implemented within three days of their receipt, the toma de razón practice described in an earlier chapter. All meetings of ayuntamientos, diputaciones provinciales, as well as Parliament in Mexico City, were open to the public; only in special cases were secret sessions permitted.[12] Just as Iturbide had suggested, patriotic societies helped to enlighten public opinion in their communities. Diputaciones provinciales and ayuntamientos selected their most illustrious citizens to serve on all manner of committees that supplied government with vital information. Elected officials visited jails periodically to protect the rights of prisoners and to maintain proper conditions.[13] Mexico City insisted upon a scrupulous observance of the chain of command outlined in the Ordinances of June 23, 1813, requiring town councils and deputations to work through their jefes políticos. Guatemala City officials, in particular, adhered carefully to this order, much more so than had been the practice in previous constitutional periods.[14] In the case of the Guatemalan D.P., this behavior seems to have resulted from the confidence inspired by Gaínza and Filísola. It was the system that Agustín Argüelles had defended with eloquence at Cádiz, and it worked adequately in Mexico and Guatemala during these years. The Consejo de Estado became a reality when Agustín I ascended the throne, although not for long. Florencio Castillo, the erstwhile defender of Costa Rica's interests in the former parliament at Cádiz, served on that body.

With only a few exceptions, the electoral procedures of constitutional Mexico followed the Spanish prototype. As noted in the previous chapter, the Mexican government allowed every three districts to elect two deputies to the Cortes—a deviation from the Cádiz system that Central Americans refused to follow, it will be recalled. Mexican authorities permitted the exception. Although the number of people for each deputy was smaller, the steps in the electoral system were identical to the Spanish model. Whenever irregularities occurred, the Guatemalan D.P. judged them according to the precedents in Spanish constitutional law. The obligation to serve the public was a demand that characterized the Mexican constitutional experiment as much as it did its Spanish predecessor. Only special cases of hardship could relieve a man from an obligation to serve the public. Judging from the example of the Guatemalan Diputación Provincial, there were only rare occasions when an application for relief from duty passed its scrutiny. The same applied to municipal positions. Public service was a responsibility and an obligation of every citizen.[15]

Economic and social reforms likewise characterized the Mexican period in Central America, in theory if not in fact. As usual, the problem was basically financial. Without a sound economic base, many reform projects never left the drawing board. The awareness of the need for measures of modernization, however, was a commendable first step in the right direction. The Guatemalan D.P., for example, recognized that Central America was in the throes of a depression. It therefore asked knowledgeable corporations and officials to draw up reports that examined the causes for depression and suggested viable remedies. The research in these reports was exhaustive and perceptive, especially one analysis written up by the Royal Consulado.[16] The shortage of capital in Central America, however, precluded any effective implementation of suggestions and programs of economic development. What little funds became available usually went into military expenditures of one kind or another.

An advocate of free trade for the area, the Guatemalan Deputation welcomed the tariff of February 1822 which Valle and his colleagues had drawn up. On the other hand, the protectionist Ayuntamiento of Guatemala City reflected the artisans' concern for the unrestricted entry of British imports. In realistic fashion, the D.P. acknowledged that imports from Belize harmed the textile crafts of Guatemala and posed a special security problem. In other words, it was not disposed to abandon all considerations for the sake of free trade. The artisans also had a stake in the nation's economy. In initiating economies to improve the government's financial predicament, the Diputación made many cutbacks at the expense of the Church. This is particularly meaningful if we recall that the Deputation formed on March 29, 1822, consisted of three clerics and one civilian. It speaks well for the public spirit and nationalism of the religious men involved, among them the Archbishop Ramón Casaus. Usually characterized as an arch-conservative in Guatemalan historiography, Casaus did not live up to that image in his career as a member of the Guatemalan D.P. during the Mexican annexation.[17]

Monopoly abuse was a primary concern of the Guatemalan Deputation. Faced with the need for money, however, it was not willing to forsake the revenue that derived from the sale of aguardiente and chicha. Following the lead of its predecessor, it restricted the number of licenses and kept the public stands in open locations, thus hoping to limit public drunkenness and crime.[18] The D.P. insisted successfully on the operations of free enterprise for the meat supply of the city, despite the opposition of vested interests in the Ayuntamiento.[19] Tobacco was another matter, and expediency dictated a policy to increase revenues wherever possible, as had been the case in Spain earlier. The fragmentation of political power in Central America, furthermore, led to the usurpation of tobacco revenues by local interests. It was not until late October 1822 that Mexico City announced its tobacco policy, which followed the pattern set in Madrid during the second constitutional period. The tobacco monopoly would continue for a two-year term, after which free enterprise would take over.[20]

Educational reform was a persistent objective throughout Central America—and primary education especially concerned the ayuntamientos of the area. Costa Rica's record was commendable despite the lack of funds for a more extensive system. A Honduran document alluded to the "glorious period" in which education would permit merit to overcome the advantages of class and race.[21] The Lancasterian system of education still attracted many followers; the problem, however, was one of getting qualified teachers to start the program in Central America.[22] Whenever resources existed, town councils welcomed the establishment of special chairs of medicine to help in the program of public health.[23] In every respect the thrust was identical to that of Charles III's program and the Cádiz Experiment's hopes for the youth of the Spanish nation.

In the reforms of cemeteries, the Guatemalan D.P. followed the recommendations made at Cádiz and the exploratory measures that were taken by the Ayuntamiento of Guatemala City in early 1814. The burial of bodies within churches and in the city limits posed a health hazard for urban dwellers, not to mention the offensive and putrid odors that polluted the environment. Cádiz legislators therefore ordered that in the future all cemeteries were to be located in unpopulated areas. Dr. Narcisco Esparragosa recommended a special site in 1814, just as the first reform period ended. Nothing happened, however, until the Mexican years, when the Guatemalan D.P. decided to implement the project. As jefe político superior, Vicente Filísola made up his mind to carry out the cemetery reform at all costs. He contributed some of his own money for the project; and so did Archbishop Casaus. The magnanimity of both Casaus and Filísola was noted in the D.P.'s records, thanks to the resolution urged by a member who complimented his two colleagues' public spirit. Irony would have it that the man in question later was destined to be the bitter enemy of both men. He was José Francisco Barrundia.[24]

Equality of the races was one of the main guarantees of the Plan of Iguala. It was nothing new, since it harked back to the Indianist program of the Cádiz Experiment. Envisioning the Indian's integration into society, the Mexican government insisted upon the red man's equality by outlawing all badges of inferiority. It abolished the degrading tribute payment, prohibited public beatings (*azotes*), discarded the compulsory contributions to the community treasuries, and outlawed the imposts for the support of local priests.[25] These issues had all been debated at Cádiz. There was no question about the sincerity of Mexican officials in honoring the pledge for racial equality in the Plan of Iguala. In fact, Mexicans were far more insistent upon these reforms than the Guatemalans.

The Indianist program in Central America led to considerable instability in a time of economic depression. Interpreting the release from tribute payments as the beginning of a new order without taxes, Indians could not understand such subtleties as equality with the whites and the payment of taxes like everyone else. Moreover, it was virtually impossible to collect any revenues from Indian communities in what is now the nation of Guatemala. Since Indians comprised at least 70 percent of the population, the effect on the government's financial condition was crucial. Furthermore, Indian leaders who were elected to office were uncooperative with authorities in Guatemala City. Many of them were illiterate and did not understand Spanish, the government's language. Oftentimes, they merely feigned ignorance of the white man's tongue. At any rate, the result was a widespread disobedience of orders emanating from Guatemala City. This irritated and frustrated the Guatemalan D.P., who saw its carefully conceived laws and projects ignored by Indian communities.[26]

Practically without financial resources, the Guatemalan Deputation balked at implementing the Indianist program advocated by the Mexican government. It insisted instead upon collecting revenues from the Indians even though they were no longer called tributes. In practice the policy was not consistent, and it ended up by depending upon the amount of force that was applied to a given Indian community. Moreover, Archbishop Casaus worked out a special series of minor taxes that would help his religious brethern to survive in Indian communities, again in defiance of express orders from Mexico City.[27] The D.P. met the disobedience of Indian magistrates with a strong policy that allowed Filísola to appoint *jefes subalternos*, or assistant chiefs, until the establishment of the juez-de-letras program. It was hoped that by then the educational program for Indians would be well underway.[28]

Influenced by financial realities, D.P. members struggled with their conscience on the Indian question. The three thoughtful clerics on the D.P. were Archbishop Casaus, Dean Antonio García Redondo, and José María Castilla. The civilians included Santiago Milla of Honduras, José Nájera, Manuel Pavón, and José Francisco Barrundia, the latter elected to the D.P. by the district of Escuintla. Of the seven, the most avid defender of the Indians was Barrundia. The debate on the Indianist program warmed up on May 15, 1822, when Gaínza described the "fatal state" of the government's finances, "so poor that the treasury could not pay the salaries of troops and employees." The Chief therefore asked for a loan of 8,000 pesos to be drawn from Indian community resources. When Barrundia questioned the need for such a step, Gaínza assured him that the emergency was real.[29]

Dissatisfied with the Chief's reply, the future ideologue of Central American liberalism launched a brilliant defense of the Indian that would warm the hearts of modern indigenistas. He reminded his distinguished colleagues that the funds in the community treasuries were "the product of the Indian's sweat," intended to protect him in an emergency. To withdraw money from these funds would be defrauding the Indian and living at his expense, a reprehensible action since "the afflicted class is poor and miserable." The rich, in the meantime, escaped by not paying taxes at all. As a student of the law for many years, Barrundia noted that borrowing from Indian community sources was prohibited even by the Recopilación de Leyes of the Spanish Empire. Moreover, the Spanish

Constitution of 1812 charged provincial deputations with the responsibility of investing funds properly and with reporting all infractions of the constitution. To proceed as suggested by Gaínza would therefore be in direct violation of the D.P.'s major responsibilities. Besides, article 172 of the "sacred code" of 1812 forbade even the King from taking property from any individual or corporation; and the D.P. was not above the law. Finally, young Barrundia pointed out to his colleagues that money borrowed from the Indians in the past had not been returned to them. During the Consolidación, for example, 300,000 pesos had been taken from the Indian treasuries and none of this money was ever returned.[30] These were harsh truths that his colleagues could not deny.

In a subsequent meeting, Barrundia made a proposal that was acceptable to the Mexican government. Pointing out that the Spanish Constitution of 1812 had made the Indian an equal in rights, it therefore guaranteed his property as a citizen. The Cádiz charter made no mention whatsoever of community treasuries because "it does not recognize any tax that is not general to the other classes." Indians, therefore, should not have to pay taxes which are not demanded of ladinos. If Indian municipalities had been able to administer their funds during the colonial centuries, they would not have contributed to so many donativos. Barrundia's point was an obvious one: Indians should be responsible for their own treasuries, just as any other group of citizens. He closed his case with the demand that all monies in the central treasury belonging to Indians should be returned to their municipalities.[31] The authorities in Mexico City supported Barrundia's proposal. The victory was academic, however. By the end of the year most funds from Indian sources had already been exhausted.[32] The constant reference to the Cádiz precedent by José Francisco Barrundia, nevertheless, underscored the indebtedness of Mexican and Central American liberalism to the Spanish prototype.

Despite good intentions, the fact remains that a weak financial base nullified the reform program of Mexican and Central American leaders. This continued weakness, in turn, led to a disillusionment and disenchantment with the Mexican connection throughout Central America. The economic situation failed to improve, and the vaunted subsidy of 100,000 pesos annually was not forthcoming from Mexico City. In fact, the financial predicament worsened during the Mexican period. Gaínza's expenditures against Comayagua and San Salvador were covered by Indian community funds, for the most part. From mid-June of 1822 forward, the presence of a Mexican expeditionary force continued the drain. The decision to attack San Salvador in December 1822, as well as the hostilities of the months that followed, brought about the financial bankruptcy of the Guatemalan government.

Although exact figures are difficult to come by, the inherited debt of the Guatemalan government must have been considerable. It included substantial amounts owed to the Indian communities, in addition to the interest on that money. The government owed at least 90,000 pesos to deputies who had served as constitutional representatives in the Spanish Cortes—a statistic that has a significant implication for the Cádiz Experiment and that reflects the long-term economic plight of Central America.[33] In addition, Guatemalans now had to supply per diems and traveling expenses for their sizable delegation at the Mexican Cortes—a serious obligation that remained unfulfilled despite Iturbide's menacing language. Recognizing that the Emperor's patience was wearing thin, Filísola urged his D.P. to avoid any further delays. The Deputation at this point notified all town councils to hold open town meetings (cabildos abiertos) in which the local citizenry could determine what tax resources might be used to pay the expenses of their deputies in the Cortes. The suggestion fell on deaf ears. The ayuntamientos of Central America were simply not willing to tax themselves for that purpose, such was the economic crisis in their jurisdiction. The Guatemalan D.P. despaired at the lack of support among the towns and their unwillingness to pay for a constitutional order. As a result, Central America never had more than twenty deputies in Mexico City at any one time, only half the number authorized.[34] This lack of representation was one of the alleged reasons for breaking with the Mexicans in 1823.

The inability to establish a viable fiscal system compounded the money problems of the Central American governments. The departure of trained Spanish bureaucrats, with their two-month severance pay, left a serious vacuum that was not filled at all during the Mexican years. The Spanish Tariff of 1820, it will be recalled, dropped the hated alcabala tax and abolished all interior customs houses. Valle's program of February 1822 followed the same orientation, although the duties were lower. Neither one was implemented, however. No taxes were collected, and contrabandists had an easy time of it. The Mexican customs law was not announced until September 7, 1822. Until then there was utter confusion throughout Central America on the matter of taxes. The vacuum, in short, had not disappeared. It persisted into 1823, after the break with Mexico.[35] Moreover, as General Filísola passed through the northern highland communities on his way to Guatemala City, he insisted upon carrying out Mexico City's orders on relieving the Indians of the tribute payments. The Guatemala City government was thus penniless. Able men on the Guatemalan D.P. could do nothing to carry out their projects.

The Mexican connection was a bitter disappointment to all Central Americans, who expected their rich neighbor to supply the wherewithal for their ambitious developmental schemes. Mexico's financial plight, it turned out, was even more serious. On April 19, 1822, the Regency implored the provincial bodies and municipalities to contribute generously to a voluntary loan that would defray the military expenses of the nation, since the nation's treasury was exhausted. On these occasions, the Guatemalan D.P. usually promised to help its Mexican colleagues, while at the same time reminding them that there were no revenues at its disposal.[36] On June 5, 1822, the Regency urged the Guatemalan Deputation to raise 50,000 pesos for the fortification of San Felipe, a worthy security measure that also could not be executed for want of funds.[37] General Filísola made the following interesting comment to his superiors in Mexico City. Noting that Central America was a difficult and expensive area to defend, he estimated that it required an investment of 400,000 to 500,000 pesos. He also pointed out that all Central America, not just Guatemala City, was experiencing a depression. Yet the money to pay for the Mexican expeditionary force came from the Guatemalan jurisdiction. The other provinces were not able, or not willing, to contribute to the common Mexican expense despite Filísola's urgings on this issue.[38]

Under ordinary circumstances, the collection of taxes would have been a difficult task. It was doubly hopeless in the case of the alcabala, that odious reminder of the colonial regime. It tarnished the Mexican image in the process. As late as June 10, 1822, Gaínza received 2,000 pesos from Indian resources; thereafter, the sums declined precipitously. By December 1822, the treasuries were empty.[39] Filísola was left with no alternative but to restore the alcabala at 4 percent, the level for Central America during the colonial years. Moreover, the Mexican leadership imposed a special *alcabala de viento* on certain foodstuffs sold in the market place, an impost that had never been collected in Central America at any time. The poor people of Guatemala City clamored against this unpopular Mexican tax, and Barrundia attacked it fervently in many meetings of the Guatemalan D.P. Such a tax, he maintained, was leaving a bad impression among the people about the connection with Mexico.[40]

As time passed, Central Americans disabused themselves of the notion that their rich Mexican neighbor would solve their financial problems. In fact, it became increasingly evident that Mexicans expected a helping hand from the provinces of Central America. When Iturbide threatened the Guatemalan D.P. for not meeting the expenses of deputies in Mexico City, it reluctantly turned over the 9,000 pesos of tobacco revenues that it had on credit in Oaxaca, scraping the bottom of the barrel.[41] In a final, desperate measure, the Deputation voted to impose a head tax of 3 percent on its constituents. There is no evidence that this "odious" and extraordinary impost was ever collected in Central America. It does reveal, however, how serious the financial question was during the Mexican period. It had been that way for years throughout Central America.[42]

Mexico's tariff schedule of August 22, 1822, was not calculated to win friends in Central America. In fact, even advocates of annexation to Mexico lamented the contents of that particular economic document, according to Vicente Filísola. Two of its fifteen articles proved to be distasteful to Central Americans, and the Guatemalan Deputation held them in abeyance until Mexico City acted upon its protest. Article 5 imposed a 20 percent tax on cane brandy. The Guatemalans protested that in Central America the brandy contractors stood to lose; it was only fair to wait until their contracts expired before imposing the tax. The real stumbling block was Article 8, raising the sales tax to 12 percent on many products. In Mexico, the government had been collecting a tax of 8 percent; but Central America had never paid more than 4 percent because economic conditions were not so favorable, according to Spanish authorities. One member of the D.P. noted that the restoration of the unpopular tax, not to mention the "increase," would "contribute to making the Empire odious." Recommending the non-imposition of the tax at the 12 percent level, the Guatemalan D.P. urged Filísola to collect the 4 percent duty, while at the same time educating the public to the need for raising the levy. This was an exaggerated case of wishful thinking.[43] By appealing both objectionable articles of the Mexican Tariff, the Guatemalan D.P. in fact suspended its implementation in Central America. When ships pulled into Central American ports, they were charged duties according to Valle's tariff of February 1822, which were much lower than those indicated by Mexican officials.[44]

Mexico's tariff schedule was only a mild harbinger of the expensive connection with the northern power. On November 5, 1822, the Mexican government announced that a forced loan of 2,800,000 pesos was needed to meet the public expenses of 1822.[45] In mid-December, the same officials estimated that 6 million pesos would be necessary to cover the imperial expenses for fiscal 1823. In preparation for paying Central America's share of these expenses, the Mexican government ordered surveys to determine the tax load throughout the area.[46] The financial demands of the Mexican government, in other words, were impossibly high for residents of Central America. The costs of Filísola's expedition to San Salvador further discouraged whatever hopes might have existed for a continuation of Central America's union with Mexico.[47]

〰〰〰

The Mexican annexation, moreover, did not solve the disunity of Central America. Nor did it satisfy the home-rule proclivities of the various provinces. When Guatemala City joined Mexico on January 5, 1822, a virtual state of war existed between Gaínza's forces and those of Comayagua. Hostilities were imminent as San Salvador refused to recognize the legality of the annexation process to Mexico. Quezaltenango had anticipated annexation to Mexico City, hoping thus to relieve itself of control from the former capital. León had declared her allegiance to the Mexicans; and Costa Rica, capitalizing upon her out-of-the-way location, drifted along with deliberate vagueness, determined not to fall under the control of the Leonese government.

How then could the Mexican connection affect these relationships within Central America? Provincial leaders hoped that their aspirations for home rule would be realized. On the other hand, Gabino Gaínza aspired to the restoration of Guatemala's hegemony over the former provinces, a consistent policy even before January 5, 1822.[48] In Honduras his troops supported the cause of Tegucigalpa against Comayagua. He appointed the Colombian Víctor Guardia to head the government of Granada, as opposed to the rule of León. Furthermore, it was no coincidence that in mid-1822 the town of Nicoya withdrew its allegiance from León and joined the cause of Granada and Guatemala City.[49] San José, Costa Rica, sustained its republican sympathies toward Guatemala City. In San Salvador, Gaínza favored a strong, military policy in opposition to José del Valle, who advocated a conciliatory policy in the deliberations of the Junta Provisional Consultiva. That is why Mariano Aycinena urged Iturbide to dissolve the Junta and form a diputación provincial, which became operational on March 29, 1822. Gaínza hoped that Quezaltenango might be restored to the control of Guatemala City by the annexation to Mexico City; the same applied to Sololá. When Chiquimula threatened to leave the city's authority, a military force intervened.[50]

Aspiring for the centralization of power in Central America, the Guatemalan D.P. authorized Archbishop Casaus to compose a position paper on the subject. The public's opposition to this proposal, however, was strong enough to deter the writing of the Archbishop's report.[51] Nevertheless, the sentiment of the Deputation was strongly in favor of a unionist movement controlled by Guatemala City. Gaínza left no doubt about his feelings on the issue, and his colleagues on the D.P. supported him wholeheartedly. Even José Francisco Barrundia shared this vision.

The Mexican presence, however, was not conducive to the control of Guatemala City over the provinces of Central America. Mexican authorities preferred to follow a conciliatory policy throughout the region. After all, Iturbide and his associates were not unmindful of the republican tendencies among those sections of Central America that supported the hegemony of the former capital. Nor did they forget the political sympathies of León, Comayagua, and Quezaltenango when they joined the Plan of Iguala. Disapproving of Gaínza's forceful policy in Honduras, Iturbide ordered those troops to join Filísola on the Salvadoran front.[52] When León and Comayagua complained of mail interference in Guatemala City, Iturbide hastened to place them temporarily under the control of the government in Puebla, Mexico.[53] In the meantime, Mexican authorities tried to improve relations between Honduras and Guatemala.[54] The situation in Nicaragua remained tense, however. Filísola diagnosed the crisis accurately when he noted that Miguel González Saraiva, the political chief, was the major obstacle to peace. He recommended the Spaniard's transfer to another post.[55]

Gaínza's government was particularly incensed at the defiance of communities that it had always controlled. It could not countenance the independence of Quezaltenango. On one occasion, in fact, Gaínza heatedly accused Filísola of supporting agitators in that city, such was his frustration.[56] He was especially irate when Sololá assumed an independent stance and again when Chiquimula openly defied the city's orders. He immediately sent troops to quash the move. As far as Chiapas was concerned, its commitment to Mexico City was unquestioned.[57]

Despite Gaínza's efforts to maintain a semblance of strength, his influence waned noticeably as his successor approached from the north. Filísola was astute enough to recognize that men identified with an old order of things could no longer maintain harmony in an area like Central America. He had a decided advantage as the outsider. Gaínza, in turn, was subsequently used effectively in the heartland of Mexico by Agustín Iturbide.[58]

In hopes of undermining Guatemala City's ambitions, the provinciano deputies in Mexico City, especially the Honduran delegation, lobbied incessantly for home rule. On May 8, 1822, the Hondurans urged the Mexican Cortes to nullify all advances of the Guatemalan authorities in Honduras and Nicaragua, referring to the titles and recognition that had been accorded to Tegucigalpa and Granada.[59] The Committee was impressed by these arguments, judging from its recommendation on July 10, 1822. Since the provinces of the ex-Kingdom of Guatemala no longer desired control from the former capital, the Committee suggested that all of these units govern themselves until the Cortes fixed a definite territorial division. At any rate, the provinces should be dependent solely upon Mexico City.[60]

The Committee's report led to a fierce debate in the Mexican Cortes. The same old points about abusive, distant government in Guatemala City came out in the provinciano argument; and the polarization of opinion led to a postponement of the vote for months, much to the chagrin of representatives from Honduras and Nicaragua.[61] Agustín I settled the issue on November 4, 1822, when he proclaimed the three-way territorial division of the former Kingdom of Guatemala into commandancies-general. It was a temporary solution. The northern unit, centered at Ciudad Real, included Chiapas, the districts of Tabasco and Chontales, and the *alcaldías mayores* of Totonicapam and Quezaltenango. Miguel González Saraiva, the former Chief at León, was the general in charge of that military commandancy. The second unit, headed by Filísola, had Guatemala City as its capital and included Sacatepéquez, Sololá, Chimaltenango, Vera Paz, Suchitepéquez, Chiquimula, the intendancy of San Salvador, and the port of Omoa. The southernmost commandancy located at León, Nicaragua, included the intendancies of Comayagua and Nicaragua, the province of Costa Rica, and the port of Trujillo.[62]

Advocates of home rule in Central America found the addendum to the November 4 order especially offensive. Each commandancy general would be independent, with authorization to deal directly with the appropriate ministries in Mexico City. For the time being, their military leaders would serve as jefes políticos superiores within their jurisdictions. For judicial questions, the Chiapas unit would use the Audiencia of Mexico City, while the two other commandancies would resort to the Audiencia of Guatemala City, an arrangement that would prevail until there was a permanent assignment of judicial territories.

Although the November 4 order was never put into effect in Central America, it had great potential for mischief. It linked Chiapas with the Mexican heartland and thus encouraged an orientation that many of its residents favored for economic and political reasons. Quezaltenango resented Iturbide's order because it ignored its aspirations for provincial status. On the other hand, its separation from Guatemala City nursed the highland city's secessionist tendencies—the thorny Los Altos issue of the national period.[63] The middle commandancy made more sense historically. Yet it had the potential of alienating San Salvador as a subordinate of Guatemala City and Comayagua, as well, by removing the port of Omoa from its jurisdiction. The southernmost unit was offensive to Costa Rica, whose antipathy toward León was of long standing. In addition, both Comayagua and Tegucigalpa would be subordinate to León. Comayagua was especially incensed since the commandancy order deprived her of all political authority.[64] In short, Iturbide's division of the Central American area was one more stress upon the connection with Mexico City, helping to explain the willingness of former enemies in that region to seek some kind of rapprochement in 1823.

The Salvadoran question took much of Vicente Filísola's time when he assumed direction of the government in June 1822. Pursuing a conciliatory policy, he abandoned the threatening posture of his predecessor's administration. In the meantime, Salvadorans were negotiating for concessions before submitting to the Mexican Empire, not an unusual tactic for the period. Valle and others in Guatemala City had hoped for concessions from Iturbide before January 5, 1822. Costa Ricans had also demanded fantastic concessions to home rule, which prompted Father Castillo to scold his brothers for being unrealistic in their demands.[65] In Mexico City, the Salvadoran agent, Juan de Dios Mayorga, negotiated feverishly to win promises for his province and to create a favorable image of the government in San Salvador under Father José Matías Delgado. Dios Mayorga was successful to the extent that he convinced the Mexican Cortes to pursue a peaceful solution to the Salvadoran question. In August 1822, the situation changed. Dios Mayorga was implicated in the "Republican Conspiracy," not surprisingly, since his province was well known for its republican sympathies.[66]

Negotiations between Filísola and the Salvadoran government followed the pattern in Mexico City. By October 1822 Filísola recognized that only an aggressive military move would secure Salvadoran cooperation. He therefore issued an ultimatum on the twenty-sixth of that month. Father Delgado countered with a quixotic and much publicized proclamation in favor of union with the United States of America on December 5, 1822. Praising the republicanism of the northern republic, Delgado looked forward to the day that Salvadorans would enjoy the protection of "the happiest power of the world."[67] A three-man mission proceeded to the United States; but nothing came of this measure of desperation—a flourish before the battle. In February 1823, San Salvador capitulated to the victorious forces of General Filísola. It was now officially part of the Mexican Empire.

~~~

By the end of the first year, the relationship with Mexico was becoming increasingly unpalatable to most Central Americans, especially as Agustín I resorted to authoritarianism. On August 27, 1822, he imprisoned a group of politicians who as republicans were allegedly conspiring against the Empire. Many Central Americans were included, yet only Dios Mayorga was a declared republican. José del Valle was implicated in the conspiracy. The publicity given to the imprisonment of leading Central Americans put another stress on the Mexican connection. The Emperor's dissolution of Parliament on October 31, 1822, further weakened his popularity in Central America. The Junta that replaced the Cortes was nothing more than a tool of the despotic Agustín I, despite the lip service to constitutionalism. Persecutions continued; and, significantly, financial demands of large proportions coincided with the government's authoritarian ways. In early December of 1822, the government violated individual rights by permitting special military tribunals to determine who was guilty of sedition or conspiracy, thus denying citizens the protection in article 176 of the Spanish Constitution against such bodies. Furthermore, Mexico declared war on Spain, a measure that angered Guatemalan merchants who wanted to maintain contacts with Cuba. Mexican generals raised the standard of revolt; and by early March 1823, the insurrection was on the verge of success.[68] Mexican events were thus creating an opportunity for Central Americans to emancipate themselves from a connection that had proven useless to them. Considering the animosities of the provincianos toward Guatemala City, the prospects for Central American union were not promising. But it was also obvious that each little province could not survive as a nation.

The catalyst for the union of Central America was a native of Naples, Italy, who had fought in Spain for the cause of liberalism and later enhanced his military reputation in Mexico. Vicente Filísola followed political events in Mexico with close attention, notifying the leading authorities throughout Central America. On March 12, 1823, he reported that the Mexican army was about to reestablish the "National Representation" in Mexico City, preparing for the return to normalcy in Mexico. The social contract had not been broken as yet; and there was therefore no cause for taking independent action.[69] On March 13, Filísola advised the officials in Chiapas, Comayagua, and Nicaragua to continue their allegiance to the central government. Despite these reassuring words, everyone suspected that the Mexican government was breaking down. This reawakened the dreams of Guatemala's republicans. Rumor had it that José Francisco Barrundia was planning to introduce a motion for absolute independence in the Guatemalan Diputación Provincial.[70]

After reading the mail from Mexico on March 28, 1823—Good Friday—Filísola evaluated the news with discernment. Iturbide's faction had invited Central Americans to send their deputies to a Cortes that would open on March 4, 1823; and the rival generals of the Army of Liberation would have nothing to do with the constitutional farce in Mexico City. The liberating army was driving toward the capital of the nation to restore the authentic constitutional regime of Mexico; and the authorities of Puebla urged the provinces of Central America to join the movement against the tyrant Iturbide. At this point, General Filísola consulted with a group of distinguished Guatemalans, including Father Fernando Antonio Dávila. They urged him to reactivate the program in the Declaration of Independence of September 15, 1821. His military associates also counseled him to support the people's clamor for a constituent assembly: "Since these provinces have the same rights as ours, it is equally just that they gather together their representatives and that they be the ones who declare if they wish to continue united to the Provinces of Mexico." This did not mean separation as such. It merely allowed Central Americans to determine where their best interests lay, especially since it was financially impossible to send their deputies to Mexico City.[71]

Filísola's momentous decision was made public in the decree of March 29, 1823, that assured Central America of her absolute sovereignty.[72] Faced with the reports from Mexico, the general chose to rely on the document of September 15, 1821, calling for a reunion of Central American representatives to decide the area's future. Although the document presented some legal deficiencies, Filísola maintained that the people had an undeniable right "to examine and rectify their pact and especially to provide for their security in the great crises of states." It was a known fact, moreover, that Central Americans were inadequately represented in the Mexican Parliament, largely because of financial inadequacy. It was doubtful that the Iturbide Congress could improve upon the matter of representation. Therefore, it was to the best interests of all Central Americans to join together at a constituent assembly according to the terms indicated in the September 15 declaration.

Filísola's decree of March 29, 1823, was remarkable for the under-standing it showed of the historical perspective of Central America. Con-sisting of twenty-three articles, it opened with an invitation to all com-munities that had been under the authority of Guatemala City on January 5, 1822, to send representatives to the special congress. Elections for deputies, one for every 15,000 persons, would follow the procedures of the Cádiz Experiment. Once two-thirds of the representatives had assem-bled, Congress would open its sessions. At that time, the deputies would decide whether or not to change the locale of the meeting, a concession to the provinciano point of view. One of the key questions to be answered by the Assembly was the validity of the January 5, 1822, decision to join Mexico, and the area's future relationship with the northern power. In the first five items of the decree, it is noteworthy that Filísola had only included territory of proven loyalty to Guatemala City, a pragmatic and sensible approach to the problem of union in Central America. Article 6, however, politely invited the provinces of Nicaragua, Costa Rica, Comayagua, Chiapas, and Quezaltenango to join the congress in which they had a common interest. If their decision were favorable, Congress would act in behalf of the entire Central American area, once two-thirds of the delegates had appeared.

In the interim, Filísola promised to guarantee order and harmony in Central America. There would not be any governmental changes at any level, and the Spanish Constitution of 1812 and pertinent laws would remain in effect with the exception of the treasury regulations. The cus-toms schedule of February 1822 was operable, not the Tariff of the Mexi-can Empire. Central American provinces were to maintain peaceful rela-tions with Spain; and there would be no interference with the trade to Habana, providing the Spanish government had no objections. Filísola was well aware that these last points were grievances against the Iturbide connection. Article 9 declared the government's peaceful relations with all the Americas and particularly with Mexico, Nicaragua, Costa Rica, Comayagua, and Chiapas. This would apply regardless of their decision to join or reject the Central American government. Striving to avoid any note of compulsion, Filísola hoped to attract the provincianos into the fold.

Assuring the public that his government and troops would support the decisions of the Constituent Assembly, General Filísola promised to maintain the status quo in government. Once the congress convened, and if it decided against the continued relationship with Mexico, the army would expect certain guarantees and separation pay for those who chose to return to the North. The rights to offices would also be respected to those who opted to stay in Central America. Article 17 authorized the Guatemalan D.P. to appoint a special committee to gather the research materials for the Assembly and to prepare an agenda. Filísola also reminded local governments that it was their responsibility to maintain order in their jurisdictions and to raise funds for their deputies' expenses at the congress. The final article promised to send copies of the March 29 decree to all Mexican officials who might be interested.

The Guatemalan Deputation supported its Chief enthusiastically, precisely because it understood the implications of the March 29 decree for the freedom of Central America. In backing Filísola, D.P. members restated their major grievances with regard to the Mexican connection. First, they noted the violent manner by which annexation had taken place on January 5, 1822, alluding to the military pressure exerted by Mexico and the resistance that it provoked in San Salvador, Granada, Costa Rica, and elsewhere. They objected to the dissolution of the Mexican Cortes on October 31, 1822, a measure that worked against the general welfare. Thirdly, they cited the unfair Mexican Tariff that provided equal duties for areas of different potential and conditions. Next, they objected to the martial law that violated the constitutional rights of individuals by subjecting them to military tribunals; and, fifth, they opposed the division of Central America into three commandancies.[73] These were all grievances that General Vicente Filísola had been pointing out in his various reports to the Mexican government.

Thanks to a military leader born in Naples, Central Americans had finally reached the threshold of their absolute independence. It was a courageous act on the part of Central America's government, one that underscored a deep faith and enthusiasm in the potential of that area. To what extent this vision was justified will be our next concern.

9. The Nation in the Cádiz Tradition

Without rejecting useful and needed reforms, she [the National Constituent Assembly] knew how to avoid the precipice of premature and indiscreet innovations to which she might have been led by the fanaticism of exalted opinions, private interest, disguised with the veil of public interest, and all the multitude of causes that gather and combine to upset and destroy nations, under the pretext of regenerating them.

JOSÉ GERÓNIMO ZELAYA, *January 23, 1825*[1]

THE Asamblea Nacional Constituyente de las Provincias Unidas del Centro de América opened its doors on June 24, 1823, in the spartan quarters of the University of San Carlos. Only forty-one deputies, roughly half of the Assembly's final membership, attended the initial sessions of that body. Most of them were representatives of Guatemala and El Salvador, since the delegates of the faraway provinces had not arrived yet in any significant numbers. The spokesmen for major corporations in Guatemala City greeted the deputies with flowery expressions of optimism; and General Filísola welcomed them briefly, reiterating his sincere interest in calling Central Americans together for such a meeting. Filísola's ideas received more detailed attention on June 29, the first working session of the A.N.C. Describing the instability that had plagued Central America in previous years, the General reminded his listeners that Mexicans had helped to stabilize the situation. His words seemed to suggest that Central Americans should not proceed in a spirit of vindictiveness toward their northern neighbor. Mexican troops were there to make possible the reunion of Central America's delegates and to uphold the decisions of the Constituent Assembly.[2]

The Asamblea's mood, however, was not at all sympathetic to Filísola's advice. On the contrary, its leaders were determined to make a complete break with Mexico and to bring about the absolute independence of Central America. As republicans who had fought the Mexicans on the battlefield, Salvadorans joined Pedro Molina, José Francisco Barrundia, and other republican stalwarts in Guatemala City to paint the Mexican connection in darkest tones. On the same day that Filísola's speech was read to the A.N.C., a special committee reported its recommendations to the Assembly. The main authors of the document were Pedro Molina, José Matías Delgado, and Simeón Cañas. They pictured the annexation to Mexico as a conspiracy of "imperialists" and agents of Servilismo, that pro-European group throughout Central America that aspired to sell out to the Empire of Agustín Iturbide. Gabino Gaínza was the typical "European Spaniard" who had worked toward that objective. Moreover, the threat of force that was implicit in Iturbide's letter of mid-October 1821 was mainly responsible for the surrender of January 5, 1822. Only a few patriots like José del Valle had dared to question the unconstitutional proceedings in Guatemala City. Because of such violence, treachery, and blatant sycophancy, Central America was delivered in chains to Mexico. Annexation was a product of violence and tyranny, and it was therefore null and void. The Asamblea agreed with the Committee's conclusion; and on July 1, 1823, it declared the absolute independence of Central America. Later, when other delegates from the distant provinces had arrived at the capital, they too signed the declaration of absolute independence.[3]

Following the Cádiz pattern, a highly organized group of "Exaltados," or radical liberals, seized the initiative and maintained its leadership during the first three months by an appeal to patriotic emotionalism. They referred to themselves as the leaders of liberalism in Central America, while they characterized their opposition as servile agents of European imperialism. Thanks to their historical role as republicans who had opposed the annexation process, they enjoyed the initial advantage and were thus able to write their interpretation of Central American history into the official record. The polarization of politics that followed, however, did not augur well for Central America's political future.

In the three months that preceded the events described above, Vicente Filísola had labored conscientiously with the Diputación Provincial in completing the preparations for the Assembly. A special junta of men who had served in the Mexican and Spanish parliaments combined their talents to compile the necessary documentation and resources for the A.N.C. All detail received their attention. Despite limited resources, they were able to appeal successfully to many corporations and private parties for the furniture, books, and supplies that were put at the disposal of the deputies. Father Fernando Antonio Dávila was the Chairman of the Junta, a deputy who had served Chiapas in Spain. Father Antonio Larrazábal was also expected to participate but ill health limited his contribution. By the way, it was José Francisco Barrundia's proposal in the Guatemalan Diputación Provincial that had urged the use on that committee of men with parliamentary experience in either Spain or Mexico.[4] General Filísola worked closely with the preparatory junta, offering his advice on occasion and contributing money from his salary. He appeared to be sincere in furthering Central American union. Leaders from the outlying provinces, at least, felt reassured as he told them of his sincerity in protecting their interests. The more moderate and conservative elements throughout Central America actually welcomed his presence in Guatemala City. On the other hand, the republicans wanted Filísola and his troops to leave the country. Costa Rica even insisted upon the departure of the Mexican force as a condition for sending her deputies to Guatemala City.[5]

Although Filísola cooperated in preparing for the convocation of the Assembly, a serious question arose concerning his motivation in issuing the decree of March 29, 1823. Republicans like Barrundia were almost paranoid on this point, convinced that Filísola was insincere and that he would eventually resort to military force to perpetuate himself in power. He would repeat, in short, Iturbide's record, that of the opportunistic tyrant. This was a widely circulated stereotype of General Filísola. In fact, even in Mexico City republicans like Carlos Bustamante used it effectively to force the withdrawal of Filísola's troops from Guatemala.[6]

By May 1823, Barrundia and Filísola were at each other's throats in the discussions of the Guatemalan Provincial Deputation. The former chose to overlook the many occasions when the Mexican Chief had sided with him on ideological points. Filísola's comportment in the D.P. confirms the fact that he was a strong believer in the constitutionalism that he had fought for in Spain and Mexico.[7] The problem was that Filísola was an advocate of constitutional monarchy, not republicanism; and the popularity of this particular European was a clear threat to the objectives of Central American republicans. Therefore, Barrundia and followers chose to capitalize upon the anti-Mexicanism of the Guatemalan populace in order to advance their political fortunes. They deliberately minimized the political importance of the popular foreigner, Vicente Filísola. In addition, there is convincing evidence to support the view that Filísola had sponsored the March 29 decree in order to enhance his political future in Central America.[8]

Whatever the truth of the matter, the controversy was out in the open by mid-May 1823, weeks before the installation of the Asamblea. Various incidents of clashes between the Mexican soldiery and the populace of Guatemala City kept the issue raging hot at all times, especially since the presence of the military force was costly. Barrundia thus proposed to his colleagues in the D.P. that the troops should return to Mexico and be replaced with less expensive militia forces—a proposal that infuriated Filísola.[9] Although responsible Guatemalans felt that Barrundia was too brash in bearding the Mexicans, they could not deny the heavy financial burden of maintaining the troops. It was agreed finally that Filísola should withdraw his troops from Central America and that Guatemala City capitalists would finance his move back into Mexico. Bitter about these decisions, especially since the Mexican government had ordered his return, Filísola evacuated his troops from Central America in August 1823. Guatemalans like Barrundia took much pride in ridding their country of a potential military menace. Yet, their antagonism to Filísola had other historical consequences as well. Filísola's intervention in Chiapas on his way back to Mexico, for example, was a deciding factor in that province's continued association with the northern power.[10] At any rate, nationalistic historians have not done justice to General Filísola and his contribution to Central American unionism.

Disillusioned with the Mexican connection, the ex-provinces of the Kingdom of Guatemala were generally receptive to Filísola's call for union on March 29, 1823. They believed that it was worth investigating despite their misgivings about the former capital. Costa Ricans had reservations about a reunion of delegates in the midst of Mexican armed forces; and, as a matter of principle, they delayed their appearance at the ex-capital until the departure of Filísola's troops. On the other hand, Salvadorans rejoiced at the call for a constituent assembly as stipulated in the document of September 15, 1821. During the early months, it will be recalled, they flaunted their republicanism and patriotism before the A.N.C.; and, along with colleagues in Guatemala City, they wrote the republican version of Central America's history into the official records. Their innuendoes on the null-and-void adherence to the Mexican Empire reflected the same biased interpretation. Yet, the insistence upon this terminology noticeably angered many delegates from the distant provinces, especially from Nicaragua and Honduras. They resented the implication that their provinces had blundered into the Mexican connection. This alienation of provincial delegates, as we shall see, facilitated new political alignments in the Asamblea later in the year.

When news of Iturbide's impending downfall reached Costa Rica in March of 1823, the provisional government canceled its tenuous connection with the Empire on the grounds of non-fulfillment of promises. Some leaders considered the possibility of joining the Republic of Colombia. The city of San José seized the opportunity to locate the Costa Rican capital within its confines, taking advantage of an incident of rebellion and the alleged conservatism of Cartago. The denizens of the former capital were furious.[11]

Acting as if she were sovereign, Costa Rica intervened in Nicaragua's affairs in order to promote her own developmental projects along the San Juan River. This intervention took the form of treaties with the cities of Granada and León, thus inaugurating a tradition that became commonplace among the sovereign entities of Central America. Although these treaties were never implemented, they revealed the ambitious aspirations of the provinces in the post-Independence years. Mariano Montealegre negotiated the Leonese treaty for Costa Rica on September 9, 1823. It stipulated that the signatories were free and independent governments until the Asamblea in Guatemala City created the nation. Pledging themselves to peace and mutual defense in the event of an attack, the document called for intervention in each other's internal affairs if there were any attempt to unseat the constitutional government. Yet, there was one significant exception: Costa Rica would remain neutral in the struggle between León and Granada. In a context of peaceful trade relations, Costa Rica promised to supply good quality tobacco to the Leonese government; and for the time being, she would continue to use León's higher courts. One interesting article committed the Leonese to serve as guarantors for Granada's 3,000-peso debt to Costa Rica. In return, Costa Rica would use her influence to get Granadian recognition of León as their capital. With regards to the territory of Nicoya, the signatories agreed to await the Asamblea's decision, whether it should belong to the "Ticos" or the Leonese.

The Granadian Treaty of August 25, 1823, made evident Costa Rican designs on the San Juan River area via the Sarapique line. It will be recalled that Víctor Guardia, as the Jefe Político of Granada, had encouraged this contact. According to the pact, Granada's representative in Guatemala City was committed to help Costa Rica gain control of Nicoya.[12] In this manner, Costa Ricans artfully promoted their territorial and economic objectives in Central America, while at the same time asserting their equality with the former capital of León.

The Tegucigalpa-Comayagua struggle for power was not so easily settled, and it threatened to explode into civil war. It paralleled the Nicaraguan feud between León and Granada, which seriously drained the financial structure of Central America. Under no conditions were the inhabitants of Tegucigalpa disposed to give up the independent status that Gaínza had given them. Moreover, Filísola continued the pattern of directly controlling Tegucigalpa and other Honduran towns that had recognized the hegemony of Guatemala City. To their confusion and consternation, the residents of Tegucigalpa were angry to learn of Juan Lindo's appointment as Jefe Político Superior of Comayagua on October 12, 1822. An appointee of Agustín Iturbide, Lindo proposed to unite the Honduran province under his direction. Writing to the municipality of Tegucigalpa, he reminded it of his birth in that city and the years that he had spent there in his youth, as if to reassure them that his government would respect their wishes. In fact, he looked forward to a profitable and enlightened relationship with Tegucigalpa. Promising to do all that he could for the economic development of the province, he concluded with these words: "let us put into use the plough, the hoe, and the crowbar."[13]

Despite these reassurances, the thought of returning to a dependency upon Comayagua horrified the city fathers of Tegucigalpa. They assumed, of course, that Iturbide had authorized Lindo to reunite the Province of Honduras. Although prepared to remonstrate vigorously to the authorities in Mexico City, the aldermen first decided to find out if Lindo was acting on his own initiative. They had a feeling that this might be the case. They asked General Filísola if the annexation of Tegucigalpa to its former capital was authentic; and the chief replied that it was not. Although overjoyed at this news, the municipal authorities of Tegucigalpa complained to Filísola that Lindo's letters to other towns in its jurisdiction were not conducive to stability. The situation worsened in the months that followed.[14] By the time that the March 29 call for a convention reached Honduras, the two rival cities were fast losing patience with each other.

The situation changed with the arrival of Filísola's call for a constituent assembly. In hopes of capitalizing on this opportunity to unite the Province of Honduras, Chief Lindo asked Tegucigalpa what it planned to do about the decree of March 29, 1823. The reply was consistent: Honduras' division into two provinces was harmful and unfortunate; and she should be united, an objective that would benefit both Comayagua and Tegucigalpa. Since the latter had always been on record in favor of a convention in Guatemala City, this fact would strengthen Honduras' hand in the constituent assembly. To avoid the domination of Guatemala City in the national government—a point that Lindo had been stressing in his correspondence—Tegucigalpa suggested the tactic of insisting upon a new meeting place for the A.N.C. There the delegates from a united Honduras would defend the rights of "both provinces" and work for "a common happiness." The city fathers also felt that José del Valle should occupy a top national post where he could advance the interests of Honduras.[15] A steadfast supporter of the A.N.C., the city government of Tegucigalpa politely refused León's invitation to a convention that would have nothing to do with Filísola's call of March 29. The Leonese counter-movement, by the way, had encouraged the treaty negotiations between Costa Rica and León, referred to above.[16]

In the Asamblea Nacional Constituyente, Tegucigalpa's deputies tenaciously maintained their independence from Comayagua.[17] In fact, Tegucigalpa refused to accept any orders from the federal government that came via Comayagua.[18] Dionisio Herrera, Valle's cousin and the Mayor of Tegucigalpa, also carried the title of Jefe Político. Moreover, when the A.N.C. awarded Tegucigalpa the right to produce coins in competition with the mint in Comayagua, the officials of the latter city deposed Jefe Político Lindo for trying to implement the order. The rivalry of the two Honduran cities, in other words, was another explosive legacy inherited by the national government.

Mexican influence was still vital in the highland areas of Chiapas and Quezaltenango. Working under Lucas Alamán, the Foreign Minister of Mexico, General Filísola had an opportunity to intervene in the politics of Chiapas, thus assuring its continued commitment to Mexico. As noted earlier, Filísola's quarrel with the Guatemalan "Exaltados" had much to do with this intervention. It colored his reports to Alamán, making the minister receptive to the notion of interference. Chiapas was henceforth a diplomatic issue; and she remained Mexican. The district of Soconusco, however, seceded from Chiapas and opted to join the A.N.C. in Guatemala City, one more illustration of the exaggerated regionalism of the colonial period.

The major threat of the times, however, was that the entire highlands, especially the region of Los Altos, might secede to Mexico in exchange for provincial status. To counter this possibility, the Asamblea in Guatemala City held out the promise that a new state might be formed if the highlands could prove that they had the requisite elements. The districts included Quezaltenango, Suchitepéquez, Sololá, and Totonicapam; and the statistical presentation of the authorities in question was impressive. Not counting Soconusco, which was expected to join Los Altos, there were 129 villages (pueblos) with a population of 210,000. The total taxes paid by the four districts (partidos) amounted to nearly 124,000 pesos annually. Los Altos could easily meet its quota of federal expenses. On paper, the highlands area of Guatemala seemed to have a stronger economic and financial base than most states of the union, even if allowance is made for some padding of statistics. The drawback, however, was that the population was overwhelmingly Indian, and the inability to communicate with them in Spanish constituted a serious weakness in the equation.[19]

The provincial delegates in the Asamblea had a vested interest in the establishment of Los Altos, since such a unit would weaken the power of the former capital. It would draw away elements that normally would have gone to Guatemala City. Moreover, the Quezaltecos' animosity toward Guatemala City was no secret. The political importance of the highland area in the balancing of power in Central America helps to explain the fierce determination of both liberal and conservative politicians in Guatemala to delay the statehood of Los Altos until 1836.

The majority of delegates from Honduras and Nicaragua affixed their signatures to the Declaration of Independence on October 1, 1823. The decree of that date also explained that letters from Costa Rica favored the move, even though their representatives had not yet arrived in Guatemala City.[20] As the provincianos gained in numbers, it was conceded that they had a right to question decrees that had been passed before their arrival in Guatemala City. Determined to minimize the political power of the Guatemalans and the Salvadorans in the Asamblea, the provincianos formed a new coalition which insisted upon a renovation of the executive branch.[21] This was on October 4, 1823. Two days later, a Honduran deputy proposed moving the nation's capital to another "point in the provinces."[22] Fearful that the new coalition might undermine their position, the Salvadorans arose to offer their "heroic province" as the site for the new capital of the nation. It was evident that the provincianos were venting their suspicions of the former capital.[23]

The impotence of the Central American government was the major factor in bringing about a change in the executive power. Filísola's departure from Guatemala City in August 1823 created a serious vacuum in the defense structure of the nation. Unable to pay the few military men at its disposal, the Asamblea was helpless in facing two disturbances that occurred in September and October of 1823. The first incident revolved around the uprising of a military opportunist; and the second was caused by the presence of the Salvadoran expeditionary force that occupied the capital in order to sustain the Asamblea's power. The net political result was to further the clamor for a new executive power in the government. The provincianos joined with the moderates of Guatemala to replace the first executive triumvirate, all appointees of the "Exaltados," which had dominated the Asamblea since mid-year.[24]

Since the Cádiz Experiment was Central America's major source of parliamentary experience, its precedents were visible everywhere as the Asamblea Nacional Constituyente began its labors. As noted earlier, the junta that prepared the ground for the Asamblea had been trained in that tradition and thus followed that example. The Asamblea did likewise. Faced with the problem of establishing an executive branch of the government, the Assembly chose to form a triumvirate, the Supremo Poder Ejecutivo. Its relationship to the congress was identical to that of the Spanish Regency that governed after September 24, 1810. In fact, Central Americans used the Spanish Reglamento of 1811 as the pattern for the S.P.E.'s ordinance, with only minor changes in terminology to meet the republican context.[25] Similarly, the S.P.E. had limited power and was essentially a tool of the Assembly, where the basic decisions on policy and appointments were made. The three-way division of power was also distorted in favor of the Assembly; and this permitted the leaders of that body in the early months—the "Exaltados" of San Salvador and Guatemala City—to put their friends in office. They exploited their position to remove from governmental posts anyone whom they suspected was not a true "patriot" and a republican. This abusive practice goes far to explain much of the instability of the government after the departure of General Filísola.[26] The "Imperialists" and "Serviles" were thus excluded from political office during the early months of the Assembly's existence. For example, Filísola himself had no chance for an appointment to the executive power, because the "Exaltados," his enemies, had passed a bill that required a seven-year-residence for any man chosen to serve in that branch.[27] As a result, the first S.P.E. consisted of two Salvadorans, Manuel Arce and Juan Vicente Villacorta, and Pedro Molina from Guatemala City. Since Arce was in the United States on a diplomatic mission, Antonio Rivera Cabezas from Guatemala, a good "Exaltado," served in his stead.

As the delegates from the distant provinces reached the capital, they joined with the political moderates of Guatemala to demand a new executive triumvirate. The "Exaltados" were beside themselves, calling all their opponents "Serviles" and "Nobles"—the language of polarization. Many *moderates* like José Francisco Córdoba were practical realists who felt that their ex-comrades—Barrundia, Molina, and others were too idealistic and impractical. Many had supported the annexation to Mexico, including Mariano Aycinena and other members of the "families." Although not liberals by "Exaltado" standards, they were nonetheless fervent believers in constitutionalism, as we have seen in earlier chapters. At any rate, the new political coalition of provincianos and moderates changed the political rules and provided more give-and-take in politics. The new coalition, of course, manipulated the government for its benefit. Since it wanted Tomás O'Horan to serve on the S.P.E., it changed the rules accordingly, permitting any American to serve on the executive after five years' residence in the area. A native of Yucatán, O'Horan was a respected lawyer who had served as Jefe Político Superior in Guatemala City. The new regulation made his election to the executive possible. It should be noted that the "Exaltados" referred to O'Horan as a tool of the "Nobles," conveniently overlooking the fact that the first S.P.E. had chosen him for the head position in Guatemala City. Manuel Arce, from El Salvador, remained on the new executive power; and the third appointee was José Cecilio del Valle, a Honduran who by no stretch of the imagination could be called an ally of the "families." Valle took over his office in February 1824, when he returned from Mexico City. Until then, José Santiago Milla filled in for him. Also maligned as a reactionary, the Honduran substitute had likewise received an appointment from the first executive power. In short, the second executive body of Central America reflected the coalition of provincial delegates and the moderates in the Assembly. If the Barrundias and Molinas aspired to play leading roles in the national body, they had to adjust their sights to the new reality. A strong current of federalism was evident in Guatemala City in December 1823. No one could afford to ignore it.[28]

Once Valle joined his colleagues on the second S.P.E., he moved to strengthen the executive branch of government. The A.N.C. supported his call for reforms. On March 19, 1824, O'Horan outlined the powers that the S.P.E. should possess. Above all, it had to be free to make all appointments for civil, military, and judicial posts with the authority to depose all members on its own. It should also be able to deploy the nation's military forces whenever necessary. In accepting these conditions, the Asamblea Nacional Constituyente made it possible to bring some balance to government. This responsible decision enhanced respect for the national assembly and gave it an image of strength that was sorely needed in Central America. It was a distinct improvement over the Cádiz model.[29]

The diputaciones provinciales and jefes políticos of old remained in operation throughout the nineteen months of the A.N.C.'s tenure. Governments followed the precedents of Spanish law, those that concorded with the new republican regime. Central Americans, however, abandoned the titles and rankings of the monarchical system. They now called the town governments *municipalidades*; but their attributes remained the same with only a few changes in terminology. One qualification was that there would be an abbreviated municipal structure in localities with less than 1,000 population.[30] Learning from the weakness of the Mexican period, the Assembly insisted that all mayors (*alcaldes primeros*) had to know Spanish. This avoided the paralysis of government that had characterized the Indian communities during Mexico's rule.[31] On the motion of Father Fernando Antonio Dávila, the A.N.C. agreed to separate political and military commands except at strategic points, where it was not feasible. Elsewhere, no political chief could command troops; the hope was to avoid the growth of a military dictatorship.[32] As the political chief of Guatemala City before joining the second S.P.E., Tomás O'Horan revived the elaborate Spanish ritual of posting and announcing orders from the government—a practice that suspicious colonials had formerly insisted upon in order to protect the Spanish constitutional order.[33]

The A.N.C. likewise followed the Cádiz example in providing for the defense of the nation. It established a special Junta de Guerra that adopted the ordinances framed in Spain. Hoping to satisfy the yearning for regionalism, the Assembly allowed every province to have a Commandant General answerable to the executive. His attributes were those authorized in the Spanish ordinances for a captain general. The military *fuero* was continued.[34] Moreover, the militias that Barrundia had recommended in the last months of Filísola's command also followed the regulations drawn up on the Peninsula. Despite Barrundia's optimism for the citizen-soldier, not many young men enlisted in the militia forces during the early months of nationhood.[35]

In judicial matters, the Central American Republic adhered to Spanish precedents, again with slight changes in terminology. The Audiencias of the colonial centuries became *cortes territoriales* at Cádiz; and they were essentially the same in the independent regime. The Alta Corte de Justicia was the equivalent of the Suprema de Justicia in Spain. Moreover, the request made by Dr. Mariano Gálvez to study the resources of the Spanish Supreme Court merely underscored the reliance and indebtedness to the peninsular experience.[36] The quarterly visits to jails, both civil and religious, became part of the national system in Central America; the same applied to district judges (jueces de letras). The freedom of the press and the machinery to protect the citizen against libel was identical to the Spanish and Mexican precursors. All of the cherished freedoms of speech, writing, and assembly became part and parcel of the new nation's arsenal in behalf of the individual's rights.[37]

Finally, the A.N.C. adapted the electoral procedures of Spanish constitutionalism to the new republican system. It was only in the Federal Constitution of 1824 and in the contemporaneous state constitutions that some innovations were attempted to correct faults that had been observed in the Cádiz Experiment. A more democratically selected electoral commission became standard in the state charters. The three electoral stages changed their terminology from *parroquias* to *juntas populares*, from *partidos* to *distritos*, and from *provincias* to *departamentos*. The essence of the electoral system, however, was identical; it was still indirect.[38] This was no coincidence. A.N.C. deputies, as well as their counterparts in the constituent assemblies of the states, were constantly citing Jeremy Bentham's dictum that governments should avoid drastic reforms and should take into account the experience of their people. Since the Spanish constitutional experience was traditional by now, and because its essence was basically liberal, it served as the guide for the congressmen of Central America. The close modeling of the Central American Republic upon the Cádiz blueprint was annoying at times to the more innovative spirits in the A.N.C.; but the majority persisted. It is interesting to note that even the "Exaltados" referred to Spanish precedents in order to convince their colleagues on certain reforms, as if it added a note of respectability to the measure. There was a parallel at Cádiz, when Argüelles and his companions sought historical precedents in the constitutional history of some kingdom of Spain, to avoid the derogatory suggestion that they were advocating a frenchified reform.[39]

This is not to say that the members of the A.N.C. ignored other constitutional systems. On the contrary, the Constitutional Committee frequently cited examples from charters of the United States, Venezuela, and Colombia, as well as the writings of Condorcet, Montesquieu, Sieyès, and others. The point is that the founding fathers of Central America were familiar with all of the constitutional writings of the Enlightenment and early nineteenth century. Nor did they ignore the example of the Greeks and the Romans. Just as their Spanish brethren before them, Central American legislators drew from many authorities, especially those whose reforms were best suited to the conditions that prevailed in their nation. Valle captured this point with these words:

> To govern is not to copy measures that are drawn up in other countries with different climate, morality, character, and customs; it is not to command what appeals to the whim or the interest of the moment. It is to master the most difficult science among those that man's talent has devised; it is to know how to apply its principles with exactitude; it is to apply them to the totality of the circumstances that make up the condition of the nation that is being governed.[40]

The Asamblea Nacional Constituyente proclaimed a "new social order" in Central America on December 17, 1823, "the most appropriate to the best lights [*luces*] of the century." The reference was to the document entitled *Bases de la Constitución Federal*.[41] It determined the guidelines for the future constitution of the Republic. Advocating the sovereignty of the people and the three-way division of power, the *Bases* guaranteed the citizen's rights to the "eternal principles of liberty, equality, security, and property." The form of government was *republicana representativa federal*. The article on religion followed the Cádiz version almost to the letter. However, the *Bases* declared the Judiciary to be elective, a notable departure from the Spanish precedent. No government in Central America could deprive the citizen of the freedom of thought, of the press, and of writing; and the right of petition was sacrosanct. There would be no entails, no torture, no constraints, no confiscation of goods, no beatings or cruel penalties, no exclusive privileges for commercial companies or corporations, and no restrictions upon economic enterprise. Central America would be a free and open society.

A remarkable reform of the Constitution of 1824 was the type of Senate called for at the national and state levels, an innovation that was peculiar to Central America. Moderates complained that the Senate violated the doctrine of the three-way division of power because it shared all three sources of power. José Francisco Barrundia and Dr. Mariano Gálvez argued that by doing so the Senate would assure stability in government. In a sense it would act as a conservative or restraining force (*cuerpo conservador*), but the opposition did not believe that this type of Senate would achieve that end.[42]

The Senate in the Central American constitution can be explained in the context of the Cádiz Experiment and the manner in which it was implemented in Central America. To begin with, the Senate at the national level consisted of two representatives from each state. At the state level, the Upper House (*Cuerpo Representativo*) had one delegate from each department, usually seven in number.

Both bodies served as consultative units for their respective executives. They functioned much like the Consejo de Estado with the Spanish King, and the Diputación Provincial with the Jefe Político Superior. Moreover, in Central America the historical trend was for these advisory units to share executive power, thanks to the nature of such leaders as Carlos Urrutia, Gabino Gaínza, Vicente Filísola, as well as the chiefs O'Horan and Cabeza de Vaca in the post-independence period. In short, it was not a question of experimentation. The pattern had a historical basis, and it only failed when an uncooperative chief like José de Bustamante refused to work with the Cádiz system.

The Senate, moreover, offered triple lists for all appointments to the government: military, civil, and religious. Again, this resembled the prerogative of the Consejo de Estado; only now the Senate, rather than the Cortes, had the right to submit the triple lists for appointments. The Senate's diplomatic function paralleled the activities of the Council of State with the significant difference that its role was not exclusively consultative although the basic responsibility was identical.

The most crucial prerogative of the Senate and the Upper House was the power to sanction the law drawn up by the Legislature. This permitted them to share an executive function of government. If congress at the state or national levels chose to assert the principle of proportional representation, they could easily pass a law that was objectionable to a given state. The Senate's power to veto a bill was therefore a major guarantee for the less-populated states. A veto could be overridden only by a two-thirds vote; and some states—Costa Rica, in particular—insisted that on financial issues a three-fourths vote was necessary to override. The Senate was required to sanction or veto a law within ten days. If the law passed, the Senate would then forward it to the executive for its implementation.[43]

There were obvious deviations from the original Cádiz model, but the parallels were nevertheless striking. In a sense, Barrundia and Gálvez were right that the Upper House could exercise a moderating influence.

By sharing executive power, the Central Americans were merely continuing a practice that had been standard since 1820 and one that worked well. The upper houses in the states were patterned after the diputaciones provinciales of the Cádiz Experiment; and the interest of the state government in economic development accounts for its support of this institution. It is hardly a coincidence that most of the states had seven units, like the seven partidos of the old diputaciones provinciales. Moreover, the overwhelming presence of provincial delegates in the Asamblea—who became the new majority coalition by October—dictated the emphasis upon federalism in the *Bases*. The Constitution of 1824, furthermore, had to be framed within these federalistic limits. This was a historical reality that could not be ignored by politicians.

The moderates in Guatemala City were centralists at heart, but they understood perfectly the reality we have just described. Nevertheless, they questioned and challenged every federalist plank that was introduced by the Constitutional Committee, led by the "Exaltados" Barrundia and Gálvez. Yet, they had no illusions that the provincianos would agree to a centralist regime. They therefore chose to work within the federalist structure, hoping to strengthen executive power and the central government wherever possible. By the same token, we can appreciate how the "Exaltados," posing as federalists, might regain their leadership in the Asamblea after the downfall of the first executive triumvirate.[44]

The influence of the Cádiz tradition was evident in still other aspects of the program that was patiently elaborated upon by members of the Constitutional Assembly. To prepare for the nation's ambitious objectives in economic development, it was imperative to have accurate statistics— "the soul of a government," they were called in the decree of November 15, 1823. A government needed to know its people, its resources, and the potential of the nation. Then it could levy taxes fairly, enlist the civic forces, and "measure the progress or decline of agriculture, industry, and commerce which are the channels of national wealth." Outlining in detail how these surveys were to be taken, the Asamblea urged political chiefs to make their compilations available to the national government within fifteen days. In another article of the same decree, the legislators reminded the jefes políticos of Chapter 13 in the Cádiz Ordinances of June 23, 1813—namely, they were responsible for updating their statistics and population figures in January of each year.[45]

Their experience under the Spanish and Mexican constitutional governments likewise influenced the fiscal program adopted by the A.N.C. The problem was critical, and the Assembly performed in a commendable and pragmatic manner. The dislocation of the area's financial structure since the days before independence was a lingering deterrent. The government needed experienced personnel. The public refused to pay old Spanish taxes that were associated with the concepts of despotism and tyranny. And, as José del Valle noted perceptively, the governments of Central America had increased their expenditures because of new expectations and tastes of the citizenry. There was also a proliferation of the bureaucracy in each of the provinces. This was costly. It was a stubborn problem that inevitably entangled itself in the relations between the federal and state governments—the subject of our last chapter.

Aware of the mistakes made by Spanish and Mexican constitutionalists, the A.N.C. recognized that old taxes should not be removed until there were acceptable substitutes. It preferred to follow the English example on these matters rather than the more innovative approach of the French. First, the A.N.C. began by recognizing the colonial debt. Then it announced the continuation of old Spanish taxes but in modified form, on a temporary basis only. Although the alcabala or sales tax was contrary "to the interests of national industry," it was still expedient to maintain it for the time being at the 4 percent level. However, basic foodstuffs would not be subject to that tax, and the A.N.C. dispensed with the odious alcabala de viento that had enraged the people of Guatemala City in Filísola's day. By lowering the tax and by providing some exemptions, the A.N.C. hoped to make it palatable to the citizens of the new nation for the short run.[46]

The same approach applied to the tobacco tax that Americans had fought so tenaciously at Cádiz. It would be kept on until another tax source could replace it. The concessions followed: tobacco growers did not have to pay the alcabala, and the government promised to stimulate the exportation of tobacco overseas.[47] Later, the A.N.C. likewise continued the gunpowder tax of the Spanish period. All three tax sources were to cover the Republic's general expenses; and the internal tobacco tax of each state would help to meet its quota for the expenses of the national government. The revenue from tobacco exports overseas, however, belonged exclusively to the Republic. In all these tax measures, the A.N.C. streamlined the administrative apparatus and cut down many posts in the process.

These were not enough taxes to meet the greater expenditures of a modern state with ambitious developmental plans, and the A.N.C. knew this. On December 1, 1823, therefore, the government announced its income tax program, based upon the ability-to-pay concept. The tax applied to all men, except for the members of certain religious orders that did social work. The new statistics, of course, would provide the requisite information to determine everyone's assessment. At that point, treasury officials would cooperate with the municipalities in collecting the revenues.[48] By January 12, 1824, the A.N.C. had finished the implementing ordinance. It was a reasonable tax schedule that ranged from 4 reales a year for servants and day workers, ages 18 to 50, to an annual tax of 20 pesos for owners of large haciendas and wholesale houses. Large cattlemen paid a tax of 15 pesos, the medium, 7½, and the small, 2. Medium-sized hacendados were assigned 5 pesos, and small ones, 1. Shopkeepers paid 10 pesos; printers, 8; owners of brandy stalls, 5; chicha stalls, 3; and lawyers, doctors, and surgeons, 5 pesos per year.[49]

It was assumed that citizens would be able to pay their income tax when the government's ambitious development program got underway. In hopes of creating wealth, the S.P.E. under José del Valle and Tomás O'Horan ordered the political chiefs to submit reports on the developmental projects for their respective provinces.[50] Valle and his colleagues were using the diputaciones provinciales in the manner intended by the Cádiz system. A constant concern of the executive branch was the construction and maintenance of an adequate infrastructure; and political chiefs received many reminders to do their utmost in opening up new communications or improving the existing facilities, which were so important for the encouragement of economic enterprise.[51] They were to notify their constituents that the S.P.E. desired to know their wishes and grievances. In the immediate vicinity of Guatemala City, Valle and O'Horan held weekly meetings with the jefe político and other officials who advised the executive on economic matters.[52] The government's interest in opening up the system to all knowledgeable people became evident in the decree of June 16, 1825. It invited all citizens to present their ideas at the National Palace in Guatemala City every Wednesday and Saturday from noon onward. The doors of the government would remain open to consider all worthy projects.[53]

Although the evidence is fragmentary, it suggests that the federal government tried its best to implement many of the developmental projects that were proposed by political chiefs and private parties. New ports were authorized in various parts of Central America, and special incentives were given to others such as Iztapa on the coast near Escuintla and the Salvadoran sites of Libertad and Conchagua.[54] As population figures came in, new municipalities were founded. The government authorized special fairs in Masaya, Nicaragua, and in Comayagua, Honduras.[55] To encourage the "national iron" industry, it freed it of all duties.[56] Tegucigalpa received permission to have a die for coining money; and Mariano Gálvez further proposed the establishment there of a mint to produce certain coins—measures that provoked angry and violent responses from the rival city of Comayagua.[57] José del Valle promoted his favorite project of bringing in a Mexican mining expert to fill the Chair in Mineralogy. It materialized when Francisco Echeverría of Guanajuato, Mexico, accepted the offer.[58] Foreigners were encouraged to participate in all manner of activities. The English company headed by William M. Simonds, for example, received a mining concession.[59]

In fact, the protection and encouragement of foreign entrepreneurs was a basic tenet of Central America's developmental program, which recognized the need for the outsider's capital and "know-how." The decree of January 22, 1824, invited foreigners to undertake colonization programs for the nation. Early in the A.N.C. deliberations, Barrundia and Gálvez presented a resolution that in praise of "liberty, of the rights of man and of the general prosperity," the United Provinces of Central America should extend its protection to all foreigners who were fleeing from persecution. Their colleagues agreed; and an appropriate committee then consulted the law of asylum that had been passed by the Spanish Cortes.[60] The appreciation for the foreigner's role in the economy was so great that even staunch Catholics in the A.N.C. were willing to make religious concessions to him: the right to practice his religion in his own house and the erection of special cemeteries for non-Catholics. There was opposition to these measures, of course; but it is interesting to note that it was Father Dávila who led the move in the A.N.C. justifying the concessions on developmental grounds.[61]

Since the latter part of the eighteenth century, Central American leaders had planned to encourage the colonization of empty lands in the north and east, attempts that did not succeed for one reason or another. The Consulado of Guatemala revived the projects from 1802 to 1819 without much success, but the interest was still there. And the S.P.E. tried to stimulate it again although the Consulado was no longer willing to do it at its own expense. Nevertheless, a group of merchants involved themselves in a project to move some eight families of Caribs to the sites of the Castillo de San Felipe and Ysabal, thus improving the defense of Guatemala's northern coast and reopening the commercial route to the

Gulf of Dulce. The S.P.E. hoped that this venture would stimulate the spread of agriculture into the area of Chiquimula. The entrepreneurs were especially determined to grow tobacco in those lands.[62] The above-mentioned Colonization Law of January 22, 1824, promised land to all foreigners who came to live in "the provinces of Costa Rica, Nicaragua, Honduras, San Salvador, Guatemala, and Quezaltenango," providing they developed their grants within a term of eight years. Under Valle's direction, the S.P.E. popularized the northern coast of Guatemala as a colonizing site. It was determined to open up that frontier by construct-ing the necessary roads and infrastructure.[63] Capital, of course, was the basic ingredient for all the projects sponsored by the S.P.E. Since it was in short supply, Valle and his colleagues welcomed many ventures with a minimum of financing, hoping that the bountiful resources of Central America would sustain the enterprise and produce further capital. In fact, the S.P.E. seemed to count on this.

The achievement of absolute independence in 1823 coincided hap-pily with the revival of Central America's economy, which finally pulled out of a deep depression that had plagued the area since the 1790s. Just how much the activities described in the previous section may have stimu-lated this revival it is difficult to say in the absence of adequate documen-tation. Certainly, the government's promotional policies did not deter the return of prosperity; and it is conceivable that it was the governmental stability of the Guatemalan and Costa Rican areas that encouraged the economic growth. In 1825, a special committee studied Central Ameri-ca's economic production in the five years before and after September 15, 1821. Despite the obvious tendency to enhance the image of a liberal government in one of the richest sections of America, the report con-cluded that there had been a doubling of production in the national years. The price of indigo increased and its production doubled; the most strik-ing rise was in cochineal, a product that had been stimulated by govern-ments since the Cádiz era. From 25 bales in 1821, it had jumped to 500 in 1825; and the Committee predicted that it would double in the next year.[64] Other products that appeared to hold promise were: vanilla, tor-toise shells, balsam, cacao, tobacco, sugar, woods, and cotton. The pros-pects for the cattle industry were good for Nicaragua and Honduras; and entrepreneurs were attracted by the mining potential of Honduras and Costa Rica. As a member of the S.P.E. and as the editor of periodicals in

Guatemala City, José del Valle exuded confidence and optimism in Central America's economic future.[65] He wrote a circular letter to the governors of Central America on September 7, 1825, reminding them of the area's fertile soil and untapped wealth. He urged them to invite men with capital and know-how to discover the region's riches—he thought especially Englishmen, whose speculative nature was so well developed. Valle proposed inviting a group of English specialists to survey the area; and he expected the state governments to assist the expedition's work in every way.[66] George Thompson conducted such a survey in those years, but it is not clear whether it was by coincidence or by invitation. At any rate, there is no doubt that English investors were sanguine about Central America's resources.

The most ambitious developmental project entertained by the legislators of the Central American Republic was the construction of an interoceanic canal through Nicaragua. The newspaper *El Liberal* of Guatemala City ranked the canal enterprise second in importance only to the independence movement itself.[67] Several foreign companies presented offers to the government, but no final decision was forthcoming until June 16, 1825. The decree of that date envisioned a canal system that was the exclusive responsibility of the nation. Private enterprise would only construct and fund the project. It would enjoy such incentives as the permission to exploit the nearby wood resources, the free introduction of machinery and instruments, and attractive profit margins on the construction of the canal as well as on the money invested. No company was mentioned, but there was a preference for an English one. When completed, the total cost of the canal would be assigned to the public debt. The federal government was responsible for setting and regulating the duties on the canal traffic. All friendly and neutral nations could use the passageway on the basis of equality; and the nation would provide the warships for the defense of the canal. In the event the project did not materialize, the Republic would not be responsible for any indemnization whatsoever.[68] The problem, of course, was to find investors who would be satisfied with those conditions, so modern and nationalistic in conception. The Central American public was optimistic about the canal. One newspaper editor predicted annual revenues from the canal at 2 to 3 million pesos, or twice the total of federal expenditures. In some years, it might even bring in more than 9 million pesos. The opening of the interoceanic route, moreover, would increase general economic activity throughout Central America, thus enhancing the average citizen's ability to pay his annual taxes.[69] Who is to say what might have been the future of Central America if such dreams had materialized.

To supplement its regular revenues, the Asamblea Nacional Constituyente decided to negotiate a loan with the House of Barclay and Herring in London. Mariano Aycinena's influence apparently determined the choice of this particular firm among those who competed for the loan. The A.N.C. authorized a loan of 8 million pesos, although the final figure was closer to 7 million, or 1,421,000 pounds sterling. These monies were for the defense of the nation and to take up the slack in the nation's financial structure until the tax system became operable. In announcing the foreign loan to the states, the federal government asked them to submit developmental projects that might be funded from the loan money.[70] The negotiation of the English loan was a significant achievement for the Republic because it promised to put Central America's financial affairs in order for the first time since the winning of independence. With the economy on the upswing and the canal project promising to open up lands that previously had been marginal because of the distance to markets, it is not difficult to understand José del Valle's optimism in the nation's future. If English Americans had succeeded in the North, Spanish Americans certainly could duplicate that record. They all shared the same bountiful New World, one with an unlimited potential for economic, political, and social progress. This was a blind faith that captured the minds of many Americans; it was the basis for what Professor Arthur P. Whitaker has called "The Western Hemisphere Idea." Valle and his liberal colleagues in Guatemala City had this faith and this vision. They had no way of knowing that the future would not be so kind to them.

Education was a prime ingredient in the grandiose schemes for economic development. The country needed learned men to lead it forward, Valle remarked on one occasion. It did not need the manipulators of the old Spanish order.[71] The creation of a constructive public opinion was a basic requirement for instilling pride in the citizen's community, his district and department, and his state and nation. Governmental leaders thus officially encouraged *tertulias patrióticas*, whose contribution to the modernization of Central American society was significant. These organizations had official sanction and operated in accordance with the regulations of the government.[72] In addition, the government also encouraged the establishment of economic societies in every province of Central America, just as Gaspar de Jovellanos had suggested decades earlier. Their work was vital to the improvement of the economy.[73] Newspapers likewise stimulated reforms with encouraging editorials and reports: the official *Gazeta de Guatemala* and the private organs *La Tribuna* (José Francisco Barrundia), *Redactor General* (José del Valle), *El Indicador* (moderates), and *El Liberal* ("Exaltados"). As their predecessors of the pre-Independence period, they kept the public informed of the "useful knowledge" that was circulating throughout the world. The government encouraged the dissemination of information by allowing these papers a franking privilege, all as part of the movement to encourage the economic development of the nation.[74]

As for the regular educational program, the leaders of national Central America followed the same trends of the Cádiz period. Valle and others were still hopeful of establishing the Lancasterian system by bringing in instructors from either the United States or Mexico. It was not until the 1830s, however, that the program was finally introduced. In the meantime, the Guatemalans turned to the system worked out by Father Matías de Córdoba, a graduate of the University of San Carlos who worked with the Indians of Chiapas. It apparently achieved the same objectives as the Lancasterian program; students taught each other at a minimum of expense. Father Córdoba sent his manuscripts to Guatemala City, where they were published and circulated throughout Central America.[75] As a member of the S.P.E., Valle urged the jefes políticos to promote "useful teachings" in their communities. Since money was scarce, they should appeal to learned citizens to volunteer their services for classes in the exact sciences, as well as those in the natural, economic, political, and moral fields. The chiefs could help these volunteers by providing classroom space; and their names would be kept on an official record for future honors or posts that might become available.[76] Many public spirited men offered such classes. A case in point was the philosophy class held in San José, Costa Rica, by Rafael Osejo.[77]

As a preliminary to educational reforms, the S.P.E. ordered a survey taken of all the schools in Central America: how many students did they have, what methods were being used, what library resources were available, the salaries of teachers and administrators, their income, and so on. While these compilations were in progress, the S.P.E. asked for the translation into Spanish of projects in public education that had been presented to the French government by the Marquis de Condorcet and colleagues. Although the S.P.E. recognized that the programs might not be suitable to Central America, it felt that at least the general principles employed might prove useful in framing a workable educational program for the area.[78] The arrival of the French chemist Dr. Jean Baptiste

Fauconnier from the University of Paris strengthened the offerings of the University of San Carlos. He became the first naturalized citizen of Central America; and the politicians and educators of Central America rejoiced at having such a distinguished scientist in their midst.[79]

The S.P.E. under Valle's leadership encouraged many projects to advance the goals of education in Central America. On March 9, 1824, it offered a prize for the best *catecismo*, a booklet in question-and-answer form that explained the merits of Central America's republican system. On the following day, the government authorized a special committee to translate a new method of studying Latin that had been published for French schools. On April 3, 1824, classes began in the fields of botany and agriculture. Later in the same month, the S.P.E. asked the diplomats who were about to leave for their posts in North and South America to champion a scientific expedition to survey the resources of the New World. Hopefully, all the American Republics would encourage such a study, inviting key scientists to participate. The search would be useful and productive, yielding significant documents on the flora and fauna of the Americas, detailed maps and sketches, etc. On May 13, 1824, military cadets began their classes in mathematics and geography. In November, the S.P.E. was supporting the study of a new method of teaching history; and plans for a military college were nearing completion.[80]

The Federal Congress of 1825 followed Valle's aggressive lead in educational matters, focussing on an educational system that had commanded the attention of the Spanish Cortes during the second constitutional period. It was one drawn up by the French educator J. L. Voidet de Beaufort; and Father Dávila, while he was in Spain, may have been responsible for inviting Beaufort to Central America. Beaufort's plans called for the establishment of a National School of Sciences, Arts, and Skills where the emphasis would be on vocational education for artisans, mechanics, industrial workers, and agricultural specialists. Since it complemented their developmental programs, the system appealed to both Spaniards and Central Americans. The Federal Congress published Beaufort's treatise, which also envisioned the establishment of agricultural colonies throughout Central America. The discussion of this program was still going on in 1826 when civil war broke out. Thus, it never materialized. In its objectives, however, the Beaufort plan seemed to be the prototype for Guatemala's Society of Agriculture, which was founded in 1833, during the administration of Governor Pedro Molina.[81]

In keeping with the Cádiz tradition, the founding fathers of Central

America were vitally interested in the integration of the Indian. Religious men like fathers Matías de Córdoba and Fernando Antonio Dávila were in the vanguard of the movement. Concerned for the plight of the Indians in the highlands, Father Córdoba wrote a strong memorial to the A.N.C. that contained suggestions on how to help the Indian.[82] Father Dávila carried on the offensive in the legislative halls. Noting that religious men were still requiring personal services from the Indian, he declared that such practices had to cease. He made his complaint on July 11, 1823. A year later, there were still reports of such abuses reaching congress. The government ordered all *alcaldes* (town magistrates) to desist from requiring forced services from the Indians, citing a Spanish decree on that same subject.[83] The constant repetition of these admonitions, however, was proof that the abuses continued into the national period.[84] The attempt to discourage the use of Indian languages in the highlands of Guatemala likewise had little effect.[85] Heading the special committee on Indian matters, Father Dávila strongly recommended the need for a law that would divide the ejidos among the Indians with individual titles. There was no follow-through on Dávila's suggestion. In fact, the documentation on the special committee is not available.[86]

Considering the emotionalism of the Castas issue at Cádiz, Central Americans welcomed the emancipation of the black man and his complete integration into society. It will be recalled that Guatemalans, as early as 1812, had ignored the restrictions on the Castas, and that the instructions to Urruela in December 1820 demanded the equality of the blacks. Since there were only about five hundred slaves in all of Central America, the emancipation movement was a popular issue. On April 17, 1825, the Central American Republic freed the slaves; and any man caught in the slave traffic automatically lost his citizenship.[87]

The manner in which the emancipation of slaves took place reflected credit on the young Central American nation. It sustained the image of a government that respected the property rights of the individual. If masters were willing to comply with a lengthy ordinance, they were eligible to receive compensation for their ex-slaves. Claims for compensation could be made within two months of the emancipation proclamation. Masters who gave up their slaves without compensation, moreover, would be congratulated publicly in the government press. Valle and O'Horan set the example by releasing their slaves. Regional juntas were responsible for paying off the ex-masters, using funds that derived from inheritance sources of various types. In the absence of documentation, we cannot say how many received compensation. It would appear that most masters followed O'Horan and Valle's example.[88]

With a deep commitment to development, the Central American Republic consciously evoked the image of a modern nation that was dedicated to private enterprise and a free society. Following the Cádiz tradition, the Republic believed in a positive and constructive role for government in the field of economic development. Recognizing that its lands were exceptionally fertile and laden with untapped resources, governmental leaders hoped to develop these resources with outside capital and know-how. Strategically located astride the two oceans where an interoceanic canal seemed a distinct possibility, Central America was an attractive area of the world to many foreign investors who competed vigorously for various contracts—loans, the canal, banking facilities, and mines. By comparison with other regions of Hispanic America, there was relative political stability in most of the area, with the glaring exception of Nicaragua. Central America's future looked auspicious to most contemporaries; and the respect gained by such leaders as José del Valle was an asset for the Republic's future.

10. Federalism and the Abyss

In the combination of powers that comprise different forms of government, there is not a single one that considered from some aspect does not present advantages, and perceived from another point of view, does not prognosticate some disadvantages. All works of man have this stamp: and governments are the least perfect of those that come from his hands.

A.N.C. *May 20, 1824*[1]

Let me cry over the terrible evils of my country: permit me to lament her ruin and perdition.

GASPAR DE JOVELLANOS[2]

DURING the crucial months of founding a nation, the Asamblea Nacional Constituyente of Central America put together an impressive record of accomplishments. The nation's most talented men comprised its membership of eighty deputies, and most of them were conscious of the pitfalls in carrying out a revolution too rapidly. Fond of the liberal and traditional experiment at Cádiz, they knew that its precepts were acceptable to the citizenry of Central America. An aggressive and imaginative executive branch, moreover, contributed to the stability of the new nation in the nineteen months that it took to establish the United Provinces of the Center of America (*Provincias Unidas del Centro de América*). The name changed subsequently to the Federated States of Central America. Many referred to it as the Federation; others, perhaps in hopes of a greater concentration of power in Guatemala City called it the Republic of Central America. The conflict in terminology underscored the political struggle between centralists and federalists (states' righters).

The Supremo Poder Ejecutivo wrote to the state governments of

Central America on May 20, 1824, offering some insights on the merits and drawbacks of federalism. It congratulated a glorious federal system that permitted effective and energetic rule by multiplying and consolidating the centers of power and wealth. Opening up new sources of enlightenment, the federal state increased the number of governmental units working for the general welfare and encouraged men to think of their country. As a result, patriotism and civic duty replaced the private interests of the past. Federalism distributed the wealth evenly among the states and thus eliminated the causes that had formerly concentrated it in one place. It also improved the administration of justice by bringing those facilities to each unit.

José del Valle and Tomás O'Horan warned, however, that there might be other possible consequences: "Unity, the origin of energy, is weakened and can disappear completely." Since all states have their own vested interests, the central government's actions might be thwarted by a divided will. It was doubly imperative, therefore, to choose leaders wisely. That would be the key to Central America's success as a nation. To prove this final point, the executive reminded the state leaders of the historical contrast between the Count of Floridablanca and Manuel Godoy, Charles IV's favorite. Both men worked within the same system for all practical purposes. Yet, while one gave body to an emerging nation, the other "threw her into the abyss."[3]

Despite some misgivings about meeting in the old capital of the Kingdom, the deputies of the distant provinces eagerly advanced their special objectives in the sessions of the Asamblea Nacional Constituyente; and they joined with the moderates in the political coalition of October 1823, which overthrew the first executive triumvirate. At this juncture, the Salvadorans decided upon a course of action that proved to be fatal for the Central American Republic. It may have been pique at the treatment of their troops in the disturbances of mid-October; possibly it was resentment over their loss of leadership when the second executive took over; or it may have been a strategy to reassert their leadership in the Assembly as the champions of states rights. Whatever the reason, San Salvador changed the name of its government on October 21, 1823, from diputación provincial to that of junta gubernativa.[4] Although it appeared to be a minor change in terminology, it opened the door for irresponsible federalism and set an example for other states of the union.[5] The change in Salvadoran policy, the realization among the "Exaltados" in Guatemala City that provincial delegates would not settle for less than federalism, and the aggressive stance of the delegates from Honduras, Nicaragua, and Costa Rica all dictated the *Bases of the Constitution* in December 1823.

San Salvador proceeded straightaway to an extreme federalist position. Fearful that Guatemalan moderates would centralize the government—and their opposition to the *Bases* seem to indicate as much—the Salvadorans seized the initiative and acted independently of the Asamblea in Guatemala City. They did not wait for permission to do anything, reporting only accomplished facts to the national body. On February 17, 1824, the Salvadorans informed the A.N.C. that they had decided to establish themselves as a state. In the process, they annexed the territory of Sonsonate.[6] Suspecting an adverse decision on annexation from the authorities in Guatemala City, the Salvadorans had simply taken the law into their own hands. A Constituent Assembly gathered in San Salvador on March 5, 1824; and by June, it had completed its "Holy Charter," the first in northern Spanish America, boasted the Salvadorans. Sovereign in every respect, El Salvador abolished slavery on its own. It established its own bishopric in May 1824, and appointed the venerable José Matías Delgado as the first bishop. Throughout these various acts of sovereignty, the Salvadorans acknowledged their indebtedness to the precedents of the Cádiz Experiment, which were liberal in orientation and familiar to the people.[7]

Fearing the disintegration of the federal government because of El Salvador's independent ways, delegates from other provinces asked for permission to convene their own state legislatures. The Asamblea had no alternative but to respond favorably to these demands; the Salvadorans had forced its hand in the matter.[8] On March 15, 1824, the A.N.C. recognized the provinces as states; and, five days later, another order authorized them to form their respective congresses, following the *Bases of the Constitution* as their model. The Assembly recommended, however, that they await the specific ordinance that was being prepared on elections and other relevant materials.[9] The instructions of May 5, 1824, contained information on how to set up the states; and they recognized the existence of El Salvador. For the remaining units, the ordinance stipulated that Guatemala's constituent assembly would consist of 18 proprietors and 13 suplentes; Honduras, 11 proprietarios and 8 suplentes; Nicaragua, 13 and 9; and Costa Rica, 11 and 4. The initial meeting points would be Antigua, Guatemala; Managua, Nicaragua; San José, Costa Rica; and Aguanqueteric, Honduras. The point was to avoid or minimize intrastate rivalries. Delegates could choose another locale after their first meeting. Los Altos' statehood depended upon the evaluation of its statistics. All states, including El Salvador, would hold elections for federal offices, the Presidency, Vice-Presidency, Senators, and the Federal Judiciary. Soconusco would remain part of El Salvador until determined otherwise by the Federal Congress. Males from eighteen years of age up were eligible to vote, although twenty-five was the age for holding office. The electoral procedures followed the Cádiz model with only minor changes.[10] The states were expected to comply with these instructions, including El Salvador.[11]

Except for Nicaragua, where instability reigned throughout 1824, the state governments of Central America organized themselves expeditiously and tried to settle their differences. They were consistent in supporting their tertulias patrióticas and in establishing adequate educational facilities, especially the obligation to found a university, which was the responsibility of each state.[12] Cartago was disconsolate at losing her status as capital, but the power balance in Costa Rica pointed toward the city of San José, a leader in republicanism.[13]

If we recall the deep bitterness of the rivalry between Comayagua and Tegucigalpa, the Hondurans arrived at a unique settlement of differences on August 31, 1824. It was agreed that the capital would alternate yearly between Tegucigalpa and Comayagua with the exception of the first two years, unless a two-thirds majority insisted upon it. Tegucigalpa was the first victor; subsequently, a suspicious and close vote gave Comayagua the capital in 1825. It was a palatable shift, however, since Dionisio Herrera, the leader of Tegucigalpa, headed the government.[14] Following the Cádiz pattern, the Honduran government consisted of seven departments, each with its jefe político. This was also the case in the State of Guatemala.[15]

The Asamblea Nacional Constituyente commenced the debates on the Constitution in July 1824. There were four "Exaltados" on the Constitutional Committee, a veritable "brain trust" as in the Cádiz prototype. Two Guatemalans, José Francisco Barrundia and Mariano Gálvez, one Nicaraguan, Isidro Menéndez, and one Salvadoran, José Matías Delgado, led the discussions on the future charter of Central America. The first three were centralists, although they posed on occasion as champions of federalism to please the galleries; Delgado, however, was a sincere states' righter. The centralist or nationalist conception of government prevailed in the discussion of civil rights and the Federal Judiciary's authority to guarantee the rights of all individual citizens.[16] The insistence upon uniformity in the codification of state laws and the centralization of the tax system were points that Barrundia, Gálvez, and Menéndez defended brilliantly while displaying a vast erudition and command of the literature on legal systems of all times. As the representative of the independent-minded government of El Salvador, Father Delgado did not always agree with them.[17]

The *moderates* tried vainly to reverse the Committee's handiwork. Their job was made difficult because of the extensive support of the *Bases of the Constitution* throughout the towns of Central America and the specific instructions that provinciano delegates had brought with them to Guatemala City.[18] Whenever anyone questioned a premise of federalism, the Committee reminded him that substantive points in the *Bases* were not subject to change.[19] Angry at the notion of predetermined guidelines, José Francisco Córdoba, as leader of the moderates, sneered that the Constitution being framed was the work of angels, just like the Cádiz charter of 1812.[20] Although intended as a facetious remark, "Cordobita's" parallel was perceptive. The "brain trust" in Guatemala City had much in common with Argüelles and company; both were groups of brilliant and persuasive men who managed to sway votes by an appeal to intellect and emotion. Moreover, there was that same effort to blend centralist and federalist concepts. The debate over the nature of the Senate was especially bitter, but Barrundia and Gálvez persuaded the majority that the veto power of ten men offered more protection to the nation than that of one man, the executive. They reminded provincianos that the Senate could distribute governmental posts equitably among the states, whereas a single executive would tend to prefer his native state.[21]

The moderate opposition performed a constructive function in exposing the weaknesses of the *Bases of the Constitution*. A respected figure in the A.N.C. who had served in Spain, Father Fernando Dávila quoted noted publicists who attacked the flaws of a federal system. In his opinion, the federal constitution did not take into account the state of civilization in Central America, thus violating one of Jeremy Bentham's cardinal rules of government.[22] Another deputy who had served Chiapas in Spain, Mariano Córdoba, felt that the "Exaltados" were too theoretical and idealistic, and lacked sufficient experience in the study of law. This was a reference to José Francisco Barrundia.[23] José Francisco Córdoba debated constantly with his former allies, Barrundia and Molina, drawing from the political experience of Guatemala under the Cádiz constitutional system. Barrundia accused him of having "aristocratic" inclinations with regard to government.[24] A hard-headed realist, "Cordobita" admitted that he favored a restricted suffrage, fewer elections, the appointment of senators by state legislatures, and a more powerful executive.[25] On the other hand, he convincingly exposed the obstacles to federalism in Central America. The financial structure of the nation could not support the proliferation of governments in the area; there were not enough qualified men to fill governmental posts; the people lacked the enlightenment that characterized a country like the United States; and, finally, provincial rivalries would produce disorders.[26]

Following a page from the American Question at Cádiz—one of many that the Americans did not win—the Asamblea agreed that the first Federal Congress rather than the Constituent Assembly itself, should ratify the Constitution. The Constitutional Committee recommended that the new body take over the government once two-thirds of the representatives were present, a clause that provoked strong objections from the provincianos. The Honduran Lindo protested that this rule would penalize the more distant states. "Cordobita" could not resist the temptation to remind his colleagues that such a provision had made it possible for Guatemalan and Salvadoran "Exaltados" to dominate the A.N.C. in its early months. Barrundia and Gálvez defended the two-thirds majority rule with emotion, citing the examples of Spain, France, and Mexico. The Honduran Milla supplied the acceptable compromise: to follow the Cádiz precedent of setting a date for the reunion of the first Congress, allowing sufficient time for the deputies from faraway states to reach the capital. The date was January 15, 1825.[27]

The members of the Asamblea Nacional Constituyente signed the Constitution on November 22, 1824. By that time, preparations were well underway for the national elections. Although the deputies reached Guatemala City by the designated date, there were delays until the Constitution was published and absolute majorities were present for each state delegation.[28] The installation of the first Federal Congress took place on February 6, 1825. On February 20 Congress was ready to start its work.[29]

The A.N.C. finished its sessions on January 23, 1825, after nineteen full months of constructive labors and concern for the Central American nation. The sacrifice of its members was notorious, since very few men received any pay from their constituents. Considering Central America's past experience, the Asamblea Nacional Constituyente did an outstanding job of bringing unity and stability to the area, despite the warfare in Nicaragua and the serious drain of that conflict upon the depleted coffers of the national treasury. The economy had picked up, however; and there were many projects and reforms that held promise for the young nation. Yet, the bane of provincialism was in the air. It remained to be seen if it could be contained long enough to bring about the economic recovery of Central America. Foreign investors were excited at the prospects of a stable and prosperous nation.[30]

～～～～～
～～～～～

While politics during the Assembly's tenure seemed to balance out despite occasional fits of partisanship, there was a clearcut polarization in the federal congresses of 1825 and 1826. The moderates controlled the first federal body and the "Exaltados" the second. Two themes dominated politics in those years, eventually leading the Republic to civil war in mid-1826: the financial question and the religious issue. The first one is not surprising since it had plagued Central America for decades. The second, however, resulted from the polarization of the political scene. Here, too, Central Americans followed the Cádiz pattern. Both questions were inextricably entwined in the federalist-centralist controversy, so characteristic of all Hispanic American countries during the early years of nationhood.

Although the Assembly had prepared the financial bases for the country in a sound and pragmatic manner, the fact is that the system was not implemented to any substantial extent before the outbreak of war. The public simply would not allow itself to be counted and vigorously resisted the income tax law of December 1, 1823. The municipal records of Guatemala City register this resistance graphically, as aldermen complained of the abuses they had received from citizens in their wards.[31] If this was the case in Guatemala City, the home of the federal government and later of the State of Guatemala, it is not difficult to imagine the resistance in less affluent and distant towns throughout Central America.[32] This reluctance to be counted, moreover, had a major political impact. People did not register for elections because they did not want their names included in tax statistics. Therefore, a well-organized party could do well in the elections even though it represented only a minority. This is what happened in the first congressional elections. The moderates went out and got the vote; they thus formed the majority bloc in the 1825 Congress. Recognizing that the Guatemala City interests were mainly moderates, who wanted to centralize government, the provincianos found themselves annoyed by the political maneuvers of the centralists. In the election of 1825, however, the "Exaltados" pushed their cause effectively among the abbreviated electorate; and with provinciano support, they were able to dominate the political activities of the second Federal Congress, at least until civil war broke out.[33]

Whether the leadership was moderate or "Exaltado," the State of El Salvador wanted no part of a government based in Guatemala City, the hated ex-capital. In this context, the immediate incidents that produced the holocaust of 1826 become meaningful. Although the documentation is not conclusive, it would appear that the interests of Guatemala predominated in the federal government mainly because the outlying states did not have the resources to pay the salaries and travel expenses of the men elected to federal office. There was, in short, a repetition of the Mexican experience. Provincianos were inadequately represented in the national government; and their elected representatives were no longer willing to labor free of charge in Guatemala City, far from home. Thus, Guatemalan interests filled the vacuum; and whether their affiliation was moderate or "Exaltado," the result appeared to be the same to jealous provincianos who, of course, absolved themselves from any responsibility for this political development. That was the pattern in mid-1826 when government broke down in Guatemala City, ushering in three years of disastrous civil war.[34]

The financial weakness of the Central American nation was fatal. Without a viable revenue system, no country could survive or implement any kind of a program of modernization. Without resources, the Asamblea Nacional Constituyente had turned in desperation to the city government at the capital, asking for funds. The city fathers, however, resisted the pressure and held their ground stubbornly in late 1823 and the early months of 1824, exasperating the Jefe Político and the Supremo Poder Ejecutivo.[35] A minor crisis of sorts occurred when the testy city fathers told the federal government that it should cut down on its expenditures, especially such frill assignments as sending representatives to Panama City for a congress of the Americas or hiring military officers from Colombia. Angered at the presumptuousness of the municipal authorities, the executive retorted with a stinging reprimand that occasioned some resignations from the city council.[36] There were hurt feelings on all sides, but there was still no money forthcoming. When Valle joined the S.P.E. in February, 1824, matters improved only slightly. It convinced him that the centralization of the tax structure was essential for Central America. The nation could not survive the drain through loopholes in its financial system, hoping that these deliberate concessions would make the tax schedule acceptable to the people. For example, state authorities had authorization to collect the sales tax (alcabala) that was destined for the use of federal authorities. In practice, what happened was that the states borrowed from the alcabala funds, much as colonial officials had resorted to the community treasuries of the Indians.[37]

Guatemala was the only state that contributed substantial amounts of money to the federal government during these years. The other governments found one excuse after another to relieve themselves of any tax payments. The A.N.C. in its decree of January 21, 1825—its last action—was still lecturing the states on their obligations in financial matters. Insisting upon its sole responsibility for the foreign loan and for public credit, the A.N.C. asked the state bodies to submit proposals for funding economic projects within their jurisdictions. It warned, however, that federal authorities would provide funds only to stable and obedient governments.[38] The gesture was a futile one. Another illustration of desperation on money matters occurred on February 7, 1824, when the A.N.C. notified the Church that its lands would be taxed 7 percent during the present emergency. The religious community might select its own evaluators, such was the Asamblea's need for money.[39] On another occasion, the Assembly raised customs duties by 4 percent on a temporary basis. The sums collected, however, did not balance the books; and salaries had to be pared in order to keep the administration going.[40]

The states, furthermore, resented all moves to centralize the nation's fiscal structure, desperately trying to make ends meet themselves. Costa Ricans argued that taxes within their jurisdiction could only be levied by the state legislature; and in the constitutional debates of mid-1824, two deputies from Costa Rica fought vigorously all attempts to centralize the tax system.[41] By September 3, 1823, the A.N.C. had not yet collected any of the old taxes that it had revived, except perhaps in Guatemala. The state governments were also in a financial bind, unable to pay the salaries for the host of new positions that had been created under the Republic. State legislators learned, moreover, that their citizens were not willing to be counted for tax purposes. As a result, state governments seized federal revenues, the tobacco tax in particular. Some of them, the State of Guatemala, for example, resorted to forced loans; and by the end of 1825, it had levied a state income tax of 2 percent on rented property and a tax on Indians of 8 reales, half of the old tribute payment.[42] States had no more success in collecting taxes and statistics than their federal counterpart. The conservative Guatemalan government of Mariano Aycinena faced the same problem during the Civil War, thus prompting it to ask for a forced loan from the moneyed interests of the City.

There was no reason to expect the Federal Congress of 1825 to have any better luck in collecting taxes than its predecessors. Dominated by fiscal conservatives (moderates), Congress insisted upon a centralized fiscal system, and this put further stress on relations with the states. It announced on July 20, 1825, that the federal government, not the states, would collect the internal alcabala in the future.[43] In November, Congress turned down the state loans that Costa Rica and Honduras had negotiated with an English banking firm. The majority bloc argued that the nation's public credit would suffer if the states were allowed to negotiate their own loans; and the default of state loans, in turn, would contribute to humiliating diplomatic relations with other powers. On the other hand, Honduras maintained that it desperately needed the loan to develop her resources. She had the same needs, as well as rights, as the federal government in negotiating the Barclay-Herring Loan.[44] A strong fiscal centralist as a member of the executive, José del Valle was now the responsible party in negotiating the above mentioned Honduran loan of 1.5 million pesos from the Louis Biré Company in London. He also recommended an equivalent loan for Costa Rica. The Barclay-Herring House, of course, lobbied sucessfully against the state loans.[45]

In addition to the English loan, the impoverished government of Honduras asked for 25,000 pesos from the federal government, a request that was turned down by the committee in question. Both moderate and "Exaltado" deputies on that committee, including Mariano Gálvez, complained that the states were defying national decrees on financial matters. Alluding especially to the action of the Salvadoran government, the committee noted that states were examining federal decrees as if that were their prerogative. Then they blatantly resisted the laws of the nation by appropriating revenues that belonged to the federal government. Wayward states should be deterred from such actions, the committee recommended. If allowed to continue their defiance, the State of Guatemala was fully justified in taking over the tax resources that it had turned over to the federal government. In short, the committee represented the views of both moderate and "Exaltado" politicians. Guatemalans were tired of footing the bills for the national government while other states, notably El Salvador, acted independently of the authorities in Guatemala City.[46]

Salvadoran defiance of the federal government was especially objectionable to politicians in Guatemala City, making compromise difficult. The government in San Salvador acted as an absolute sovereign, often an abusive one. For example, it ordered the suspension of individual rights for those who resisted or disobeyed laws, forcing them into exile. The federal government declared that particular Salvadoran order unconstitutional. In March 1825, a Salvadoran spokesman urged his government to appoint the administrators of the tobacco units without consulting federal authorities. He insisted that the gunpowder tax should revert to the state in order to meet its expenses for defense. In a spirited rebuff, the Federal Congress countered that its resolutions were not subject to the sanction of state assemblies.[47]

The seriousness of El Salvador's defiance provoked a stinging reprimand from *El Liberal*, José Francisco Barrundia's paper. Noting that the Salvadoran government had passed the recommendation to take over the tobacco and gunpowder revenues, Barrundia condemned the "disorganizing measures" of the state legislature. In the past, he had supported Salvadorans and their federalist program; but now he had to speak out against their defiance of the tobacco law of December 15, 1823, which he had helped to frame. If Salvadorans had a real grievance, he reminded them that they should resort to Article 89 of the Constitution. Why had El Salvador failed to do so? How could a state of the union set itself above the federal law? If a state could do so, what would prevent any district within that state from doing likewise? Anarchy would be the result of such irresponsible liberalism. On another occasion, *El Liberal* editorialized on the usurpation of the federal gunpowder tax.[48]

With "Exaltados" like Barrundia and Gálvez joining the moderates in defending the federal government from states' rights actions, Salvadorans and other provincianos reached the conclusion that both liberal and conservative Guatemalans were against the cause of the provinces. It was thus doubly imperative to remove the national capital to a new location, preferably in El Salvador.[49]

The religious issue further irritated the centrifugal forces that were leading the nation to civil war. Considering the traditional position of Central Americans in the period from Cádiz through independence, it is surprising that it even surfaced at all. The first ripple, ever so slight, appeared on July 2, 1823, when a deputy (Isidro Martínez of Nicaragua) observed that by following Spanish precedents the Asamblea National Constituyente was precluding any "just reforms" of religious abuses. Desirous of avoiding this touchy question, Dr. Mariano Gálvez convinced his colleague that it should be deferred to a more settled period. It came up again in Article 6 on the restoration of "civil, military, and ecclesiastical" authorities. Fathers Dávila and Castilla insisted emphatically that religious authorities were not subject to civil power, raising the old controversy between regalists and ultramontanes. While the clerics supported canonical authority, Gálvez, Menéndez, and "Cordobita" defended the regalist or nationalist position.[50] On the issue of the fuero, the legislators followed the Cádiz pattern, and the religious lobbyists carried the day. It was understood, however, that eventually there would be an adjustment whereby all persons would be treated equally in the courts.[51]

A spirit of compromise prevailed among the members of the A.N.C. On July 8, 1823, they agreed that at the appropriate time the executive would have the right of presentation of candidates to religious posts. For the time being, however, these matters were left for subsequent negotiations with the Papacy. The financial straits of the government prevented the government's mission from proceeding to Rome. In the meantime, El Salvador seized the initiative by establishing a bishopric, a reform that had been approved by the Spanish Parliament. The Costa Ricans likewise proposed the establishment of a bishopric, hoping to separate from the religious leaders in León. Both proposals were sent to a federal committee. In the investigations that followed committeemen wanted to know what resources would help pay for the bishopric in Costa Rica. If the federal mission had been able to proceed to Rome, it is likely that the Asamblea would have supported the Salvadoran move.[52]

The leaders in San Salvador, however, were very impatient, suspecting that perhaps Archbishop Ramón Casaus would enlist the moderates to fight their proposal. They therefore created their own bishopric in May, 1824, and elected their first bishop, hoping that papal approval would ensue. In their state constitution of June, 1824, certain clauses indicated that the *patronato real* (royal patronage prerogatives) belonged to the sovereign power that had replaced the Spanish King. Guatemalan rivals argued against this thesis: El Salvador was not a sovereign unit and thus could not assume a prerogative that belonged to the Republic. *El Indicador* of Guatemala City minced no words in attacking the assumptions of Salvadorans on this issue; and the latter were now convinced beyond the shadow of a doubt that the "Serviles" in Guatemala City were following orders from Archbishop Casaus.[53]

A war of pamphlets ensued that presented the rival viewpoints. Defending El Salvador, Dr. José Simeón Cañas wrote at least two treatises that received wide circulation throughout Central America. Father Cañas argued the regalist view, which ironically meant the "states' rights" position in Central America. He especially took issue with the publication entitled *The Roman Catholic Letter to the Faithful of the State of San Salvador* which accused the State of being schismatic. Just as America had broken with Spain, Cañas emphasized, the American clergy no longer obeyed the orders of the Patriarch, the Nuncio, and the general prelates of Spain, nor did they send the money payments that had been customary in the past. Moreover, historical authorities and documents were available that justified the appointment of a Bishop. He hoped that the Pope would honor the appointment. Throughout the erudite discussion, which ran to twenty-one pages, the basic assumption was that El Salvador constituted a sovereign nation and therefore could exercise the former royal patronage. Cañas also insisted that the State of El Salvador had the right to do what it wanted about the tithes (*diezmos*), even suppress them as the Spanish Cortes had done recently.[54] In a second and shorter tract, the cleric offered a rebuttal to the arguments of Father José Mariano Herrarte, pointing out those precedents in canonical law that justified the Salvadoran action in selecting Dr. José Matías Delgado as their first bishop.[55]

Other states, especially Costa Rica and Nicaragua, followed the religious dispute closely. In hopes of enlisting their support, Salvadorans maintained a steady correspondence with them. They were informed of the latest moves of the federal government, and Salvadoran reports highlighted the "states' right" viewpoint. Costa Ricans and Nicaraguans had no trouble receiving the message: the real monsters were the "Serviles" and Archbishop Casaus, those enemies of federalism who lived in Guatemala City. The religious question, in other words, was regarded by the provincianos as a power play on the part of the hated interests of the old capital who had always opposed their sincere aspirations for home rule. San Salvador's responsibility for this polarization was evident in its promotion of the stereotype concerning Guatemala City. The objective of its correspondence was to secure independent bishoprics everywhere in Central America, even in Nicaragua, all of them free from Guatemala City's control.[56]

When the moderate majority in the Federal Congress voted against El Salvador's right to establish a bishopric in July 1825, it deliberately circulated copies of this decision throughout the dissident state. A serious rupture was imminent. At this point, the Federal Senate vetoed the act of the Lower House. Controlled by Guatemalan "Exaltados" and liberals from the provinces, the Senate pointed out that the Constitution did not expressly give the royal patronage to the federal government. It therefore was a right inherent in the sovereignty of each state as stipulated in Article 10.[57] Whatever the merits of the Senate's veto, it was hardly an action to give solace to a Central American nationalist. It was a severe blow to the credibility of the federal government, bringing much joy to the followers of states' rights. Resentful of the City's centralizing tax measures, the states were now happy with the victory for their cause as sovereign entities. Such a humiliating defeat for the Archbishop and the ultramontane point of view, however, led to a tragic polarization on the religious question.

With the battle joined, the ultramontanes continued their forceful defense of the Church in Central America, subject to the authority of

Archbishop Ramón Casaus. Based on canon law, their interpretation supported papal authority. It condemned such movements as Gallicanism that undermined the Pope's position in the Church. These religious men were not at all pleased, therefore, with the federal decree of February 26, 1825, honoring the ex-Bishop of Blois (Gregoire) for his publication on the Gallican Church as well as his contribution to the emancipation of the Americas. The moderate majority apparently was not yet in existence. At any rate, Congress agreed to publish and translate the Bishop's book for circulation throughout Central America.[58]

To counteract this dangerous trend, Casaus' agents warned their flocks about the acts and words of the liberals, who were clearly heretics. Sensitive to the propaganda of the ultramontanes, states' rights liberals mounted a counter-campaign to prove to the faithful that they were good Catholics. The priests who told the people such lies were not believers in the Constitution; they were vicious men who were inciting Central Americans to war, rather than functioning as "ministers of Jesus Christ." They were acting like "agents of the King of Spain" and of the "aristocrats."[59] They were the instruments of outside powers, trying to force a "dependency" upon other countries. The liberals, on the other hand, were the true nationalists and the guarantors of the nation's independence. In Costa Rica, some committeemen who were studying the prospects for a bishopric noted that "a nation should not receive the law from foreigners, nor suffer them to intervene in its affairs."[60] The correspondence of El Salvador, Costa Rica, and Nicaragua referred frequently to the non-nationalists in their midst, thus exacerbating the tension between liberals and conservatives. Governor Dionisio Herrera of Honduras issued a decree which, in the name of the Holy Bible, denounced the opposition to liberalism. Jesus Christ had influenced "our constitution," he said. The people should therefore not be deceived by the reactionaries.[61]

Anticlericalism thus became a reality in Central America, springing initially from the regalist versus ultramontane controversy. Later, it mixed itself in the ideological arena and produced dangerous stereotypes: impious liberals who did not respect the Church as opposed to conservatives who were against reforms and favored dependence upon outside powers and institutions. Incident after incident fed these distortions and led the Central American people toward war. A few incidents should illustrate the point.

El Liberal narrated the case of a friar, presumably a Spaniard, who was expounding against federalism. When challenged by a Guatemalan underling, the Spaniard ordered Manuel Urrutia out of his house. Fortunately, Father Dávila learned of the event and had it brought to court. The Spanish cleric, however, managed to escape on a technicality. When Urrutia tried to join the order in question at a later date, he was turned down, allegedly for being a republican. The informer was a close associate of Archbishop Casaus. Urrutia reapplied and was turned down again. *El Liberal* lamented the implications of that particular story: entry into the religious orders was for those who favored "the foul breath of servilismo."[62]

Another incident reminded the editor of *El Liberal* of the quarrel that Archbishop Casaus had raised with the Municipality of Guatemala City back in 1813. In this case, the Dominican prelate, Miguel Aycinena, refused to acknowledge the right of the Superior Court to investigate religious prisoners, remarking that such presumptuousness resulted from reading the works of Voltaire and Robespierre. The same friar allegedly encouraged others to defy the government, for example, on the payment of the 7 percent tax on religious property. The courts, as might be expected, announced the decision that religious men had to abide by the laws of the state and that individual guarantees applied to religious men as well.[63] The name of Aycinena, already becoming obnoxious to irritable liberals in Guatemala, gave the incident its crucial importance.

As civil war approached, there was a pronounced anticlericalism among the liberals of Central America. In the State of Guatemala, Governor Juan Barrundia, José Francisco's brother, was especially determined to control the Church within his borders. A decree of July 20, 1826, stipulated the age brackets and prerequisites of men who wanted to serve in a religious capacity. The objective was to improve their qualifications. Futhermore, the Guatemalan government forbade the use of sermons to combat liberal ideas.[64] On July 22, the State of Guatemala issued the Organic Law of the Tribunals. Like the Cádiz counterpart, it called for a certain number of visits to all jails within its boundaries. Articles 128 and 129, however, stipulated that all religious men were subject to the same laws as other citizens of the State. In short, Guatemalans had declared the desafuero, just as the Spanish liberals had done in Madrid.[65] This development caused great concern among priests and devout Catholics throughout Central America, especially in Guatemala itself.[66] Civil war was now a fact of life in Guatemala; and it was perhaps no coincidence that the Vice-Chief of Guatemala, Cirilo Flores, lost his life at the hands of angry Indians in Quezaltenango.

The financial question also led to the breakdown of order in Central America. When the State Government of Guatemala began its existence in Antigua, it soon found out that financing its operations would be no easy matter. Since the largest concentration of the population was in Guatemala City, state officials counted on substantial revenues from the urban center, just as the federal government had done without much success. In November, 1824, Guatemala levied a 2 percent tax on rented property, a source that did not yield much revenue. The state then turned to a tax on aguardiente and chicha.[67] In February 1825, Barrundia's government exacted a forced loan of 80,000 pesos from the state's leading citizens, many of whom lived in Guatemala City. The Jefe Político Antonio Rivera encountered the same type of resistance as before. The residents of the City were in no mood for further taxes.[68] Because of this defiance and to expedite matters in all walks of government, Juan Barrundia and his colleagues decided to move to Guatemala City on July 1, 1825, thus exposing the nation to a possible clash between federal and state authorities since both shared the same locale.[69] There had been tension between the two governments on earlier occasions over touchy items of protocol.

The financial condition of the State did not improve after the transfer to Guatemala City. The deficit was 100,000 pesos by the end of 1825. To liquidate this debt and to guard against future imbalances, Governor Barrundia convinced his legislature that a direct tax was needed. He announced it on December 31, 1825. Henceforth every citizen of the State had to pay an annual impost of eight reales, or one peso. Statistics were now the order of the day. State officials, however, encountered the same problems that had confronted their federal counterparts. Nobody wanted to be counted for tax purposes, especially the Indians at whom the direct tax was aimed, and they were 70 percent of the population. It was no consolation to them that the tax in question was only one-half the tribute that they had paid Spain, a point that state authorities had stressed in order to make the tax palatable to the Indians.[70] At this juncture, it is conceivable that the financial and religious issues merged in the minds of dissatisfied Indians, especially since the Barrundia government had taken an anticlerical stance. Enemies of the liberal state government fed this dissatisfaction.

There is no intention to deal here with the immediate events that led to civil war in Central America by mid-1826. That story has been thrashed out in other studies.[71] It was not just a clash between two strong personalities: Manual José de Arce as President of the Republic and Governor Juan Barrundia of Guatemala, brother of Senator José Francisco Barrundia. Despite some inconsistencies, the product of personal and emotional factors, it makes more sense to see the conflict as the struggle between federalism and centralism. As the break was in the offing, Governor Barrundia seized the tobacco revenues in his state which previously had been turned over dutifully to the federal authorities. The Salvadorans had likewise taken over those revenues at a much earlier date, so the defiance of the federal government was nothing new in Central America. The difference was that Guatemala's defiance touched off a military confrontation; on August 15, 1826, the state legislature authorized military preparedness. Civil War had begun. On September 5, 1826, President Arce arrested Governor Barrundia; and the State government set up offices in Quezaltenango. Vice-Chief Flores met his untimely death on October 13. By the end of that month, President Arce controlled the recalcitrant state; and in the elections that followed, Mariano Aycinena won the governorship, the recognized leader of the hated "Serviles." He proceeded to cooperate closely with President Arce. Thus, one of the states, the largest one at that, had been brought to heel by the central government in Guatemala City. This was hardly a day of rejoicing for the cause of federalism.

Consistency should have dictated the support of Governor Barrundia by the states' righters of Central America. After all, Barrundia had forcefully demonstrated the states' cause in financial, political, and religious matters. To be sure, they eventually came over to the proper side, against President Arce. The provincianos' inconsistency in the early days of the Civil War reveals the impact of other factors that were personal and regional as well. The Salvadoran government chose to support Arce because he was a native of that state; its desire to move the national capital to El Salvador had also become a virtual obsession by this time. Salvadorans glossed over the fact that the 1826 Federal Congress was virtually under the control of Guatemalan "Exaltados" and that the provincianos' inability to dominate the discussion there was due to the failure of the states to send their deputies to Guatemala City. They did not have the money to pay the per diems and travel expenses. By default, therefore, the balance of power in the federal government rested in the Guatemalan delegation, either "Exaltado" or moderate. Angry at the reprimands of such former allies as Senator José Francisco Barrundia, Salvadorans, who were almost paranoid on this point, chose to believe that all Guatemalans, liberal or conservative, were determined to grind down the provincianos, just as they had done during the colonial centuries. It is interesting to note that Salvadorans compared the situation with that of the Americans at Cádiz. The oppressor now was Guatemala.[72]

Moreover, the government in San Salvador succeeded in convincing other provincianos to their point of view. Costa Ricans, for example, charged the old capital of wanting to dominate the provinces for its own selfish interest.[73] When they learned of Arce's close cooperation with the "Serviles," Costa Ricans recognized their error and returned to the position that consistency dictated.

The Civil War of 1826–1829 marks a tragic end to the early movement of constructive constitutionalism in Central America. As it turned out, it was the beginning of the end for the Central American Republic, which never recovered from the effects of that war. The financial situation went from bad to worse, and the ideological polarization deprived Central Americans of an orderly and prosperous economic development for the next half-century. There were other signs of weakness on the horizon before the outbreak of hostilities. To begin with, the bankruptcy of the House of Barclay and Herring in the financial panic of the 1820s denied Central America a much-needed loan. Moreover, the canal project was left in abeyance because no foreign company was able, or willing, to supply the 200,000 pesos that had been stipulated by the federal government.[74] The major fault in the historical picture, however, was the exaggerated provincialism of the Central American area, a heritage that fixed its roots in three hundred years of colonial rule. A weak economic base furthered the process of disintegration.

≈≈≈

The Cádiz Experiment was basically an adaptation of enlightened thought to the process of modernization in the Spanish-speaking world. It followed the Enlightenment in its emphasis upon the dignity, freedom, and capacity of man to regenerate himself and his environment—a faith in the individual and in the reform process that challenged the premises and institutions of the Old Regime. The Bourbon dynasty of eighteenth-century Spain was a firm advocate of change and strove to unify and modernize the nation state of Spain. The reign of Charles III (1759–1788) was particularly significant in this regard. These were the years when men like Floridablanca, Campomanes, Gálvez, Jovellanos, and others put into effect many reforms, especially economic and political programs that established guidelines for the process of modernization. Furthermore, an important elite throughout the Spanish world welcomed this new vision of Hispanic life, especially in the economic societies of their regions. The world was in a mood for change, and the belief in progress dominated the thinking of governmental leaders. Spain and her Empire were no exception.

It is significant that the study of history was in vogue during the reign of Charles III. The nationalistic ministers of the regime, moreover, played leading roles in the rebirth of historical studies. The results were far-reaching. It reminded Spaniards and Spanish Creoles that they had a tradition of long standing in constitutionalism, not only of the compact between a monarch and his people but also of man's "natural rights" as a child of God. These concepts circulated widely throughout the Spanish world. They made a deep impression, for example, in the Kingdom of Guatemala. We have noted how well Central Americans blended these notions with the secular origins of "natural rights" of John Locke and others, whose works often were quoted in public documents in order to prove a given point on a constitutional issue. With this type of preparation, the Cádiz Experiment was a logical result.

The literature of the first constitutional period in Spain acknowledged the indebtedness of Spanish constitutionalism to the reforming spirit of Charles III and his leading ministers. The Bad Government of Manuel Godoy, coupled with the invasion of Napoleon's forces, provided the opportunity to establish a constitutional monarchy in Spain. It also brought about a reconsideration of the relationship between the mother country and the overseas colonies. For various reasons, anticolonialism was a reality by 1808, spurred on by the memorable events of that year. Spain's involvement in the diplomacy of the French Revolution and the Napoleonic Era weakened her financially and isolated her from her colonies. The popularity of laissez-faire economics in the Americas, as well as in Spain, inevitably came into conflict with the mercantilistic doctrines of the past. The innate rivalry of European Spaniards and American Spaniards was another vital pressure for change in colonial relationships. Moreover, the success of the American Revolution and its product, the United States of America, inspired Spanish Americans to seek adequate concessions from the weakened mother country in Europe. Spain's urgent need for money to fight the French further emboldened Americans and Asians to equalize their rights with those of Peninsulars in any new nation that might emerge from the deliberations at the Cortes of Cádiz.

Despite the distorted views about the Cádiz Experiment, resulting from the bitter rivalry of liberals and conservatives, the reforms were both traditional and progressive. Although Spaniards and Americans desired to modernize society, they believed in a moderate or gradualist approach to change. The strong religious influence was evident in the preservation of the ecclesiastical fuero, the role of the clergy in elections, and the insistence upon "moral and virtuous" citizens. The large presence of clergymen at Cádiz helps to explain these measures, but it is also notable that the electorate seemed to prefer enlightened prelates as their representatives in Parliament. The same pattern held in the Central American and Mexican phases of the Experiment.

The Consejo de Estado with its concession to the "Estates" reflected a traditional concern for stability and for the restraint of absolute power by a moderating force that represented the intellectual elite of the nation. The humanitarian concern of the Cádiz legislators, especially with regard to the Indian and the helpless in general, was in part an extension of the Christian ethic of helping one's brother regardless of color, a tradition which had deep roots in the Spanish world. The indirect procedures of elections and the restrictions in the suffrage, on the other hand, gave the Cádiz system a decided traditionalist and elitist cast.

It was nonetheless a program that was modern in its political, economic, legal, and social reforms. The assumption of modern nationalism—indeed, this may have been the major weakness of the Cádiz Experiment—underlay the political system. Believing in efficient and open government, the leaders at Cádiz elaborated a compromise which was basically highly centralized. Yet it also made key concessions to regionalism in the institution of the Diputación Provincial and its component Ayuntamientos (municipalities). Contrary to a standard distortion of the Cádiz period, executive power was strong from the level of the King down to the jefe político of a province. There were, however, checks and balances: the Consejo de Estado was an effective curb on both the executive and legislature, thanks to its prestige and moral power among the people. The diputación provincial and the ayuntamiento of a capital had ways of exposing an abusive political chief—the fate of José de Bustamante in Guatemala was a case in point. Enlightened public opinion was a key factor in the Cádiz Experiment. It was to be cultivated in the schools, in the press, in tertulias patrióticas, in economic societies, and in the electoral system.

Determined to uproot the barbaric practices of the past and to preserve the rights of individual citizens, even those who happened to run afoul of the law, the judicial system was modern, humanitarian, comprehensive, and fair. Moreover, the Cádiz Experiment had a social conscience. The concern for the Indians, among the non-whites, was exemplary, although very little of the reform program was actually implemented because of the resistance of vested interests. Religious, humanitarian, and economic factors had influenced the legislation to integrate such an important group in American society. The Cádiz legislators were not yet ready for the issue of slavery, although there were some preliminary discussions about it. They did, however, begin preparations for ending the slave trade, despite the opposition of slaveowners in Cuba and elsewhere. As for the Castas, the Cádiz deputies offered only minor concessions, because of the implications for the political power balance between Americans and Peninsulars. In practice, judging from the Central American example, the Castas were allowed to vote.

Following the lead of the Bourbon reforms, the Cádiz Experiment put its greatest emphasis upon economic development, and it strongly advocated laissez-faire thinking. The main purpose of the Diputación Provincial was to serve as a development corporation for its region, conducting surveys of potential resources and industries, promoting education and the construction of an adequate infrastructure, supervising the municipalities for fiscal responsibility, and so on. The ayuntamientos had specific instructions to nurture the three main sources of wealth: agriculture, commerce, and industry. Free competition was imperative, and the system attacked monopoly in all forms. In Spain, this meant freeing the land from medieval encumbrances and levies so that the private entrepreneur might increase the productivity of the soil. In America, the Cádiz legislators envisioned a program of agrarian reform; and it was hoped that the main beneficiary of the distribution of lands would be the Indians. With a stake in a free society, the Indian would work his land, prosper, and augment his numbers. The increase of the population in the Americas was a desideratum of Spanish and American planners; colonization projects and the encouragement of foreign immigrants with "know-how" and capital were also vital aspects of the developmental program.

The Cádiz legislators emphasized the promotion of agriculture, just as Gaspar de Jovellanos had urged in his famous *Informe de Ley Agraria*. After all, it was the key activity in Spain and in the Americas. Commerce and industry were secondary; and the feeling prevailed that these activities would be stimulated by the increase in agricultural production. In this respect, the Spanish world was largely indebted to the French physiocrats.

The educational system forged by the deputies in the parliaments of Cádiz and Madrid was functional as well as classical. In any case, it was modern with textbooks drawn from the best authorities at all levels— elementary schools, secondary schools, universities, and polytechnic institutes. A corporation of intellectuals advised national authorities on policy and texts. The result was a uniform educational plan, controlled by the State. In its orientation and objectives, it already anticipated the educational programs of philosophical Positivism in the late nineteenth century.

American delegates welcomed this blueprint for an open society. Consistently in favor of the program of modernization, they introduced many of the reforms and concepts that were adopted at Cádiz. Central American deputies took representative stands on many issues, reflecting the desires of their New World colleagues. The American defense of "free trade" was constant and noteworthy, although thwarted by the selfish merchant interests in the port city. The attack upon the tobacco monopoly likewise emphasized a fierce commitment to free competition. The overseas delegation led the way on Indian reforms, and it heatedly contested the Peninsulars on the rights of the Castas—not an entirely disinterested stand, it will be recalled. On the American Question, which involved the political control of the new Spanish nation, the overseas deputies failed time and time again, in part because of the polarization of American versus Spaniard. The unflattering stereotypes of each other did not help matters. This lack of success, moreover, provoked a sense of alienation that brought about the independence of most of Spain's colonies in the New World. The anticlericalism of legislators in Madrid completed the process of alienation in Mexico and Central America during the second constitutional period. Although leaders from those two countries might admire and even adopt reforms passed in Madrid, they no longer were willing to tolerate Spanish rule.

Since military conditions prevailed in Spain, South America, and Mexico during the first constitutional period, it was difficult to determine how practical the Cádiz reforms were in fact. Fortunately, the relative peace of Central America provided an adequate testing ground for the Cádiz Experiment; and the implementation of the program revealed some basic deficiencies that would torment the area's future: a weak economic base and an exaggerated spirit of regionalism.

Central American society welcomed the news that constitutionalism was scheduled to replace the old colonial order. It had been preparing itself for this eventuality since the reign of Charles III. The Spanish defense against Napoleon's forces bestirred the loyalty of subjects in the Kingdom of Guatemala, whose contributions were deeply appreciated in Spain. A sense of independence and demands of equality and justice permeated their correspondence with the beleagured mother country. Although Central Americans cooperated with the Spanish hierarchy in the defense of their homeland, the latent animosity of European versus American impinged upon the common effort against the enemy. As the subjects of the New World readied themselves to send representatives to Spain—to serve on the Junta Central, the Regency, and the Cortes of Cádiz—they began to grasp the full significance of the change that was occurring in the colonial relationship. Armed with the knowledge of the Enlightenment and their aspirations for a better existence, Central Americans anticipated much of the reform program that emerged from the deliberations at Cádiz. They opted for biennial elections in their municipalities and instructed their delegates in parliament to secure home rule for themselves as well as a progressive order of things. In every respect, Central Americans were ideologically ready for the Cádiz Experiment.

Under the direction of Captain General José de Bustamante, the Spanish hierarchy worked out satisfactorily the preliminary arrangements for establishing a constitutional regime. The electoral ordinance and instructions were drawn up with dispatch and imagination, allowing Central America a maximum representation. The organizing genius of the Honduran José del Valle was especially notable on that occasion. As a result, the municipal elections of late 1812 came off smoothly. The lower classes, however, were apathetic. Younger members of the elite around Guatemala City were the conspicuous victors of the first constitutional elections. Among them were future founding fathers of Central America, who gained valuable political training under the Cádiz system.

The animosity between Iberian and American, however, frustrated and delayed the national set of elections in early 1813 and committed Central Americans irretrievably to constitutionalism. Just as Spaniard and Creole had polarized at Cádiz over the American Question, the Spanish hierarchy in Central America became convinced that the native-born were treacherously planning for a break from Spain. Guatemalans, on the other hand, viewed the obstructionism of Spanish officials as the perverse actions of anticonstitutionalists. Letter after letter to the authorities in Cádiz registered the unconstitutional procedures of Bustamante and his colleagues. Hoping for redress, Americans anxiously awaited the verdict from Cádiz, carrying out, in the meantime, the dictates of the Cádiz Experiment as best as they could under the circumstances. Bustamante deliberately stalled the establishment of the Diputaciones Provinciales in Guatemala City and León for almost a year; fortunately, the Municipality of Guatemala City corrected the situation somewhat by assuming provincial functions in the interim. The devotion of Central Americans to constitutionalism was unquestionably the salient characteristic of this first trial.

The timidity and unwillingness of the Spanish Parliament to support Guatemalans against Bustamante and his associates was a source of great disillusionment to many Creoles, preparing some of them for eventual independence from Spain. That was the significance of the conspiracy that aborted in Guatemala City during the waning days of 1813. After the return of Ferdinand VII to the throne of Spain, Bustamante's vindictive program simply reinforced the determination of certain leaders throughout Central America to separate from the mother country at the appropriate time.

During the second constitutional period, the hostility between European and American assured the expected break with Spain. The resistance of Spanish treasury officials on the tariff and customs issues was particularly annoying to Central American leaders, not to mention its crucial effect upon the worsening financial situation. Yet there was a notable contrast in the cooperation of Spanish political chiefs with their American colleagues on the provincial deputation of Guatemala City, establishing a precedent that affected the nature of the upper house in the future national and state governments of Central America.

Although Central Americans admired the Cádiz system and tried to implement its institutions throughout their area, the fact was that the program suffered from a lack of financial resources. Central America had been experiencing an economic depression since the end of the eighteenth century. This stubborn fact of life, plus the distance involved in traveling to Spain, meant that Creoles would never have an adequate representation in the Spanish National Parliament. As it turned out, the same factors worked against the connection with Mexico City and later within Central America itself, fanning regionalist fires everywhere.

To fail in the collection of taxes during a depression was understandable enough, but it was even more difficult to make ends meet in the psychological context of Independence. Along with political freedom, the liberated parties expected a respite from the onerous taxation of the colonial order. When this turned out to be an empty dream, dissension became widespread throughout Central America. It was difficult, for example, to convince the masses of Indians that relief from the degrading tribute payment meant that they would now be expected to pay their proper share of duties as integrated citizens of the body politic, especially since the new tax load exceeded the previous one. The non-Indians were no more sophisticated in their expectations. They opted for a more complex and expensive form of government without being willing to subject themselves to the responsibility of paying taxes. Many would not even permit themselves to be counted and others did not vote in elections in order to avoid taxation—a condition that prevailed throughout Central America at all levels of government. Such resistance, of course, precluded the establishment of viable political order.

The endemic regionalism of the colonial centuries surfaced with a vengeance in the early nineteenth century and eventually overwhelmed the Central American Republic. Although the Cádiz experiment did not create "federalism" it did in fact encourage it by permitting regional elements to articulate their aspirations and needs. All future states of Central America, at one time or another, lobbied for the major institutions of home rule: an intendancy (financial control), a seminary or university (educational system), a bishopric (religious establishment), and a diputación provincial (economic and political administration). Furthermore, the Cortes of Cádiz sanctioned and encouraged the sundry provincial projects submitted to it by the representatives of Central America. Many of these concessions—the Salvadoran bishopric, for example—loomed as major issues during the early years of the Republic, dividing states' righters and centralists.

The hostility of provincial interests toward Guatemala City, the old capital of the Kingdom, conditioned the shifting political alignments of Central America. Costa Rica, so distant from the capital, found it advantageous to side with Guatemala City in order to escape from León's control over her. San José in particular favored this strategy which also undermined its rival Cartago, the former center of the Costa Rican area. Moreover, San José's republicanism aided the same goals. León, Nicaragua, resented the subservience of its provincial deputation to the authorities in Guatemala City in religious and judicial matters. The Leonese aspired to complete independence from the Guatemalan capital and for a larger jurisdiction within Central America. Thus, León's officials resisted the pressure of Gabino Gaínza in Guatemala City during the post-Independence period and openly sided with the Mexican Empire as a more convenient alternative. After all, Mexico reportedly had a stronger financial base; and, considering the distance to Mexico City, it was reasonable to expect a greater degree of autonomy for Nicaragua in joining the Mexicans. On the other hand, Guatemala City allied itself with Granada, who openly defied the government at León. A tragic bloodbath ensued that drained Nicaragua and Central America for many years to come. Republicanism was also a bond between Granada and Guatemala City.

The pattern in Honduras was similar. Comayagua wanted full control of her former ports, Omoa and Tujillo. She was the first in Central

America to announce in favor of a separate provincial deputation of her own. Guatemalan authorities countered this initiative successfully with military force; the cooperation of Tegucigalpa, another center of republicanism, strengthened the cause of Guatemala City. Salvadorans likewise opted for republicanism and resisted the general move toward the Mexican Empire until military actions brought them back into the fold. Chiapas' secession to Mexico was never reversed; and this pattern influenced the provincial aspirations of Los Altos, led by the highland city of Quezaltenango. The Mexican connection, however, did nothing to assuage the regional hostilities of Central America. They merely smoldered, only to revive again in the deliberations of the National Constituent Assembly in Guatemala City.

Federalism was the dominant voice in the framing of the Constitution of 1824. The Central American charter, like its Spanish model, tried to maintain a blend of centralism and federalism without satisfying either position. Disgruntled Salvadorans set the pattern of secession by declaring the existence of the State of El Salvador; thereafter they reported only accomplished facts to the National Assembly. The Salvadoran defiance on financial and religious questions, imitated by other states as well, helped to bring civil war to Central America in 1826, thus marking the end of the Experiment for all practical purposes.

The Cádiz reforms served as the parliamentary tradition of Central America in the immediate years after Independence. The political structures of the Spanish system were adapted to the national and state governments of the region. Economic developmental plans and techniques, educational objectives and forms, social goals and measures, racial and cultural integration of the Indian, and the general program of freedoms associated with Central American liberalism underscored its deep indebtedness to the Spanish precursor. The utilitarian features of the Spanish experiment, moreover, reappeared in Central America during the Revolution of 1870, headed by Justo Rufino Barrios of Guatemala.

Notes

CHAPTER ONE

1. Gaspar de Jovellanos, "Elogio Fúnebre," Madrid, December 8, 1788, Venceslao de Linares y Pacheco, ed., *Obras de Jovellanos* (8 vols., Barcelona, 1839–1840), III, 273.
2. *Ibid.*, p. 265.
3. *Ibid.*, p. 266.
4. *Ibid.*, p. 270.
5. *Ibid.*, pp. 271–272.
6. *Ibid.*, p. 272.
7. *Ibid.*, p. 277.
8. *Ibid.*, pp. 275–276.
9. Gaspar de Jovellanos, "Informe de la Sociedad Económica de Madrid al Real y Supremo Consejo de Castilla en el expediente de Ley Agraria," *Obras*, VII, 29–185. Also see "Noticia histórica del Excmo. Señor Don Gaspar Melchor de Jovellanos," by the editor of *Obras*, VIII, 205–228, containing a brief biography of Jovellanos and a digest of the *Informe*.
10. Richard Herr, *The Eighteenth Century Revolution in Spain* (Princeton, New Jersey, 1958), p. 379.
11. Jovellanos, *Obras*, VII, 83–84, and 372, footnote 9 on Smith.
12. *Ibid.*, p. 35.
13. *Ibid.*, p. 37–38.
14. *Ibid.*, pp. 72–79, 123–126, 139–141.
15. *Ibid.*, p. 83.
16. *Ibid.*, pp. 46–47.
17. *Ibid.*, pp. 94–95, 103–104.
18. *Ibid.*, pp. 58–59.
19. *Ibid.*, pp. 141–142.
20. *Ibid.*, pp. 142–145.
21. *Ibid.*, pp. 146–147.
22. *Ibid.*, p. 149.
23. *Ibid.*, pp. 155–157.
24. *Ibid.*, pp. 158–159.
25. *Ibid.*, p. 168.
26. *Ibid.*, pp. 171.
27. *Ibid.*, p. 176.
28. *Ibid.*, pp. 176–178.
29. *Ibid.*, p. 181.

30. *Ibid.*, p. 179.
31. The work by Dr. Troy Floyd, *The Anglo-Spanish Struggle for Mosquitia* (Albuquerque, 1967), describes in detail the manner in which this exaggerated localism hampered the defense effort in Central America; also see François Chevalier, *Land and Society in Colonial Mexico: The Great Hacienda* (Berkeley, 1963), which reveals how the royal will was often thwarted locally. Subsequently the Crown legalized the usurpation of power. William H. Dusenberry, *The Mexican Mesta* (Urbana, Illinois, 1963), likewise exposes the effective power of cattlemen.
32. John Lynch, *The Spanish-American Revolutions, 1808–1826* (New York, 1973), pp. 5–7.
33. Herr, *Spain*, devotes Chapter II to "Regalism and Jansenism in Spain," pp. 11–36; also see Henry Kamen, *The War of Succession in Spain, 1700–15* (Bloomington, Indiana, 1969), pp. 361–395.
34. Herr, *Spain*, p. 147.
35. Real Consulado, "Apuntamientos sobre la agricultura y el comercio del Reyno de Guatemala, March 29, 1811, in *Economía guatemalteca en los siglos XVIII y XIX* (Guatemala City, 3rd ed., 1970), p. 63. See also my articles in the *Hispanic American Historical Review*, Vol. XXXVI (May 1956), 171–189, and Vol. XXXVIII (May 1958), 179–208, dealing with the economic history of seventeenth-century South America.
36. Royal cédula, April 22, 1804, Archivo General de Centro América (hereafter cited as AGCA), Guatemala City, Al. 23, legajo 1536, expediente 10091; also see cédula, May 31, 1789, AGCA, Al. 23, leg. 1532, exp. 10087, a printed set of rules on how the slaves were to be treated so that they might be made "useful," especially in the development of agriculture.
37. Arthur F. Corwin, *Spain and the Abolition of Slavery in Cuba, 1817–1886* (Austin, Texas, 1967), pp. 13–16.
38. Consulado, "Apuntamientos," p. 24.
39. *Ibid.*, pp. 23–28.
40. Murdo J. MacLeod, *Spanish Central America: A Socioeconomic History, 1520–1720* (Berkeley, Los Angeles, London, 1973), is authoritative in these matters.
41. Royal cédula, April 22, 1804, cited in note 36; also see the excellent discussion on the colonial economy by Robert C. West and John P. Augelli, *Middle America, Its Lands and Peoples* (Englewood Cliffs, New Jersey, 1966), pp. 276–307, and Robert S. Smith, "Indigo Production and Trade in Colonial Guatemala," *Hispanic American Historical Review*, Vol. XXXIX, No. 2 (May 1959), 181–211.
42. Troy S. Floyd, "The Guatemalan Merchants, the Government, and the *Provincianos*, 1750–1800," *HAHR*, Vol. XLI, No. 1 (February 1961), 90–110; also, translated into Spanish in *Economía guatemalteca en los siglos XVIII y XIX* (Guatemala City, 3rd ed., 1970), pp. 1–20.
43. Royal cédula, December 17, 1794, AGCA, Al. 23, leg. 4638, exp. 39591.
44. Royal cédulas. September 19, 1800, and December 16, 1803, AGCA, Al. 23, leg. 1536, exp. 10091; Royal Order, March 24, 1796, AGCA, Al. 5, leg. 2266, exp. 16445, that also promised free public lands for anyone wishing to cultivate flax and hemp in Central America.
45. Consulado, "Apuntamientos," pp. 62–63.
46. Royal order, June 1, 1792, AGCA, A3.9, leg. 158, exp. 3076.
47. Consulado, "Apuntamientos," pp. 53–55; also see the excellent analysis of these colonization schemes in William S. Sorsby, "Spanish Colonization of the Mosquito Coast, 1787–1800," *Revista Historia de América*, Nos. 73–74 (January–December 1972), pp. 145–153.

48. Royal cédula, December 23, 1786, AGCA, Al. 40, leg. 4797, which called for setting up the Intendancy of Comayagua: "por cuanto siendo conveniente a mi servicio y al bien de mis vasallos fomentar la provincia de Comayagua . . . y auxiliarla por todos los medios conducentes, para que restableciéndose sus havitantes, floresca en utilidad suya el comercio, y experimenten todas las ventajas y alivios que les deceo." Also see Al. 40, leg. 4797, folios 6r to 8r and Al. 23, leg. 4638, fol. 26v (El Salvador); Al. 23, leg. 4635 (Chiapas); Al. 23, leg. 1532, fol. 216r (Costa Rica); and Al. 23, leg. 4573, exp. 39.460.

49. Royal cédula, December 17, 1794, cited in note 43; also see the well-documented study of Ligia Estrada Molina, *La Costa Rica de don Tomás de Acosta* (San José, Costa Rica, 1965), who governed from 1797 to 1810.

50. This account is based on the excellent study of Professor Floyd on the Anglo-Spanish rivalry (see note 31).

51. (Ithaca, New York, 1956). It was awarded the Herbert Eugene Bolton Prize by the Conference on Latin American History (American Historical Association) in 1956.

52. Carlos Martínez Durán, *Las ciencias médicas en Guatemala* (Guatemala City, 1941) is excellent on this topic. Other key studies focusing on the intellectual ferment of this period are: John Tate Lanning, *The University in the Kingdom of Guatemala* (Ithaca, New York, 1955); Virgilio Rodríguez Beteta, *Evolución de las ideas* (Paris, 1929); Ramón A. Salazar, *Historia del desenvolvimiento intelectual de Guatemala* . . . (Tomo 1, Guatemala City, 1897), available in paperback (vols. 11–13, Editorial del Ministerio de Educación Pública, Guatemala City, 1951).

53. Fr. José Antonio Goicoechea to Rector of University, November 8, 1782, AGCA, Al. 3–1, leg. 1906, exp. 12633; Lanning, *Eighteenth-Century*, pp. 67–72, evaluates this key document. Since most documents do not include the surname Liendo, the name Goicoechea has been used instead.

54. *Ibid.*, p. 124.

55. *Gazeta* (Guatemala), no. 219, 1801, Tomo V, in which Goicoechea observed as follows about the faculty at the University: "cuerpo entre los más distinguidos, no sólo de América, sino aún de mucha parte de Europa. Sus doctores en lo general son sabios, piadosos, y reflexivos: sus Catedráticos enseñan las ciencias del modo más sólido que se puede imaginar. La filosofía Wolfi Loki Condillaciana, dictada con la firme persuasión de que sin muchos conocimientos matemáticos no será filosofía ni calabaza; la aritmética, geometría, óptica, estática, y geografía, componen hoy la mayor parte de un buen curso filosófico. Ya se pasó el tiempo de *mi nanita Chana*, en que hasta las muchachas se hacían partidarias de los *Tomistas, Escotistas*, y *Suaristas:* un *contra sic argumentor* hacía entonces más ruido que la atración Neutoniana. Una ú otra reliquia, que ha quedado de aquel tiempo, sirve para acordarnos el motivo de nuestros pasados atrasos."

56. *Gazeta* (Guatemala), no. 334, December 19, 1803, Tomo VII.

57. Robert J. Shafer, *The Economic Societies in the Spanish World (1763–1821)* (Syracuse, New York, 1958), pp. 215–218, discusses the alleged and perhaps valid reasons for the Sociedad's suspension in 1801.

58. *Ibid.*, pp. 195–198, 210, 213, 247–248, 312; *El Editor Constitucional* (Guatemala City), Supplement to No. 10, July 30, 1821, pp. 707–709; Actas, Guatemala City, No. 82, Sept. 28, 1820, No. 86, Oct. 7, 1820, No. 87, Oct. 9, No. 88, Oct. 10, 1820, AGCA/ Al.2.2, exp. 15746, leg. 2193; Acta, Guatemala City, No. 9, Jan. 30, 1821, AGCA/ Al.2.2, exp. 15747, leg. 2194.

59. This is evident in many issues of the *Gazeta*; see, for example, no. 9, April 10, 1797, containing a very meaningful quotation on all the reform institutions of the King-dom; no. 32, Sept. 11, 1797; no. 61, May 14, 1798; and no. 104, May 13, 1799.

60. The Consulado has received considerable attention from scholars. In English, see the works of Ralph Lee Woodward, Jr., *Class Privilege and Economic Development: The Consulado de Comercio of Guatemala, 1793–1871* (Chapel Hill, North Carolina, 1966), and Robert Sidney Smith, "Origins of the Consulado of Guatemala," *HAHR*, Vol. XXVI, No. 2 (May 1946), 150–161. Manuel Rubio Sánchez has produced the first installment of his monograph, "El real consulado de comercio," *Antropología e Historia de Guatemala*, 19:2 (July-Dec. 1967), pp. 59–73, covering the years 1781 to 1800. In 1787, when the parties who wanted the organization established wrote to the Crown, they provided an excellent overview of economic life in Central America. They wanted all non-whites excluded as well as those entrepreneurs with less than 20,000 pesos (see AGCA, A1.5, leg. 2266, exp. 16437, "Reglas porque se ha de governar el nuebo Consulado que se debe establecer en la Nueba Ciudad de Goathemala . . ." October 24, 1787).

61. *Reglamento para la propagación y estabilidad de la vacuna en el Reyno de Guatemala* (Nueva Guatemala, Ignacio Beteta, 1805), 29 pages, AGCA, A1. 38, leg. 1745, exp. 11716.

62. *Gazeta* (Guatemala), Prospectus, February 13, 1797, Tomo I.

63. *Ibid.*, No. 163, June 30, 1800, Tomo IV, "hombre de pelo en pecho, y de una imaginativa mui sugeta a la razón."

64. *Ibid.*, No. 151, March 7, 1800, Tomo IV.

65. *Ibid.*, No. 212, July 13, 1801, Tomo V; No. 354, July 9, 1804, Tomo VIII.

66. *Ibid.*, No. 221, Sept. 7, 1801, Tomo V.

67. *Ibid.*, No. 46, December 18, 1797, Tomo I.

68. *Ibid.*, No. 13, May 8, 1797 (De Pauw); No. 18, June 5, 1797 (Robertson); No. 25, July 14, 1797 (Morvilliers), Tomo I. In the earlier issues (No. 1, Nov. 27, 1797, and No. 4, March 6, 1797), the *Gazeta* had questioned similar views, especially on the effects of climate, by Montesquieu, Bodin, Chardin, Fontenelle, and the Greek historian Diodoro de Sincilia. This theme is treated in the excellent study by Antonello Gerbi, *The Dispute of the New World: The History of a Polemic, 1750–1900* (Pittsburg, 1973, translated by Jeremy Moyle).

69. *Gazeta* (Guatemala), No. 22, July 3, 1797, Tomo I.

70. Rodríguez Beteta, *Evolución*, pp. 27–31, reproduces the pertinent extracts of the treatise that appear in Nos. 49–51, Tomo II, of the *Gazeta*.

71. Rodríguez Beteta, *Evolución*, pp. 89–100 reproduces the article "El primer problema político económico del país—la despoblación de lleno en el libre comercio," which may have been prepared for the Economic Society.

72. Shafer, *Economic Societies*, pp. 131–132, and note 37, p. 134.

73. *Gazeta* (Guatemala), No. 22, July 3, 1797, Tomo I, in which the editor attacks race prejudice in general whether against the Indian or the ladino, saying "considero solamente que es un hombre, que en su semblante está impresa la imagen del Criador, lo mismo que en el mío." No. 172, Sept. 1, 1800, Tomo IV, reports the success of Tomás Ruiz, an Indian who subsequently received his Doctorate in Philosophy; he also taught at the seminario in León, Nicaragua, that eventually was given university status: see No. 290, Feb. 7, 1803, Tomo VII, praising Ruiz and Juan de los Santos Zuazo.

74. Rodríguez Beteta, *Evolución*, reproduces the article on pages 220–235 and 238–243. The last quotation appears on page 228.

75. *Ibid.*, p. 232 forward.

76. Royal cédula, Sept. 6, 1788, AGCA, A1. 23, leg. 1532, exp. 10087, concerns the Indians in Nicaragua and the malpractice of royal officials collecting tribute in kind at a fixed price and then selling it at a much higher price on the market. The intendente was ordered to prevent this abuse; whether he did or not is another question.

77. Lanning, *Eighteenth-Century*, pp. 9–19.
78. Royal cédula, June 7, 1815, AGCA, Al.23, leg. 1543, exp. 10098; also reproduced in John Tate Lanning, *Reales Cédulas de la Real y Pontífica Universidad de San Carlos de Guatemala* (Guatemala City, 1954), pp. 300–303.
79. Consulado, "Apuntamientos," pp. 21–70 for the entire document (see note 34).
80. *Ibid.*, p. 41.
81. *Ibid.*, p. 46.
82. *Ibid.*, p. 48.
83. *Ibid.*, p. 49.
84. *Ibid.*, p. 50.
85. *Ibid.*, p. 51.
86. *Ibid.*, pp. 62–64.

CHAPTER TWO

1. Decree, Cádiz, February 14, 1810, Archivos Nacionales de Costa Rica (hereinafter ANCR), *Actas, 1800–1810*, doc. no. 336, p. 130; also in Luciano de la Calzada Rodríguez, *La evolución institucional; las Cortes de Cádiz: precedentes y consecuencias* (Zaragoza, 1959) Publicación no. 220 de la Institución "Fernando El Católico," p. 33.
2. For the events of this date, see the *Diario de las discusiones y actas de las Cortes* (Cádiz, 20 vols., 1811–1813), September 24, 1810, and *El Conciso* (Cádiz), September 26, 1810, both in my personal collection; and *El Español* (London), Oct. 7, 1810, which contains the report of Nicolás María de Sierra, Secretario de Estado y del Despacho Universal de Gracia y Justicia, September 24, 1810.
3. Junta Central Decree, Sevilla, January 29, 1810, in Gaspar de Jovellanos, *Obras de Jovellanos* (8 vols., Barcelona, 1839–1840), VIII, 113–119. For an excellent description of the conditions at Cádiz during this period, see Ramón Solís, *El Cádiz de las Cortes* (Madrid, 1958). He discusses the make-up of Parliament on pages 250–251.
4. *Diario*, September 24, 1810.
5. *El Conciso* (Cádiz), September 26, 1810.
6. *Diario*, September 24; January 29 decree, *Obras de Jovellanos*, VIII, 113–119.
7. *Diario*, September 25, Oct. 1–3, 1810; and James F. King, "The Colored Castes and American Representation in the Cortes of Cádiz," *HAHR*, XXXIII, No. 1 (February 1953), pp. 38–42, for a detailed analysis and description of the American maneuver.
8. Consulta de Gaspar de Jovellanos, Sevilla, May 21, 1809, *Obras*, VIII, 84.
9. Geoffry A. Cabat, "The Consolidation of 1803 in Guatemala," *The Americas*, Vol. XXVIII, No. 1 (July 1971), 20–38, and especially Asunción Lavrín's article, "The Execution of the Law of *Consolidación* in New Spain: Economic Aims and Results," *Hispanic American Historical Review*, Vol. 53, No. 1 (February 1973), 27–49, provide excellent treatment on the impact of Godoy's measure in those parts of the Spanish world. Also see the remarks about the Consolidación in *Obras de Jovellanos*, VIII, 244–245, and the *Diario*, Tomo III, 278–279, and Tomo XV, 62.
10. Royal cédula, November 23, 1799, Archivo General de Centro América (hereafter AGCA), Guatemala City, Al.38, leg. 1904, exp. 12573; *Gazeta de Guatemala* (Guatemala City), March 11, 1811.
11. Gabriel H. Lovett, *Napoleon and the Birth of Modern Spain* (2 vols., New York, 1965) provides an excellent description of military events, especially in Volume One.
12. See the documents on this topic in *Obras de Jovellanos*, VII, 222, and in *El Español* (London), April 30, 1810. The indispensable authority on this period is Miguel

Artola, *Los orígenes de la España contemporánea* (2 vols., Madrid, 1959). And for French-occupied Spain also see his study, *Los afrancesados* (Madrid, 1953).

13. *El Español*, April 30, 1810; *Semanario Patriótico* (Cádiz), September 1, 1808; *Obras de Jovellanos*, VII, 229, 251–252, 318–319; Jovellanos and Romana to Junta de Valencia, Sevilla, October 23, 1809, Archivo Histórico Nacional, Madrid (hereafter AHNM), Estado, leg. 11.

14. *Obras de Jovellanos*, VII, 265; *El Español*, February 30, 1810.

15. *Obras de Jovellanos*, VII, 306–309; *Semanario Patriótico*, January 2, 1812, reviews Jovellanos' contribution. Agustín Argüelles, for example, served on the constitutional committee, and Antonio Capmany headed the special committee on the History of Parliaments in Spain.

16. See documents 67–78, AHNM, Estado, leg. 54, exp. D. Document 71 is the Jan. 22 decree, which was reissued on June 5, 1809; also see the documents and Blanco-White's commentary on them in *El Español*, Sept. 30, 1810, and January 30, 1811.

17. Consulta, Sevilla, May 21, 1809, *Obras de Jovellanos*, VIII, 78–89.

18. *Ibid.*, VII, 313, 315, 325–326.

19. *Ibid.*, 316–317, 322–323, and VIII, 93–95.

20. *El Español*, Sept. 30, 1810; the decree of January 29 can be consulted in *Obras de Jovellanos*, VIII, 113–119. Also see Jovellanos' comments, VII, 333–344. Fernando Jiménez de Gregorio, *La convocación a Cortes Constituyentes en 1810. Estado de la opinión española en punto a la reforma constitucional* (Madrid, 1955), pp. 251–253, has demonstrated that Spanish public opinion supported Jovellanos' traditional approach to constitutional reform. Also see his discussion of the Junta Central's last decree (pp. 270–271).

21. *Gazeta de Regencia* (Cádiz), March 13, 1810, and Jan. 29, 1810, decree, cited in note 20; also see *Obras de Jovellanos*, VII, 341.

22. *El Español*, July 30, 1810, reproduces the pertinent documentation along with Blanco-White's commentary of same.

23. Acta, No. 36, October 15, 1810, Junta de Cádiz, AHNM, Estado, leg. 944; Agustín de Argüelles, *Examen histórico de la reforma constitucional que hicieron las Cortes Generales y Extraordinarias* (2 vols., London, 1835), I, 174–175, 247.

24. Acta, No. 42, June 10, 1810, Junta de Cádiz, AHNM, Estado, leg. 943; *El Español*, July 30, 1810; Argüelles, *Examen histórico*, I, 175–176; Alvaro Flórez Estrada, *Examen imparcial de las disensiones de América con España* (Cádiz, 1812), pp. 23–24.

25. Actas, No. 72, July 5, 1810, and No. 75, July 6, 1810, Junta de Cádiz, AHNM, Estado, leg. 943; *El Español*, September 30, 1810, reproducing the Regency's order of August 30, 1810; Argüelles, *Examen histórico*, I, 178–179.

26. *Diario*, February 15, 1811.

27. Acta, June 10, 1810, cited in note 24; *El Español*, July 30, 1810; Argüelles, *Examen histórico*, I, 180–181.

28. See documents 6–42, AHNM, Estado, leg. 57, exp. C; on the loans, see number 23 and 24, January 18, 1809, and González's four-page broadside, "Donativo patriótico voluntario."

29. Actas, Ayuntamiento de Guatemala, Nos. 68–72, August 14–23, 1808, AGCA, Guatemala City, Al.2.2, exp. 15734, leg. 2188; acta, No. 23, March 14, 1809, Guatemala City, AGCA, Al.2.2., exp. 15735, leg. 2188, which includes González's publication of February 20, 1809. It is interesting to note that on May 1, 1811, González Sarabia was seriously being considered for the post of Viceroy of Mexico, but some gentlemen in Parliament (the Llanos?) argued that he was not qualified for the post. The nomination was dropped. See, acta secreta, Cádiz, May 1, 1811, in *Actas de*

las sesiones secretas de las Cortes Generales Extraordinarias de la nación española (Madrid, 1874), p. 270.

30. Publication of February 20, 1809, cited in note 29, with enclosure, Ceballos to González, Aranjuez, November 1, 1808; decree, Junta Central, Aranjuez, October 13, 1808, in *Gazeta de Guatemala* (Guatemala City), February 2, 1809, contributing to the same stereotype.

31. González to Central Americans, Guatemala City, February 20, 1809, in acta, No. 23, March 14, 1809, cited in note 29; acta, No. 101, Guatemala City, November 16, 1810, AGCA, Al.2.2, exp. 15736, leg. 2189, which reviews all the correspondence on the incident.

32. Ayuntamiento de Guatemala to Junta Central, Guatemala City, January 24, 1809, AHNM, Estado, leg. 57, Exp. C, doc. 26.

33. Acta, No. 99, November 15, 1808; actas, No. 11 (February 3), and No. 12 (Feb. 7), No. 28 (April 7), No. 37 (May 5, 1809).

34. Ayuntamiento de Comayagua to Spanish government, 1808, AHNM, Estado, leg. 57, exp. C, Doc. 23; actas, September 24 and July 1806, February 6, 1808, Tegucigalpa, Archivo Nacional de Honduras, leg. 13, paquete 13; acta, No. 12, Quezaltenango, March 26, 1806, *Libro de Quezaltenango* (edited by Francis Gall, consulted in manuscript form); acta, May 30, 1809, Cartago, ANCR, *Actas, 1800–1810*, p. 67. It should be noted that interest in municipal reforms before 1812 was lacking in Mexico as contrasted to Central America according to Roger L. Cunniff, "Mexican Municipal Electoral Reform, 1810–1822," in Nettie Lee Benson, ed., *Mexico and the Spanish Cortes, 1810–1822; Eight Essays* (Austin, Texas, 1966), pp. 59–86.

35. Actas, Guatemala City, No. 112 (December 22), No. 113 (December 23, 1808), and No. 9 (January 27, 1809).

36. Actas, Guatemala City, Nos. 10 (January 30), 26 (March 23), 31 (April 18), 32 (April 19), 33 (April 21), 34 (April 25), 36 (May 2), 42 (May 24), 47 (June 6), 48 (June 8), 50 (June 16), 52 (June 21), 54 (June 27), 95 (November 11, 1809) and 1 (January 2, 1811).

37. Actas, Quezaltenango, May 26, Sept. 1 and 5, October 27, 31, 1809 and August 17, Sept. 25, 1810; acta, Cartago, May 30, 1809, pp. 79–80; actas, Tegucigalpa, May 22, December 22, 1809; actas, Guatemala City, Nos. 79 (Sept. 22), 80 (Sept. 26), 95 (November 11, 1809) and 19 (March 2), 20 March 9, 1810. For the choices of 14 cities that voted, see *Boletín del Archivo General de Central América*, Tomo 3, No. 3 (April 1938), note 16, p. 381.

38. Acta, Guatemala City, No. 4, January 11, 1811, AGCA, A1.2.2, exp. 15737, leg. 2189, Libro de Cabildo, 1811; Acta, Quezaltenango, February 12, 1811; acta, Tegucigalpa, March 6, 1811.

39. Actas, Quezaltenango, January 22, 1811 (on Father López Rayón) and July 13, 1810 (on instructions). The Regent Miguel de Lardizábal was sent a copy of the instructions (acta, July 27, 1810).

40. Actas, Guatemala City, No. 102, November 20, 1810, No. 12 (Feb. 1), No. 71 (August 20), No. 81 (Sept. 24), No. 82 (Sept. 27), No. 85 (October 8, 1811).

41. Tomás Acosta to King, Cartago, April 19, 1810, ANCR, *Actas, 1800–1810*, pp. 109–113.

42. *Gazeta de Guatemala* (Guatemala City), July 21, 1810.

43. Actas, Guatemala City, No. 66 (August 9), and No. 75 (Sept. 2, 1808).

44. Acta, Guatemala City, No. 15, February 17, 1809, plus enclosure by González "Aviso al público" of February 15, 1809.

45. Acta, Guatemala City, No. 104, December 11, 1809, and minutes Nos. 13–15, and No. 26 in 1810; and González's published reports of April 20 and May 15, 1810, in ANCR, *Actas 1800–1810*, pp. 132–135.

46. Actas, Guatemala City, No. 56 (June 19) and No. 64 (July 10, 1810); *Gazeta de Guatemala* (Guatemala City), No. 219, May 22, 1811.

47. Acta, Guatemala City, No. 10, January 30, 1810; also see the analysis of this document in Fernando Jiménez de Gregorio, *La convocación a Cortes*, pp. 250–251 and in Jorge Mario García Laguardia, "Estado de la opinión sobre convocatoria a Cortes Constituyentes en 1810: Actitud del Ayuntamiento de Guatemala," *Estudios* (Universidad de San Carlos, Departamento de la Facultad de Humanidades, Guatemala), No. 3 (1969), pp. 23–39. The document is reproduced in the latter reference, along with an interpretive introduction which challenges the Jiménez view.

48. Acta, No. 10, January 30, 1810; Ayuntamiento de Bogotá to Junta Central, Bogotá, November 20, 1809, in Camilo Torres, *El memorial de agravios, pregón de la independencia* (Tunja, Colombia, 1960, ed. by Rafael Salamanca Aguilera), pp. 42–61.

49. Acta, Guatemala City, No. 10, January 30, 1810.

50. Acta, Guatemala City, No. 45, May 22, 1810.

51. Actas, No. 53 (June 8) and No. 63 (July 6, 1810).

52. For details on the elections see, *Boletín del Archivo de Centro América,* Tomo 3, No. 4 (July 1938), p. 470, and Sofonías Salvatierra, *Contribución a la historia de Centro América* (2 vols., Managua, 1939), II, 288–290; *Gazeta de Guatemala* (Guatemala City), July 28, December 19, 1810.

53. Acta, Guatemala City, No. 89, October 9, 1810; acta, Cartago, November 2, 1810, plus enclosures, ANCR, *Actas, 1800–1810*, pp. 162–163, 172–173, and Castillo to Ayuntamiento de Cartago, Cádiz, July 18, 1811, ANCR, CC 2344.

54. *Instrucciones para la constitución fundamental de la monarquía española y su gobierno de que ha de tratarse en las próximas cortes generales de la nación . . . .* (Guatemala City, 1953). First published in Cádiz in 1811. Sofonías Salvatierra (cited, note 52) discovered a manuscript copy in the Archivo General de Indias (Sevilla), the one edited and footnoted by Captain General José de Bustamante. It was reproduced in the *Anales de la Sociedad de Geografía e Historia de Guatemala* in 1943. The present reproduction honors the centennial of Antonio Larrazábal's death; César Brañas, a noted literary figure in Guatemala, wrote the excellent introduction to the document (hereafter called "Instrucciones"); for an expanded version of this introduction, see César Brañas, *Antonio Larrazábal, un guatemalteco en la historia* (2 vols., Guatemala, 1969); it is a digest of all that has been written about Larrazábal to date and it reproduces many key documents concerning him.

55. "Apuntes Instructivos pa. el Diputado de Cortes de Guatemala," Guatemala City, December 20, 1810, *Revista de la Facultad de Ciencias Jurídicas y Sociales de Guatemala*, Epoca 3.a, Tomo II, No. 1 (March-April 1939), 136–159 (hereafter "Apuntes").

56. "Instrucciones," p. 9.

57. *Ibid.*, pp. 10–13 for all 30 points.

58. In all, six points dealt with religion, *ibid.*, pp. 13–15.

59. *Ibid.*, pp. 19–24.

60. Article 83, *ibid.*, p. 27, on Indians.

61. "Apuntes," p. 152.

62. "Instrucciones," p. 42.

63. *Ibid.*, p. 50.

64. *Ibid.*, pp. 52.

65. *Ibid.*, pp. 52–54.

66. *Ibid.*, pp. 55–58.

67. Acta, Guatemala City, No. 84, September 20, 1810, erroneously numbered 34.

68. "Instrucciones," pp. 70–77.
69. *Ibid.*, p. 85.
70. "Apuntes," p. 143.
71. *Ibid.*, pp. 150–151.
72. *Ibid.*, p. 158.

CHAPTER THREE

1. *El Español* (London), August 30, 1811.
2. *Diario* (Cádiz), March 29, 1813.
3. José Alvarez de Toledo y Dubois, *Manifiesto o satisfacción pundonorosa a todos los buenos españoles europeos, y a todos los pueblos de la América, por un diputado de las Cortes reunidas en Cádiz* (Philadelphia, 1811), which is available in the Rare Book Room, Library of Congress, Washington, D.C. I have used what amounts to the second edition of this pamphlet, entitled *Objecciones satisfactorias del mundo imparcial al folleto dado a luz por el marte-filósofo de Delaware Don José Alvarez de Toledo* (Charleston, 1812), which reproduces the original manifesto as well as a scathing rebuttal by Terso Machuca, a Cuban-based Spaniard. James F. King, "The Colored Castes and American Representation in the Cortes of Cádiz," *HAHR*, XXXIII, No. 1 (February 1953), pp. 33–48, stresses the importance of the Castas issue from September 25, 1810, forward; and his documentaiton is convincing although not conclusive.
4. Actas secretas, Cádiz, October 10, 11, 14, pp. 15–16, 19, in *Actas de las sesiones secretas de las Cortes Generales Extraordinarias de la nación española* (Madrid, 1874). Although valuable, these minutes of the secret meetings are much too brief. More important for the present interpretation are the innuendoes in the public debates of January and February 1811, the editorials in the Cádiz press, and the subsequent publications of participants.
5. Decree, Cádiz, October 15, 1810, in José Muro Martínez, comp., *Decretos y órdenes de Cortes en las dos épocas de 1810 a 1814, y 1820 a 1823* (Valladolid, 1875), p. 5; *Diario*, January 9, 1811.
6. "Proposiciones que hacen al Congreso Nacional los diputados de América y Asia," Isla de León, December 16, 1810, in Alvarez de Toledo y Dubois, *Objecciones*, pp. 43–47. For an English translation and evaluation of the propositions, see William Walton, *An Exposé on the Dissentions of Spanish America* (London, 1814), pp. 282–289.
7. *Diario* (Cádiz), January 11, 1811.
8. *Ibid.*, February 7 and 9, 1811; acta, Guatemala City, No. 92, October 16, 1810, AGCA, Al.2.2, exp. 15736, leg. 2189.
9. Alvarez de Toledo y Dubois, *Objecciones*, pp. 48–52; *Diario*, January 2, 1811.
10. See, for example, Argüelles, *Examen histórico*, I, 310–374, and II, 24–58; *Diario*, January 9 and 18, 1811, and February 13, 1811.
11. *Semanario Patriótico* (Cádiz), February 21, 1811, edited by Manuel José Quintana, one of Spain's great poets. He analyzes the eleven demands in this issue.
12. *Diario*, January 9 and 18, 1811, for the remarks of Mejía and Guridi Alcocer.
13. *El Telégrafo Americano* (Cádiz), December 11, 1811, January 1, 8, and 15, 1812.
14. *Diario*, January 18, 20, 23, and February 7, 1811; *Semanario Patriótico*, February 21, 1811.
15. *Diario*, January 27 and February 9, 1811. Some propositions were deferred until the discussion of the Constitution, later in 1811 and early 1812.
16. Demetrio Ramos, "Las Cortes de Cádiz y América," *Revista de Estudios Políticos* (Madrid, No. 126, Nov.-Dec. 1962), pp. 537–538, 552. His entire monograph appears on pages 433–639).
17. Juan López Cancelada, *Ruina de la Nueva España si se declara el comercio libre con los*

estrangeros (Cádiz, 1811), iii–vii, 12–13, 18–19, 46–47, 49, 54–58; also see, actas secretas, Cádiz, June 1, 2, 1811, in which Americans complained of this pamphlet, to no avail it seems.

18. Walton, *An Exposé*, pp. 285, 310; actas secretas, Cádiz, August 13, 15, and September 30, 1811.

19. "Representación de la Diputación Americana a las Cortes de España," Cádiz, August 1, 1811, in *El Español*, March 30, 1812, pp. 370–389; also available in the Rare Book Room, Library of Congress, Washington, D.C. *Pamphlets*, Vol. 144:35. Surprisingly, Ramos "Cortes," p. 572, mentions this document but does not analyze it at all.

20. *El Español*, March 30, 1812, pp. 374–375.

21. *Ibid.*, p. 387. It will be recalled that Jovellanos had made this point in the *Informe de Ley Agraria* of 1795.

22. *Diario*, June 3 and July 11, 1811.

23. Argüelles, *Examen histórico*, II, pp. 24–25; Conde de Toreno, "Information on the principal events which took place in the government of Spain from the commencement of the insurrection in 1808 . . . ." *Pamphleteer* (London), trans. William Walton, XVII, No. 33 (1820), 16.

24. *Diario*, Sept. 3, 4, 10, 1811.

25. For an excellent evaluation of Article 22, see James F. King, "The Colored Castes," pp. 53–64.

26. *Diario*, Sept. 6, 1811; also see minutes of January 25, 1811, in which Guridi admitted that the suplentes had agreed to exclude the Castas but, he observed, "ni la voluntad de los Sres Diputados Americanos hace ley."

27. *Ibid.*, Sept. 6.

28. *Ibid.*, Sept. 5, 7, 1811.

29. *Ibid.*, Sept. 4, 1811.

30. *Ibid.*, Sept. 6, 1811.

31. *Ibid.*, Sept. 10, 1811.

32. *Ibid.*, Sept. 11, 1811.

33. *Ibid.*, January 26, 1812.

34. *Ibid.*, Sept. 14, 1811.

35. *Ibid.*, Sept. 15, 1811.

36. *Ibid.*, Sept. 14, 15, 20, 1811.

37. *Ibid.*, Sept. 16, 17, 18, 19, 20, 1811.

38. *Ibid.*, Sept. 27, 29, 1811.

39. *Ibid.*, October 23, November 9, and December 17, 1811, when Argüelles made the final argument.

40. *Ibid.*, January 10, 17, 1812.

41. *Ibid.*, January 17, 20, 1812.

42. *Ibid.*, January 23, 1812.

43. Argüelles, *Examen histórico*, I, 180–181.

44. *Ibid.*, II, 32–33.

45. *Diario*, Jan. 10, 12, 13, 14, 17, 1812.

46. *Ibid.*, June 5, 12, 16, 1813; in Muro Martínez, *Decretos*, June 23, 1813, pp. 168–185.

47. *Diario*, February 7, 1812, plus the Ayuntamiento's letter published in the minutes.

48. *Ibid.*, February 18, 1812.

49. *Ibid.*, February 23, 1812.

50. *Ibid.*, April 20, 1812.

51. *Ibid.*, April 27, 1812.

52. *Ibid.*, April 28, May 1, 1812.
53. Camilo Destruge, comp., *Discursos de Don José Mejía en las Cortes Españolas de 1810– 1813* (Guayaquil, 1909), and Alfredo Flores y Caamaño, *Don José Mejía Lequerica en las Cortes de Cádiz de 1810 a 1813 (o sea el principal defensor de los intereses de la América española en la más grade asamblea de la península* (Barcelona, 1913).
54. See, Ayuntamiento to Andrés and Manuel Llano, Guatemala City, February 10, 1811, in *Diario*, June 3, 1811; actas secretas, February 4, 7, 1812, pp. 554, 557, when Andrés was considered for a position on the Consejo de Estado.
55. *Ibid.*, December 14 and 17, 1810.
56. *Ibid.*, April 3 and July 3, 1811; also see minutes for January 5, February 6, Nov. 18, Dec. 30, 1811, January 16, March 5, and June 20, 1812.
57. Rafael Labra has analyzed the terms of the ten American presidents in his book *Los presidentes Americanos en las Cortes de Cádiz* (Cádiz, 1912).
58. See *Diario* for dates cited.
59. *Ibid.*, February 15, 1813; *Gazeta de Guatemala* (Guatemala City), March 29 and July 3, 1811; decree, Cádiz, June 28, 1812, in Muro Martínez, *Decretos*, p. 79.
60. *Diario*, October 24, 26, 1811, January 12, 1812, and February 16, 1813.
61. Decree, Cádiz, July 15, 1812, in Muro Martínez, *Decretos*, p. 80.
62. Actas, Guatemala City, Nos. 68 (August 13) and 86 (October 11, 1811), Al.2.2, exp. 15737, leg. 2189, Libro de Cabildo, 1811.
63. Actas, Consejo de Estado, Cádiz, August 28 and September 1, 1813, AHNM, Sección Estado, Libro 12; consultas, Consejo de Estado, Cádiz, September 18 and October 6, 1813, AHNM, Sección Estado, Libro 59.
64. Decrees, October 16, 1813, p. 204, December 1, 1811 (Matina) and April 29, 1814 (Punta de Arenas), p. 234 in Muro Martínez, *Decretos*; also in ANCR, CC, expediente 4238; consultas, Consejo de Estado, Cádiz, June 19, August 18, 1813, libro 59. The latter recommended the establishment of a bishopric. *Diario*, August 16, 1813, in which Castillo proposed the lowering of a tax on cacao.
65. *Diario*, March 21, 1812.
66. *Ibid.*, December 4, 1812.
67. *Ibid.*, May 29, 1813; Sofonías Salvatierra, *Contribución a la historia de Centro América* (2 vols, Managua, 1939), II, 310; and consultas, Consejo de Estado, Cádiz, July 3 and August 14, 1813. In *Diario* (Cádiz), October 3, 1813, consult the enclosure "Memoria, Secretaría del Despacho de la Governación de Ultramar," Cádiz, September 30, 1813, which reveals the progress made in Chiapas in the harvesting of grana (cochineal) since 1810 and plans for its expansion to the Lake Atitlán area of Guatemala. It also indicates that the Spanish government was seriously considering the canal recommended by Mariano Robles.

   Diario (Madrid), November 18, 1813, which includes the decision of the appropriate committee to commence the investigation on the feasibility of establishing a diputación provincial in Chiapas. The results of the inquiries would be forwarded to Guatemala City so that its diputación provincial could add its recommendations on the matter. *Diario*, October 27, 1813, reports on the disposition of Robles' many propositions—almost all of them favorably accepted.
68. *Diario*, August 27 and December 15, 1811.
69. Acta, Consejo de Estado, Cádiz, December 2, 1812, AHNM, Sección Estado, Libro 12.
70. Salvatierra, *"Contribución,"* II, 231–275; also see, *Diario*, July 13, August 16, 1813.
71. Salvatierra, *"Contribución,"* II, 310.
72. *Diario*, March 2, 29, 1813; consulta, Consejo de Estado, Cádiz, July 13, 1813.
73. *Diario*, November 22, 1811.

74. *Ibid.*, June 23, 1813.
75. *Ibid.*
76. Consulta, Consejo de Estado, Cádiz, May 3 and June 26, 1813.

CHAPTER FOUR

1. *Diario* (Cádiz), June 10, 1811.
2. *Redactor General de España* (Madrid), January 29, 1814.
3. For an excellent review of the polemical literature of the first constitutional period, see Fernando Jiménez de Gregorio, *La convocación a Cortes Constituyentes en 1810. Estado de la opinión española en punto a la reforma constitucional* (Madrid, 1955), pp. 224–239. That the controversy is still alive today can be illustrated in the work of Luciano de la Calzada Rodríguez, *La evolución institucional; las Cortes de Cádiz: precedentes y consecuencias* (Zaragoza, 1959), Publicación #220 de la Institución "Fernando el Católico," pp. 36–43.
4. Dictamen, Comisión de Constitución, December 24, 1811, in *Constitución política de la monarquía española* (Madrid, 1820), consulted in the Arturo Taracena Collection, Guatemala City. In explaining the theoretical bases for their recommendations to the Cortes, committee members acknowledged their debt to the precedents in the *Fuero Juzgo*, the code of laws of the Visigoths. Thus, the constitutional project, in their opinion, was "nacional y antiguo en la substancia, nuevo solamente en el orden y método de su disposición."
5. *Diario*, November 16, 18, 1811. Also see Article 248 of the Constitution.
6. *Diario*, September 25, 1811.
7. *Ibid.*, August 31, 1811.
8. Dictamen, December 24, 1811, in *Constitución política*.
9. Jiménez de Gregorio, *La convocación*, pp. 262–264, indicates that there was considerable resentment toward the nobility for its unwillingness to resist the French intruders. Also see *Diario*, August 11, 13, 1811.
10. *Ibid.*, June 4, 5, 1811.
11. *Ibid.*, June 6, 1811; decrees, August 6, 1811, and July 19, 1813, in José Muro Martínez, comp., *Decretos y órdenes de Cortes en las dos épocas de 1810 a 1814, y 1820 a 1823* (Valladolid, 1875), pp. 35, 189.
12. Guridi of Mexico explained this point well; see, *Diario*, June 10, 1811; also, June 11 and June 17, 1811.
13. Title 4 of the Constitution includes Articles 168 to 241, dealing with the executive power.
14. *El Censor* (Madrid), August 26, 1820, contains an excellent analysis of this institution, pp. 259–383; also see *Diario*, October 27, 29, 31, 1811, for the opinion of Agustín Argüelles and the Conde de Toreno.
15. *Ibid.*, January 2, 3, and February 19, 1812.
16. In the columns of *El Español* (London), Blanco-White frequently commented on the distorted power situation in Cádiz: see, for example, the issue of March 30, 1812.
17. Consulta, Consejo de Estado, June 23, 1813, libro 50, on Belize; resolution, Regency, July 4, 1813, AHNM, Sección Estado, leg. 64, on same; acta, Consejo de Estado, August 6, 1812, and January 30, 1813, libro 13, on U.S. aggression; consulta, Consejo de Estado, March 17, 1813, libro 50, on tobacco.
18. See Articles 18 to 26 in Constitution.
19. *Diario*, September 6, 1813, which gives details on the voting that took place in the Cortes for the first and only diputación permanente of the Cádiz era. Father Larrazábal received the highest vote of any of the seven deputies. The Peninsulars won the seventh position.

20. Article 366.
21. *Catecismo político para instrucción del pueblo* (Guatemala City, Casa de Beteta, 1811), based on Cádiz version of the fall of 1810.
22. See, for example, *Semanario Patriótico* (Cádiz), March 19, 1811; *Gazeta de Madrid* (Cádiz), November 20, 1810; and *El Robespierre Español* (Cádiz), July, 1811.
23. Article 371 in the Constitution prepared the ground for the decree issued in Madrid, August 6, 1820, during the second constitutional period. It was published and widely circulated by Guatemalan authorities in February 1821, AGCA, Al.39, leg. 1906, exp. 12642.
24. For a good bibliographical treatment of this topic, see Fray Cesáreo de Armellada, *La causa indígena americana en las Cortes de Cádiz* (Madrid, 1959); it is short on interpretation, however.
25. *Diario*, May 13, 1811; Juan López Cancelada, and his paper *El Telégrafo Americano* (Cádiz) reported the abuses in many issues.
26. *Diario*, August 21, 1811.
27. *Ibid.,* March 12, 13, 1811; decree, March 13, 1811, in Muro Martínez, *Decretos,* pp. 18–19.
28. *Diario*, October 21, 1812.
29. Actas, Quezaltenango, Nos. 3 and 4, January 10, 14, 1812, *Libro de Quezaltenango* (Francis Gall); also see *Diario*, May 4, 1812, describing the reaction to the tribute decree in Peru, and January 25 and February 13, 1812, the delays in Central America.
30. Asesor's expediente, Guatemala City, August 9, 1821, AGCA, A3.16, leg. 2569, exp. 37.716. For Peru, see *Diario*, August 13, 1813, containing a letter from Trujillo, in which the Indians complained of efforts to force them to pay the tribute, dated February 13, 1813.
31. Ayuntamiento, Guatemala City, to Cortes, November 8, 1811, published in *Diario*, April 20, 1812. Father Larrazábal read the document into the minutes, a very perceptive analysis of ejido abuses.
32. *Ibid.*, for Larrazábal's recommendation.
33. *Ibid.*, March 12, 1811, in which Argüelles remarked: "Las Tierras en manos de los indios sin capitales para reducirlas a cultivo son inútiles, pues que no pueden producir fruto alguno espontáneamente." For details on the Regency's actions, see *Diario*, Oct. 3, 1813, with enclosure, Memoria, Secretario del Despacho de la Gobernacíon de Ultramar, Sept. 30, 1813, pp. 69–75 (p. 72 for specific information).
34. *Ibid.*, February 14, 1812; also see May 29, 1813, for Mariano Robles' recommendations for Indian scholarships.
35. *Ibid.*, April 14, 1812, when Father Castillo's bills were first introduced; on August 12, 1812, the committee reported its findings to Parliament.
36. *Ibid.*, August 12.
37. *Ibid.*, October 21 and November 9, 1812; decree, Cortes, Cádiz, September 8, 1813, in Muro Martínez, *Decretos*, outlawing public beatings (*azotes*) as degrading punishment for the Indian.
38. *El Español*, May 30, 1811, presents a realistic view on the abolition of slavery although it favors the end of the slave trade (pp. 149–154).
39. *Diario*, April 2, 1811, which reproduces the project.
40. Arthur F. Corwin, *Spain and the Abolition of Slavery in Cuba, 1817–1886* (Austin, Texas, 1967), p. 23, claims that Argüelles had made this statement to José Antonio Saco of Cuba.
41. *Diario*, April 2, 1811; also see April 19 minutes.
42. *Ibid.*, December 14, 1811.
43. *Ibid.*, March 14, 1812; also, Ayuntamiento, Guatemala city, to Larrazábal, August

13, 1811, *Boletín del Archivo General de Centro América*, Tomo III, No. 4 (July 1938), 493–498.

44. Larrazábal to Ayuntamiento, Cádiz, January 13, 1813, *ibid.*, 507–508; *Diario*, March 14, 1812.

45. Consulta, Consejo de Estado, Cádiz, March 17, 1813, AHNM, Sección Estado, Libro 50, consisting of 104 folios.

46. Actas secretas, Cádiz, June 1, 16, 17, 18, 1811, *Actas de las sesiones secretas de las Cortes Generales Extraordinarias de la nación española* (Madrid, 1874), pp. 299, 315–317; *El Español* (London), August 30, 1811, and the issue of April 30, 1811; William Walton, *An Exposé on the Dissentions of Spanish America* (London, 1814), pp. 307–318; Demetrio Ramos, "Las Cortes de Cádiz y América," *Revista de Estudios Políticos* (Madrid, No. 126, Nov.–Dec. 1962), 538–543, 559–591, for an extensive treatment of these negotiations.

47. Actas secretas, Cádiz, July 16, 17, 18, 1812, pp. 681–684; Walton, *Exposé*, pp. 319–321, for the remarks of an Englishman wholly in sympathy with the Americans.

48. *Diario*, March 29, 1813.

49. *Ibid.*

50. Resolution, Regency, Cádiz, October 18, 1812, AHNM, Sección Estado, leg. 63.

51. *Diario*, March 29 and April 10, 1813.

52. Instructions, Cádiz, June 23, 1813, in Muro Martínez, *Decretos*, pp. 168–185.

53. *Diario*, June 5, 1813.

54. *Ibid.*

55. *Ibid.*, June 10, 1813.

56. *Ibid.*, June 12, June 16, 1813.

57. *Ibid.*, March 18, 1813.

58. *El Español* (London), November 30, 1811.

59. *El Español* (January 10, 1811, September 30 and November 30, 1812, reproduce the key documents, as well as Blanco-White's commentary; also see *Semanario Patriótico* (Cádiz), November 29, 1810, opposing the Bishop's refusal in the initial stages of the incident; *Diario*, February 3, 1811, August 17, 1812; resolution, Regency, Cádiz, September 26, 1813, AHNM, Sección Estado, Leg. 64.

60. *Diario*, October 14, 15, 28, 1811; *El Español*, November 30, 1811, reviews the Cortes' reaction to the *Manifiesto* during October and pictures Argüelles as fearful of a "League" that had placed obstacles before Parliament since September 24, 1810—in short, the liberal leader was overly sensitive, perhaps even paranoid, in suggesting a conspiracy was afoot. Or was he playing to the galleries?

61. *Diario*, August 28, 29, 1811.

62. See, for example, Lardizábal to Ayuntamiento of Guatemala City, Cádiz, July 16, 1810, *Boletín AGCA*, Tomo III, No. 4 (July 1938), 474, in which he promises to carry out his instructions until the Americans were "legitimately represented." Also see, acta secreta, October 10, 1810, p. 14, which discusses a letter that Lardizábal had sent to the Cortes arguing that his instructions forbade any substantive changes in laws for the Americas until the arrival of proprietary deputies from overseas. The Cortes, however, denied the validity of those instructions on the grounds that they were issued for service on the Junta Central and not the present Parliament.

63. *El Español*, October 30, 1812, and enclosures.

64. Another incident involved the publication of Gregorio Vicente Gil, *España vindicada en sus clases*, which followed the position of Orense and Lardizábal; moreover, he criticized the Cortes for the rhetoric against the nobility in treating entailed estates, thus pitting classes against each other. Blanco-White again provided all the documents in *El Español*, November 30, 1811, and shamed Argüelles for using "the mother country is in danger" justification in violating the freedom-of-the-press principle.

65. In fact, Blanco-White, a clergyman himself, attacked the Cortes' abolition of the Inquisition on the grounds that it was too traditional. See *El Español*, Feb. 1813. For details on the Inquisition, see the special compilation; *Discusión del proyecto sobre el tribunal de la inquisición* (Madrid, 1870), also numbered Tomo VI.

66. "Manifiesto en que se exponen los motivos del decreto anterior," *ibid*, pp. 4533–4535; *Diario*, March 8, 9, and July 9, 1813; *El Español* (March 30, April 30, May 30, June 30, and August 30, 1813) for documents on this issue plus the usual perceptive insights; and *Abeja Española* (Cádiz), February 10, 1813, reflecting the polarization of the times on the clerical issue.

67. *Diario*, October 28, 1811; *El Español*, October 30, 1812, is excellent on this subject.

68. *El Español*, June 30, July 30, Sept. 30, and Oct. 30, 1813; *Abeja Española* (Cádiz), August 27, 1813, also perceptive on the disintegration of Spain.

69. *Redactor General* (Madrid), January 18, 1814.

70. *Ibid.*, Jan. 21, 22, 23, 1814.

71. *Ibid.*, February 5, 1814.

72. *El Censor* (Madrid), October 21, 1820; *Representación y manifiesto* . . . (Madrid, 1820), which reproduces the document signed by the 69 deputies, a stinging indictment of the entire Cádiz Experiment.

CHAPTER FIVE

1. Acta, Guatemala City, Cabildo Extraordinario, No. 9, September 18, 1812, folio 146, in which Bustamante said: "a nadie más toca el convite que a mí," Archivo General de Centro América (Guatemala City), Libros de Cabildo, 1812, Al.22, expediente 15738, legajo 2190 (hereafter: AGCA, L.C., 1812).

2. José de Bustamante to Regency, Guatemala City, May 18, 1814, León Fernández, ed., *Colección de documentos para la historia de Costa Rica* (10 vols., San José, Costa Rica, 1881–1907), X, 484 (hereafter, Col. Fernández).

3. *Gazeta del Gobierno de Guatemala* (Guatemala City), October 2, 1812, enclosed in Acta, Guatemala City, No. 13, September 26, 1812, AGCA, L.C., 1812.

4. *Ibid.*

5. *Ibid.*

6. *Diario de las discusiones y actas de las Cortes* (20 vols., Cádiz, 1811–1813), March 20, 1813 (hereafter, *Diario* [Cádiz]).

7. His service record is in the Archivo Histórico Nacional, Sección Estado, legajo 54, expediente E, documentos 89–98 (July 28, 1809 forward), putting him on a preferred list for a key appointment in the Kingdom of Guatemala.

8. "Manifiesto," Guatemala City, March 24, 1811, *Boletín del Archivo General de Centro América*, Tomo III, No. 4 (July 1938), 491–492; also see *Gazeta de Guatemala* (Guatemala City), March 29, 1811, and Acta, Guatemala City, No. 28, March 26, 1811, AGCA, Libros de Cabildo, 1811, Al.2.2, exp. 15737, leg. 2189 (hereafter, AGCA, L.C., 1811).

9. Actas, Guatemala City, Nos. 34 (April 26), 50 (June 14), 51 (June 17), 53 (June 21), and 86 (October 11, 1811), AGCA, L.C. 1811; and Acta, Quezaltenango, September 27 and October 29, 1811, Francis Gall's unpublished version of "Libro de Quezaltenango."

10. Actas, Guatemala City, Nos. 37 (May 4), 81 (September 24), and 103 (November 29, 1811), AGCA, L.C. 1811.

11. Acta, Guatemala City, No. 51, June 17, 1811, AGCA, L.C., 1811.

12. Actas, Quezaltenango, September 27, November 26, 1811, and January 7, May 5, 1812, "Libro de Quezaltenango"; and Acta, Guatemala City, No. 96, November 8, 1811, with enclosure "Lista . . . Cuerpo de Voluntarios," Guatemala City, November 8, 1811, AGCA, L.C. 1811.

13. Acta, Guatemala City, No. 97, November 12; 1811, containing the circular that was sent out on that date to all other ayuntamientos; also see Acta, No. 100, November 19, 1811, with its enclosures, AGCA, L.C., 1811; and Acta, Cartago, December 28, 1811, Col. Fernández, X, 344–345.

14. Actas, Guatemala City, Nos. 11 (January 29) and 99 (November 16, 1811), AGCA, L.C., 1811; Louis E. Bumgartner, *José del Valle of Central America* (Durham, North Carolina, 1963), pp. 64–65.

15. Acta, Guatemala City, No. 83, October 1, 1811, AGCA, L.C., 1811.

16. Actas, Guatemala City, Nos. 38 (May 20), 39 (May 22), 40 (May 29), 41 (June 2), 43 (June 9, 1812), plus an enclosed copy of the *Gazeta* in No. 40, AGCA, L.C., 1812.

17. Actas, Guatemala City, Nos. 9 (Cabildo Extraordinario, September 18, plus enclosure), 11 (September 23), 12 (September 25), and 13 (September 26, 1812) with enclosed letter, AGCA, L.C., 1812.

18. José de Bustamante to Ayuntamiento de Tegucigalpa, Guatemala City, January 20, 1812, Archivo Nacional de Honduras (Tegucigalpa), legajo 15, paquete 15 (hereafter ANH-T).

19. Bumgartner, *Valle*, Chapter 3, entitled "Steadfast Royal Servant, 1808–1815," pp. 54–84.

20. Universidad de San Carlos de Guatemala, *Economía guatemalteca en los siglos XVIII y XIX* (Guatemala City, 3rd. ed., 1970), p. 24, listing 313, 344 for Castas and Negroes. These statistics appear in the report of the Real Consulado, entitled "Apuntamientos sobre la agricultura y el comercio del Reyno de Guatemala," Guatemala City, March 29, 1811, pp. 21–70.

21. The Ayuntamiento of Guatemala City had made this recommendation to the Junta, who found it acceptable; see Acta, Guatemala City, No. 3, September 9, 1812, AGCA, L.C., 1812.

22. Acta, Guatemala City, No. 96, December 4, 1812, with enclosures "Tabla para facilitar la elección de los diputados de cortes, suplentes, y de provincia de Guatemala, 1812," and "Instrucción formada de orden de la junta preparatoria para facilitar las elecciones de diputados y oficios consejiles," Guatemala City, November 11, 1812, (40 pp. published by Beteta), AGCA, L.C., 1812.

23. Acta, Guatemala City, No. 98, November 20, 1812, AGCA, L.C., 1812; and Acta, Guatemala City, No. 1, December 7, 1812, AGCA, Libros de Cabildo, 1812–1813, Al.22, exp. 15739, leg. 2190 (hereafter, AGCA, L.C., 1812–1813).

24. Actas, Guatemala City, Nos. 1–4, December 7–18, 1812, AGCA, L.C., 1812–1813.

25. Acta, Guatemala City, No. 66, July 16, 1813, AGCA, L.C., 1812–1813.

26. Actas, Guatemala City, Nos. 22 (February 12 with enclosure "Proclama," Regency, Cádiz, August 30, 1812), and 46 (May 11, 1813), AGCA, L.C., 1812–1813.

27. Acta, Guatemala City, No. 18, January 29, 1813, AGCA, L.C., 1812–1813.

28. Actas, Guatemala City, Nos. 32 (March 18), 53 (June 4), 55 (June 11), 57 (June 18), 76 (August 20), 79 (August 31), and 81 (September 3, 1813), AGCA, L.C., 1812–1813.

29. Actas, Guatemala City, Nos. 89 (September 28), 90 (October 1), and 91 (October 5, 1813), AGCA, L.C., 1812–1813.

30. The following Actas, Guatemala City, are in AGCA, L.C., 1812–1813, if they are dated in 1813; or in AGCA, Libros de Cabildo, 1814, Al.2.2, exp. 15740, leg. 2191 (hereafter, AGCA, L.C., 1814) if it deals with the following year. On new business licenses, see No. 60, June 28, 1813; on meat supply, Nos. 62 (July 5), 63 (July 6), 64 (July 9), and 91 (October 15, 1813); on public health, Nos. 33 (April 29), 38 (May 17), and 65 (July 16, 1814); on *gremios* or guilds, No. 31, March 16, 1813; on

food supply, Nos. 13 (January 13), 35 (March 30), and 38 (April 8, 1813); on prizes for the economic society, Nos. 15 (January 19), and 49 (May 21, 1813); on infrastructure, especially Juarros' plan for a bridge across the Motagua River, No. 48, May 18, 1813; and on water, No. 73, August 9, 1813.

31. Decree, Cádiz, June 8, 1813, and subsequent action and documentation on this theme in AGCA, Al.385, exp. 12609, leg. 1905.

32. Actas, Guatemala City, Nos. 4 (December 18) and 5 (December 22, 1812), AGCA, L.C., 1812–1813.

33. Acta, Guatemala City, No. 6, December 24, 1812, AGCA, L.C., 1812–1813.

34. Actas, Guatemala City, Nos. 7 (January 2) and 8 (January 5, 1813), AGCA, L.C., 1812–1813.

35. Actas, Guatemala City, Nos. 8 (January 5), 9 (January 7), and especially 10 (January 8, 1813), for Aycinena's remarks.

36. See the enclosure in Acta, No. 8, January 5, 1813.

37. There are many minutes that contain information on the elections: see, for example, Actas, Guatemala City, Nos. 20 (February 13), 27 (March 3), 35 (March 30), 48 (May 18), 51 (May 28), 72 (August 6), 80 (September 2), and 89 (September 28, 1813), AGCA, L.C., 1812–1813.

38. Acta, Guatemala City, No. 25, March 24, 1814, plus enclosure, AGCA, L.C., 1814.

39. Actas, Guatemala City, Nos. 15 (January 19) and 24 (February 19, 1813), AGCA, L.C., 1812–1813.

40. Actas, Guatemala City, Nos. 65 (July 16), 68 (July 23), 91 (October 5), 107 (November 23, 1813), AGCA, L.C., 1812–1813. Diputación Provincial to Ayuntamiento de Cartago, León, November 29, 1813, Archivos Nacionales de Costa Rica (San José), Complementario Colonial, .2513 (hereafter: ANCR, C.C.).

41. Actas, Guatemala City, Nos. 33 (March 23), referring to the decree of November 11, 1811, and 78 (August 27, 1813), AGCA, L.C., 1812–1813; also see, *Diario* (Cádiz), March 18, 1813.

42. Actas, Guatemala City, Nos. 34 (March 26), 39 (April 10), 52 (June 1), and 86 (September 17, 1813), AGCA, L.C., 1812–1813.

43. Acta, Guatemala City, No. 31, March 16, 1813, AGCA, L.C., 1812–1813; also see my monograph *La Conspiración de Belén en Nueva Perspectiva* (Guatemala City, 1965), dealing with the abortive plot in Guatemala City known as the "Belén Conspiracy."

44. Actas, Guatemala City, Nos. 40 (April 21), 53 (June 4), 54 (June 9), 58 (June 22) plus enclosures, 59 (June 25), and 60 (June 28, 1813), AGCA, L.C., 1812–1813.

45. Actas, Guatemala City, Nos. 19 (January 26), 35 (March 30), and 36 (April 2, 1813), AGCA, L.C., 1812–1813.

46. Acta, Guatemala City, May 28, 1813, AGCA, L.C., 1812–1813.

47. Acta, Guatemala City, No. 67, July 20, 1813, AGCA, L.C., 1812–1813.

48. Miguel González Saraiva to Juan Manuel de Cañas, León, August 9, 1820, in ANCR, C.C. 3841.

49. Acta, Guatemala City, No. 96, October 22, 1813, AGCA, L.C., 1812–1813; Acta, Diputación Provincial, León, January 27, 1814, ANCR, Sección Histórica (hereafter, ANCR, S.H.), exp. 3369.

50. Actas, Guatemala City, Nos. 59 (July 27, 1814), AGCA, L.C., 1814, and 91 (October 15, 1813), AGCA, L.C., 1812–1813.

51. Juan Antonio Tornos to José de Bustamante, Comayagua, No. 394, May 21, 1814, and Ayuntamiento de Comayagua to Tornos, Comayagua, May 24, 1814, AGCA, Al.22.5, exp. 90, leg. 82.

52. Diputación Provincial de Nicaragua to Regency, León, March 23, 1814, and J.B.

Gual to José de Bustamante, León, April 27, 1814, Col. Fernández, X, 448–457 and 465 respectively.

53. Diputación Provincial de Nicaragua to Regency, León, March 23, 1814, *ibid.*, X, 448–457.
54. Ayuntamiento de Cartago to José de Bustamante, Cartago, October 3, 1811: *idem* to Juan de Dios Ayala, Cartago, August 16, 1813, *ibid.*, X, 338–340 and 419–423 (see p. 421 for the specific quotation).
55. "Exposición de Síndicos," Cartago, October 23, 1820, *ibid.*, X, 564–571; also see Juan de Dios Ayala's letter, September 27, 1813, *ibid.*, X, 433–435, on the Panama trade and the *"inoservancia de nuestra sabia constitución."*
56. Acta, Guatemala City, No. 72, August 6, 1813, AGCA, L.C., 1812–1813.
57. Acta, Guatemala City, Nos. 82 (September 7) and 91 (October 5, 1813), AGCA, L.C., 1812–1813.
58. Actas, Guatemala City, Nos. 86 (September 17) and 89 (September 28, 1813), AGCA, L.C., 1812–1813.
59. Acta, Guatemala City, No. 108, November 26, 1813, AGCA, L.C., 1812–1813.
60. Rodríguez, *Belén*, pp. 5, 7, 49–50; and for the Salvadoran uprisings, see Miguel Angel García, *Procesos por Infidencia, 1811–1815* (San Salvador, 1940).
61. Sofonías Salvatierra, *Contribución a la historia de Centro América* (2 vols., Managua, 1939), II, 338, referring to the session of September 3, 1813.
62. *El Universal* (Madrid), March 3, 1814, reproduced in *Boletín del Archivo General de Centro América*, Tomo III, No. 4 (July 1938), 521; also see, Salvatierra, *Contribución*, II, 462.
63. José de Bustamante to Ramón Casaus, Guatemala City, August 25, 1814, *Boletín*, Tomo III, No. 4 (July 1938), 522–524.
64. Acta, Guatemala City, March 22, 1814, AGCA, L.C., 1814, in which he mentions for the first time the leave granted to him on February 19, 1814; also see Salvatierra, *Contribución*, II, 463.
65. Acta, Guatemala City, No. 14, February 18, 1814, AGCA, L.C., 1814.
66. Acta, Guatemala City, No. 14, February 18, 1814, AGCA, L.C., 1814, with enclosure, José de Aycinena to Ayuntamiento de Guatemala, Cádiz, September 14, 1813.
67. Actas, Guatemala City, Nos. 71 (August 3, 1813), AGCA, L.C., 1812–1813, and 64 (August 26, 1814), AGCA, L.C., 1814; also see, Salvatierra, *Contribución*, II, 463.
68. José Bustamante to Regency, Guatemala City, May 18, 1814, Col. Fernández, X, 467–491: also in Archivo General de Indias (Sevilla), Audiencia de Guatemala, Estante 101, Cajón 3, leg. 7.

CHAPTER SIX

1. "Manifiesto de los americanos que residen en Madrid a las naciones de la Europa, y principalmente á la España, demonstrado las razones legales que tienen para no concurrir el día 28 de mayo á elegir diputados que representen los pueblos ultramarinos donde nacieron," Madrid, 1820, Biblioteca Nacional (Guatemala City), Hojas Sueltas, 1820 (hereafter, BNG, H.S., 1820).
2. Royal cédula, Valencia, May 4, 1814, enclosed in Acta, Guatemala City, September 2, 1814, Archivo General de Centro América (Guatemala City), Libros de Cabildo, 1814, Al.2.2, exp. 15740, leg. 2191 (hereafter, AGCA, L.C., 1814).
3. Actas, Guatemala City, Nos. 46 (May 23, 1815), plus enclosures, and 11 (February 10, 1818) AGCA, L.C. 1815, Al.2.2, exp. 15741, leg. 2191 and AGCA, L.C., 1818, Al.2.2, exp. 15744, leg. 2193 (hereafter, AGCA, L.C., 1815, and AGCA, L.C. 1818).

4. Enoch F. Resnick, "The Council of State and Spanish America, 1814–1820," unpublished Ph.D dissertation, American University (Washington, D.C.), 1970, is a carefully documented study of the interregnum that demonstrates the points made here.
5. Manifesto, Madrid, July 20, 1814, Archivos Nacionales de Costa Rica (San José), Complementario Colonial 2504, f.11 (hereafter, ANCR, C.C.).
6. Royal Order, Madrid, May 24, 1814, *ibid.*
7. "Informe," Madrid, July 11, 1815, ANCR, C.C. 3380, which includes the demands of both deputies; also see documents in León Fernández, ed., *Colección de documentos para la historia de Costa Rica* (10 vols., San José, Costa Rica, 1881–1907), X, 494–504 (hereafter, Col. Fernández).
8. Royal cédulas, Madrid, June 17, 1814 (erroneously dated 1813), AGCA, Al.23, leg. 1543, and March 14, 1816, plus attached expediente, AGCA, Al.1, exp. 910, leg. 30; also, Sofonías Salvatierra, *Contribución a la historia de Centro América* (2 vols., Managua, 1939), II, 347.
9. For example, see Acta, Ayuntamiento de Tegucigalpa, November 29, 1814, Archivo Nacional de Honduras (Tegucigalpa), leg. 15, paquete 15 (hereafter, ANH-T), replying to the cédula of June 25, 1814, on erasure and Bustamante's order of November 18, 1814. This particular ayuntamiento complied; in other areas, especially in Guatemala City, Bustamante was unable to destroy all of the documentation, fortunately for subsequent historians.
10. For example, see Actas, Guatemala City, Nos. 67 (August 22), 73 (September 9), 88 (November 4), and 97 (December 3, 1814), AGCA, L.C., 1814.
11. Ironically, it is the only extant copy; it was first published in the 1930s in the *Boletín* of AGCA; the most recent version, with an excellent introduction by César Brañas, *Instrucciones para la constitución fundamental de la monarquía española y su gobierno . . . Antonio de Larrazábal . . .* (Guatemala City, 1953).
12. Royal cédula, Madrid, June 13, 1817, AGCA, Al.2, esp. 1130, leg. 40, reviewing all the correspondence up to this date.
13. Bustamante to Ayuntamiento, Guatemala City, December 22, 1815, in Acta, No. 107, December 22, 1815, AGCA, L.C., 1815.
14. See, Actas, Guatemala City, Nos. 62 (July 27), 72 (August 22), and 86 (October 10, 1815), AGCA, L.C., 1815; Nos. 4 (January 14), 23 (March 23), 24 (March 29), and 25 (April 9, 1817), AGCA, Libros de Cabildo, 1817, Al.2.2, exp. 15743, leg. 2192 (hereafter: AGCA, L.C., 1817); and Nos. 11 (February 10) and 26 (April 7, 1818), AGCA, L.C., 1818.
15. "Memorial de la residencia . . . José de Bustamante," Guatemala City, October 16, 1820, AGCA, Al.30-4, exp. 11581, leg. 1739 (hereafter, Memorial de Bustamante).
16. Royal cédula, Madrid, June 13, 1817 (see note 12).
17. *Ibid.*; also see Actas, Guatemala City, Nos. 70 (August 29, 1814), AGCA, L.C., 1814; 46 (May 23) and 47 (May 26, 1815), plus enclosures, AGCA, L.C., 1815.
18. Memorial de Bustamante, October 16, 1820. One of the judges, Francisco de Paula Vilches, asserted that it was men like Bustamante who, in effect, convinced Americans that they should seek independence from Spain.
19. Expediente in royal cédula, Madrid, June 17, 1817, AGCA, exp. 1130, leg. 44; Actas, Consejo de Estado, Madrid, April 15 and May 17, 1820, Archivo Histórico Nacional, Sección de Estado, Libro 13 (hereafter, AHN-M, S.E.); Consulta, Consejo de Estado, Madrid, May 1, 1820, AHN-M, S.E., Libro 51.
20. Charge 4 of Memorial de Bustamante, 1820; also see, Acta, Guatemala City, November 28, 1817, AGCA, L.C., 1817.
21. Actas, Guatemala City, Nos. 32 (April 24) and 35 (May 5, 1818), AGCA, L.C., 1818; Nos. 23 (March 18), 26 (March 30), 36 (April 30), 44 (May 21, 1819), and others in August 1819, AGCA, Libros de Cabildo, 1819, Al.2.2, exp. 15745, leg. 2193 (hereafter, AGCA, L.C., 1819).

22. Acta extraordinaria, Consejo de Estado, Madrid, April 2, 1820, AHN-M, S.E., Libro 22.
23. Acta, Guatemala City, No. 35, May 5, 1820, AGCA, Libros de Cabildo, 1820, Al.2.2, exp. 15746, leg. 2193 (hereafter, AGCA, L.C., 1820).
24. Instructions, Madrid, March 22, 1820, AGCA, Al.23, leg. 1543 (printed). They include the electoral instructions for Spain and for the overseas area, as well as a supplement with key articles from the Constitution of 1812, bearing upon elections. Also see, Acta, Guatemala City, No. 46, June 12, 1820, with enclosure, AGCA, L.C., 1820.
25. Acta, Guatemala City, No. 70, August 22, 1820, AGCA, L.C., 1820.
26. Acta, Guatemala City, No. 46, June 12, 1820, AGCA, L.C., 1820; and *El Editor Constitucional* (Guatemala City), November 13, 1820, *Escritos del Doctor Pedro Molina* (3 vols., Guatemala, 1954), p. 283. The pagination is consecutive throughout all three volumes. See the Bibliography for the chronological order of the set.
27. Actas, Guatemala City, Nos. 51 (June 28), 52 (June 30), 53 (July 4), and 54 (July 7, 1820), AGCA, L.C., 1820.
28. Acta, Guatemala City, No. 62, July 27, 1820, AGCA, L.C., 1820.
29. Actas, Guatemala City, Nos. 64 (August 1), 78 (September 16), and 94 (October 30, 1820), AGCA, L.C., 1820.
30. Louis E. Bumgartner, *José del Valle of Central America* (Durham, North Carolina, 1963), pp. 121–122.
31. Actas, Guatemala City, Nos. 58 (July 17) and 68 (August 16, 1820), AGCA, L.C., 1820.
32. Actas, Guatemala City, Nos. 64 (August 1), 67 (August 11), 70 (August 22), 73 (August 31), 76 (September 9), and 91 (October 20, 1820), AGCA, L.C., 1820; Acta, D.P., Guatemala City, No. 19, October 18, 1820, AGCA, Diputación Provincial de Guatemala, B1.13, exp. 479, leg. 16 (hereafter, AGCA, D.P.-G, 1820).
33. "Prospectus," *El Editor Constitucional* (Guatemala City), I, 1-3; "Prospectus," *El Amigo de la Patria* (Guatemala City), October 16, 1820 (See Bibliography for location of volumes). On the Indian and economic development, see *Amigo*, October 26, 1820, and August 7, 1821; and on education, May 22 and 24, 1821.
34. Bumgartner, *Valle*, pp. 108–109, and throughout the earlier chapters has documented Valle's motivation and character. In *El Amigo de la Patria* (Guatemala City), November 3, 1820, Valle criticized the aristocratic leanings of the 1810 Instructions to Antonio Larrazábal as a rebuttal to *El Editor Constitucional*'s charges against him. For Valle's attack upon the free trade policies of the "families," see issues of November 11, 24, and December 23, 1820. And for *El Editor*'s mixed stand on free trade, see supplement to No. 7, August 21, 1821, pp. 79–83, supplement to No. 9, September 4, 1820, pp. 109–113. On the other hand, see No. 11, September 18, 1820, pp. 139–145.
35. Acta, Guatemala City, No. 3, January 9, 1821, AGCA, Libros de Cabildo, 1821, Al.2.2, exp. 15747, leg. 2194, 1st semester (hereafter, AGCA, L.C., 1821A).
36. Acta, Guatemala City, No. 25, March 20, 1821, AGCA, L.C., 1821A.
37. Actas, Guatemala City, Nos. 10 (February 1) and 11 (February 6, 1821), AGCA, L.C., 1821A.
38. Actas, Guatemala City, Nos. 5 (January 16), 6 (January 9), and 18 (February 27, 1821), AGCA, L.C., 1821A.
39. Acta, Guatemala City, No. 18, February 27, 1821, AGCA, L.C., 1821A. It was to be called the *Mensual de los Acuerdos del Ayuntamiento de Guatemala*. I have not found any issues, and it could be that the idea was dropped when Valle, the editor, left his post as Mayor.
40. Actas, Guatemala City, Nos. 27 (March 27) and 33 (April 25, 1821), AGCA, L.C.,

1821A; and Acta, D.P., Guatemala City, No. 64, April 9, 1821, AGCA, Diputación Provincial de Guatemala, B1.13, exp. 478, leg. 16 (hereafter, AGCA, D.P.-G, 1820–1821); Bumgartner, *Valle*, pp. 121–125.

41. *Ibid.*, p. 134.

42. *Ibid.*, p. 133, in which Bumgartner mistakenly refers to his appointment as a juez de letras. See the list of 48 judges in Actas, Guatemala City, Nos. 39 (May 14) and 56 (July 7, 1821), AGCA, L.C., 1821A; also see, Decreto, Madrid, October 22, 1820, José Muro Martínez, comp., *Decretos y órdenes de Cortes en las dos épocas de 1810 a 1814, y 1820 a 1823* (Valladolid, 1875), pp. 286–288.

43. Actas, D.P., Guatemala City, Nos. 6 (September 15), 15 (October 19), 25 (October 30), 26 (November 2), 28 (November 6, 1820), which pointed out the obstructionism of the political leaders in Chiquimula who refused to allow the Indians to vote, AGCA, D.P.-G, 1820; Nos. 9 (November 27), 13 (December 9), 19 (December 21, 1820), and 37 (February 5), 56 (March 22), and 64 (April 19, 1821), AGCA, D.P.-G, 1820–1821; Nos. 14 (July 17), and 20 (August 7, 1821), AGCA, Diputación Provincial de Guatemala, B1.13, exp. 520, leg. 17 (hereafter, AGCA, D.P.-G, 1821).

44. Actas, Guatemala City, Nos. 10 (February 1), 11 (February 6), 14 (February 16, 1821), AGCA, L.C., 1821A.

45. Actas, D.P., Guatemala City, Nos. 49 (March 7), 64 (April 9), 65 (April 11), 68 (April 27, 1821), AGCA, D.P.-G, 1820–1821; also, Nos. 9 (June 30) and 12 (July 12, 1821), AGCA, D.P.-G, 1821.

46. Acta, Guatemala City, No. 31, April 10, 1821, AGCA, L.C., 1821A.

47. Actas, Guatemala City, Nos. 14 (July 17), 21 (August 9), and 29 (August 31, 1821), AGCA, L.C., 1821A; Miguel González Saraiva to Governor Cañas, León, May 23, 1821, ANCR, C.C. 3318.

48. Actas, Guatemala City, Nos. 51 (June 28), 56 (July 14, 1821), AGCA, L.C., 1821A; Acta, D.P., Guatemala City, No. 18, December 20, 1820, AGCA, D.P.-G, 1820–1821.

49. Acta, D.P., Guatemala City, No. 75, May 14, 1821, AGCA, D.P.-G, 1820–1821; Actas, Guatemala City, Nos. 11 (February 6), 13 (February 13), and 39 (May 14, 1821), AGCA, L.C., 1820–1821; No. 82 (September 28, 1820), AGCA, D.P.-G, 1820.

50. Actas, D.P., Guatemala City, Nos. 20 (December 22, 1820), 28 (January 12), and 49 (March 7, 1821), for the quotation in the text, AGCA, D.P.-G, 1820–1821; and Nos. 1 (June 4), 2 (June 8), 4 (June 14), 5 (June 16), and 28 (August 29, 1821), AGCA, D.P.-G, 1821.

51. Acta, D.P., Guatemala City, No. 27, January 10, 1821, AGCA, D.P.-G, 1820–1821.

52. Actas, D.P., Guatemala City, Nos. 20 (December 22, 1820) and 28 (January 12, 1821), AGCA, D.P.-G, 1820–1821.

53. Acta, D.P., Guatemala City, No. 4, June 14, 1821, AGCA, D.P.-G, 1821.

54. Actas, D.P., Guatemala City, Nos. 6 (June 19), 7 (June 22), 24 (August 17), and 27 (August 27, 1821), AGCA, D.P.-G, 1821.

55. Acta, D.P., Guatemala City, No. 49, March 7, 1821, AGCA, D.P.-G, 1820–1821; José Tinoco to Jefe Político Subalterno in Tegucigalpa, Comayagua, November 16, 1820, containing the names of the seven provinciales. See the "Expediente sobre la excepción de la Alcaldía Mayor de Comayagua," 1818, ANH-T, leg. 27, paquete 15, exp. 59.

56. Actas, D.P., Guatemala City, Nos. 7 (November 23, 1820), 23 (January 2), 55 (March 21), 68 (April 27), and 71 (May 5, 1821), AGCA, D.P.-G, 1820–1821; 15 (July 20, 1821), AGCA, D.P.-G, 1821, reporting the election of Justo de los

Campos to the Guatemalan D.P.; also see, "Expediente," 1818, ANH-T, leg. 27, paquete 15, exp. 59.

57. Ayuntamiento de Ciudad Real to Gavino Gaínza, C. Real, August 17, 1821, plus enclosures, AGCA, B1.13, exp. 540, leg. 18.

58. Manual José de Arce to Pedro Molina, San Salvador, September 13, 1821, *Documentos relacionados con la historia de Centro América*, in *Folletín de "La República"* (Guatemala, 1896), pp. 55–56.

59. Acta, Cartago, October 25, 1820, and "Instrucciones," José María Zamora, Cartago, December 16, 1820, Col. Fernández, X, 567–571 and 576–580.

60. The influence of Benjamin Constant is stressed by Charles A. Hale, *Mexican Liberalism in the Age of Mora* (New Haven, 1968). This was probably because there were striking parallels between his thought and the Cádiz movement. Considering the publication date of his work, however, it is conceivable that he may have drawn from the Cádiz Experiment himself.

61. Decreto, Madrid, June 27, 1821, in Muro Martínez, *Decretos*, pp. 361–362.

62. See, for example, Acta, Consejo de Estado, Madrid, February 6, 1821, AHN-M, S.E., Libro 23. Both Molina's *Editor* and Valle's *Amigo* kept their readers informed on the instability of Spanish life.

63. Decretos, Madrid, August 17, September 26, and October 1, 1820, in Muro Martínez, *Decretos*, pp. 249–250, 268–269, 274–276.

64. Actas, Guatemala City, Nos. 33 (April 25) and 35 (April 30, 1821), AGCA, L.C., 1821A, in which the Ayuntamiento supported the request.

65. Actas, Consejo de Estado, Madrid, April, October 20, and October 22, 1821, AHN-M, S.E., Libro 13 for the first, Libro 24 for the last two.

66. Acta, Consejo de Estado, Madrid, October 17, 1821, AHN-M, S.E., Libro 24; decretos, August 14, 1820 (p. 249), August 6, 1820 (pp. 246–247), June 26, 1822 (pp. 467–468), June 29, 1820 (p. 473), in Muro Martínez, *Decretos*; "Manifiesto," Madrid, May 28, 1820, BNG, H.S., 1820; José Sacasa to Ayuntamiento de Cartago, Madrid, July 24, 1820, ANCR, C.C., exp. 9691.

67. Actas, Guatemala City, Nos. 9 (January 30), 36 (May 4), and 44 (June 1, 1821), AGCA, L.C., 1821A; José Sacasa to Ayuntamiento de Cartago, Madrid, August 30, 1820, ANCR, C.C., exp. 3193.

68. *El Editor Constitucional* (Guatemala City), July 31, 1820, pp. 24–26; "Instrucciones," Julián Urruela, Guatemala City, December 6, 1820, enclosed in Acta, Guatemala City, No. 2, November 26, 1820, folios 138–145 vuelto, AGCA, L.C., 1820.

69. *El Amigo de la Patria* (Guatemala City), June 5 and August 4, 1821; also see Bumgartner, *Valle*, pp. 149–154, on José's changing viewpoint of the colonial past.

70. *El Editor Constitucional* (Guatemala City), February 5, 1821, pp. 427–429; also see articles on pp. 173–179, 236, 378–381, 599.

71. *Ibid.*, May 28, 1821, p. 599.

72. *Ibid.*, (June 4, 1821), pp. 613–616, which used the anagram Airebi (Iberia) and Odnanref le Otargni (Fernando El Ingrato). It was first published in England.

73. Actas, Junta de Censura, Guatemala City, July 27 and August 23, 1821, AGCA, A1.1, exp. 57305, leg. 6931.

74. *El Editor Constitucional* (Guatemala City), June 12, 1821, p. 626.

75. *Ibid.*, June 5, 1821, pp. 643–646.

76. *Ibid.*, July 23, 1821, pp. 691–693.

77. *Ibid.*, August 27, 1821, pp. 747–748; "Exposición," Madrid, June 25, 1821, *Boletín del Archivo General de Centro América* (Guatemala), Tomo 1, No. 4 (July, 1936), 398–411.

78. *El Genio de la Libertad* (Guatemala City), September 3, 10, 15, 1821, pp. 754–755, 757, 773–775 (for quotation see the latter).

79. Acta, Guatemala City, No. 72, September 4, 1821, AGCA, L.C., 1821B.
80. Acta, Guatemala City, No. 75, September 14, 1821, AGCA, L.C., 1821B.
81. José Sacasa to Miguel Larreynaga, Madrid, January 13, 1822, a document which I was permitted to see by my friend Esperanza Zeceña, granddaughter of Larreynaga.

CHAPTER SEVEN

1. Joaquín Lindo (Secretary of Comayagua's D.P.) to Manual Ramírez, Comayagua, October 19, 1821, Rafael Heliodoro Valle, *La Anexión de Centro América a México* (6 tomos, Mexico City, 1924–1949), I, 54 (hereafter: Valle, *Anexión*).
2. For an excellent commentary on the events of that day, see Rafael Obregón Loria, *De nuestra historia patria: los primeros días de Independencia* (San José, Costa Rica, 1971), pp. 27–88; also the emotional description in José Francisco Barrundia, "Al nacimiento de la patria en el 15 de setiembre," *Revista Conservadora del Pensamiento Centroamericano*, Vol. 25, No. 123 (December 1970), 9–12, written in the 1830s.
3. *El Genio de la Libertad* (Guatemala City), October 1, 1821, pp. 792–793, which includes the voto particular that they signed on September 15, 1821. It was forwarded to the Junta Provisional Consultiva on September 18.
4. The September 15, 1815, document has been reproduced in numerous texts and compilations of documents. See the commentary in Andrés Townsend Ezcurra, *Las Provincias Unidas de Centroamérica: Fundación de la República* (2d. ed., only complete one, San José, Costa Rica, 1973), pp. 21–24.
5. Actas, J.P.C., Guatemala City, September 25, 26, and October 3, 1821, Archivo General de Centro América (Guatemala City), Actas de la Junta Provisional Consultiva, B1.13, exp. 562, leg. 19 (hereafter, AGCA, J.P.C., 1821–1822); and *El Genio*, October 4, 1821, pp. 802–803.
6. J.P.C.'s circular, Guatemala City, October 3, 1821, *El Genio*, October 3, 1821, pp. 801–802; and also the issue of October 4, 1821, pp. 802–803.
7. *Ibid.*, p. 810, and the issue of October 1, 1821, pp. 792–793, which includes their voto.
8. Acta, Guatemala City, No. 78, September 28, 1821, AGCA, Libros de Cabildo, Segundo semestre, 1821 (hereafter, AGCA, L.C., 1821B).
9. Acta, Guatemala City, No. 84, October 9, 1821, AGCA, L.C., 1821B.
10. *El Genio* (Guatemala City), October 4, 1821, pp. 802–810.
11. Acta, J.P.C., Guatemala City, No. 49, November 14, 1821, AGCA, J.P.C., 1821–1822.
12. Acta, J.P.C., Guatemala City, No. 57, November 23, 1821, AGCA, J.P.C., 1821–1822.
13. Circular, J.P.C., Guatemala City, October 3, 1821, *El Genio*, October 4, 1821, pp. 801–802.
14. *Ibid.*, October 22, 1821, pp. 831–834, reproducing Ayuntamiento de San Vicente to J.P.C., San Vicente, October 2, 1821.
15. Acta, J.P.C., Guatemala City, No. 56, November 22, 1821, AGCA, J.P.C., 1821–1822.
16. Acta, J.P.C., Guatemala City, No. 94, January 11, 1822, AGCA, J.P.C., 1821–1822, concerning a case that involved Indians in Chiquimula.
17. Acta, J.P.C., Guatemala City, No. 12, September 30, 1821, AGCA, J.P.C., 1821–1822.
18. Citizens to G. Gaínza, Guatemala City, October 13, 1821, *Boletín del Archivo General de Centro América*, Tomo II, No. 1 (October 1936), 55–59.
19. Acta, J.P.C., Guatemala City, No. 26, October 16, 1821, AGCA, J.P.C., 1821–1822.

20. Acta, J.P.C., Guatemala City, No. 74, December 15, 1821, AGCA, J.P.C., 1821–1822.
21. Actas, J.P.C., Guatemala City, Nos. 24 (October 13), 42 (November 7, 1821), and 115 (February 12, 1822), AGCA, J.P.C., 1821–1822.
22. Acta, J.P.C., Guatemala City, No. 104, January 28, 1822, AGCA, J.P.C., 1821–1822, indicating that Valle and his colleagues had signed the report on December 14, 1821.
23. Acta, J.P.C., Guatemala City, No. 35, October 27, 1821, AGCA, J.P.C., 1821–1822.
24. Actas, J.P.C., Guatemala City, Nos. 27 (October 18), 41 (November 6), and 49 (November 14, 1821), AGCA, J.P.C., 1821–1822.
25. Actas, J.P.C., Guatemala City, Nos. 17 (October 5), 22 (October 11), 40 (November 5), and 61 (November 28, 1821), with an enclosure by Dr. José Delgado, AGCA, J.P.C., 1821–1822.
26. Actas, J.P.C., Guatemala City, Nos. 52 (November 17) and 55 (November 21, 1821), AGCA, J.P.C., 1821–1822.
27. Manuel Mier y Terán to Agustín Iturbide, Ciudad Real, October 24, 1821, Valle, Anexión, I, 60.
28. Acta de Independencia, Comayagua, September 28, 1821, ibid., 14–16.
29. Actas, J.P.C., Guatemala City, Nos. 39 (November 3) and 41 (November 6, 1821), AGCA, J.P.C., 1821–1822.
30. Actas, J.P.C., Guatemala City, Nos. 48 (November 13), 50 (November 15), 51 (November 16), for the quotes, and 54 (November 19, 1821), on Tegucigalpa as a D.P., AGCA, J.P.C., 1821–1822.
31. Acta, J.P.C., Guatemala City, No. 65, December 3, 1821, AGCA, J.P.C., 1821–1822.
32. Acta, J.P.C., Guatemala City, No. 71, December 11, 1821, AGCA, J.P.C., 1821–1822.
33. Acta, J.P.C., Guatemala City, No. 87, January 4, 1822, AGCA, J.P.C., 1821–1822.
34. Acta, J.P.C., Guatemala City, No. 90, January 7, 1822, AGCA, J.P.C., 1821–1822.
35. Bando, M. González Saraiva, León, September 28, 1821, Obregón, Independencia, pp. 222–223.
36. Ibid., pp. 223–225.
37. D.P. Nicaragua to Miguel González Saraiva, September 29, and idem to Manuel Mier y Terán, León, December 7, 1821, in Valle, Anexión, I, 17–19 and 109–114.
38. Ibid., pp. 112 and 49–62; the latter includes a "Manifiesto," D.P. Nicaragua, León, February 7, 1822.
39. Actas, J.P.C., Guatemala City, Nos. 22 (October 11), 56 (November 22), and 70 (December 20, 1821), AGCA, J.P.C., 1821–1822; "Proclama," Pablo Alvarado, Guatemala City, October 22, 1821, Archivos Nacionales de Costa Rica (San José), Provincial Independiente, exp. 77 (hereafter, ANCR, P.I.); "Manifiesto de Los Patriotas," Guatemala City, October 17, 1821, in Valle, Anexión, I, 45–48.
40. Actas, J.P.C., Guatemala City, No. 29, October 20, 1821, AGCA, J.P.C., 1821–1822.
41. Actas, J.P.C., Guatemala City, Nos. 55 (November 21), Castillo's appointment, and 79 (December 22, 1821), La Guardia's assignment, AGCA, J.P.C., 1821–1822; Miguel González Saraiva to Crisanto Sacasa, León, December 1, 1821, and Víctor de la Guardia to Junta Gubernativa de Costa Rica, Granada, January 16, 1822, in Valle, Anexión, II, doc. 5, p. 12.
42. See the exhaustive study of Obregón Loria, Independencia, pp. 89–207; also Hernán G. Peralta, El Pacto de Concordia (San José, 1952); "Proyecto del Pacto Social Funda-

mental Interino de Costa Rica," December 1, 1821, in Francisco María Iglesias, comp., *Documentos Relativos a la Independencia* (3 vols., San José, Costa Rica, 1899–1902), II, 38–49 (hereafter, Iglesias, *Documentos*).

43. Acta, J.P.C., Guatemala City, No. 85, January 2, 1822, AGCA, J.P.C., 1821–1822.

44. Acta, J.P.C., Guatemala City, No. 30, October 21, 1821, with a draft of a letter written by the Marquis de Aycinena. Also see Gaínza to D.P. Nicaragua, Guatemala City, October 7, 1821, *El Genio de la Libertad* (Guatemala City), October 29, 1821, pp. 849–851.

45. *Ibid.*, November 5, 1821, pp. 854–859, 861–862.

46. *Ibid.*, October 22, 1821, pp. 840–841, for a report on the first session of the tertulia patriótica (October 17); also see pp. 873–879 (November 19) and 885 (December 10, 1821); also, Actas, J.P.C., Guatemala City, Nos. 22 (October 11), 24 (October 13), 39 (November 3, 1821), AGCA, J.P.C., 1821–1822.

47. *El Genio de la Libertad* (Guatemala City), October 15, 1821, pp. 821–827.

48. Acta, J.P.C., Guatemala City, No. 35, October 27, 1821, AGCA, J.P.C., 1821–1822.

49. Actas, Guatemala City, Nos. 106 (December 11), when the poll was proposed, and 112 (December 29, 1821), Cabildo Extraordinario, AGCA, L.C., 1821B.

50. Acta, J.P.C., Guatemala City, No. 18, October 6, 1821, AGCA, J.P.C., 1821–1822.

51. Agustín Iturbide to Gavino Gaínza, Mexico City, October 19, 1821, in Valle, *Anexión*, I, 49–53.

52. See especially Iturbide to Conde de la Cadena, Mexico City, November 29, 1821, *ibid.*, 99–101.

53. Actas, J.P.C., Guatemala City, Nos. 61 (November 28), 62 (November 29, 1821), and 85 (January 2, 1822), AGCA, J.P.C., 1821–1822.

54. Acta, J.P.C., Guatemala City, No. 60, November 27, 1821, AGCA, J.P.C., 1821–1822.

55. Actas, J.P.C., Guatemala City, Nos. 63 (November 30), 64 (December 1), 65 (December 3), 66 (December 4), and 67 (December 5, 1821), AGCA, J.P.C., 1821–1822; also see, José de Oñate to Iturbide, Guatemala City, December 3, 1821, in Valle, *Anexión*, I, 103–106.

56. Acta, J.P.C., Guatemala City, December 1, 1821, AGCA, J.P.C., 1821–1822.

57. Acta, J.P.C., Guatemala City, No. 85, January 2, 1822, AGCA, J.P.C., 1821–1822.

58. Diario de las sesiones de la Soberana Junta Provisional Gubernativa del Imperio Mexicano, Sesión, November 12, 1821, in Valle, *Anexión*, II, 12.

59. Gaínza to Iturbide, Guatemala City, January 12, 1822, and José Manuel Herrera to Gaínza, Mexico City, February 17, 1822, *ibid.*, 74, 38–40.

60. Acta, J.P.C., Guatemala City, unnumbered, Janaury 14, 1822, AGCA, J.P.C., 1821–1822.

61. Junta de Censura to Gaínza, January 17, 18, 1822, and Gaínza to Junta de Censura, Guatemala City, January 29, 1822, A1.1, exp. 57, 305, leg. 6931.

62. Gaínza to Iturbide, Guatemala City, December 18, 1821, in Valle, *Anexión*, I, 143–145.

63. Iturbide to Junta Gubernativa del Imperio, Mexico City, February 11, 1822, and Iturbide's order, February 16, 1822, *ibid.*, II, 66–67, 71.

64. Acta, J.P.C., Guatemala City, No. 59, November 26, 1821, AGCA, J.P.C., 1821–1822.

65. Actas, J.P.C., Guatemala City, Nos. 76 (December 18, 1821), 100 (January 21), 107 (February 1), and 115 (February 12, 1822), AGCA, J.P.C., 1821–1822.

66. Ayuntamiento de Quezaltenango to Filísola, Quezaltenango, February 5, 1822, and other pertinent documents, in Valle, *Anexión*, II, 48, 67–69.
67. Actas, J.P.C., Guatemala City, Nos. 76 (December 18, 1821) and January 16, 1822 (unnumbered), AGCA, J.P.C., 1821–1822.
68. D. P. Salvador to D. P. León and D. P. Comayagua, San Salvador, December 25, 1821, in Valle, *Anexión*, I, 160–162.
69. Acta, J.P.C., Guatemala City, No. 101, January 28, 1822, AGCA, J.P.C., 1821–1822.
70. Actas, J.P.C., Guatemala City, Nos. 109 (February 5), 110 (February 6), and 111 (February 7, 1822), AGCA, J.P.C., 1821–1822.

CHAPTER EIGHT

1. Agustín Iturbide to Mariano Aycinena, Mexico City, January 30, 1822, in Rafael Heliodoro Valle, *La Anexión de Centro América a México* (6 tomos, Mexico City, 1924–1949), III, 160–161 (hereafter, Valle, *Anexión*).
2. Mariano Aycinena to Agustín Iturbide, Guatemala City, December 18, 1821, and Iturbide to *idem*, Mexico City, December 31, 1821, and January 3, 1822, in Valle, *Anexión*, III, 58, 80–81.
3. Iturbide to Gaínza, Mexico City, December 28, 1821, *ibid.*, p. 75.
4. Iturbide to Gaínza, Mexico City, January 23, 1822, *ibid.*, p. 151.
5. Mariano Aycinena to Iturbide, Guatemala City, January 18, 1822, *ibid.*, p. 141.
6. Spy to Gaínza, San Salvador, January 12, 1822, *ibid.*, 132–133.
7. Aycinena to Iturbide, Guatemala City, January 18, 1822, *ibid.*, pp. 141–142.
8. See, for example, Filísola's letters of September 16 and October 18, 1822, *ibid.*, pp. 406–418. Louis E. Bumgartner, *José del Valle of Central America* (Durham, N. Carolina, 1963), pp. 193–194, does not see this connection.
9. Iturbide to Gaínza, Mexico City, January 23, 1822, in Valle, *Anexión*, III, 151.
10. *Ibid.*, pp. 149–150.
11. Decree, Regency, Mexico City, March 11, 1822, on freedom of the press, Archivo General de Centro América, B5.8, exp. 92, 796, leg. 4123; Acta, J.P.C., Guatemala City, No. 99, January 19, 1822, plus enclosure, AGCA, Actas de la Junta Provincial Consultiva, B1.13, exp. 562, leg. 19 (hereafter, AGCA, J.P.C., 1821–1822); and Gaínza to Junta de Censura, Guatemala City, January 29, 1822, AGCA, A1.1, exp. 57, 305, leg. 6931.
12. Acta, D.P., Guatemala City, No. 19, June 20, 1822, AGCA, Actas de la Diputación Provincial de Guatemala, B5.7, exp. 1849, leg. 68 (hereafter, AGCA, D.P. 1822–1823); Actas, Guatemala City, Nos. 43 (May 21), 46 (May 31), and 47 (June 4, 1822), AGCA, Libros de Cabildo, B78.1, exp. 10101, leg. 529 (hereafter, AGCA, L.C., 1822).
13. Acta, Guatemala City, No. 28, March 28, 1822, AGCA, L.C., 1822.
14. Actas, D.P., Guatemala City, Nos. 28 (July 29, 1822), AGCA, D.P., 1822–1823, and 6 (February 3, 1823), AGCA, Actas de la Diputación Provincial de Guatemala, B5.7, exp. 1854, leg. 68 (hereafter, AGCA, D.P., 1823).
15. Actas, D.P., Guatemala City, Nos. 45 (September 26), 46 (September 30), and 47 (October 10, 1822), AGCA, D.P., 1822–1823, involving two members elected to the D.P.; both were rejected; also see, Acta, Guatemala City, No. 9, January 25, 1822, AGCA, L.C., 1822.
16. Report of Consulado, Guatemala City, August 6, 1822, AGCA, B5.7, exp. 1847, leg. 67; also see, Actas, D.P., Guatemala City, Nos. 4 (April 18), 5 (April 22), 32 (August 22), and 38 (September 5, 1822), AGCA, D.P., 1822–1823.
17. Actas, D.P., Guatemala City, Nos. 1 (April 1), 18 (June 7), and 20 (June 25, 1822),

AGCA, D.P., 1822–1823; also, *Arancel Provisional para las aduanas de Guatemala*, February 10, 1822, Guatemala City, Biblioteca Nacional, Hojas Sueltas, 1821–1823, 12 pages (hereafter, BNG, H.S. 1821–1823).

18. Actas, D.P., Guatemala City, Nos. 48 (October 10), 55 (November 4), and 57 (November 11, 1822), AGCA, D.P., 1822–1823.

19. Actas, D.P., Guatemala City, Nos. 48 (October 10), 55 (November 4), and 57 (November 11, 1822), AGCA, D.P., 1822–1823.

20. Decreto, Mexico City, No. 54, October 29, 1822, AGCA, B5.8, exp. 92, 796, leg. 4123.

21. Actas, D.P., Guatemala City, Nos. 6 (April 21), 9 (May 2), 10 (May 13, 1822), AGCA, D.P., 1822–1823; Junta Gubernativa, Alajuela, Nos. 98 (September 28) and 99 (September 29, 1822), in Francisco María Iglesias, comp., *Documentos Relativos a la Independencia* (3 vols., San José, Costa Rica, 1899–1902), II, 225–227 (hereafter, Iglesias, *Documentos*); and "Estados de la Casa de Enseñanza," San José, October 2, 1822, República de Costa Rica, *Documentos Históricos Posteriores a la Independencia* (San José, Costa Rica, 1923), I, 86–92 (hereafter, Costa Rica, *Documentos*); and Licenciado Juan N. F. Lindo to people of Honduras, Comayagua, October 30, 1822, in Valle, *Anexión*, III, 427–428, for quotation in the text.

22. Acta, Guatemala City, October 11, 1822, AGCA, L.C., 1822.

23. Acta, D.P., Guatemala City, No. 5, February 1, 1823, AGCA, D.P., 1823.

24. Actas, D.P., Guatemala City, Nos. 7 (April 29), 21 (June 27), 33 (August 19), 34 (August 22), in which Barrundia referred to their motivation as follows: "rasgo de generosidad, patriotismo y amor a la humanidad," 42 (September 16), 43 (September 19), 46 (September 30), 50 (October 17), 53 (October 28), 54 (October 31), 56 (November 7), and 59 (December 16, 1822), AGCA, D.P., 1822–1823.

25. Decree, Regency, Mexico City, February 21, 1822, AGCA, B5.8, exp. 92,796, leg. 4123; also Actas, D.P., Guatemala City, Nos. 2 (April 11), 3 (April 15), and 20 (June 25, 1822), AGCA, D.P., 1822–1823.

26. Actas, D.P., Guatemala City, Nos. 30 (August 5) and 50 (October 17, 1822), AGCA, D.P., 1822–1823. Well versed in the Spanish Constitution of 1812, José Francisco Barrundia used it to defend Indian rights in the D.P. Father Antonio García Redondo was instrumental in exposing the weakness of the reform program for the Indians.

27. Acta, D.P., Guatemala City, No. 45, September 26, 1822, AGCA, D.P., 1822–1823.

28. Actas, D.P., Guatemala City, Nos. 32 (August 12), 50 (October 17), and 56 (November 7, 1822), AGCA, D.P., 1822–1823.

29. Acta, D.P., Guatemala City, No. 11, May 15, 1822, AGCA, D.P., 1822–1823.

30. *Ibid.*; also, Acta, D.P., Guatemala City, No. 56, November 7, 1822, AGCA, D.P., 1822–1823.

31. Acta, D.P., Guatemala City, No. 12, May 23, 1822, AGCA, D.P., 1822–1823.

32. Acta, D.P., Guatemala City, No. 62, January 1, 1823, AGCA, D.P., 1822–1823.

33. Actas, D.P., Guatemala City, Nos. 1 (April 1) and 25 (July 11, 1822), AGCA, D.P., 1822–1823.

34. Actas, D.P., Guatemala City, Nos. 49 (October 14), 55 (November 4), 59 (December 16, 1822), and 62 (January 7, 1823), AGCA, D.P., 1822–1823; also see, Sesión, Congreso Constituyente, Mexico City, March 29, 1823, in Valle, *Anexión*, IV, 199.

35. Actas, D.P., Guatemala City, Nos. 12 (May 23), 16 (June 10), 18 (June 17), 20 (June 25), and 54 (October 31, 1822), AGCA, D.P., 1822–1823.

36. Acta, D.P., Guatemala City, No. 13, May 30, 1822, AGCA, D.P., 1822–1823.

37. Acta, D.P., Guatemala City, No. 25, July 11, 1822, AGCA, D.P., 1822–1823.

38. Filísola to Secretario de Hacienda del Imperio, Guatemala City, August 3, 1822, in Valle, *Anexión*, III, 375–377; and Sesión, Junta Nacional Instituyente del Imperio Mexicano, Mexico City, November 26, 1822, *ibid.*, II, 381.

39. Actas, D.P., Guatemala City, Nos. 16 (June 10, 1822) and 62 (January 7, 1823), AGCA, D.P., 1822–1823.

40. Actas, D.P., Guatemala City, Nos. 56 (November 7, 1822), AGCA, D.P., 1822–1823; and 4 (January 30, 1823), AGCA, D.P., 1823.

41. Acta, D.P., Guatemala City, No. 55 (November 4, 1822), AGCA, D.P., 1822–1823.

42. Acta, D.P., Guatemala City, No. 49, October 14, 1822, AGCA, D.P., 1822–1823 (the 3 percent tax); also see, Filísola to Iturbide, Ciudad Real, February 25, 1822, in Valle, *Anexión*, III, 215–216.

43. Actas, D.P., Guatemala City, Nos. 41 (September 14), and 42 (September 16, 1822), AGCA, D.P., 1822–1823.

44. For example, see, Acta, D.P., Guatemala City, No. 54, October 31, 1822, AGCA, D.P., 1822–1823.

45. Decree, Mexico City, November 5, 1822, AGCA, B5.8, exp. 92,796, leg. 4123.

46. Decree, Mexico City, December 20, 1822, Archivos Nacionales de Costa Rica (San José), Anexión a México, exp. 8 (hereafter: ANCR, A.M.); also see Acta, D.P., Guatemala City, No. 9, February 25, 1823, AGCA, D.P., 1823.

47. Antonio José Arrivillaga to Miguel Larreinaga, Guatemala City, December 3, 1822, in Doña Esperanza Zeceña's private collection, Guatemala City.

48. Filísola to Iturbide, Ciudad Real, February 25, 1822; Gaínza to Iturbide, Guatemala City, March 3, 1822; and Mariano Aycinena to Iturbide, Guatemala City, March 3, 1822, in Valle, *Anexión*, III, 214–216, 223–224, and 225–226.

49. Víctor de la Guardia to Junta de Costa Rica, Granada, January 16, 1822, Archivos Nacionales de Costa Rica (San José), Provincial Independiente, exp. 886 (hereafter, ANCR, P.I.); Ayuntamiento de Nicoya to Junta de Costa Rica, Nicoya, July 20, 1822, ANCR, P.I., exp. 361; and Gaínza to Iturbide, Guatemala City, March 3, 1822, in Valle, *Anexión,* III, 223–224.

50. Actas, J.P.C., Guatemala City, Nos. 119 (February 16), about Chiquimula, and 121 (February 20, 1822), AGCA, J.P.C., 1821–1822; also see, Gaínza to Filísola, Guatemala City, February 16, 1822, and Aycinena to Filísola, Guatemala City, February 18, 1822, in Valle, *Anexión*, III, 192–193, 198–200.

51. Actas, D.P., Guatemala City, Nos. 9 (May 2), 21 (June 27), 22 (July 4), and 24 (July 8, 1822), AGCA, D.P. 1822–1823.

52. Iturbide to Gaínza, Mexico City, December 28, 1821, in Valle, *Anexión*, III, 75.

53. Iturbide to Regency, Mexico City, January 19, 1822, and *idem* to Gaínza, January 23, 1822, in Valle, *Anexión*, III, 143, 147; also see, Iturbide to Junta Gubernativa del Imperio, Mexico City, February 11, 1822, *ibid.*, II, 66–67.

54. Regency to pueblos de Guatemala, February 15, 1822, and Ayuntamiento de Tegucigalpa to Col. Simón Gutiérrez, Tegucigalpa, January 31, 1822, *ibid.*, III, 191, 163; and Secretario de Relaciones Exteriores del Imperio to Gaínza, Mexico City, February 17, 1822, *ibid.*, II, 74.

55. Filísola to Secretario de Guerra y Marina, Guatemala City, August 3, 1822, *ibid.*, III, 379–381.

56. Filísola to Gaínza, Ciudad Real, February 1822, *ibid.*, II, 85–90.

57. *Ibid.*, III, 223–224, 328; Actas, J.P.C., Guatemala City, Nos. 119 (February 16) and 121 (February 20, 1822), AGCA, J.P.C., 1821–1822.

58. Filísola to Secretario de Guerra y Marina, Guatemala City, August 3, 1822, in Valle, *Anexión*, III, 381; also see, Actas, Guatemala City, Nos. 19 (March 1) and 53 (June 21, 1822), AGCA, L.C., 1822.

59. Memorial, Representantes de la Provincia de Honduras (Joaquín Lindo, Juan Lindo, and Cayetano Bosque), Mexico City, May 8, 1822, in Valle, *Anexión*, II, 142–146.

60. Dictamen, Comisión de Relaciones Exteriores del Congreso Constitucional Mexicano, Mexico City, July 8, 1822, *ibid.*, 238–243. The report was presented in the session of July 10.

61. *Ibid.*, pp. 244–250; Sesión de Cortes, Mexico City, September 6, 1822, *ibid.*, p. 321.

62. Circular, Ministerio de Guerra y Marina del Imperio Mexicano, and order of Agustín I, Mexico City, November 4, 1822, *ibid.*, 358–359.

63. Ayuntamiento de Quezaltenango to Filísola, Quezaltenango, December 17, 1822, *ibid.*, 419–420.

64. Ayuntamiento de Comayagua to Iturbide, Comayagua, December 28, 1822, *ibid.*, 437–440.

65. Florencio Castillo to Junta Provincial de Costa Rica, Mexico City, December 8, 1822, ANCR, A.M., exp. 21.

66. Manifiesto, Vincente Filísola, Guatemala City, November 10, 1822, in Valle, *Anexión*, II, 366–370.

67. Proclama, José Matías Delgado, San Salvador, December 5, 1822, *ibid.*, 400–403.

68. *Redactor General* (Guatemala City), October 3, 1825; and Antonio José Arrivillaga to Miguel Larreinaga, Guatemala City, December 17, 1827, in Esperanza Zeceña's private collection, Guatemala City.

69. Manifiesto, Vicente Filísola, Guatemala City, March 12, 1823, *Boletín del Archivo General de Centro América*, Tomo IV, No. 2 (January 1938), 372.

70. Andrés Townsend Ezcurra, *Las Provincias Unidas de Centroamérica: Fundación de la República* (San José, 1973), pp. 47–48.

71. As quoted in *ibid.*, p. 48.

72. Decree, Vicente Filísola, Guatemala City, March 29, 1823, *ibid.*, pp. 49–52; also in Acta, D.P., Guatemala City, No. 12, March 29, 1823, plus enclosure, AGCA, D.P., 1823.

73. Townsend Ezcurra, *Las Provincias*, pp. 53–56; and *Redactor General* (Guatemala City), August 25, 1825, by José del Valle, reproducing the D.P.'s memorial to the Mexican Cortes, April 1823. I was unable to locate a copy of this memorial in AGCA, D.P., 1823.

CHAPTER NINE

1. Speech, José Gerónimo Zelaya, Guatemala City, January 23, 1825, *El Indicador* (Guatemala City), January 31, 1825.

2. Exposition, Vicente Filísola, Guatemala City, June 24, 1823, Rafael Heliodoro Valle, *La Anexión de Centro América a México* (6 tomos, Mexico City, 1924–1949), IV, 315–321 (hereafter, Valle, *Anexión*).

3. A detailed and excellent analysis of the Assembly's earlier sessions is in Andrés Townsend Ezcurra, *Las Provincias de Centroamérica: Fundación de la República* (San José, 1973), especially pp. 111–191. Many of the key documents are reproduced in part or in their entirety.

4. *Ibid.*, pp. 57–60, 85–109; Moción, José Francisco Barrundia, Guatemala City, 1823, Archivo General de Centro América, B5.7, exp. 1827, leg. 67.

5. Filísola to Ministro de Estado y Relaciones Interiores y Exteriores, Guatemala City, June 1, 1823, in Valle, *Anexión*, IV, 298–301; also see, document in *ibid.*, pp. 301–303. For Filísola's cooperation with the D.P. in Guatemala City, see Actas, D.P., Guatemala City, Nos. 14 (April 11), 15 (April 17), 19 (May 12), 22 (May 30),

and 27 (June 19, 1823), Archivo General de Centro América (Guatemala City), Actas de la Diputación Provincial de Guatemala, B5.7, exp. 1854, leg. 68 (hereafter, AGCA, D.P., 1823).

6. Acta, D.P., Guatemala City, No. 23, May 31, 1823, AGCA, D.P., 1823; also see, Sesión, Congreso Constituyente de México, Mexico City, April 1, 1823, in Valle, *Anexión*, IV, 208–215, as well as documents on pp. 242–243, 257–258, 309.

7. See, for example, Actas, D.P., Guatemala City, Nos. 34 (August 22), 48 (October 10), 55 (November 4), and 57 (November 11, 1822), AGCA, Actas de la Diputación Provincial de Guatemala, B5.7, exp. 1849, leg. 68 (hereafter, AGCA, D.P., 1822–1823).

8. The major points in this bitter controversy can be studied in Filísola's manifestoes of May 12, 1825, and October 2, 1824, in Valle, *Anexión*, VI, 52–67 and 102–156, responding to the attacks of Barrundia, Molina, and Mariano Gálvez, in *La Tribuna* (Guatemala City), Nos. 16 and 18. Also see Barrundia's "Al manifiesto de Vicente Filísola, agente de Iturbide en Guatemala," August 10, 1825, published by M. Arévalo in Guatemala City (18 pp.)

9. The major dispute first arose in Acta, D.P., Guatemala City, No. 18, May 5, 1823; also see Actas Nos. 20 (May 26), 22 (May 30), and 23 (May 31, 1823), AGCA, D.P., 1823.

10. Filísola's bitterness is reflected in many letters that he wrote to Lucas Alamán who was Secretario de Estado y del Despacho de Relaciones de México; see, for example, Valle, *Anexión*, V, 108–110, on the action in Chiapas.

11. See the documents in Francisco María Iglesias, comp., *Documentos Relativos a la Independencia* (3 vols., San José, Costa Rica, 1899–1902), II, 14, 216, 238–239, 343–351 (hereafter, Iglesias, *Documentos*).

12. José Carmen Salazar (Jefe Político Superior e Intendente de León) to Junta de Costa Rica, León, August 25, 1823, which includes the Treaty of September 9, 1823, signed in León, ANCR, Provincial Independiente, exp. 445 (hereafter, ANCR, P.I.); and Treaty of August 25, 1823, enclosed in Montealegre to Junta de Costa Rica, León, August 25, 1823, ANCR, P.I., exp. 444.

13. Juan Lindo to Municipalidad de Tegucigalpa, Comayagua, October 17, 1822, Archivo Nacional de Honduras (Tegucigalpa), 1822, Paquete II, leg. 6 (hereafter, ANH-T).

14. Ayuntamiento to Filísola, Tegucigalpa, October 8, 1822; *idem* to *idem*, November 9, 1822; *idem* to Juan Lindo, February 13, 1823; and *idem* to Filísola, March 24, 1823, ANH-T, 1823, Paquete, II, leg. 7.

15. Ayuntamiento to Juan Lindo, Tegucigalpa, April 19, 1823, ANH-T, 1823, Paquete II, leg. 7.

16. Ayuntamiento to Junta Gubernativa de León, Tegucigalpa, May 9, 1823, ANH-T, 1823, Paquete II, leg. 7.

17. Francisco Márquez to Ayuntamiento de Tegucigalpa, Guatemala City, November 15, 1823, and Próspero Herrera and Francisco Márquez to Ayuntamiento de Tegucigalpa, Guatemala City, March 19, 1824, ANH-T, 1823, Paq. III, leg. 21.

18. Ministerio del Estado Federal to Jefe Político de Tegucigalpa (Dionisio Herrera), Guatemala City, 1823, ANH-T, Paq. III, leg. 21.

19. Acta, Quezaltenango, April 27, 1825, "Libro de Quezaltenango," Francis Gall's original manuscript (hereafter, Gall, "Libro de Quezaltenango"); also published in 1836 as "Informe . . . Los Altos," April 27, 1825, 12 pp.

20. Decree, A.N.C., Guatemala City, October 1, 1823, BNG, Hojas Sueltas, 1821–1823 (hereafter, BNG, H.S., 1821–1823); also see Andrés Townsend Ezcurra, *Las Provincias Unidas de Centroamérica: Fundación de la República* (San José, 1973), pp. 144–145.

21. Decree, A.N.C., Guatemala City, October 4, 1823, BNG, H.S., 1821–1823.

22. Ponencia, Juan Esteban Milla, Guatemala City, October 6, 1823, Archivo General de Centro América (hereafter, AGCA), B6.2, exp. 2456, leg. 91.
23. Ponencia, Juan Francisco Sosa and Simón Vasconcelos, Guatemala City, October 6, 1823, AGCA, B6.2, exp. 2456, leg. 91.
24. For details on the Ariza incident of September, 1823, and the presence of the Salvadoran expedition in Guatemala City in the following month, see Townsend Ezcurra, *Las Provincias*, pp. 203–215 and 224–231, respectively.
25. *Ibid.*, pp. 162–167, comparing the Spanish text with the one agreed upon in Guatemala City; also see "Reglamento del Poder Ejecutivo," Guatemala City, July 8, 1823, Biblioteca Nacional (Guatemala City), Hojas Sueltas, 1821–1823 (hereafter, BNG, H.S., 1821–1823).
26. Filísola to Secretario Lucas Alamán, July 31 and August 29, 1823, in Valle, *Anexión*, V, 116–127 and 143, containing valuable insights into the politics of the period despite his bias.
27. Townsend Ezcurra, *Las Provincias*, p. 177.
28. For a perceptive discussion of the political change, see *ibid.*, pp. 216–231, dealing with the second S.P.E.; also see, "Manifiesto . . . Supremo Poder Ejecutivo," Guatemala City, November 14, 1823 (34 pp.) and A.N.C. degree, October 4, 1823, BNG, H.S., 1821–1823; and Acta, D.P., Guatemala City, No. 29, July 18, 1823, AGCA, D.P., 1823.
29. Memoria, José del Valle, Guatemala City, 1825, pp. 7–8, BNG, Hojas Sueltas, 1825 (hereafter, BNG, H.S., 1825).
30. Decree, A.N.C., Guatemala City, May 10, 1824, Archivos Nacionales de Costa Rica (San José), Sección Federal, Año 1824, exp. 741 (hereafter, ANCR, S.F., 1824); Acta, Guatemala City, No. 65, August 8, 1823, AGCA, Libros de Cabildo, 1823 (hereafter, AGCA, L.C., 1823).
31. Decree, A.N.C., Guatemala City, May 12, 1824, AGCA, B5.8, exp. 2037, leg. 77.
32. Ponencia, Fernando Antonio Dávila, Guatemala City, July 11, 1823, AGCA, B6.8, exp. 2658, leg. 97. José Francisco Barrundia was especially concerned with this point in the debates on the Constitution from July, 1824, forward.
33. Acta, Extraordinaria, Guatemala City, No. 57, July 20, 1823, AGCA, L.C., 1823.
34. Decree, A.N.C., Guatemala City, August 5, 1823, AGCA, B6.17, exp. 92,800, leg. 4124, and BNG, Hojas Sueltas, 1824 (hereafter, BNG, H.S., 1824).
35. Acta, Guatemala City, No. 5, January 9, 1824, AGCA, Libros de Cabildo, 1824, B78.1, exp. 10103, leg. 530 (hereafter, AGCA, L.C., 1824); and Townsend, *Las Provincias*, pp. 250–251.
36. Decrees, A.N.C., Guatemala City, June 9, 1824, AGCA, B5.8, exp. 2037, leg. 72, and July 23, 1824, AGCA, B6.17, exp. 92,799, leg. 4124; and ponencia, Mariano Gálvez, Guatemala City, May 28, 1824, AGCA, B6.2, exp. 2463, leg. 91.
37. Acta, Guatemala City, No. 5, January 14, 1825, AGCA, B78.1, exp. 10104, leg. 530, Libros de Cabildo, 1825 (hereafter: AGCA, L.C., 1825); and *El Indicador* (Guatemala City), October 24, 1823, has a good review of the freedom-of-the-press issue from 1820 to 1824.
38. For example, see State Decree, San Salvador, October 8, 1824, BNG, H.S., 1824; Decree, A.N.C., Guatemala City, May 5, 1824, *ibid.*; Actas, Guatemala City, Nos. 58 (May 28) and 117 (December 5, 1824), AGCA, L.C., 1824; Sesiones, A.N.C., Guatemala City, July 19, 21, 1824, AGCA, B6.26, exp. 2968, leg. 115.
39. Sesiones, A.N.C., Guatemala City, July 5, 18, 21, September 1 and 10, AGCA, B6.26, exp. 2970, leg. 116.
40. Valle, Memoria, 1825, pp. 8–9, BNG, H.S., 1825.
41. *Bases de la Constitución*, Guatemala City, December 17, 1823, AGCA, 1h, --920.
42. Sesión, A.N.C.'s Constitutional Committee, Guatemala City, August 13, 1824, AGCA, B6.26, exp. 2969, leg. 116 (hereafter, AGCA, C.C. Aug.).

43. Sesiones, A.N.C.'s Const. Committee, Guatemala City, August 4, 7, 9, 12, 13, 16, 17, and 23, *ibid.*

44. *El Indicador* (Guatemala City), November 15, 1824.

45. Decree, A.N.C., Guatemala City, November 15, 1823, Archivos Nacionales de Costa Rica (San José), Sección Federal, Año 1823, exp. 429 (hereafter, ANCR, S.F., 1823).

46. Decree, A.N.C., Guatemala City, November 27, 1823, BNG, H.S., 1821–1823.

47. *Ibid.*

48. Decree, A.N.C., Guatemala City, December 1, 1823, *ibid.*, which was put into effect by the S.P.E. on December 11.

49. Decree, A.N.C., Guatemala City, January 12, 1824 (S.P.E.'s order on January 22), BNG, H.S., 1824.

50. Acta, Guatemala City, No. 34, March 9, 1824, AGCA, L.C., 1824.

51. Acta, Guatemala City, No. 81, July 6, 1824, *ibid.*

52. Valle's Memoria, 1825, p. 12, BNG, H.S., 1825; also, Acta, Guatemala City, No. 45, April 8, 1824, AGCA, L.C., 1824.

53. Federal Decrees, Guatemala City, No. 207, ANCR, Sección Federal, Año 1825, exp. 8 (hereafter, ANCR, S.F., 1825).

54. Federal Decree, Guatemala City, June 21, 1826, BNG, Hojas Sueltas, 1826, rescinding these concessions (hereafter, BNG, H.S., 1826).

55. Decrees, A.N.C., Guatemala City, Nos. 92 (May 10), 113 (September 9), and 121 (November 30, 1824), AGCA, B6.7, exp. 2907, leg. 108.

56. Decree, A.N.C., Guatemala City, No. 61, Janaury 17, 1824, AGCA, B6.7, exp. 92,803, leg. 4125.

57. Mariano Gálvez to A.N.C., Guatemala City, August 14, 1823, AGCA, B6.2, exp. 2454, leg. 91; and Actas, Comayagua, February 5, 11, 1824, AGCA, B6.2, exp. 2462, leg. 91. Comayagua's municipality ousted the jefe político who tried to implement the law.

58. José del Valle to A.N.C., Guatemala City, February 28, 1824, in Valle, *Anexión*, VI, 29; Ponencia, J.F. Córdoba, Guatemala City, February 21, 1824, AGCA, B6.7, exp. 2551, leg. 93; and Decree, A.N.C., Guatemala City, No. 63, August 25, 1824, ANCR, Sección Federal, 1823–1825, "Indice" (hereafter, ANCR, S.E., 1823–1825).

59. Decree, A.N.C., Guatemala City, January 22, 1824, specifically invited foreign investors; also see, Decree, A.N.C., Guatemala City, June 27, 1825, ANCR, S.F., 1825, exp. 548, and *El Indicador* (Guatemala City), July 11, 1825.

60. Motion, J.F. Barrundia and Mariano Gálvez, Guatemala City, July 16, 1823, AGCA, B6.2, exp. 2453, leg. 91; Decree, A.N.C., Guatemala City, December 31, 1823, BNG, H.S., 1824; and Proposal, Fernando Antonio Dávila, no date, Guatemala City, AGCA, B6.8, exp. 2680, leg. 97, on checking the Spanish law.

61. Sesión, A.N.C., Constitutional Committee, Guatemala City, July 9, 1824, AGCA, B6.26, exp. 2968, leg. 116 (hereafter, AGCA, C.C., July).

62. Miguel González Saraiva *et al.* to Jefe Político Superior, Guatemala City, August 31, 1824, plus enclosures, AGCA, B10.8, exp. 3483, leg. 79641.

63. Valle's Memoria, 1825, BNG, H.S., 1825.

64. *El Indicador* (Guatemala City), January 16, 1826, is valuable for its statistics on the economy. See the issue of July 11, 1825, covering the years 1816–1825.

65. *Ibid.*, July 18, 1825; also see, *El Redactor General* (Guatemala City), edited by José del Valle; the prospectus appears in the issue of June 12, 1825, and 32 issues follow, up to October 26, 1826.

66. Valle to Governor of Costa Rica, Guatemala City, September 7, 1825, ANCR, S.F., 1825, exp. 535.

67. *El Liberal* (Guatemala City), May 17, 1826.

68. Federal decree, Guatemala City, June 16, 1825, ANCR, S.F., 1825, exp. 548; also published in BNG, H.S., 1825.
69. *El Liberal* (Guatemala City), May 17, 1826.
70. Decree, A.N.C., Guatemala City, January 21, 1825, BNG, H.S., 1824.
71. Valle's Memoria, 1825, p. 14, BNG, 1825.
72. Decree, A.N.C., Guatemala City, August 8, 1823, BNG, H.S., 1821–1823; Acta, Guatemala City, No. 108, November 21, 1823, AGCA, L.C., 1823.
73. J. Bernardo Escobar to Secretario General de Guatemala, Guatemala City, December 13, 1825, AGCA, B92.4, exp. 32,288, leg. 1394, reveals that the tertulia patriótica had been responsible for reviving the Economic Society of Guatemala.
74. Decree, A.N.C., Guatemala City, August 16, 1823, BNG, H.S., 1824.
75. *El Indicador* (Guatemala City), December 6, 1824; *El Liberal* (Guatemala City), April 30, 1826; Actas, Guatemala City, Nos. 32 (March 5), 56 (May 21), 57 (May 25), 58 (May 28) and 72 (July 6, 1824), AGCA, L.C., 1824; also, Actas, Guatemala City, Nos. 25 (April 4), 31 (April 25), and 44 (June 6, 1826), AGCA, Libros de Cabildo, 1826, B78.1, exp. 10105, leg. 531 (hereafter, AGCA, L.C., 1826).
76. Enclosed in Acta, Guatemala City, April 7, 1824, AGCA, L.C., 1824.
77. Manuel Aguilar to Municipalidad de Cartago, San José, January 7, 1826, ANCR, Sección Federal, Año 1826, exp. 877 (hereafter, ANCR, S.F., 1826).
78. Decree, A.N.C., Guatemala City, May 12, 1824, ANCR, S.F., 1824, exp. 741; Valle's Memoria, 1825, p. 15, BNG, H.S., 1825.
79. *El Liberal* (Guatemala City), March 20, 1825.
80. Valle's Memoria, 1825, pp. 16–19, BNG, H.S., 1825.
81. *El Liberal* (Guatemala City), June 1, 1826; Beaufort to Ministerio de Relaciones, Guatemala City, July (?), 1825, AGCA, B10.8, exp. 79,641, leg. 3483; "Proyecto de reglamento de una Sociedad de Agricultura . . .," Guatemala City, September 12, 1833, AGCA, B80.2, exp. 22,720, leg. 1074.
82. Sesión, A.N.C., July 3, 1824, AGCA, B6.26, exp. 2987, leg. 118.
83. Ponencia, Fernando Antonio Dávila, Guatemala City, July 11, 1823, AGCA, B6.2, exp. 2453, leg. 91; Ponencia, Eusebio Arzate, Guatemala City, January 6, 1824, AGCA, B6.2, exp. 2459, leg. 91; Actas, Guatemala City, No. 76, July 20, 1824, AGCA, L.C., 1824, and No. 11, February 6, 1825, AGCA, L.C., 1825.
84. State Decree, Guatemala City, No. 66, November 9, 1825, BNG, H.S., 1825.
85. Acta, Guatemala City, No. 111, November 12, 1824, AGCA, L.C., 1824.
86. Ponencia, Fernando Antonio Dávila, Guatemala City, January 2, 1824, AGCA, B6.2, exp. 2473, leg. 91.
87. Decrees, A.N.C., Guatemala City, April 17, 1824, BNG, H.S., 1824, and April 23, 1824, ANCR, S.F., 1824, exp. 741.
88. Decree, A.N.C., Guatemala City, April 17, 1824, plus enclosed ordinance of April 24, 1824, ANCR, S.F., 1824, exp. 429.

CHAPTER TEN

1. Decree, Supremo Poder Ejecutivo, Guatemala City, May 20, 1824, Archivos Nacionales de Costa Rica (San José), Sección Federal, Año 1824, exp. 741 (hereafter, ANCR, S.F., 1824).
2. As cited in *Redactor General* (Guatemala City), October 26, 1826, José del Valle's periodical.
3. S.P.E. to State Governments, Guatemala City, May 20, 1824, ANCR, S.F., 1824, exp. 741.
4. Acta, D.P., San Salvador, October 21, 1823, BNG, H.S., 1821–1823.
5. Salvadoran Government to Junta de Costa Rica, San Salvador, October 27, 1823, ANCR, P.I., exp. 504.

6. Salvadoran Junta to A.N.C., San Salvador, February 17, 1824, AGCA, B6.11, exp. 2867, leg. 102.
7. Congreso Constituyente del Estado del Salvador a sus comitentes, San Salvador, November 23, 1824, BNG, Hojas Sueltas, 1824 (hereafter, BNG, H.S., 1824).
8. Ponencia, Joaquín Lindo, Guatemala City, March 12, 1824, AGCA, B6.2, exp. 2461, leg. 91; and Acta, Guatemala City, No. 31, March 2, 1824, AGCA, Libros de Cabildo, 1824, B78.1, exp. 10103, leg. 530 (hereafter: AGCA, L.C., 1824).
9. Actas, Guatemala City, Nos. 40 (March 26) and 45 (April 8, 1824), AGCA, L.C., 1824.
10. Decree, A.N.C., Guatemala City, May 5, 1824, BNG, H.S., 1824.
11. Salvadoran Decree, San Salvador, October 8, 1824, BNG, H.S., 1824.
12. El Indicador (Guatemala City), November 1, 1824; Sesión, Costa Rican Government, San José, June 26, 1824, in Iglesias, Documentos, III, 290–291; A.N.C.'s order, Guatemala City, December 24, 1824, B11.6, exp. 4330, leg. 195, on states and their universities.
13. Acta, Cabildo Abierto, Cartago, No. 32, July 4, 1824, in República de Costa Rica, Documentos Históricos Posteriores a la Independencia (Tomo 1, San José, Costa Rica, 1923), 1, 227 (hereafter, Costa Rica, Documentos Posteriores).
14. Decree, Constituent Assembly, Comayagua, No. 3, August 30, 1824, containing a copy of the August 31 agreement, ANH-T, Paq. 5, leg. 40; also Dionisio Herrera to Tegucigalpa's citizens, Comayagua, September 9, 1825, ANH-T, Paq. 5, leg. 37.
15. Decree, Constituent Assembly, Comayagua, June 28, 1825, ANH-T, Paq. 5, leg. 40; Decree, Guatemala State, Antigua, No. 38, November 9, 1825, BNG, Hojas Sueltas, 1825 (hereafter, BNG, H.S., 1825).
16. Sesión, A.N.C., Constitutional Committee, Guatemala City, July 8, 1824, AGCA, B6.26, exp. 2968, leg. 116 (hereafter, AGCA, C.C., July), and August 2, 1824, AGCA, B6.26, exp. 2969, leg. 116 (hereafter, AGCA, C.C., August).
17. Sesiones, A.N.C., Guatemala City, July 28, 31, 1824, AGCA, C.C., July, and August 2, 1824, AGCA, C.C., August.
18. El Indicador (Guatemala City), November 15, 1824.
19. For example, see, Sesiones, A.N.C., Guatemala City, July 9, 24, 1824, AGCA, C.C., July, and August 12, 1824, AGCA, C.C., August.
20. Sesión, A.N.C., Guatemala City, August 12, 1825, in which "Cordobita" made this comparison, AGCA, C.C., August.
21. Sesión, A.N.C., Guatemala City, August 4, 12, 1824, ibid.
22. Sesión, A.N.C., Guatemala City, July 5, 1824, AGCA, C.C., July.
23. Sesión, A.N.C., Constitutional Committee, Guatemala City, September 3, 1824, AGCA, B6.26, exp. 2970, leg. 116 (hereafter, AGCA, C.C., September).
24. Sesión, A.N.C., Guatemala City, August 25, 1824, AGCA, C.C., August.
25. Sesiones, A.N.C., Guatemala City, July 27, AGCA, C.C., July, and August 2, 1824, AGCA, C.C., August.
26. Sesiones, A.N.C., Guatemala City, July 7, 1824, AGCA, C.C., July, and August 12 and 13, 1824, AGCA, C.C., August.
27. Sesiones, August 31, August 31 (Extraordinario), AGCA, C.C., August, and September 1824, AGCA, C.C., September.
28. Decree, A.N.C., Guatemala City, September 16, 1824, BNG, H.S., 1824; Acta, Guatemala City, No. 113, November 19, 1824, AGCA, L.C., 1824.
29. El Indicador (Guatemala City), February 7, 1825.
30. Redactor General (Guatemala City), August 31, 1825, in which Valle cited the remarks of publicists on Central America and her population.
31. For example, see, Actas, Guatemala City, Nos. 5 (January 9), 9 Extraordinario (January 17), 51 (May 4), and 88 (August 27, 1824), AGCA, L.C., 1824; Nos. 35 (April 19), 47 (May 27), and 69 (August 9, 1825), AGCA, Libros de Cabildo, 1825,

B78.1, exp. 10104, leg. 530 (hereafter, AGCA, L.C., 1825); Nos. 11 (February 7) and 69 (August 18, 1826), AGCA, Libros de Cabildo, 1826, B78.1, exp. 10105, leg. 531 (hereafter, AGCA, L.C., 1826).

32. For example, see, "Actas de la Diputación Supletoria," Guatemala City, installed on March 4, 1824, with the main objective of setting up the new system. The last acta (No. 10, May 26, 1824) exposes the problems involved (AGCA, B8.10, exp. 2807, leg. 101).

33. Although it had a strong moderate bias, *El Indicador* (Guatemala City), January 23, 1826, is exceptional in revealing political realities of the times.

34. Actas, Guatemala City, Nos. 24 (February 13) and 107 (October 29, 1824), AGCA, L.C., 1824; *El Indicador* (Guatemala City), January 17, 31, 1825; José Santos Madriz to Ministro de Relaciones de Costa Rica, Guatemala City, February 15, 1825, Costa Rica, *Documentos Posteriores*, 1, 248, complaining that he had not received any money for six months.

35. Actas, Guatemala City, Nos. 4, Extraordinario (January 8), and 9 (January 17, 1824), AGCA, L.C., 1824. Complicating matters was the fact that Tomás O'Horan had been the political chief in question; later he continued the feud as a member of the S.P.E.

36. Actas, Guatemala City, Nos. 14, Extraordinario (January 26), 19 (February 3), 20 (February 6), 21 (February 7), and 22 (February 10, 1824), AGCA, L.C., 1824.

37. Valle's Memoria, 1825, pp. 23–27, BNG, H.S., 1825; also see Decree, A.N.C., Guatemala City, April 20, 1824, ANCR, S.F., 1824, exp. 745.

38. Decree, A.N.C., Guatemala City, January 21, 1825, BNG, H.S., 1824.

39. Decree, A.N.C., Guatemala City, February 7, 1824, BNG, H.S., 1824; Jefe Político Vaca to Municipalidad de Guatemala, Guatemala City, April 20, 1824, AGCA, B78.50, exp. 21278, leg. 8641.

40. Decree, A.N.C., Guatemala City, January 23, 1824, BNG, H.S., 1824; Acta, Guatemala City, No. 93, September 10, 1824, AGCA, L.C., 1824, setting September 6, 1824, as the date the raise was authorized.

41. Costa Rican delegation to Government of Costa Rica, Guatemala City, March 5, 1824, ANCR, P.I., exp. 1069; Sesión, A.N.C., Guatemala City, July 30, 31, 1824, AGCA, B6.26, exp. 2968, leg. 115.

42. Many decrees of the A.N.C. register complaints about the usurpations of the state governments. For the Guatemalan case, see, State decrees, November 20, 1824 and December 31, 1825, BNG, H.S., 1824 and 1825; Acta, Guatemala City, No. 14, Extraordinario, February 11, 1825, AGCA, L.C., 1825.

43. *El Indicador* (Guatemala City), August 8, 1824, was a moderate organ and therefore very useful on the financial issue.

44. Dictamen, Guatemala City, November 11, 1825, ANCR, Sección Federal, Año 1825, exp. 645 (hereafter, ANCR, S.F., 1825), which includes the Committee's report on the two loans; "Discurso del C. Presbítero Urbano Ugarte, Dip. de Honduras," Guatemala City, ANCR, S.F., 1825, exp. 10.

45. José Antonio Alvarado to Ministerio General de Costa Rica, Guatemala City, July 22, 1827, and *idem* to Valle, Guatemala City, July 21, 1825, ANCR, S.F., 1825, exp. 536–537.

46. Dictamen, Guatemala City, November 7, 1825, in Orden, No. 266, Guatemala City, November 11, 1825, BNG, Hojas Sueltas, 1825 (hereafter, BNG, H.S., 1825).

47. Congreso Constituyente del Estado de Salvador a sus comitentes, San Salvador, November 23, 1824, and "Manifiesto," San Salvador, November 27, 1824, BNG, H.S., 1824; Dictamen, Comisión de Hacienda, San Salvador, March 28, 1825, BNG, H.S., 1825; and Acta, Guatemala City, September 20, 1825, AGCA, L.C., 1825.

48. *El Liberal* (Guatemala City), June 14, 27, 1825.
49. "Dictamen de la Comisión Especial," San Salvador, October 16, 1826, ANCR, Sección Histórica, Año 1826, exp. 712 (hereafter, ANCR, S.E., 1826).
50. Townsend Ezcurra, *Las Provincias*, pp. 147–148, 150–153.
51. *El Indicador* (Guatemala City), September 16, 1826, especially the article entitled "Carta del viajero." This newspaper defended the ultramontane position, yet it was fairly objective in doing so.
52. *Ibid.*, October 24, 1824.
53. *Ibid.*, November 29, 1824, and June 7, 1825.
54. *Refutación a los enemigos encubiertos de la patria y manifiestos calumniadores del Estado del Salvador por dos diputados de su Congreso Constituyente* (San Salvador, September 7, 1824, 21 pp.), in ANCR, P.I., 1036.
55. *Segunda advertencia patriótica del Doctor Cañas* (Guatemala City, October 28, 1824, 9 pp.), followed by an appendix *Adivinanza piadosa* (5 pp.), ANCR, P.I., exp. 1033.
56. For example, see, Ministerio General del Salvador to Secretario General de Costa Rica, San Salvador, August 22, 1825; *idem* to *idem*, San Salvador, November 10, 1825; Min. Costa Rica to Government of El Salvador, San José, December 3, 1825; *idem* to Government of Nicaragua, San José, December 18, 1825; and broadside, Government of El Salvador, December 20, 1825, plus enclosures, ANCR, S.F., 1825, exp. 19, 596, and 704.
57. Senate's decision, Guatemala City, August 5, 1825, published by El Salvador's government, ANCR, S.F., 1825, exp. 532.
58. *El Liberal* (Guatemala City), April 8, and June 6, 1825.
59. *Ibid.*, June 6, 1825.
60. "Expediente . . . Obispado," San José, September 2, 1825, ANCR, Congreso, Año 1825–1827, doc. 4116 (hereafter, ANCR, Con. 1825–1827).
61. State Decree, Herrera to Honduras, Comayagua, November 15, 1826, BNG, Hojas Sueltas, 1826 (hereafter, BNG, H.S., 1826).
62. *El Liberal* (Guatemala City), April 8, 1825.
63. *Ibid.*, March 22 and April 10, 1826.
64. *El Indicador* (Guatemala City), August 24 and September 2, 1826.
65. State Decree, Guatemala City, July 22, 1826, BNG, H.S., 1826.
66. Acta, Guatemala City, No. 104, Extraordinario, November 25, 1826, AGCA, L.C., 1826.
67. State Decree, Antigua, Nos. 19 (November 20) and 23 (December 15, 1824), BNG, H.S., 1824.
68. Actas, Guatemala City, Nos. 14, Extraordinaria (February 11), 20, Extraordinaria (February 26), 21, Extraordinaria (February 27), and 22 (March 1, 1825), AGCA, L.C., 1825.
69. State decree, Antigua, No. 49, June 22, 1825, BNG, H.S., 1825, claiming that the move was due to the desire to protect the "rights" of the State and to bring "economy to the treasury."
70. State decree, Guatemala City, December 31, 1825, BNG, H.S., 1825.
71. One of the best treatments is Adam Szasdi, *Nicolás Raoul y la República Federal de Centro América* (Madrid, 1958).
72. For example, see, Salvadoran Government to Federal Government, San Salvador, March 9, 1826, and *idem* to Secretario de Costa Rica, San Salvador, June 7, 1826, ANCR, S.F., 1826, exp. 24.
73. Ministro General de Costa Rica to Senator Mariano Córdoba, San José, October 3, 1826, and *idem* to Ministerio de Guerra, San José, October 18, 1826, ANCR, S.F., 1826, exp. 596.
74. Federal decree, Guatemala City, August 25, 1826, BNG, H.S., 1826.

Glossary

A

afrancesados — Spanish subjects who collaborated with the Napoleonic government in Spain

aguardiente — brandy

alcabala(s) — sales tax(es) of varying amounts

alcabala de viento — a special Mexican tax levied on food products sold in the market-place

alcalde(s) — town magistrate(s)

alcaldes mayores — protectors of Indians in extended jurisdiction

alcaldía(s) mayor(es) — governmental unit(s) for larger towns or settlements of Indians

alcalde primero (1) — mayor

Alta Corte de Justicia — Supreme Court

amortización — alienation of lands

arancel — a tariff schedule

arribadas — ships in distress (see navíos de arribada)

Asamblea Nacional Constituyente de las Provincias Unidas del Centro de América — National Constituent Assembly of the Provinces of the Center of America (Guatemala City)

Asamblea Nacional Constituyente — (abbr. of above)

A.N.C. — (abbr. of above)

asiento — contract, especially for the slave trade in the Hispanic world

audiencia(s) — regional courts overseas during the colonial period

ayuntamiento(s) — town council(s)

azotes — public beatings

B

"Bacos" — "The Drunks," a derogatory term applied to a political faction in Guatemala City

baldíos	public lands
Bases de la Constitución Federal (December 1823)	Bases of the Federal Constitution

C

cabildo	the session of a corporation, as applied to the meetings of the town council or the ecclesiastical corporation (sometimes used as a synonym for *ayuntamiento* or *municipalidad*)
cabildos abiertos	special town meetings to discuss major decisions for the community; open to bona fide residents
cabildo eclesiástico	a session of the ecclesiastical corporation; also, used as the name of that body
"*Cacos*"	"The Thieves," an uncomplimentary term applied to a political party in Guatemala City
cajas de communidad	community treasuries for Indians, or trust funds for Indians
Caja de Consolidación	Funding Reserves
cartillas técnicas	technical manuals or booklets
Casta(s)	non-white(s); mixed blood(s); or at Cádiz, anyone with African blood, whatever the degree
catecismo(s)	Catechism(s)
catecismo político	political manual (catechism)
cédula(s)	royal decree(s)
Centrales	members of the Junta Central in Spain
chicha	spirits (or drink) of commoners in Guatemala
chicherías	stalls where the drink (*chicha*) is sold
colegios	grammar schools (secondary)
compromisario(s)	elector(s) in the national series of elections (Constitution of 1812)
conquistador(es)	conqueror(s)
Consejo de Castilla	Council of Castile
Consejo de Estado	Council of State
Consejo de Indias	Council of the Indies
consulado(s)	merchant guild(s)
consulta(s)	a consultative report(s)
corregidores (de indios)	Royal officials supervising Indian villages
cortes	parliament
cortes territoriales	regional courts under the Cádiz system (same as the colonial *audiencia*)
cuerpo conservador	conservative or moderative body (force)
cuerpo representativo	representative body; the Upper House of state governments in Central America

D

departamentos	departments or provinces (same as *provincias* of Cádiz system)
desafuero	a denial of *fuero*, a special privilege or jurisdiction
diezmo(s)	tithe(s)
diputación permanente	a permanent deputation which represents Parliament while it is not in session
diputación(es) provincial(es)	provincial deputation(s)
D.P.	abbr. for *diputación provincial*
diputado(s)	deputy(ies) of Parliament
distritos	districts (same as *partidos* of Cádiz system)
dolce farniente (Italian)	sweet leisure ("sweet doing nothing")
donativos	voluntary donations to the Crown of Spain by subjects

E

ejidos	commons, communal lands of the Indians
El dos de mayo	May 2, 1808, when the people of Madrid began the resistance movement against Napoleon's forces
El Genio de la Libertad	*The Genius of Liberty*, a Guatemalan newspaper at the time of Independence from Spain
El Misterio de la Concepción Purisma de María Nuestra Señora	The Mystery of the Immaculate Conception of Mary, Our Lady
escudo	a coin, financial unit
españoles	"Spaniards" who might be from America *"españoles Americanos"* or *"españoles europeos"* from Europe
estanco (estanquillos)	stall(s) or franchises for the sale of liquor (see *aguardiente* and *chicha*); also means a "monopoly"
"*Exaltados*"	"Exalted Ones," a term applied to the radical liberals
exposición	a presentation, exposition

F

fuero	a special privilege which permits a member of an ecclesiastical or military corporation, for example, to be tried for special cases in his own corporate jurisdiction

G

gobierno	a governmental unit, such as that of Costa Rica in the colonial era
gremios	artisan guilds

H

hacendado(s)	farm or plantation owner(s)
hacienda(s)	a farm or plantation
hojas sueltas	broadsides (publication)

I

indigenismo	Indianism: study of the Indian, Indian reforms, Indian themes in the arts, literature, politics, etc.
indigenista	a supporter of Indianism (see above)
Informe de Ley Agraria (1795)	Report on Agrarian Law
intendente	Intendant: a royal official who dealt with treasury, justice, administration, and military matters

J

jefe(s) político(s)	political chief(s)
Jefe Político Superior	Superior Political Chief who outranked other political chiefs in a given jurisdiction
jefes subalternos	assistant chiefs, "subordinate chiefs"
jueces de hecho	local judges in the freedom-of-the-press system (second)
juez(ces) de letras	"judge(s) of letters" who are district magistrates
junta(s)	gathering(s) of key personages, leading governmental unit(s)
Junta Central Suprema y Gubernativa de España	Central and Supreme Governing Junta of Spain
Junta Central	(abbr. of above)
J.C.	(abbr. of above)
Junta de Cádiz	political government of the Province of Cádiz
junta de censura	censorship board
juntas de defensa	defense units of Spain after May 2, 1808
junta gubernativa	governing board
Junta Gubernativa Subalterna	Subordinate Governing Board
juntas populares	parish assemblies (same as *parroquias* of Cádiz system)

Junta Preparatoria	The Electoral Board under the Constitution of 1812 empowered to supervise elections in a given region
juntas protectoras	protective or supervisory bodies
juntas provinciales	provincial units
junta provisional	temporary junta (board)
Junta Provisional Consultiva	Consultative Provisional Government in Guatemala City after September 15, 1821
juntas superiores	higher councils or juntas
Junta Suprema de Guerra	Supreme War Council

L

ladinos	a mixed blood (Indian and White), thus same as *mestizos*; also, anyone not culturally an Indian
laissez-faire	free enterprise, "to leave alone"

M

mandamiento(s)	compulsory work levies of Indians
mayorazgos	civil entails
Mesta	Sheepherder's organization in the Middle Ages (Spain)
mestizo	a mixed blood (white and Indian)
Ministro Universal de las Indias	Universal Minister of the Indies
mita(s)	compulsory work levies by Indians
Montepío, Monte Pío	a financial reserve; a bank or loan association. Indigo Growers' Association (*Montepío de Cosecheros de Añil*
Muy Noble y Leal Ayuntamiento de Guatemala	The Very Noble and Loyal Municipality of Guatemala

N

nacional(es)	national(s)
navíos de arribada	ships in distress, thus allowed to frequent a Spanish port; also called *arribadas*
"*Nobles*"	the moderate and conservative party in Guatemala called this by the liberals to emphasize its relationship with the area's elite

O

oidor(es)	judge(s) of an *audiencia*

P

Pacto de Concordia	The Unity Compact (referring to Costa Rica)
Pacto Social	Social Compact (referring to Costa Rica)
pardos	mixture of Indian and Black; also *zambos*
partido(s)	district(s)
patria	homeland, "mother country"
patrón(es)	boss(es), landlord(s), master(s)
patronato real	royal patronage
peso(s)	monetary unit(s) of varying value, consisting usually of eight *reales*
pesos fuertes	a *peso* of eight *reales*
Plaza de la Constitución	Constitution Square
primeras letras	elementary education, "to read, write, and count"
propietario(s)	proprietor(s); deputies elected to office, thus having a proprietary stake in the government
protomédico	head of the public medical and health services
provinciano(s)	man (men) from the outlying provinces (of Central America)
Provincias Unidas del Centro de América	United Provinces of the Center of America
pueblo	village

Q

quetzales	a Guatemalan financial unit worth a dollar today
Quezaltecos	residents of the highland city of Quezaltenango (Guatemala)

R

real	royal (adjective)
real(es)	coin(s); one-eighth of a *peso*
real(es) de minas	mining association(s)
Recopilación de Leyes	famous compilation of Spanish laws on the colonies (1680)
regidor(es)	alderman (men)
regidores perpétuos	aldermen or town councillors whose office is for life
Reglamento de Comercio Libre (1778)	Free Trade Ordinance
repartimiento(s)	compulsory work levies of Indians; or obligatory purchase of manufactures by Indians from royal officials
residencia	an investigation held at the end of an official's term of office

S

Santo Oficio	Inquisition
señoría	a title or ranking for certain municipalities, as well as key personages
señorío	an entailed estate
"Serviles"	"servile" people
síndico(s)	city attorneys (syndics)
suplente(s)	substitute(s) who hold office provisionally, until the appearance of the proprietary deputy
Suprema de Justicia	Supreme Court

T

ternas	a listing of three names, one of which will receive a given position in government
Terror Bustamantino	"The Reign of Terror" under Captain General Bustamante in Central America
tertulia patriótica	patriotic reunion; a club whose primary objective was to enlighten the public on major issues; licensed by the state
Ticos	a nickname for Costa Ricans
tierras baldías	public lands (see *baldíos*)
tierras realengas	royal lands, domain
toma de razón	acknowledgment and receipt of a given governmental decree
Tribunal de Vigilancia	Security Tribunal

V

voto particular	private or individual vote with an explanation for the choice
voz activa	"active voice," which, according to the Guatemalan Larrazábal, could elect officers to government
voz pasiva	"passive voice", which, according to the Guatemalan Larrazábal, could not be elected to office

Z

zambos	mixture of Indian and black; also *pardos*
zeladores	informants, spies

Bibliography

I. ESSAY ON AUTHORITIES

The Cádiz years in Spanish history have attracted writers from many parts of the world, especially on commemorative occasions, and the literature has been plentiful and of varying quality. Central Americans became interested in the Cádiz story during the 1930s, when the well-known Nicaraguan historian, Sofonías Salvatierra, discovered in the Spanish archives José de Bustamante's unfavorable edition of the 1810 instructions to Father Antonio Larrazábal. Sensing the importance of this document to Guatemalans, he allowed them to reprint it in the *Anales de la Sociedad Geográfica e Histórica de Guatemala* (Guatemala City, 1941), while he contented himself with analyzing the instructions and providing a historical setting for them in his *Contribución a la historia de Centro América* (2 vols., Managua, 1939). It was the first real exposure of the role played by Central Americans at Cádiz, an account that is essentially accurate in its main lines. A more elaborate copy of Larrazábal's orders appeared in Guatemala City on the centennial of his death, 1953, with a well-organized and sensitive preface by César Brañas, one of Guatemala's great poets. Later, Brañas wrote *Antonio Larrazábal, un guatemalteco en la historia* (2 vols., Guatemala City, 1969); this sentimental study added little information about Larrazábal's public career, and did not cover the clergyman's career in Spain to any great extent. In the meantime, the Peruvian Andrés Townsend Ezcurra was bringing together the available documentation on the Asamblea Nacional Constituyente, which he published as the *Fundación de la República* (Guatemala City, 1958), presumably the first of two volumes. The completed edition, however, appeared as one volume under the title *Las Provincias Unidas de Centroamérica: Fundación de la República* (San José, Costa Rica, 1973). In certain analyses of the A.N.C.'s earlier acts, Townsend Ezcurra noted the similarities with the Cádiz Constitution of 1812. Costa Rican historians like Hernán Peralta and Rafael Obregón Loria, among others, have also recognized their indebtedness to the Spanish prototype in such documents as the *Pacto de Concordia*.

The most aggressive student of the first constitutional period in Central America is the young Guatemalan Lawyer Jorge Mario García Laguardia, whose training has been mainly in political science and law. In a pamphlet entitled *Las cortes de Cádiz y la constitución de 1812* (Guatemala City, 1967), this Guatemalan scholar provides a succinct review that is based on the standard Spanish authorities. Later, García Laguardia launched a series of articles on the subject for historical journals in Guatemala and Mexico, all of them well received. He then proceeded to bring together facsimile copies of the major documents that we have utilized for the first constitutional period under the title *La Génesis del Constitucionalismo Guatemalteco* (Guatemala City, 1971), with an introduction of his findings to date. These documents, all of them published in other sources, included the minutes and documents of the Bayonne Constitution in 1808–1809, Larrazábal's instructions, the minority report of the Ayuntamiento of Guatemala City in 1811, and the Consulado's report of the same year—a convenient compilation in every sense. For the college paperback trade, García Laguardia published *Orígenes de la democracia constitucional en Centro América* (San José, Costa Rica, 1971), in which he retells his story and attempts to evaluate the Cádiz experiment in Central America during the first constitutional period. Unfortunately, it was written hastily and some portions of the account are garbled. Moreover, his emphasis upon the importance of French influence upon Central America, and especially the Bayonne Constitution of 1809, is standard among many Latin American and Spanish legal authorities. In my opinion, it is too theoretical and uncritical and cannot be supported by historical realities as I have encountered them. García Laguardia, in addition, offers no coverage of the American Question at Cádiz, nor does he review the objectives and actions of Central Americans in Spain. His book does not treat the second constitutional period, Independence and the Mexican connection, nor the initial years of nation-building. In short, his work reveals the top of the iceberg; and it is indeed questionable to use the term "democracy" with regard to the Cádiz Experiment. It was far more representative and elitist than democratic.

As the centennial of the Cádiz Cortes approached, many Spanish Americans devoted their time to the study of a period that they recognized was crucial in their own legal formation. They took pride, of course, in the role played by their countrymen at Cádiz. A case in point was the Argentine lawyer Enrique Valle Iberlucea, who wrote *Las Cortes de Cádiz: La Revolución de España y la democracia en América* (Buenos Aires, 1912), a very general speech with penetrating insights into the American Question. He added an appendix which included *Los diputados de Buenos Aires en las Cortes de Cádiz*. Another talented student of the Cortes was the Cuban-born Rafael María de Labra y Cadrana, a representative of Puerto Rico in the Spanish Parliament, a professor of international relations in Spain, and an activist for effective commonwealth status for Puerto Rico and Cuba. His publications are prolific, usually speeches that he delivered at the Ateneo in Madrid. Among others, he published *América y la Constitución española de 1812* (Madrid, 1914), *Las declaraciones y los decretos de las Cortes de Cádiz sobre América* (Madrid, 1912), *Los diputados americanos en las Cortes de Cádiz* (Madrid, 1911),

España y América (1810–1912) (Madrid, 1912), and *Los presidentes americanos de las Cortes de Cádiz* (Cádiz, 1912). In his books and pamphlets, Labra dwelled upon the mistakes of the Peninsulars which alienated the inhabitants of the New World.

Other Americans have compiled documentation about the Spanish Cortes or have written biographies of their representatives. Among these are: Rafael de Alba, ed., *La constitución de 1812 en la Nueva España* (2 vols., Mexico City, 1912–1913); Genaro García, *Apuntes biográficos de diputados mejicanos* (Mexico City, 1911); Camilo Destruye, comp., *Don José Mexía Lequerica, Su Vida y sus discursos parlamentarios* (Guayaquil, 1909); Alfredo Flores y Caamaño, *Don José Mejía Lequerica en las Cortes de Cádiz de 1810 a 1813 (o sea el principal defensor de los intereses de la América española en la más grande asamblea de la península* (Barcelona, 1913); Luis Alayza Paz Soldán, *La constitución de Cádiz, 1812, El egregio limeño Morales y Duárez* (Lima, 1946); Victor Manuel Rendón, *Olmedo, homme d'Etat e poete américain, chantre de Bolívar* (Paris, 1904); and Pedro de Angelis, *Ramón Power, Primer diputado a Cortes de Puerto Rico* in his *Miscelánea puertorriqueñas; colección de artículos históricos biográficos* (Puerto Rico, 1894).

North Americans have likewise focussed upon the Cádiz years and their impact upon the New World. Professor James Ferguson King, "The Colored Castes and American Representation in the Cortes of Cádiz," *Hispanic American Historical Review*, XXXIII, No. 1 (February 1953), pp. 38–42, has studied in great detail the initial stages of the American Question, a version which I first heard as a graduate student in Professor King's seminar at Berkeley. Also thorough is Otto Carlos Stoetzer, "La constitución de Cádiz en la América Española," *Revista de Estudios Políticos*, No. 126 (Nov.–Dec. 1962), pp. 641–664. Professor Nettie Lee Benson has been a very active scholar on this theme since her doctoral dissertation at the University of Texas, dealing with the provincial deputations of Mexico and their contribution to Mexican federalism. It was published under the title *La diputación provincial y el federalismo mexicano* (México, 1955). She also edited *Mexico and the Spanish Cortes, 1810–1822, Eight Essays* (Austin, Texas, 1966), the results of a seminar on the Cádiz era by students of hers at the University of Texas. Others, primarily interested in peninsular history, include Edward Julius Goodman, "Nationalism in the Cortes of Cádiz," (Ph.D., Columbia University, 1952), Enoch F. Resnick, "The Council of State and Spanish America: 1814–1820," (Ph.D., the American University, Washington, D.C., 1970), and Gabriel H. Lovett, *Napoleon and the Birth of Modern Spain* (2 vols., New York, 1965).

My impression is that Spaniards do not like to write about the loss of their former colonies in the New World. It was not until the sesquicentennial that Professor Demetrio Ramos essayed his study "Las Cortes de Cádiz y América," in the *Revista de Estudios Políticos*, No. 126 (Nov.–Dec. 1962), pp. 433–639. In this lengthy work, Ramos treats the American Question up to February 1811, at which time, he prefers to think that it was settled to everyone's satisfaction. He therefore spends the remainder of the study on the British mediation attempts in the New World. Ramos does not proceed beyond the point developed by Professor King, and in the process he distorts the account.

As for the Spanish Cortes, the literature seems endless; and we propose here only to single out the major studies whose bibiographies or documentary contributions are noteworthy. Indispensable is the work of Miguel Artola, *Los orígenes de la España contemporánea* (2 vols., Madrid, 1959). In the first volume he interprets the period; and in the second, he reproduces key documentary materials and provides a bibliography. Artola's work, *Los afrancesados* (Madrid, 1953), completes the picture for the Peninsula. Other valuable bibliographies can be found in Manuel Izquierdo Hernández, *Antecedentes y comienzos del reinado de Fernando VIII* (Madrid, 1958), pp. 779–793; Ramón Solís, *El Cádiz de las Cortes* (Madrid, 1958), pp. 541–563; and Lovett's above-mentioned study, pp. 852–868.

Moreover, there are special studies that deserve mention: *Revista de Estudios Políticos* (Madrid, Institución de Estudios Políticos, Nov.–Dec. 1962) devoted an entire issue to the Cortes de Cádiz. We have already mentioned the contributions of Stoetzer and Ramos, and we now take note of the essays written there by Melchor Fernández Almagro ("Del Antiguo Régimen a las Cortes de Cádiz") and José Luis Commellas ("Las Cortes de Cádiz y la Constitución de 1812"). In addition, there is the scholarly study of Fernando Jiménez de Gregorio, *La convocación a Cortes Constituyentes en 1810; Estado de las opinión española en punto a la reforma constitucion* (Madrid, 1955), which is indispensable for the climate of opinion that preceded the Cortes. Carlos Sanz Cid, *La constitución de Bayona* (Madrid, 1922), contributes to the standard view that much that went on at Cádiz was the result of French influence as represented by the 1809 constitution in southern France. For the interregnum period, see María del Carmen Pintos Vieites, *La política de Fernando VII entre 1814 y 1820* (Madrid, 1958); José María Cordero Torres, *El consejo de estado, su trayectoria y perspectivas en España* (Madrid, 1944); and Enoch F. Resnick's dissertation, cited above. The massive work of Alberto Gil Novales, *Las sociedades patrióticas (1820–1823)* (2 vols., Madrid, 1975) covers the second constitutional period in exemplary fashion. Other useful works are: María Cruz Sevane, *El primer lenguaje constitucional español: las Cortes de Cádiz* (Madrid, 1968); Raúl Morondo y Elías Díaz, "Tendencias y grupos políticos en las Cortes de Cádiz y en las de 1820," *Cuadernos Hispanoamericanos,* No. 201 (1966), pp. 637–675; and Federico Suárez, *Conservadores, innovadores, renovadores en las postrimerías del Antiguo Régimen* (Pamplona, 1955). For the pro-clerical view, see Luciano de la Calzada Rodríguez, *La evolución institucional; las Cortes de Cádiz: precedentes y consecuencias* (Zaragoza, 1959); and P. Isidoro A. Villapadierna, *Cuestión religiosa en las Cortes de Cádiz, 1810–1813* (Madrid, extract from *Hispania Sacra*, Vol. 8, 1955). Finally, there is the sketchy outline of Indian reforms in Fray Cesáreo de Armellada, *La causa indígena en las Cortes de Cádiz* (Madrid, 1959).

Given the controversy that surrounds the Cádiz story, the student must inevitably consult the available documentation, printed and in manuscript form. Fortunately, I accumulated a sizable collection of printed materials in Guatemala City. While working in the Archivo General de Centro América, Professor Carlos Meléndez of the University of Costa Rica informed me that there was a book sale nearby later that afternoon. The collection dealt primarily with European history, and most of it was on a dirt floor in a rather damp room. The small-sized volumes sold at two dollars (*quetzales*) and the larger ones at three. When I noticed twenty volumes of the *Diario de las Cortes* (Cádiz), I scooped them up into my lap and set them aside. I also picked up the *Obras de Jovellanos* (8 vols., Barcelona, 1839–1840) edited by Venceslao de Linares Pacheco—all at the two-dollar price! I likewise found a three-volume set of José María Queipo de Llano (Conde de Toreno), *Historia del levantamiento, guerra y revolución de España* (3 vols., Paris, 1851), some volumes by Pedro Rodríguez Campomanes, and a series on the religious question during the second constitutional period. It was a remarkably worthwhile day; and it took me at least a month to dry out the books in question, thanks to the ubiquitous sunshine of a Guatemalan winter. The *Diario* was especially significant because it belonged to Marcelo Molina, the first governor of the State of Los Altos in the 1830s. When Arturo Taracena, a noted book collector in Guatemala City and a good friend of mine, found out that I had purchased his grandfather's collection of the *Diario*, he turned pale. He consoled himself with the knowledge that it at least was in good hands.

In addition to the Conde de Toreno's famous history, the student must also consult Agustín de Argüelles, *Examen histórico de la reforma constitucional que hicieron las Cortes Generales y Extraordinaries* (2 vols., London, 1835); and Alvaro Flórez Estrada, *Examen imparcial de las disensiones de América con España* (Cádiz, 1812), which attacks Spanish trade policy in the New World. Other memoirs and collections of documents include: Jorge Campos, ed., *Obras escogidas de D. Antonio Alcalá Galiano* (2 vols., Madrid, 1955); Alvaro Alonso-Castrillo, ed., *Memoria de José García de León y Pizarro (1770–1835)* (2. vols., Madrid, 1953); Carlos Seco Serrano, ed., *Obras de D. Francisco Martínez de la Rosa* (8 vols., Madrid, 1962). Many of these works can be found in the series of the *Biblioteca de Autores Españoles*. Finally, see Miguel Artola, ed., *Memoria de tiempos de Fernando VII* (2 vols., Madrid, 1957), which contains memoirs of key personages including the *Viaje a las Cortes* by Joaquín Lorenzo Villanueva, whose remarks on the secret sessions of the Cortes are especially useful.

II. ARCHIVES AND OTHER REPOSITORIES OF PRIMARY MATERIALS

A. SPAIN

1. Archivo Histórico Nacional, Madrid (AHNM), Sección Estado (S.E.).

The holdings for the period of the Junta Central are extensive and can be identified quickly by using the *Indice de los papeles de la Junta Central Suprema Gubernativa del Reino y del Consejo de Regencia* (Madrid, 1904). The *consultas* of the Consejo de Estado for both constitutional periods were useful to me; so were the minutes of the Junta de Cádiz which affected American interests. Also see the *Indice alfabético de materias* (2 vols., Madrid, 1966) to expedite the search for documents.

2. Archivo de las Cortes, Madrid.

Of limited use for me, I merely checked out certain footnotes in Professor James F. King's article on the Castas. Also, this source was mined extensively by Fernando Jiménez de Gregorio for his study of public opinion before 1810.

3. Archivo General de Indias, Sevilla.

Since I had already seen most of the documentation from the Audiencia de Guatemala in Central America, I checked only for additional materials, especially for the 1814–1815 period, to see if other Central Americans had submitted proposals to the Minister of the Indies, Miguel de Lardizábal.

4. Biblioteca Nacional, Madrid.

There are certain key catalogs that facilitate the use of this excellent repository of materials. For manuscripts dealing with the New World, see Julián Paz, *Catálogo de manuscritos de América existentes en la Biblioteca Nacional* (Madrid, 1933) and Florentino Zamora Lucas and María Casado Lucas, *Publicaciones periódicas existentes en la Biblioteca Nacional* (Madrid, 1952). Also very useful for bibliographical purposes was José Simón Díaz, *Bibliografía de la literatura hispánica* (2nd. ed., 7 vols., Madrid, 1962), especially Volume Two, which in effect is a bibliography of Hispanic bibliographies, and not restricted to literature. For my purposes, I was interested in sampling the major newspapers of the period, both in the General Library and in the Special Section called "Raros." These were the main periodicals consulted: *Abeja Española* (Cádiz), *El Censor* (Madrid), *El Conciso* (Cádiz), *El Español* (London), *El Telégrafo Americano* (Cádiz), *El Robespierre Español* (Cádiz), *Gazeta de la Regencia* (Cádiz), *Redactor General de España* (Madrid), and *Semanario Patriótico* (Cádiz).

5. Archivo de la Diputación Provincial de Guipúzcoa, San Sebastián.

My main concern here was to check generally for the Basque reaction to the reform of the Diputación Provincial. Since their *fueros*, or liberties, had in effect permitted provincial rule in the Basque area for years, the reforms were regarded as traditional.

6. Special Printed collections: *Diario de las Cortes.*

There are indices that appear frequently in the minutes of Parliament, providing the temptation to consult merely the sessions that dealt with certain themes. This saves time, but it does not allow the scholar to savor an epoch and catch the nuances that are possible when he reads the entire record and familiarizes himself with the actors involved. By doing this, I was able to develop a feeling for the parliamentary experience of Spaniards and Americans, although it was time-consuming. It complemented the impressions I formed from reading the major newspapers of the period. Blanco-White's *El Español* (London) was an especially valuable check on the discussions in the *Diario*. Since there are different editions of the *Diario*, it is pointless to include volume and page numbers. The date easily identifies the material. The following are the various sets and volumes used in this study.

(a) *Diario de las discussiones y actas de las Cortes* (23 vols., Cádiz, 1811–1813). As noted above, I have the first twenty volumes in my library.

(b) *Diario de Sesiones de las Cortes Generales y Extraordinarias* (8 vols., Madrid, 1870). I used this set to complete the coverage from June 27 to September 24, 1813. This edition also has a volume (sixth) that pulls together the major documents on the issue of the Inquisition.

(c) *Actas de las sesiones secretas de las Cortes Generales Extraordinarias de la nación española* (Madrid, 1874). They are useful but too sketchy.

(d) *Actas de las sesiones de la legislatura ordinaria de 1813* (Madrid, 1876), which cover the minutes from October 1, 1813, to February 19, 1814.

(e) *Manifiesto de la Junta Provisional a las Cortes* (Madrid, 1820). This document set up the administrative machinery for the second constitutional period in Madrid.

(f) *Actas de las sesiones secretas de las cortes ordinarias y extraordinarias de los años 1820 y 1821, de las de los 1822 y 1823, y de las celebradas por las diputaciones permanentes de las mismas cortes ordinarias* (Madrid, 1874). The minutes start on July 25, 1820.

(g) *Diario de las sesiones de Cortes* (3 vols., Madrid, 1871). This covers the legislature of 1820, starting on June 26 and ending on November 9, 1820. The volumes are paginated consecutively, which is also true for the sets that follow.

(h) *Diario de las sesiones de Cortes* (3 vols., Madrid, 1871), for the legislature of 1821, starting February 29 and ending June 29, 1821.

(i) *Diario de las sesiones de Cortes* (Madrid, 1871), for the extraordinary legislature (September 22, 1821, to February 14, 1822).

(j) *Diario de las sessiones de Cortes* (2 vols., Madrid, 1872), for another extraordinary legislature (October 1, 1822, to February 19, 1823).

(k) *Diario de las sesiones de Cortes* (2 vols., Madrid, 1885), for the ordinary legislature. Volume One covers February and part of March 1823, and the *Gaceta de Madrid* is the medium for the minutes. Volume Two deals with the legislature at Cádiz from April to September 15, 1823, which ended the second constitutional period in Spain.

B. CENTRAL AMERICA AND MEXICO

1. Archivo General de Centro América, Guatemala City, which was formerly called the Archivo General de la Nación. Its official publication is the *Boletín*. Under the directorship of the late Joaquín Pardo, it published many key documents from the archives. My own experience with documents from the Diputación Provincial de Guatemala is to warn the user not to assume that the documents in the *Boletín* are exhaustive, because they are selective or portions have been deleted. In short, he should work with the originals in the archives, just to be safe. These are the major categories of manuscripts that I have perused for this book. The following are all for Guatemala City:

(a) *L.C., 1808*: Libro de Cabildo, Guatemala City, 1808, AGCA, Al.2.2 (asignatura), 15734 (expediente), .2188 (legajo), January 2 to December 23, 1808.

L.C., 1809: Libro de Cabildo, Guatemala City, 1809, AGCA, (asignatura) Al.2.2, (expediente) 15735, (legajo) 2188, January 3 to December 22, 1809. Some volumes also carry the title "Actas Capitulares." I should note that almost all actas are numbered, but occasionally some are not. The date, of course, makes it easy to find the minute in question.

L.C., 1810: Libro de Cabildo, Guatemala City, 1810, AGCA, (asig.) Al.2.2, (exp.) 15736, (leg.) 2189, January 5 to December 24, 1810.

L.C., 1811: Libro de Cabildo, Guatemala City, 1811, AGCA, (asig.) Al.2.2, (exp.) 15737, (leg.) 2189, January 2 to November 29, 1811.

L.C., 1812: Libro de Cabildo, Guatemala City, 1812, AGCA, (asig.) Al.2.2, (exp.) 15738, (leg.) 2190, January 3 to December 4, 1812, which includes two printed documents of importance for the first constitutional elections in Central America: *Tabla para facilitar la elección de los diputados de cortes suplentes y de provincia de Guatemala* and *Instrucción formada de orden de la Junta Preparatoria para facilitar las elecciones de diputados y oficios consejiles* (Guatemala, 1812, pp. 1–40), printed by José Beteta. See folios 111 to 133.

L.C., 1812–1813: Libro de Cabildo. Actas Capitulares del Ex.mo Ayuntamiento Constitucional, Guatemala City, December 7, 1812, to December 24, 1813, plus message of thanks on December 31, 1813, AGCA, (asig.) Al.2.2, (exp.) 15739, (leg.) 2190.

L.C., 1814: Libro de Cabildo, Guatemala City, 1814, AGCA, (asig.) Al.2.2, (exp.) 15740, (leg.) 2191, January 4 to December 13, 1814.

L.C., 1815: Libro de Cabildo, Guatemala City, 1815, AGCA, (asig.) Al.2.2, (exp.) 15741, (leg.) 2191, January 3 to December 22, 1815.

L.C., 1816: Libro de Cabildo, Guatemala City, 1816, AGCA, (asig.) Al.2.2, (exp.) 15742, (leg.) 2192, January 4 to December 24, 1816.

L.C., 1817: Libro de Cabildo, Guatemala City, 1817, AGCA, (asig.) Al.2.2, (exp.) 15743, (leg.) 2192, January 3 to November 28, 1817.

L.C., 1818: Libro de Cabildo, Guatemala City, 1818, AGCA, (asig.) Al.2.2, (exp.) 15744, (leg.) 2193, January 4 to December 15, 1818.

L.C., 1819: Libro de Cabildo, Guatemala City, 1819, AGCA, (asig.) Al.2.2, (exp.) 15745, (leg.) 2193, January 5 to December 23, 1819.

L.C., 1820: Libro de Cabildo,, Guatemala City, 1820, AGCA, (asig.) Al.2.2, (exp.) 15746, (leg.) 2193, January 4 to December 29, 1820, which includes "Instrucciones . . . Julián Urruela," folios 138–145 vuelto.

L.C. 1821A: Libro de Cabildo, 1.re semestre, Guatemala City, AGCA, (asig.) Al.2.2 (exp.) 15747, (leg.) 2194, January 2 to July 17, 1821.

L.C., 1821B: Libro de Cabildo, Segundo semestre, Guatemala City, AGCA, (asig.) Al.2.2 (exp.) 15748, (leg.) 2194, July 27, 1821 to January 1, 1822.

L.C., 1822: Libro de Cabildo, Guatemala City, 1822,

AGCA, (asig.) B78.1, (exp.) 10101, (leg.) 529, January 4 to December 26, 1822.

L.C., 1823: Libro de Cabildo, Guatemala City, 1823, AGCA, (asig.) B78.1, (exp.) 10102, (leg.) 529, January 3 to December 29, 1823.

L.C., 1824: Libro de Cabildo, Guatemala City, 1824, AGCA, (asig.) B78.1, (exp.) 10103, (leg.) 529, January 1 to December 31, 1824.

L.C., 1825: Libro de Cabildo, Guatemala City, 1825, AGCA, (asig.) B78.1, (exp.) 10104, (leg.) 530, January 4 to December 30, 1825.

L.C., 1826: Libro de Cabildo, Guatemala City, 1826, AGCA, (asig.) B78.1, (exp.) 10105, (leg.) 531, January 3 to December 22, 1826.

(b) *D.P.-G.*, 1820: Actas de la Junta Provincial, Guatemala City, AGCA, (asig.) Bl.13, (exp.) 479, (leg.) 16, July 13 to November 6, 1820, the interim group that began to function once the second constitutional period had started.

D.P.-G., 1820–1821: Actas de la Ex.ma D.P. de Guatemala, Guatemala City, AGCA, (asig.) Bl.13, (exp.) 478, (leg.) 16, November 7, 1820 to May 29, 1821.

D.P.-G., 1821: Actas de la Ex.ma D.P. de Guatemala, Guatemala City, AGCA, (asig.) Bl.13, (exp.) 520, (leg.) 17, June 4 to September 11, 1821.

J.P.C., 1821–1822: Actas de la Ex.ma Junta Provisional Consultiva de Guatemala, Guatemala City, AGCA, (asig.) Bl.13, (exp.) 562, (leg.) 19, September 17, 1821, to February 21, 1822.

D.P.-G.,1822–1823: Actas de la D. Provincial de Guatemala, Guatemala City, AGCA, (asig.) B5.7, (exp.) 1849, (leg.) 68, March 29, 1822 to January 9, 1823.

"Decretos y reales órdenes, Regencia al Soberano Congreso Constituyente, Mexico City, 1822", AGCA, (asig.) B5.8, (exp.) 92.796, (leg.) 4123; and same for 1823, AGCA, B5.8, 92797, 4123.

D.P.-G., 1823: Actas de la Ex.ma D.P. de Guatemala, Guatemala City, AGCA, (asig.) B5.7, (exp.) 1854, (leg.) 68, January 13 to September 30, 1823.

D.P.-G., 1824: Actas de la D.P. Supletoria, Guatemala City, AGCA, (asig.) B5.7, (exp.) 79.426, (leg.) 3478, March 4 to May 26, 1824, dealing just with the financial issue.

(c) *Const. July, 1824*: Actas, Asamblea Nacional Constituyente, Guatemala City, Constitutional Committee Report, July,

1824, AGCA, (asig.) B6.26, (exp.) 2968, (leg.) 116.

Const. Aug. 1824: Actas, A.N.C., Guatemala City, Const. Comm. Report, August, 1824, AGCA, (asig.) B6.26, (exp.) 2969, (leg.) 116.

Const. Sept. 1824: Actas, A.N.C., Guatemala City, Const. Comm. Report, September, 1824, AGCA, (asig.) B6.26, (exp.) 2970, (leg.) 116. Also useful for the period of the A.N.C. is the "Indice de los decretos por la Asamblea Nacional Constituyente", AGCA, (asig.) B6.7, (exp.) 2907, (leg.) 108. For the Junta de Censura, 1820–1821, see AGCA, (asig.) Al.l, (exp.) 57.305, (leg.) 6931, with 44 documents.

2. Biblioteca Nacional, Guatemala City (BNG). This repository is valuable for its broadsides (*hojas sueltas*) and pamphlets, bound in yearly volumes for the most part. On the second floor is the Hemeroteca, which houses the newspapers.

(a) *BNG, H.S., 1820:* Contains, for example, the eight-page "Manifiesto de los americanos que residen en Madrid a las naciones de la Europa . . . demostrando las razones legales que tienen para no concurrir el día 28 de mayo á elegir diputados que representen los pueblos ultramarinos donde nacieron" (Madrid, 1820, reprinted in Guatemala City by José Beteta in that same year).

BNG, H.S., 1821–1823: Includes many decrees of the A.N.C., the Reglamento del Poder Ejecutivo, July 8, 1823, a manifesto by the S.P.E. on November 14, 1823, and the provisional tariff drawn up by Valle and his colleagues on February 13, 1822.

BNG, H.S., 1824: A.N.C. decrees, state decrees, José F. Barrundia's manifesto to Vicente Filísola, August 10, 1824, the prospectus for the newspaper *El Indicador* (Guatemala City), and an articulate blast against the liberals by José Francisco Córdoba, June 8, 1824, "Al público," 19 pages.

BNG, H.S., 1825: State decrees (Guatemala), Federal decrees, and José del Valle's *Memoria*, February 25, 1825, which reviews the reforms of the A.N.C. and the S.P.E. especially during Valle's tenure.

BNG, H.S., 1826: Some Honduran documents of importance.

BNG, H.S., 1827–1828: Guatemalan state decrees on loans, etc.

BNG, H.S., 1829: The waging of the war, etc.

(b) Thanks to the conscientious work and direction of Rigoberto Bran Azmitia, the Hemeroteca of the BNG has been well organized for all periods, a vast improvement over the conditions that prevailed twenty-two years ago when I first began to work on Guatemalan history. The following were the most useful newspapers for my purposes; and, oftentimes, issues of a given newspaper are scattered throughout Guatemala City.

El amigo de la patria (Guatemala City). In recent years, because of the sesquicentennial of Central American Independence, volumes of this newspaper have been published in Guatemala City and Tegucigalpa, because of José del Valle's origins (see my articles and reviews in the *Handbook of Latin American Studies*, "Central America," nos. 30, 32, 34, and 36, for example). I first worked with this periodical in the BNG, two tomos (October 16, 1820, to April 30, 1821, and May 15, 1821, to March 1, 1822). Tomo 3 was in a special collection: Facultad de Humanidades, Guatemala City.

El editor constitucional (Guatemala City), has been published (3 vols., Guatemala City, 1954) by the Editorial del Ministerio de Educación Pública; also see, *Colección de Documentos*, Nos. 10–12. *El genio de la libertad* was the new name given to the periodical as Independence became a mere matter of time. The dates for both are July 28, 1820, to December 10, 1821.

El Indicador (Guatemala City), in two volumes (1824–1825 and 1825 to 1827). There is also a duplicate set in one volume (October 11, 1824, to April 30, 1827).

El Liberal (Guatemala City), has two volumes: No. 1 (March 15, 1825 to September 28, 1825) and No. 2 (February 10 to July 6, 1826).

Gaceta de Gobierno (Guatemala City), 1824.

Gaceta de Guatemala (Guatemala City), February 13, 1797 to July 3, 1811. There were originally 18 volumes in the set, but some are missing. The Sociedad de Geografía e Historia in Guatemala City has some; the same applies to the Library of Congress in Washington, D.C., which has vols. 2, 5, 6, 11, 13, and 14. I strongly suspect that the missing volumes may be in Santiago, Chile, taken there by the famous Chilean bibliographer José Toribio Medina.

Periódico de la Sociedad Económica de Guatemala (Guatemala City), 1815–1816.

Redactor General (Guatemala City), another one edited by José del Valle, June 12, 1825, to October 26, 1826; it is found with the paper *El Liberal* (see above).

3. Others in Guatemala. The "Libro de Quezaltenango" was unpublished when I consulted it in the office of Dr. Francis Gall. It consisted of two parts: a libro of 199 hojas, covering the period from January 3, 1806, to July 13, 1812; and one called "Libros de Actas Municipales," July 1813, to May 26, 1819, consisting of 106 folios. There were two private collections in Guatemala City that I was allowed to see: one belonging to Mrs. Esperanza Zeceña, concerning the career of Miguel Larreynaga, her grandfather. It consisted of 7 bound volumes and one loose volume, apparently intended to serve as an encyclopedia of sorts. It displays impressive erudition and painstaking work. There was also one unbound volume of letters, very heavy on the period of the 1830s. I have cited a few of the documents for my period. The second collection belonged to the late Arturo Taracena, who had sold the bulk of his works to the University of Texas. See Nettie Lee Benson, *Arturo Taracena Flores Library* (No. 4 the University of Texas Institute of Latin American Studies Offprint Series, 1964). It was the remainder of that collection that my dear friend allowed me to consult. His worthwhile contributions to Central American bibliography will be sorely missed.

4. Nicaragua and El Salvador have very little manuscript materials for the years covered by this volume because of a series of earthquakes, fires, and other catastrophes. In San Salvador, the Archivo General de la Nación has one legajo of documents that covers mainly the year 1823. Nevertheless, there is a famous collection of printed documents by Miguel Angel García, *Diccionario histórico enciclopédico de la República de San Salvador*, which consists of many different numbered volumes. Special mention should be made of the volume on *Procesos de Infidencia* . . . *1811 hasta 1818* (San Salvador, 1940). Nicaraguan history has been reconstructed mainly from repositories in Costa Rica, Guatemala, and Spain.

5. Archivos Nacionales de Costa Rica, San José (ANCR). Next to Guatemala, Costa Rica possesses the largest volume of documentation, perhaps because of its geographical location vis-à-vis the other countries of Central America and its more stable development during the course of the nineteenth century. Moreover, Costa Ricans have conscientiously managed to get copies of documentation from Spain. There are various *asignaturas* that contain pertinent materials: C.C. (Complementario Colonial). Also see *Indice, Sección Colonial* of the ANCR: S.H. (Sección Histórica), P.I. (Provincial Independiente), P.C. (Provincial Costaricense), S/H.M. (Sección Histórica Municipal, 1823, Alajuela for example), and A.M. (Anexión a México).

In addition, see published documentation in the ANCR's periodical, *Revista de los Archivos Nacionales*: for example, "Actas del cabildo de Cartago, 1800–1810" (San José, January–June 1959, pp. 7–174, Año XXIII). Other government publications have likewise provided printed documents: República de Costa Rica (Publicaciones de la Secretaría de Educación Pública), *Documentos Históricos Posteriores a la Independencia* (1 volume, San José, Costa Rica, 1923), for the years 1821–1836; and *Documentos para la historia de Costa Rica, 1545–1784* (San José, Costa Rica, 1902–1905), consisting of 17 pamphlets published under the direction of Cleto González Vízquez and Faustino Vízquez. And then, of course, the useful collections of León Fernández, ed., *Colección de documentos para la historia de Costa Rica* (10 volumes, San José, Costa Rica, 1881–1907) and Francisco María Iglesias, *Documentos relativos a la independencia* (3 vols., San José, Costa Rica, 1899–1902).

6. Archivo Nacional de Honduras, Tegucigalpa (ANHT). Honduras' record on archives for this period has been similar to the Salvadoran and Nicaraguan story: fires and disorders that destroyed much of the documentation. I was therefore pleasantly surprised to find as much as I did on the pre-Independence rivalry between Tegucigalpa and Comayagua. Although the archives first started in Comayagua in 1820, they were reestablished in Tegucigalpa by late 1880. There were at least 19 legajos that were pertinent to my study, numbered 1 through 19, which proceeded chronologically to 1829.

7. Archivo Municipal, Tegucigalpa, had one volume of Actas Municipales (1801–1832). But this is misleading: the coverage is good for 1801–1809 and then there is a jump to the 1826–1832 period.

8. Archivo General de la Nación, Mexico City. My work in Mexico was limited mainly because I had seen most of the pertinent documentation in the AGCA of Guatemala City. I was anxious to find out, however, what José del Valle's contribution was to the type of senate adopted by the Mexicans; this was before I had arrived at the conclusion that the Central American Upper House was an inevitable result of the Cádiz Experiment and experience in the area. I perused the newspaper *Gaceta de México*, also called *Gaceta del Govierno Imperial de Mexico* for 1823, as well as *El Sol* at the Hemeroteca Nacional.

Moreover, there are several authorities whose volumes are indispensable for telling the Cádiz story: Rafael Heliodoro Valle, *La anexión de Centro América a México* (6 vols., Mexico City, 1924–1949), which is excellent for the Mexican years in Central

America; Lucas Alamán, *Historia de Méjico* (5 vols., 1849–1852), which amounts to the memoirs of this distinguished statesman who represented Mexico effectively in the second constitutional period at Madrid; Lorenzo de Zavala, *Ensayo histórico de las revoluciones desde 1808 hasta 1830* (2 vols., Paris, 1831); and the *Colección de órdenes de la soberana Junta Provisional Gubernativa, y soberanos congresos generales de la nación mexicana* (2 vols., Mexico City, 1829).

III. SELECTIVE BIBLIOGRAPHY: BOOKS, ARTICLES, PAMPHLETS, BROADSIDES UTILIZED IN THIS STUDY THAT HAVE NOT BEEN CITED ABOVE.

Altamira, Rafael. *Autonomía y descentralizatión legislativa en el régimen colonial español, siglo XVI a XVIII.* Coimbra, 1945.

Alvarez, José María. *Instituciones de derecho real de Castilla y de Indias.* Guatemala, 1818.

Alvarez de Toledo y Dubois, José. *Manifiesto o satisfacción pundonorosa a todos los buenos españoles europeos, y a todos los pueblos de la América, por un diputado de las Cortes reunidas en Cádiz.* Philadelphia, 1811.

————. *Objecciones satisfactorias del mundo imparcial al folleto dado a luz por el marte-filósolfo de Delaware Don José Alvarez de Toledo.* Charleston, 1812.

"Apuntes Instructivos pa. el Diputado de Cortes do Guatemala," *Revista de la Facultad de Ciencias Jurídicas y Sociales de Guatemala*, Tomo II, No. 1, March-April 1939, 136–159.

Arce, Manuel José. *Memorias del General Manuel José Arce, primer presidente de Centro Américo.* San Salvador, 1947.

Asamblea Nacional Constituyente. "Indice de la correspondencia . . . 1823, 1824, 1825, entre los Estados Federales de Centro América," Archivos Nacionales de Costa Rica (hereafter ANCR), Sección Federal, 1823–1825. San José, Costa Rica.

Aznar López, José. *El Doctor Don José de Flores: una vida al servicio de la ciencia.* Guatemala City, 1960.

Bancroft, Hubert Howe. *History of Central America.* New York, 1883–1887. 3 vols.

"Bases de la constitución Federal." Guatemala City, December 17, 1823. Archivo General de Centro América (hereafter AGCA), ih.–920.

Batres Jáuregui, Antonio. *La América Central ante la historia.* Guatemala City, 1915–1949. 3 vols.

Belda, José y Rafael María de Labra. *Las Cortes de Cádiz en el Oratorio de San Felipe.* Madrid, 1912.

Benson, Nettie Lee and Charles R. Berry, *The Central American Delegation to the First Constituent Congress of Mexico, 1822–1823* (Institute of Latin American Studies Pamphlet 95, Univ. of Texas, Austin, 1970).

Beristáin de Souza, José Mariano. *Biblioteca hispano americana septentrional; o, catálogo y noticias de los literatos, que o nacidos, o educados, o florecientes en la América septentrional española, han dado a luz algún escrito, o lo han dexado preparado para la prensa.* Mexico, 1816. 3 vols.

Blanco y Crespo, José. *The Life of the Reverend Joseph Blanco-White.* London, 1845.

Borrego, Andrés. *El libro de las elecciones; reseña histórica de las verificadas durante los tres períodos del régimen constitucional (1810 a 1814)–(1834 a 1873).* Madrid, 1874.

Bumgartner, Louis E. *José del Valle of Central America.* Durham, North Corolina, 1963.

Bustamante, Carlos María. *Historia del Emperador D. Agustín de Iturbide hasta su muerte, y sus consequencias; y establecimiento de la república popular federal.* Mexico, 1846.

Bustamante, José de. "Memorial de residencia," AGCA, A.30–4, exp. 11581, leg. 1739. Also, Royal cédula, June 13, 1817, AGCA, Al.2, exp. 1130, leg. 44, for his dismissal from office.

Cabat, Geoffry A. "The Consolidation of 1803 in Guatemala." *The Americas,* XXVIII, July 1971, 20–38.

California, University of, Library. *Spain and Spanish America in the libraries of the University of California; a catalogue of books.* New York, 1969. 2 vols. (reprint of 1928–1930 ed.)

Canga Argüelles, José. *Diccionarie de hacienda.* London, 1826–1827. 5 vols.

Cañedo, Juan de Dios. *Manifiesto de la nación española, sobre la representación de las provincias de ultramar en las próximas Cortes.* Madrid, 1820. Reimpreso en México, 1820.

————. *Manifiesto de los Americanos que residen en Madrid á las Naciones de la Europa, y principalmente á la Espãna, demostrando las razones legales que tienen para no concurrir el día 28 de mayo a elegir diputados que representen los pueblos ultramarinos donde nacieron.* Madrid, 1820. Reimpreso en Mexico, 1820.

Capmany y de Montpalou, Antonio de. *Práctica y estilo de celebrar cortes en el reino de Aragón, principiado de Cataluña y reino de Valencia. Y una noticia de las de Castilla y Navarra. Recopilado todo y ordenado por Don Antonio de Capmani. Va añadido el reglamento para el Consejo representativo de Ginebra, y los reglamentos que se observan en la Cámara de los comunes de Inglaterra.* Madrid, 1821.

Carnicero, Josef Clemente. *Historia razonada de los principales sucesos de la gloriosa revolución española.* Madrid, 1814–1815. 4 vols.

————. *El liberalismo convencido por sus mismos escritos, o Examen crítico de la constitución de la monarquía española publicada en Cádiz, y de la obra de Don F. co Marina "Teoría de las Cortes" y de otras que sostienen las mismas ideas acerca de la soberanía de la nación.* Madrid, 1830. 2 tomos en 1.

Castro y Rossi, Adolfo de. *Cádiz en la guerra de la independencia.* 2 ed. Cádiz, 1864.

Catecismo político para instrucción del pueblo. Guatemala City, 1811.

Chevalier, Francqis. *Land and Society in Colonial Mexico: The Great Hacienda.* Berkeley, 1963.

Chinchilla Aguilar, Ernesto. *El Ayuntamiento Colonial de la ciudad de Guatemala.* Guatemala City, 1961.

―――. *La inquisición en Guatemala.* Guatemala City, 1953.

Cid Fernández, Enrique del. *Don Gabino de Gaínza y otros estudios.* Guatemala City, 1959.

Contreras, J. Daniel. *Una rebelión indígena en el partido de Totonicapán en 1820. El Indio y la independencia.* Guatemala City, 1951.

Corwin, Arthur. *Spain and the Abolition of Slavery in Cuba, 1817–1886.* Austin, Texas, 1967.

Cuba, Gobernador Someruelos. *Fidelísimos habitantes de la Isla de Cuba.* Habana, 1810.

Dávila, Fernando Antonio. *Exposición del P.D. Fernando Antonio Dávila, diputado por la provincia de Chiapa en apoyo de la que presentó a las Cortes la Diputación Americana en la sesión del día 25 de junio del corriente año.* Madrid, 1821.

Delgado, Jaime. *España y México en el siglo XIX.* Madrid, 1950. 3 vols.

―――. *La independencia de América en la prensa española.* Madrid, 1949.

Desdevises de Dézert, A. *L'Espagne de L'Ancien Regime: Les Institutions.* Paris, 1899.

Diccionario bibliográfico da guerra peninsular. Coimbra, 1924. 4 vols.

Diccionario bibliográfico de la Guerra de la Independencia española (1808–1814). Madrid, 1944. 3 vols.

Durón, Rómulo, ed. *Obras de Don José Cecilio del Valle.* Tegucigalpa, 1906.

Dusenberry, William H. *The Mexican Mesta.* Urbana, Illinois, 1963.

Elorza, Antonio. *La ideología liberal en la ilustración española.* Madrid, 1970.

Estrada Molina, Ligia. *La Costa Rica de don Tomás de Acosta.* San José, Costa Rica, 1965.

"Extracto de la Conspiración de Belén, el año de 1813". *Diario de Centro América,* Guatemala City, pp. 23–45. Written by Pedro Molina, it is believed.

Farriss, Nancy M. *Crown and Clergy in Colonial Mexico, 1759–1821.* London, 1968.

Fernández Almagro, Melchor. *La emancipación de América y su reflejo en la conciencia española.* 2ª ed. Madrid, 1957.

―――. *Orígenes del Régimen Constitucional en España.* Barcelona, 1928.

Filísola, Vicente. *La cooperación de México en la independencia de Centro América (Documentos inéditos o muy raros para la historia de México, XXXVI).* Mexico, 1911.

Flemion, Philip F. "States' Rights and Partisan Politics: Manuel José Arce and the Struggle for Central American Union." *Hispanic American Historical Review,* 53, November 1973.

Floyd, Troy. *The Anglo-Spanish Struggle for Mosquitia*. Albuquerque, 1967.

————."Bourbon Palliatives and the Central American Mining Industry, 1765–1800." *The Americas*, 17:2, October 1961, pp. 103–125.

————. "The Guatemalan Merchants, the Government, and the Provincianos, 1750–1800." *Hispanic American Historical Review*, 41, 1961.

Fontana Lázaro, Joseph. *La quiebra de la monarquía absoluta, 1814–1820 (La crisis del antiguo régimen en España)*. Barcelona, 1971.

Franco, José Luciano. *Política continental americana de España en Cuba, 1812–1830*. Habana, 1947.

Gándara Durán, Carlos. *Pedro Molina*. Guatemala City, 1936.

García Laguardia, Jorge Mario. "Estado de la opinión sobre convocatoria a Cortes Constituyentes en 1810: Actitud del Ayuntamiento de Guatemala." *Estudios,* Universidad de San Carlos, No. 3, 1969.

García Peláez, Francisco de Paula. *Memorias para la historia del Antiguo Reino de Guatemala*. Guatemala City, 1943.

Gautier, D. A. *Cortes generales y extraordinarias de Cádiz*. Cádiz, 1896.

Gerbi, Antonello. *The Dispute of the New World: The History of a Polemic, 1750–1900*. Pittsburgh, 1973.

Gil, Gregorio Vicente. *España vindicada en sus clases*. Cádiz, 1811.

Gil Munilla, Octavio. "Teoría de la Emancipación." *Estudios Americanos, Revista de la Escuela de Estudios Hispano Americanos*. Sevilla. Vol. II, Núm. 7 (Sept. 1970), pp. 329–351.

Giménez Fernández, Manuel. *Las doctrinas populistas en la independencia de Hispano-América*. Sevilla, 1947.

González Mollinedo y Saravia, Antonio. *En el confuso aspecto que presentan los negocios públicos de la Europa*. Antigua, Guatemala, 1810.

González y Montoya, José. *Rasgos sueltos para la Constitución de América, anunciado por el intendente de exército Don Josef González y Montoya*. Cádiz, 1811.

Great Britain. Treaties. *A convention between H.B.M. and H. Catholic Majesty, Ferdinand the Seventh*. London, 1814.

Griffith, William J. "The Historiography of Central America Since 1830." *Hispanic American Historical Review*, Vol. 40, November 1960.

Guillén, Flavio. *Un fraile prócer y una fábula poema (estudio acerca de Fray Matías de Córdoba)*. Guatemala City, 1932.

Guridi y Alcocer, José Miguel. *Representación de la diputación americana a las Cortes de España*. London, 1812.

Guzmán, Martín Luis, ed. *México en las Cortes de Cádiz*. Mexico, 1949.

Hale, Charles A. *Mexican Liberalism in the Age of Mora*. New Haven, 1968.

Hargreaves-Mawdsley, W. N., ed. *Spain under the Bourbons, 1700–1833: A Collection of Documents*. Columbia, South Carolina, 1973.

Helman, Edith. "Some Consequences of the Publication of the *Informe de ley agraria* by Jovellanos." *Estudios hispánicos: Homenaje a Archer M. Huntington*. Wellesley, Mass., 1952. Pages 253–273.

Herr, Richard. *The Eighteenth-Century Revolution in Spain*. Princeton, 1958.

Holleran, Mary P. *Church and State in Guatemala.* New York, 1949.

Incitativa de un mejicano á todos los españoles, en defensa de la que se publicó en la península reclamando el número de diputados de ultramar para las presentes Córtes fecha en Valladolid en 30 de marzo de este año: e impugnación de los errores y proposiciones sediciosas del artículo inserto en el Suplemento al Noticioso general de 27 de septiembre. Mexico, 1820.

Juarros, Domingo. *Compendio de la historia de la Ciudad de Guatemala.* Guatemala City, 1937. 2 vols.

Kamen, Henry. *The War of Succession in Spain, 1700–15.* Bloomington, Indiana, 1969.

Kenyon, Gordon. "Gabino Gaínza and Central America's Independence from Spain." *The Americas,* XIII, 1957.

———. "Mexican Influence in Central America, 1821–1823." *Hispanic American Historical Review,* XLI, 1961.

Lamadrid, Lázaro. *Una figura centroamericana, Dr. Fr. José Liendo y Goicoechea, O.F.M.* San Salvador, 1948.

Lanning, John Tate. *The Eighteenth-Century Enlightenment in the University of San Carlos de Guatemala.* Ithaca, New York, 1956.

———. ed. *Reales cédulas de la Real y Pontífica Universidad de San Carlos de Guatemala.* Guatemala City, 1954.

———. *The University in the Kingdom of Guatemala.* Ithaca, New York, 1955.

Lavrín, Asunción. "The Execution of the Law of *Consolidación* in New Spain: Economic Aims and Results." *Hispanic American Historical Review,* 53, February 1973, pp. 27–49.

Levaggi, Abelardo. "Origen del poder legislativo en Hispanoamérica (1810–1814)." *Revista del Instituto de Historia del Derecho Ricardo Levene,* Buenos Aires, 19 (1968), pp. 30–63.

Levene, Ricardo. *La política económica de España en América y la Revolución de 1810.* Buenos Aires, 1914.

Llorente, Juan Antonio. *Memorias para la historia de la revolución española, con documentos justificativos.* Paris, 1814–1816. 3 vols.

López Cancelada, Juan. *Ruina de la Nueva España si se declara el comercio libre con los estrangeros.* Cádiz, 1811.

Lynch, John. *The Spanish-American Revolutions, 1808–1826.* New York, 1973.

Macleod, Murdo J. *Spanish Central America: A Socioeconomic History, 1520–1720.* Berkeley, 1973.

Manning, William R., ed. *Diplomatic Correspondence Concerning the Independence of the Latin-American Nations.* New York, 1925. 3 vols.

Marure, Alejandro. *Bosquejo histórica de las revoluciones de Centro América desde 1811 hasta 1834.* Guatemala City, 1877. 2 vols.

———. *Efemérides de los hechos notables acaecidos en la república desde el año de 1821 hasta el de 1842.* Guatemala City, 1844.

Maravall, José Antonio. "El pensamiento político en España a comienzos del siglo XIX: Martínez Marina." *Revista de Estudios Políticos*, Madrid, No. 81, Mayo-Junio 1955, pp. 29–82.

Martín de Balmaseda, Fermín. *Decretos del Rey Don Fernando VII.* Madrid, 1816–1819. 6 vols.

Martínez Durán, Carlos. *Las ciencias médicas en Guatemala.* Guatemala City, 1941.

―――. "Sociedad Económica de Amigos de Guatemala." *Universidad de San Carlos*, XXVI, 1952.

Martínez Marina, Francisco. *Ensayo histórico-crítico sobre la legislación y principales cuerpos legales de los reinos de León y Castilla, especialmente sobre el código de D. Alfonso el Sabio, conocido con el nombre de las Siete Partidas.* Madrid, 1808.

―――. *Teoría de las Cortes ó grandes juntas nacionales de los reinos de León y Castilla; monumentos de su constitución política y de la soberanía del pueblo. Con algunas observaciones sobre la lei fundamental de la monarquía española.* Madrid, 1813. 3 vols.

Mateos, Juan A., ed. *Historia parlamentaria de los congresos mexicanos de 1821 a 1857.* Mexico, 1877–1912. 25 vols.

Mayes, Guillermo. *Honduras en la independencia de Centro-América y anexión a México.* Guatemala, 1955.

Medina, José Toribio. *La imprenta en Guatemala (1660–1821).* Santiago, Chile, 1910.

Mexico, Laws and Statutes. *Colección de los decretos y órdenes que han espedido las Cortes generales y extraordinarias desde su instalación de 24 de Septiembre de 1810 hasta igual fecha de 1811 y desde 24 de mayo de 1812 hasta 24 febrero de 1813.* Mexico, 1852.

Michelena, Ignacio de. *Reflexiones sobre la constitución de la monarquía española.* Cádiz, 1809.

Mier Noriega y Guerra, Servando Teresa de. *Historia de la revolución de la Nueva España.* London, 1813. 2 vols.

Molina, Pedro. *Documentos Relacionados con la Historia de Centro América.* Guatemala, 1896, in Folletín "La República."

―――. "Memorias acerca de la Revolución de Centro América, desde el año de 1820 hasta el de 1840." *Centro-Americano*, XIII, 1921.

Montúfar, Lorenzo. *Reseña histórica de Centro América.* Guatemala City, 1878–1888. 7 vols.

Montúfar y Coronado, Manuel. *Memorias para la historia de la revolución de Centro América.* Guatemala City, 1934.

―――. *Recuerdos y Anécdotas.* San Luis Potosí, Mexico, 1836.

Moreno, Laudelino. "Guatemala y la invasión napoleónica de Espāna." *Anales de la Sociedad de Geografía e Historia de Guatemala*, VII, 1930.

Muller, Gene Allan. *The Making of a Nineteenth Century Revolutionary: Dr. Tomás Ruiz of Central America* (Mimeograph, El Paso, Texas, 1974).

Muro Martínez, José. *Decretos y órdenes de Cortes en las dos épocas de 1810 a 1814, y 1820 a 1823.* Valladolid, 1875.

Nieto Vélez, Armando. *Contribución a la historia del fidelismo en el Perú, 1808–1810.* Lima, 1960.

Obregón Loria, Rafael. *De Nuestra historia patria: los primeros días de independencia.* San José, Costa Rica, 1971.

Ovilo y Otero, Manuel. *Manual de biografía y de bibliografía de los escritores españoles del siglo XIX.* Paris, 1859. 2 vols.

Parker, Franklin Dallas. *José Cecilio del Valle and the Establishment of the Central American Confederation.* Tegucigalpa, 1954.

————. "José Cecilio del Valle: Scholar and Patriot." *Hispanic American Historical Review*, XXXII, 1952.

Paso, Leonardo. *De la colonia a la independencia nacional.* Buenos Aires, 1963.

Peralta, Hernán. *El Pacto de Concordia.* San José, Costa Rica, 1952.

Pérez, Dionisio. *Las Cortes de Cádiz.* Madrid, 1903.

Pineda de Mont, Manuel. *Recopilación de las leyes de Guatemala . . .* Guatemala, 1869, vol. 1.

Pradt, Dominique. *Examen del plan presentado a las Cortes, para el reconocimiento de la independencia de la América española.* Bordeaux, 1822.

Publicación de la nueva Constitución de la Monarquía Española, celebrada en Santo Domingo Retaluleuk, Provincia de Suchitepéquez. Guatemala, 1812.

Ramos Pérez, Demetrio. *Historia de las cortes tradicionales de España.* Madrid, 1944.

Reflexiones sobre el comercio de España con sus colonias en América, en tiempo de guerra. Por un español, en Philadelphia. Philadelphia, 1799.

Reglamento para la propagación y estabilidad de la vacuna en el Reyno de Guatemala. Nueva Guatemala, 1805 (AGCA, Al.38, exp. 11716, leg. 1745).

Reglamento provisorio para la elección de representantes en la legislatura del Estado de Nicaragua. Guatemala City, 1824.

Rezabal y Ugarte, José de. *Biblioteca de los escritores que han sido individuos de los seis colegios mayores.* Madrid, 1805.

Robertson, William Spence. *Iturbide of Mexico.* Durham, North Carolina, 1952.

Rodríguez, Mario. *A Palmerstonian Diplomat in Central America: Frederick Chatfield, Esq.* Tucson, Arizona, 1964.

————. *La Conspiración de Belén en Nueva Perspectiva.* Guatemala City, 1965.

Rodríguez Beteta, Virgilio. *Evolución de las ideas.* Paris, 1929.

Rosa, Ramón. *José Cecilio del Valle.* Guatemala City, 1929–1930. 2 vols.

Rosell, Avenir. *La taquigrafía en las Cortes de Cádiz, 1810–1813.* Montevideo, 1960.

Rubio, Julián María. *La Infanta Carlota Joaquina y la política de España en América (1808–1812).* Madrid, 1920.

Rubio Sánchez, Manuel. "El real consulado de comercio." *Antropología e Historia de Guatemala*, 19:2, July-December 1967.

Rydjord, John. "British Mediation between Spain and her Colonies, 1811–1813." *Hispanic American Historical Review*, XXI (February 1941), pp. 29–50.

Salamanca Aguilera, Rafael, ed. *El memorial de agravios, pregón de la independencia.* Tunja, Colombia, 1960.

Salazar, Ramón A. *Desenvolvimiento intelectual de Guatemala.* Guatemala City, 1897.

————. *Historia de veintún años; la independencia de Guatemala.* Guatemala City, 1928.

————. *Mariano Aycinena* (Biblioteca de Cultura Popular, XXII). Guatemala City, 1948.

Salillas, Rafael. *En las Cortes de Cádiz: Revelaciones acerca del estado político y social.* Madrid, 1910.

Salmón, Maestro. *Resumen histórico de la revolución de España.* Cádiz, 1808–1814. 5 vols.

Samayoa Guevara, Héctor Humberto. *Implantación del régimen de intendencias en el Reino de Guatemala.* Guatemala City, 1960.

Sánchez Agesta, Luis. *Historia del constitucionalismo español.* Madrid, 1955.

Sempere y Guarinos, Juan. *Histoire des Cortes d'Espagne.* Bordeaux, 1815.

————. *Los principios de la constitución española y los de la justicia universal aplicados a la legislación de señorío, o sea concordia entre los intereses y derechos del Estado y los de los antiguos vasallos y señores. Precede un discurso histórico legal sobre la feudalidad y los señoríos en España. Dedicado a las Cortes por un jurisconsulto español.* Madrid, 1821.

Shafer, Robert Jones. *The Economic Societies in the Spanish World (1763–1821).* Syracuse, New York, 1958.

Solano y Pérez Lila, Francisco de. *Estudio histórico y socioeconómico de Guatemala durante el siglo XVIII.* Madrid, 1970.

Smith, Robert S. "Indigo Production and Trade in Colonial Guatemala." *Hispanic American Historical Review*, XXXIX, 1959.

————. "Origins of the Consulado of Guatemala." *Hispanic American Historical Review*, XXVI, 1946.

Solórzano, Valentín F. *Evolución económica de Guatemala.* Guatemala, 1963.

Solución á la cuestión de derecho sobre la emancipación de la América, por el ciudadano Joaquín Infante, natural de la Isla de Cuba. Cádiz, 1820.

Sorsby, William S. "Spanish Colonization of the Mosquito Coast: 1787–1800." *Revista Historia de América*, Nos. 73–74, January-December 1972.

Spain. Archivo Histórico Nacional, Madrid. *Documentos de Indias, siglos XV–XIX.* Madrid, 1954.

Spain. *Constitución Política de la Monarquía Española.* Cádiz, 1812.

Spain. Cortes, 1810–1813. *Documentos de que hasta ahora se compone el expediente que principiaron las Cortes extraordinarias sobre el tráfico y esclavitud de los negros.* Madrid, 1814.

Spain. Cortes. *Representación y manifiesto que algunos diputados a las Cortes ordinarias firmaron en los mayores apuros de su opresión en Madrid, para que la magestad del Señor D. Fernando el VII, a la entrada en España de vuelta de su cautividad, se penetrase del estado de la nación, del deseo de sus provincias, y del remedio que creían oportuno; todo fué presentado á S.M. en Valencia por uno de dichos diputados, y se imprime en cumplimento de real orden.* Madrid, 1814.

Spain. Cortes. Comisión de Ultramar. *Informe sobre la memoria del señor secretario de la gobernación de Ultramar.* Madrid, 1822.

Spain. Treaties. *Tratado entre S.M. el rey de España y de las Indias, y S.M. el rey del Reino Unido de la Gran Bretaña e Irlanda . . . abolición del tráfico de negros.* Madrid, 1817.

Stanger, Francis Merriman. "The Struggle for Nationality in Central America." Unpublished Ph.D. dissertation, University of California, Berkeley, 1930.

Suasnavar, José. *Informe que sobre la erección de un Estado compuesto con los pueblos de Los Altos dió al govierno S. de la nación en 27 de Abril de de 1824.* Quezaltenango, 1836.

Szasdi, Adam. *Nicolás Raoul y la República Federal de Centro-América.* Madrid, 1958.

Tatham, William. *Communication concerning the agriculture and commerce of America: containing observations on the commerce of Spain with her American colonies in time of war. Written by a Spanish gentleman in Philadelphia in this present year, 1800. With sundry other papers concerning the Spanish interest.* London, 1800.

Thompson, George A. *Narrative of an Official Visit to Guatemala from Mexico.* London, 1829.

Tobar Cruz, Pedro. *Valle, el hombre, el político, el sabio.* Guatemala City, 1961.

Toreno, Conde de. "Information on the principal events which took place in the government of Spain from the commencement of the insurrection in 1808 . . ." *Pamphleteer,* London, XVII, No. 33 (1810). Translated by William Walton.

Torres, Camilo. *El memorial de agravios, pregón de la independencia.* Tunja, Colombia, 1960.

Torres Lanzas, Pedro, ed. *Independencia de América, fuentes para su estudio. Catálogo de documentos conservados en el Archivo General de Indias de Sevilla.* Madrid, 1912. 6 vols.

Universidad de San Carlos de Guatemala. *Economía guatemalteca en los siglos XVIII y XIX.* 3rd ed., Guatemala City, 1970.

Urquijo, José María Mariluz. *Los proyectos españoles para reconquistar el Río de la Plata, 1820–1833.* Buenos Aires, 1958.

Used, Jorge A. Lines. *Bibliografía antropológica aborigen de Costa Rica.* San José, Costa Rica, 1943.

Valenzuela, Gilberto. *La imprenta en Guatemala.* Guatemala City, 1933.

Valladares Rodríguez, Juan, ed. *El pensamiento económico de José Cecilio del Valle.* Tegucigalpa, 1958.

Valle, José del, and Jorge del Valle Matheu, eds. *Obras de José Cecilio del Valle.* Guatemala City, 1929–1930. 2 vols.

Vela, David. *Barrundia ante el espejo de su tiempo.* Guatemala City, 1956. 2 vols.

Villacorta, J. Antonio. *Historia de la Capitanía General de Guatemala.* Guatemala City, 1942.

Villanueva, Carlos A. *Fernando VII y los nuevos estados.* Paris, 1912.

Villa-Urrutia, Wenceslao R. de. *Relaciones entre España é Inglaterra durante la guerra de la independencia, apuntes para la historia diplomática de España de 1808 á 1814.* Madrid, 1911–1914. 3 vols.

Walton, William. *An Exposé on the Dissentions of Spanish America.* London, 1814.

Webster, C. K., ed. *Britain and the Independence of Latin America, 1812–1830. Select Documents from the Foreign Office.* London, 1938. 2 vols.

West, R. C. "The Mining Economy of Honduras during the Colonial Period." Actas del XXXIII Congreso Internacional de Americanistas, San José, Costa Rica, I (1959), 767–77.

West, Robert C., and John P. Augelli. *Middle America, Its Lands and Peoples.* Englewood Cliffs, New Jersey, 1966.

Woodward, Ralph Lee. *Class Privilege and Economic Development: The Consulado de Comercio of Guatemala, 1793–1871.* Chapel Hill, North Carolina, 1966.

Woodward, Jr., Ralph Lee. "Economic and Social Origins of the Guatemalan Political Parties." *Hispanic American Historical Review,* 45:4, November 1965, 544–566.

Wortman, Miles. "La Féderation d'Amérique Centrale, 1823–1839." Thesis, L'Ecole Pratique Des Hautes Etudes, Paris, 1973.

———. "Bourbon Reforms in Central America: 1750–1786." *The Americas,* Vol. 32:2, October 1975, 222–238.

———. "Government revenue and economic trends in Central America: 1787–1819." *Hispanic American Historical Review,* Vol. 55:2, May 1975. 251–286.

Zamocois, Niceto de. *Historia de Méjico desde sus tiempos más remotos hasta nuestros días.* México, 1879–1888. 18 vols.

Zamora y Coronado, José María, comp. *Biblioteca de legislación ultramarina.* Madrid, 1844–1846. 6 vols.

Index

Acosta, Tomás de, 43, 71
Agar, Pedro, 79, 98
Agriculture, 14, 25–26, 232
  Bourbon reforms, 3–4
  Jovellanos's proposals, 4–8
Aguanqueteric (Honduras), 214
Aguardiente (brandy), 103, 155
Agüero, Vicente, 117
Agustín I, 181, 183–86. *See also* Iturbide,
  Agustín
Alajuela (Costa Rica), 70
Alamán, Lucas, 193
Alcabala (sales tax), 176, 177, 219
Alcohol and drunkenness, 103, 154–55
Alfonso the Wise, 45, 91
Alta Corte de Justicia, 198
Alvarado, Pablo, 158
Amatitlán (Guatemala), 108
America, Spanish
  economic activities, 14–16
  Enlightenment in, 18–27
  geography of, 13
  Junta Central and, 35
  map of, 10–11
American delegation at Cádiz
  accomplishments of, 68–74
  and debates on Constitution, 59–68
  as lobbyists for native areas, 70–74
  loyalty to Cádiz Constitution, 100
  propositions presented by, 54–55
  and racial question, 54
American Philosophical Society, 20
"American Question" at Cádiz, 53–74
Amigo de la Patría, El, 133–34, 137,
  144–45, 151
A.N.C. *See* Asamblea Nacional
  Constituyente de las Provincias Unidas
  del Centro de América

Anticlericalism, 143, 225–26
Antigua (Guatemala), 214
Aranjuez (Spain), 33
Arce, Manuel José de, 196, 227–28
Arechavala, Joaquín, 42, 117
Arévalo, Manuel, 114
Argüelles, Agustín, 56, 96, 100, 170,
  198, 216
  in debates on Constitution, 59, 244
    on *Castas* question, 61
    on federalism, 64–65, 67–68, 74
    on Indian rights, 86
    on political power, 83, 94
    and religious question, 76
    and slavery, 88
Argüelles, José Mariano, 127–28
Argüello, Toribio, 146
Arrivillaga, Francisco, 132
Asamblea Nacional Constituyente de las
  Provincias Unidas del Centro de América
  (A.N.C.), 187–219
  accomplishments of, 212–13
  on *Castas* and slavery issue, 210–11
  Constitutional Committee, 215–16
  and Constitution of 1824, 199–200
  declares absolute independence, 188
  and economic development, 201–5
  and educational development, 208–9
  and electoral procedures, 198
  evaluation of, 217–18
  executive branch formed, 195, 198
  financial problems of, 219
  Indian policy of, 209–10
  and judicial system, 198
  on religious reforms, 222–23
  Salvadoran challenge to, 213–15
  taxation policy of, 202–3
  and Tegucigalpa-Comayagua feud, 193

Asiento, 12. *See also* Slave trade and slavery
Asturias, Juan Bautista, 109
Asturias, Prince of, 80
Avila, José Ignacio, 46, 71
Aycinena, José de, 20, 42, 102, 105, 113, 127, 146
  on Bustamante's abuses, 122, 123, 128, 129
  on Consejo de Estado, 70, 79, 105
  on Consejo de Indias, 125
  as *intendente* in San Salvador, 104
Aycinena, Mariano, 138, 143, 146, 148 179, 196, 207
  and *ayuntamiento* of Guatemala City, 131
  and Cádiz reforms, 133, 144
  as governor of Guatemala, 220, 228
  and Iturbide, 161, 167, 168–69
Aycinena, Miguel, 226
Aycinena, Vicente (Marquis de), 42, 43, 45, 47, 123, 127, 149, 156
Ayuntamientos (town councils), 5, 92–93, 231–32
  of Guatemala City, 41–42, 102, 104, 127
    in conflict with Bustamante, 104–5, 112–17, 120–23
    election of, 108–9
    and implementation of Cádiz Constitition, 110–12
    and tariff of 1822, 171–72
Azmitia, José, 132

"Bacos," 134, 150–51
Bailén (Spain), 33
Bank of Savings and Loan (Spain), 73
Barclay and Herring House, 207, 221, 229
Barrundia, José Francisco, 132, 163, 173, 180, 228
  in A.N.C., 188–90, 215–17
  career and background, ix-x, 109–10
  and Belén conspiracy, 122, 128, 129
  and capital export tax, 153–54
  on electoral reforms by J.P.C., 150
  and independence from Spain, 146, 147, 165, 184, 196
  and Indian question, 174–75
  as journalist, 134, 208
  on military reforms, 197–98
  on new Senate, 199–201
  and unionism vs. home rule question, 158–61, 222
Barrundia, Juan, 132, 226, 227–28

Barrutia, Luis, 45
Bases of the Constitution, 216
  adopted by A.N.C., 199–201
  model for state constituent assemblies, 214
Batres, Juan José, 132
Batres, Pedro, 109
Bayonne, Constitution of (1808), 35
Beaufort, J. L., 209
Belén Conspiracy, 122, 128, 132
Belize (British Honduras), 17, 79, 172
Bell, Andrew, 130
Beltranena, Manuel, 109
Bentham, Jeremy, 142, 198, 216
Betancourt, Pedro de, 48
Beteta, Ignacio, 114
Black legend, 47, 56
Blake, Joaquín, 79
Blanco y Crespo (Blanco-White), José María, 31, 36, 90, 253
  on Cádiz Constitution, 95–98
Bolívar, Simón, 152
Bonaparte, Joseph, 32
Bonaparte, Napoleon, 31–33
Borbón, Cardinal de, 98
Borbón, Luis de, 29, 98, 121
Bourbon dynasty
  and modernization of Spain, 3–8
  overseas policies of, 8–18
Buenos Aires Charter, 155
Bustamante, Carlos, 189
Bustamante y Guerra, José de, 66, 231, 234–35
  attitude toward Cádiz Experiment, 69, 70
  executive role in Guatemala, 102–23
  presentation of Cádiz Constitution by, 101-2
  and reactionary orders from Ferdinand VII, 127, 128–29
  replacement ordered, 128–30

Cabeza de Vaca, 139, 141, 200
Cabildo Eclesiástico, 140, 148
Cacao culture, 14
"Cacos," 134, 147–48, 150–51, 156, 157–60
Cádiz, 15, 130–31
  Constitutional convention in, 53–74
  Constitution of, 28, 75–100
    abolition of entailed estates, 77

Cádiz, Constitution of, (Continued)
Consejo de Estado powers, 78–79
on economic and trade policy, 89–92
educational system and, 81, 84
electoral system, 79–80
estate representation, 76–77
evaluation of, 95–100
implementation of, in Central
America, 106–12, 119–23
Indians, treatment of, 84–87, 94
on law and legal system, 81
monarch, powers of, 77–78
Parliament in, 77–78, 80–81
on political power and governance,
92–95
pragmatism of, 76, 94
and religious question, 76, 98
on slavery, 87–88, 95
Cádiz Experiment, evaluation of, 229–37
Caja de Consolidación, 31–32, 43
Campillo y Cosío, José, 23, 91
Campomanes, Count of, 41, 229
Canal, interoceanic, 206, 229
Cañas, José Simeón, 117, 188, 223–24
Candina, Angel María, 149
Canga-Argüelles, José, 90, 99, 100
Capmany, Antonio, 244
Caracas rebellion, 37–38
Cartago (Costa Rica), 16, 70, 108, 191,
215, 236
Casaus, Ramón, 102, 106, 108, 140,
148, 149, 172, 173, 223–26
on centralization, 179–80
in dispute with *ayuntamiento,* 115–16
on Indian question, 174
Castas, 13, 210–11, 232
debate over, at Cádiz, 54, 60–63,
67–68
voting rights for, 107, 149
Castilla, José María, 134, 148, 156,
174, 222
Castillo, Eusebio, 109, 154
Castillo, Florencio, 76, 89, 94, 98, 114,
126, 144, 171, 182
at Cádiz, 46, 59, 60–62, 67,
69–71, 76
on free trade, 90–91
Castillo, Manuel del, 109
Castillo de San Felipe, 204
Cattle industry, 205. See also *Mesta*
Ceballos, Pedro de, 39
Cemeteries, 173

Censorship, 104–5, 114. *See also* Freedom
of the press
Central America. *See* America, Spanish;
American delegation at Cádiz
Central American Republic, 195–211
establishment of federation, 212–13
Chamorro, Pedro, 117
Charles III, 1-3, 229, 230
Charles IV, 31–32
Chiapas (Mexico), 103, 180, 185, 193
governance of, 108, 142, 146, 151
home rule in, 149, 156, 160, 167–68
representation at Cádiz, 46, 71–72
revolution in, 147
Chicherías, 155
Chile, 35
Chimaltenango (Guatemala), 108,
149, 181
Chiquimula (Guatemala), 108, 146, 180,
181, 205
Choluteca (Honduras), 106
Chontales (Mexico), 181
Church. *See also* Religious question
in Larrazábal instructions, 48
sale and taxation of lands, 5, 220
Ciscar, Gabriel, 98
Ciudad Real de Chiapas, 16, 71
Ciudad Rodrigo (Spain), 105
Civil War, Central American, 227–29
Cochineal production, 205, 249
Cochrane, Lord Thomas, 168
Colbert, Jean-Baptiste, 8
College of Lawyers, 43
College of Surgery, 103
Colombia, Republic of, 191
Comayagua (Honduras), 146, 182, 185,
204, 236
governance of, 16, 40, 108, 151
home rule in, 141–42, 156–57, 160,
165, 175, 179, 180, 181
representation at Cádiz, 46, 72–73
struggle with Tegucigalpa, 192–93,
215
"Compact" theory of government, 44–45
Conchagua, 204
Conciso, El, 30
Concordia, Pacto de, 159–60
Condorcet, 199
Consejo de Castilla, 33
Consejo de Estado, 143, 171
composition of, 70, 78–79, 89, 125
and Constitution of 1824, 200

Consejo de Estado, (Continued)
 role in Cádiz system, 77–79, 231
Consejo de Indias, 9, 125, 129
Constant, Benjamin, 142, 260
Constituent Assembly
 in Guatemala City (1823), 148–49,
 185–86, 187–219
 in provinces, 214–15
Constitution of Bayonne (1808), 35
Constitution of Cádiz. *See* Cádiz
 Constitution
Constitution of Central American Republic
 (1824), 199–201, 217, 237
Consulado de Cádiz, 37
Consulado de Guatemala, 18, 20, 25–27,
 86, 112, 204–5
Córdoba, José Francisco (Cordobita), 109,
 132, 148, 150, 163, 168, 196, 216–17
 and Declaration of Independence, 147
 on home rule for Nicaragua, 158
 on religious reforms, 220
Córdoba, Mariano, 216
Córdoba, Matías de, Father, 22, 208, 210
Córdoba, Treaty of, 161, 167
Cordobita. *See* Córdoba, José Francisco
Correa, Eulogio, 117
Cortes, General and Extraordinary, 28–31,
 38, 143–45
 as Constitutional convention,
 53–74
Cortes, Mexican, 164
Cortés y Larraz, Pedro, Archibishop, 71
Costa Rica, 16, 43, 172, 181, 221
 colonization in, 205
 and Constituent Assembly, 185
 governance of, 108, 215
 home rule in, 119, 142, 159–60, 179,
 182, 190–92, 194, 223–25, 236
 representation at Cádiz, 46, 59, 70–71
Council of the Indies, 9, 125, 129
Cuba, 15, 35, 88, 182–83
Cueyagua, 157

Dávila, Father Fernando Antonio, 126,
 146, 197, 209, 216, 226
 in A.N.C., 189
 and independence of Central
 America, 184
 on Indian policy, 210
 on religious reforms, 222

"Declaration of the Rights of Citizens"
 of Guatemala City ayuntamiento, 47–48
Delgado, Father José Matías, 148, 153,
 166, 182
 in A.N.C., 188, 215, 216
 first bishop of Salvador, 214, 224
 on Guatemalan Diputación
 Provincial, 117
Desafuero, 143
Diario de las Cortes, 105
Diéguez, Domingo, 134, 139, 144
Dios Mayorga, Juan de, 182, 183
Diputación Provincial, 108, 114,
 122–23, 133
 and A.N.C., 197
 in Costa Rica, 159–60
 creation of, 65–67
 membership of, in Guatemala and
 Nicaragua, 117–19
 powers of, 93, 95
 role in Cádiz Experiment, 231, 232
 in second constitutional period, 137–42
Dulce, Gulf of, 204

Ecclesiastical Cabildo, 140, 148
Echeverría, Francisco, 204
Economic development, 111–12. *See also*
 Trade
 A.N.C. on, 201–5
 at Cádiz, 89–92
 in Central America, 175–76, 205–7
 J.P.C. attempt to restore, 152–54
 in Larrazábal's instructions, 49–50
 under Mexican rule, 171
Economic Society of Guatemala City. *See*
 Royal Economic Society of
 Guatemala City
Editor Constitucional, El, 133–34, 135,
 144–46
Education, 18–19, 232
 A.N.C. policies on, 207–9
 in Cádiz Constitution, 81, 84
 in Guatemala City, 110–11, 130
 under Mexican rule, 172
Elections
 of A.N.C., 198
 in Cádiz Constitution, 79–80, 234
 implementation of, 107–9
 to Constituent Assembly in Guatemala,
 148–49

Elections, (Continued)
  of delegates to Cortes, 114
  national, in 1820, 131, 137, 138–39
El Salvador
  governance of, 15, 16, 108, 228–29
  home rule in, 166, 213–15, 219,
    221–25, 228
  representation at Cádiz, 59, 71
England. *See* Great Britain
Enlightenment, 18–27
Entailed estates, 77, 89
Escuintla (Guatemala), 108, 203
Español, El, 98
Español, Juan Antonio, 132
Esparragosa, Narciso, 18, 173
Esponda, Sebastián, 46
Estachería, José de, 15-16
Estate representation in Cádiz
  Constitution, 76–77
"Exaltados," 195–96, 208, 214–15, 218,
  219, 222
Executive power in Cádiz Constitution,
  77–78

Fauconnier, Jean Baptiste, 208–9
Federal Congress, 209, 217, 218–19
Federalism, Cádiz debates and, 33, 49,
  64–67, 74
Ferdinand VII, 29–30, 32, 100
  and Cádiz Constitution, 124–27
  as Constitutional monarch, 131
Filísola, Vicente, General, 165–66, 168,
  180, 195–96, 200
  and A.N.C., 187–90
  and Central American financial
    problems, 176–78
  executive role of, 170–76, 181–83
  and unionism in Central America,
    183–86, 190, 193
Flores, Cirilio, 226, 228
Flores, José, Dr., 18, 146
Flórez Estrada, Alvaro, 56
Floridablanca, Count of, 33–34, 35, 229
France, 31, 47, 99
Free trade. *See* Trade
Freedom of the press, 68, 97–98,
  114, 136
Fuero Juzgo, 250
Funes, Dean, 155

Gaínza, Gabino, 146, 149, 155, 168,
  170, 175, 179–80, 188, 200, 236
  and Declaration of Independence, 148
  and Guatemala Diputación Provincial,
    137, 140, 141
  and J.P.C., 150
  and Mexican rule in Central America,
    160–64
  and military intervention in
    Honduras, 157
  on regionalism, 141–42
Galarza, Domingo, 117
Gálvez, Mariano, Dr., 148, 221,
  222, 229
  in A.N.C., 215–17
  and economic development, 204
  and Senate, 198–201
Garay, Martín, 125
García, Nicolás (Bishop of Léon), 70,
  156, 158, 159
Garcia, Granados, José, 109
García Peláez, Francisco, 112
García Redondo, Father Antonio, 23–24,
  47, 148, 174
García Reyes, Mariano, 117
Gazeta de Guatamala, 18, 19, 21–22,
  134, 208
Gazeta del Gobierno, 151
Genio de la Libertad, El, 146, 147, 151,
  158–59, 160–61
Godoy, Manuel, 31–32, 230
Goicoechea, Father Jose Antonio Liendo
  de, 18–19, 22
González Sarabia, Antonio, 38–42,
  43–44, 244
Gonzáles Saraiva, Miguel, 158, 159,
  180, 181
Granada (Nicaragua), 17, 103, 104,
  159, 160, 191
Granadian Treaty (1823), 192
Great Britain, 90
  and educational reform, 130
  rivalry with Spain, 16–17
  and slave trade, 12, 88
Gual, Juan Bautista, 118, 119
Guardia, Victor de la, 159, 179, 192
Guatemala, Kingdom of, 35, 46, 82–83
(map), 179, 181, 214, 220
  colonization in, 205
  Diputación Provincial in, 108, 117–19,
    172, 173, 185–86

Guatemala, Diputación Provincial in,
(Continued)
   and A.N.C., 188–90
   bankruptcy of, 175–76
   becomes J.P.C., 149
   and centralization, 179–80
   clashes with Bustamante, 122–23
   and Indian question, 174–75
   under Mexican rule, 170–71
   in second constitutional period,
     137–42
Guatemala City, 15–16, 101–3, 108–9,
  131, 146, 236
   ayuntamiento of, 39–42, 66, 70, 127,
     150–51
     on "compact" theory, 44–45
     and constitutional monarchy, 131–32
     instructions to Larrazábal, 47–52, 89
     Mexican faction in, 161–62
     and Regency, 45–46
   under Valle administration, 135–37
Guatemalan Censorship Board, 114
Gunpowder tax and law, 202, 221, 222
Guridi y Alcocer, Father José Miguel,
  59, 60, 88
Gutiérrez, Agustín, 117
Gutiérrez, Símon, 157
Haiti, 87
Hapsburg dynasty, 8
Heredia (Costa Rica), 70, 159
Hermosilla, Luis, 146
Herrarte, Father José Mariano, 224
Herrarte, Mariano, 132
Herrera, Dionisio, 193, 225
Hidalgo, Miguel, 56–57, 70, 104
Honduras, 194, 214, 221
   cattle industry in, 205
   colonization in, 205
   governance of, 215
   home rule in, 141–42, 156–57, 236
   mining industry, 16, 205
   representation at Cádiz, 59, 72–74
Humboldt, Alex von, 164

Iguala, Plan of, 149, 157, 158,
  161–63, 173, 180
Income tax program, 203, 218
Independence movement, 142–46
   and continuity with Cádiz Experiment,
     148–49
   Declaration of Independence, 147–49
Indians, treatment of, 13, 22, 23–25,
  231–32

  in Cádiz Constitution, 84–87, 94
   ejido system, 85–86
   taxation vs. tribute, 84–85
   work levy reform, 86–87
  franchise for, 56–57, 138
  under Mexican rule, 173–75
  taxation of, 84–85, 153, 174–75,
    209–10
Indicador, El, 208, 223
Indigo production, 14–15, 205
Inquisition, 98, 253
Institutions, political, and Cádiz
  Constitution, 65–67, 92–95
Instructions for the Politico-Economic
  Government of the Provinces, 92, 95
Intendancy system, 9, 16, 151
Iturbide, Agustín, 143, 147, 152, 157,
  170, 177–78, 180
  as constitutional monarch in Mexico,
    161, 167–69, 191
Iztapa, 203–4

Jamaica, 17
Jefe político (appointed political chief),
  65–66, 67, 92–93, 95, 197
Jesuits (Society of Jesus), 48, 55, 143
Jiménez, Anselmo, 117
Joseph I, 35
Jovellanos, Gaspar Melchor de, 31, 207,
  229, 232
   on constitutional monarchy, 35–36
   on education, 81
   eulogy of Charles III, 1–3
   and Junta Central, 34, 35
   Report on Agrarian Law, 3–8, 89
J.P.C. *See* Junta Provisional Consultativa
Juarros, Antonio, 20, 41–43, 45, 47,
  127, 135
   Juarros Administration, 109–13,
    120–23
Judicial system
   under A.N.C., 198
   in Cádiz Constitution, 81
   in Guatemala, 137–38
Junta Central Suprema y Gubernativa de
  España
   cedes power to Regency, 30, 36
   and constitutional convention,
    36–38, 45
   constructive measures of, 34–35
   creation of, 33–34
Junta de Censura, 133, 136, 145, 165

Junta de Guerra (Guatemalan), 197
Junta Preparatoria, 106–7
Junta Provisional Consultativa (J.P.C.),
149–56
   and creation of Central American
   Republic, 160–61
   dissolution of, 168, 179
   and home rule, 156–60
   and union with Mexico, 163–67
Junta Superior Gubernativa de Costa Rica,
159–60
Junta Suprema de Guerra (Spanish), 68
Juntas, provincial (Spanish), 33, 34

Ladino population, 13
La Guardia, Víctor de. *See* Guardia,
   Víctor
Lancaster, John, 130
Land tenure, reform of, 5, 25–27,
85–86
Lardizábal y Uribe, Miguel, 36, 97, 98,
125–26
Larrave, José Antonio, 132, 150
Larrave, Mariano, 161, 163
Larrazábal, Antonio, 79, 99, 100, 102,
105, 113, 122, 144, 148
   at Cádiz, 46–47, 55, 59, 62–72, 76
      instructions, 47–52, 127
   on Indian reforms, 85–87
   and political power question, 93, 94
   rehabilitation of, 129, 131
   on trade and taxation questions, 89–92
Larreinaga, Miguel de, 47, 70, 146,
148–50, 156
Las Casas, Bartolomé de, 87
Léon (Nicaragua), 16, 72, 108, 118, 151
179, 181, 182, 191
   and home rule, 158–59, 160,
   165, 180
   uprisings in, 103, 104
Léon, Bishop of. *See* García, Nicolás
Léon Island, 28–31
Ley Agraria, 3–8, 52, 232
Liberal, El, 206, 208, 222, 225–26
Liberalism, Spanish, 75–76, 95–96
Libertad, 204
Lindo, Juan, 158, 192–93, 217
Llano, Andrés, 58–59, 69, 157
Llano, Manuel, 58–59, 68, 69, 71, 157
Locke, John, 44
López, José, Venancio, 132
López Cancelada, Juan, 56, 58

López de la Plata, José Antonio, 46, 63,
72, 126
López Rayón, Father Mariano José, 19, 43
Los Altos region (Guatemala), 182,
194, 215
Louis Biré Company, 221
Luján, Manuel, 30

Managua (Nicaragua), 214
Mariana, Juan de, 44
Martínez, Isidro, 222
Martínez de la Rosa, Francisco, 99
Masaya (Nicaragua), 159, 160, 204
Matina (Costa Rica), 70
Meat monopoly, 111–12
Medina, Father Bruno, 117, 118
Mejía Lequerica, José María, 58, 68, 100
Melón, Sebastián, 109
Menéndez, Isidro, 215, 216, 222
Merchant Guild of Guatemala. *See*
   Consulado de Guatemala
Mesta (stock-raising monopoly), 4–5, 8
Mestizos, 56–57
Mexico
   during Agustín's authoritarian phase,
   182–83
   influence on Central America of, 160–66
   revolution in, 145–46
   rule in Central America by, 169–71
      economic and social reforms, 171–72
      educational reforms, 172
      electoral representation, 171
      home rule vs. centralism, 179–83
      Indian question, 173–75
      racial equality, 173
      tariff policy, 176–79
      taxation policy, 176–77
Miguel Hidalgo revolt, 56–57, 70, 104
Military reforms, 68, 197–98
Milla, José Santiago, 126, 148, 158,
196, 217
   and Indian question, 174
   and military intervention in
      Honduras, 157
   and Venezuelan Constitution, 155
Milla, Juan Esteban, 146
Mining industry, 16, 204, 205
Miyares, Fernando, 122
Molina, Pedro, 139, 150, 151, 163, 165,
196, 209
   in A.N.C., 188

Molina, Pedro (Continued)
  and Declaration of Independence,
    146, 147
  edits *El Editor*, 134
  on political unionism and home rule,
    156, 158, 159, 160–61
Monarch, powers of, in Cádiz
  Constitution, 77–78
Montealegre, Mariano, 191
Montepío, 15, 26, 152
Montesquieu, 51, 199
Montiel, Father José Cleto, 126
Montúfar, Manuel, 134
Morejón, José Francisco, 46, 72–74
Morelos, José, 103, 104
Moreno, Lorenzo, 109
Morvillier, Masson de, 22
Moskito Shore, 17
Muñoz Torrero, Diego, 31, 61

Nájera, José, 174
New Granada, 35
New Spain, 35
Newspapers, 56, 133–35. See also
  individual papers by name
Nicaragua, 114, 146, 149, 185, 191–92,
  214, 224, 225
  colonization in, 205
  governance of, 108, 117–19
  home rule in, 118–19, 142, 157–59, 215
  representation in Cádiz, 46, 59, 72
Nicoya, 108, 179, 191
Nueva Segovia (Nicaragua), 70

Oaxaca (Mexico), 146, 162
O'Horan, Tomás, 196, 197, 200, 203,
  210–11, 213
Olmedo, José Joaquín, 86–87
Omoa (Honduras), 15, 16, 17, 72, 73,
  74, 88, 152, 157, 181, 182, 236
Oñate, José, 163
Orense, Bishop of. *See* Quevedo y
  Quintano, Pedro
Osejo, Rafael, 208
Ostolaza, Blas, 87

Pabón, Domingo, 109
Pamplona, Bishop of, 100
Papacy, 98–99
Pardo population, 13
Parliament in Cádiz Constitution, 77, 78,
  80–81

Pauw, Cornelius de, 22
Pavón, Cayetano, 45
Pavón, Manuel José, 42, 43, 47, 127, 174
Peinado, José María, 45, 47, 49, 70, 104
  as intendant in San Salvador, 127,
    128, 130
  on taxation, 50–51
Peláez. *See* Garcia Pelaez, Francisco
Peninsular War, 32–33
Pérez, José María, 117
Peru, 35
Philip V, 9
Philippines, 35, 55, 90–91
Plata, López. *See* López de la Plata,
  José Antonio
Poggio, Félix, 109
Political parties, 132, 133–34
Political power system in Cádiz
  Constitution, 59, 61–64, 92–95
Political theory, 30, 44–45, 62, 96
Portugal, 88
Power, Ramón, 28
Pradt, Abbé de, 145
Press, 56
  and stimulation of economic
    reforms, 207–8
  two-party, 133–35
Price, Richard, 145
Protocol issue, 139
Puebla, 146
Puerto Barrios (Guatemala), 14
Puerto Rico, 35
Punta Arenas (Costa Rica), 70, 126

Quesaltepeque, 166
Quevedo y Quintano, Pedro (Bishop of
  Orense), 29, 30, 96–97, 98, 124
Quezaltenango, 103, 108, 149, 156, 185,
  205, 228
  ayuntamiento in, 41, 43
  home rule in, 160, 165, 180, 182
  Mexican influence in, 179, 193, 194
Quicksilver monopoly, 57
Quiroga, Antonio, General, 130–31

Racial question, 54, 56–57, 60–63. *See also*
  Castas; Indians, treatment of
Ramírez, Alejandro, 19–21, 23, 42
Ramírez, Manuel, 132
Ramírez, Ramón, 132
Ramos Arizpe, Father José Miguel, 59,
  60–61, 93, 94, 99, 100

Recopilación de Leyes, 174
Redactor General, 208
Regency, 30, 36, 37–38, 79, 98, 121–22
Regionalism, 141–42, 231, 236
Reglamento de Comercio Libre, 9
Religious question, 76, 87, 170, 222–26
Revolutionary movement in Central
  America, 103–4
Riego Revolt, 130–31
Río de la Plata, 35
Rivera Cabezas, Antonio, 141, 148, 196
Robles, Mariano, 46, 71
Royal Audiencia, 19
Royal Consulado. *See* Consulado de
  Guatemala
Royal Council of Castile, 4, 6
Royal Economic Society (Guatemala),
  18–20, 27, 32, 40, 42, 112, 137
Royal Economic Society (Spain), 1, 4, 6, 8
Royal Merchants Guild. *See*
  Consulado de Guatemala
Ruiz, Tomás, 116

Sacasa, Crisanto, 159
Sacasa, José, 143, 146
Sacatepéquez (Guatemala), 108, 181
Salazar, José Carmen, 117
Sales Tax. See *Alcabala*
Salmón, Francisco, 109
San Carlos, University of, 18, 19, 23,
  44, 47, 106, 109, 134
San Diego, Juan de, 148
San Felipe, 177
San José (Costa Rica), 70, 159, 179, 191,
  208, 214, 215, 236
San José de Calazans school, 111, 130
San Juan River, 16, 17, 191–92
San Martín, José de, 168
San Miguel (El Salvador), 70, 108
San Salvador (El Salvador), 70, 71, 103,
  167, 169, 181, 214
  colonization in, 205
  Filísola negotiations with, 182–83
  governance of, 108, 151, 179
  Guatemalan campaign against, 175
  representation in Cádiz, 46
  under Mexican rule, 179
Santa Ana (El Salvador), 41, 70, 108, 166
Santo Tomás (Guatemala), 14, 15
San Vicente (El Salvador), 70, 108, 152,
  153, 167
School of Design, 18

Semanario Patriótico (Cádiz), 56
Senate, 199–201
Sierra Morena, 33
Sieyès, Abbé, 199
Simonds, William M., 204
Slave trade and slavery, 12–13, 87–88,
  210–11
Smallpox, 20–21
Smith, Benjamin, Dr., 21
Soconusco (Chiapas), 71, 193, 194
Sololá, 165, 180, 181, 194
Sonsonate (El Salvador), 108, 149, 214
Sovereignty issue, 30, 62, 96
Spanish Empire, overseas possessions of,
  8–18, 10–11 map
  centralization of, 9
  economic activities, 14–16
  geography, 13
  racial composition, 13
  trade policies, 9, 12–13
Suárez, Francisco, 44
Suchitepéquez (Guatemala), 108,
  181, 194
Supreme Court, 81
Supremo Poder Ejecutivo (S.P.E.), 195–97
  and colonization projects, 204–5
  education program, 208–9
  and federalism, 212–13
  and financial crisis, 203, 219

Tabasco (Mexico), 187
Tapachula (Chiapas), 71
Tarriffs, 176–79
  of 1820, 140–41, 152, 176
  of 1822, 171–72
Taxation, 7, 85, 153–54, 175–76, 235
  A.N.C. policy, 202–3
  Federal Congress and, 218–22
  in Larrazábal's instructions, 50–51
Tegucigalpa (Honduras), 40–41, 157,
  179, 182, 236
  as alternative capital, 142, 215
  economic development in, 204
  governance of, 108
  and home rule, 160
  rivalry with Comayagua, 72–73,
    192–93
Tehuantepec, Isthmus of, 72
Telégrafo Americano, El, 56
Tertulia patriótica, 161, 169, 207
Textile industry, 118
Thompson, George, 206

Tinoco, José, 141, 157
Tobacco monopoly, 79, 165, 172, 202, 221, 222, 233
  in Cádiz debates, 57, 89–90
Tonalá (Chiapas), 71
Toreno, Conde de, 56
  and constitutional debates, 59, 68
  on federalism, 64–65, 67
Totonicapam (Guatemala), 108, 181, 194
Trade policy, 4–5, 9, 12–13, 21, 140–41, 154
  American delegation and free trade question, 48, 55, 58–59
  Cádiz discussion of, 57–58, 233
  under Mexican rule, 171–72
Tribuna, La, 208
Tribunal de Vigilancia, 43–44
Tribute payment, 84–85
Trujillo (Honduras), 16, 17, 72–74, 152, 157, 181, 236

Ujarrás (Costa Rica), 70
United States, seizure of territory by, 79
Upper House (provincial) in 1824 Constitution, 200–201
Urruela, Gregorio, 41
Urruela, José, 109
Urruela, Julián de, 144
Urrutia, Carlos, 129–30, 131, 133, 137, 140, 141–42, 200
Urrutia, Manuel, 225–26
Utrecht, Treaty of, 12

Vaca, Alejandro, 109
Valdés, José, 149
Valdez, José Francisco, 109
Valencia, Junta de, 34

Valle, José Cecilio del, 42, 136, 138, 144, 146, 154–55, 168–69, 179, 182, 183, 193, 204, 210–11, 213, 221, 234
  in A.N.C., 188, 199, 202–3
  and Declaration of Independence, 148
  on economic potential of Central America, 205–7
  on education program, 208–9
  as journalist, 134, 208
  on J.P.C., 149, 151, 153–55
  on Junta Preparatoria, 106–7
  mayor of Guatemala City, 135–37
  and S.P.E., 196, 197
  tariff and trade policies, 171, 176
  and union in Central America, 156, 157, 164
Varea, Esteban, 79, 89, 125
Venezuela, 14, 35, 92, 155
Vera Paz (Guatemala), 108, 181
Villacorte, Juan Vicente, 196
Villa Urrutia, Jacobo de, Judge, 19, 20, 23
Vitoria, Francisco de, 44
Volunteers for Ferdinand VII, 103

War of Independence, Spanish, 32–33
War of Spanish Succession, 9
Ward, Bernardo, 21
Work levies (*mita*), 86–87

Ybarra, Mateo, 146
Ysabal, 204
Yucatán, 146
Yzaguirre, Agustín, 141

Zambo population, 13